JOURNEY BACK

to

WATOOKA

A Story of Guyana

Steve Connolly

Published to coincide with the 52nd Anniversary of Guyana's Independence 1966-2018

Suite 300 - 990 Fort St
Victoria, BC, V8V 3K2
Canada

www.friesenpress.com

Copyright © 2018 by Steve Connolly
First Edition — 2018

All rights reserved.

No part of this publication may be reproduced in any form, or by any means, electronic or mechanical, including photocopying, recording, or any information browsing, storage, or retrieval system, without permission in writing from FriesenPress.

ISBN
978-1-5255-2595-7 (Hardcover)
978-1-5255-2596-4 (Paperback)
978-1-5255-2597-1 (eBook)

1. TRAVEL, CARIBBEAN & WEST INDIES

Distributed to the trade by The Ingram Book Company

TABLE OF CONTENTS

Special Endorsements vii

Preface xi

O Guyana! 1

Pathway to Watooka—the Book 31

The Rainforest 53

Journey Back to Watooka 79

The Rainforest I 117

Return to the Rainforest 137

Photos 157

My Search for Kunj 173

Return to Watooka 197

Houses of History—Watooka .221

Houses of History—Christianburg, Cockatara,
Wismar, and Georgetown 275

Guyana—The Future 307

Epilogue 331

Acknowledgements 347

Bibliography 351

Author 357

Best wishes to Frank Fernandes!

Steve Connolly
Dec. 2021

To all of my Connolly family members,
to all of my Guyanese friends,
and to … Guyana

SPECIAL ENDORSEMENTS

Steve Connolly's *Journey Back to Watooka* evokes nostalgia, not only for him, but also for an older generation of Guyanese who recall the heyday of the development of the bauxite industry at Mackenzie, British Guiana, during the colonial period leading to its nationalisation in the 1970's. At the same time, it offers younger readers valuable information on the social and economic transformation resulting from the development of the bauxite industry, particularly during the same specific period. The book also encompasses accounts of the author's three journeys to Guyana in 2016-2017 when he visited his childhood home in Watooka which, in those days of seven decades ago, was an exclusive segregated community reserved for the expatriate management and engineering staff of the industry.

Clearly, the author displays his prodigious memory and undoubtedly applies diligent research producing this volume. His storytelling recalls his childhood days in Mackenzie and provides immense details of many of the personalities involved in the early growth of the country's bauxite industry which itself is a fitting tribute to all of them. Of special interest, his account of the effects of World War II on bauxite shipping from British Guiana opens up a little-known aspect of history to the reader. And while the story brings the reader back to present day Guyana, it furnishes an insight, while giving his own perspective, into the various factors influencing the growth of the bauxite industry and the economic development of Guyana as a whole. The book makes attractive reading and its publication is a welcome addition to Guyanese literature.

Dr. Odeen Ishmael,
Ambassador Emeritus (ret.)
and Author

Journey Back to Watooka is a brilliant follow-up to Steve Connolly's first book *Children Of Watooka*. This new book is part travelogue, part autobiography, part nostalgia and part Guyana's history. Written in clear and descriptive language, the anecdotes and stories are illustrative of bygone days, the present and a venture into the future. The research is detailed and characteristic of the author who, like a true detective, leaves no stone unturned.

As a Guyanese writer, I can relate to many of the stories in Connolly's book. Guyana has always been depicted as a place with great potential. Unfortunately, this potential never seems to materialise, always a bridesmaid never a bride. Connolly brings it all together, connecting the past to the future. He describes the rainforest, towns and villages, including Watooka where he had been first raised, and much more. People, politics and personalities come under his microscope as he is a 'people person'. He throws light on many things that make Guyana so special to me.

Dr. Bernard Heydorn,
Educator, Journalist and Author

SPECIAL ENDORSEMENTS

Any book that immortalises a tiny settlement in a little known country way down in Demerara, South America, placing it on the world map in no uncertain manner, juxtaposing individuals and events to world status, is worth owning and being placed alongside other significant books in private and public libraries.

Journey Back to Watooka is such a book, swamped with stories of ordinary men and women doing extraordinary deeds. It is filled with stories of events occurring in that far away place that made significant contributions to the world and where the effects of some of those events and the works of some of those men and women are still being felt today.

Journey Back to Watooka follows admirably in the wake of the first book and first travelogue on Guyana, *The Discovery of Guiana* by Sir Walter Raleigh (1596) and a contemporary travelogue *The Sly Company Of People Who Care* by Rahul Bhatacharya (2011). An avid reader will find that *Journey Back to Watooka* is also about books and writers … the author's way of setting homework for further reading, a masterstroke!

Petamber Persaud,
Chief Librarian, National Library of Guyana
and Author

Steve Connolly's retracing of his childhood footsteps in *Journey Back to Watooka* makes a significant contribution to Guyana's history, precisely when much of our collective memory has been eroded by the ravages of time and by emigration. It is an intensely evocation of a bygone era, made all the more fascinating by a veritable cornucopia of people stories. In spite of or because of the author's Canadian upbringing, mixed with a certain nostalgia for his childhood, Steve Connolly brings interesting perspectives to bear in writing about Guyana's unique rainforest, its geography, its people, past and present, its politics and, above all, its very bright future that lies ahead. Throughout, his love for the country of our birth is palpable. I encourage Guyanese and people of all nations to read this captivating narrative of our remarkable country.

Dr. Riyad Insanally, Ambassador to the United States for the Cooperative Republic of Guyana

PREFACE

Steve Connolly states that his purpose for writing his second book *Journey Back to Watooka* is to relate history, to relate stories about interesting Guyanese people and to do so revealing how these people of many races live together under their democratic government. Steve has done this and more. He begins his narrative with a comprehensive background about the country of his birth, reminding readers of Guyana's beginnings, its varied racial composition, starting with the Amerindians, Guyana's indigenous peoples, on to the slave trade, then the arrival of different nationalities to the country, its political background, the development of the bauxite/aluminium industry, as well as other industries, and even the importance of the rainforest.

His journey begins with the author returning to Watooka in Linden where he was born and had spent part of his boyhood. Along the way, readers become acquainted with interesting Guyanese and other people … from Syeada, the Guyanese woman who feeds and even rescues stray animals, to fascinating guests at the Rainforest B. & B., Steve's base in Georgetown. They also learn about former Prime Minister/President Sam Hinds who journeys with Steve to Linden, about other presidents/prime ministers and about even more notable Guyanese people such as for Edward Ricardo Braithwaite, author of *To Sir, With Love*.

Demonstrating his belief that everybody has a story worth telling, the author relates the tragic and poignant story of Kunj Beharrysingh, a Guyanese police officer who died enigmatically of a heart attack. He takes the reader with him on his search for Kunj's tomb in the overgrown and dangerous *Le Repentir Cemetery*.

Other unique and informative sections of the narrative are the chapters dealing with historical houses, most of which are located in Linden's Watooka where Steve had lived, as well as in Christianburg, Cockatara, Wismar and even in Georgetown. These houses provide a nostalgic view of life in Guyana as well as of the storied people who had lived, or still live, in them. Finally, the author examines Guyana's future after positing on why there are so many Guyanese expatriates and why they have not returned home. Giving much hope for the country's future, he then focusses on the topics of agriculture, bauxite/precious metals/minerals mining, sugar, rum, hemp, tourism, new infrastructure and much more ... that synergistically are important for Guyana's future success. In particular, the author examines Guyana's path as it is propelled into the new era of oil production which will no doubt help to make it a world player as it once was when its bauxite industry had played a vital role to help the Allies win World War II.

This book is of special interest to me since I am a daughter of the soil who had lived on both sides of the Demerara River in old Mackenzie and I am intimately acquainted with the entire area. For the first twelve years of my life, I had lived at Retrieve ... the land where the Demerara Bauxite Company, Demba, had later built its alumina plant (1961) after acquiring the land from my mother's family, the Allicocks. My family had moved across the river to Wismar on the west bank. As a child who had crossed the river almost daily to school and to church, I had gazed in fascination at the large bauxite ships that had sailed upriver to collect bauxite from the mines. When I had received a Demba scholarship and had commenced school at Mackenzie High, my consciousness about the area had expanded and, like for Steve, I developed a fierce interest in it so that later in my life I wrote about such in my Black Water novels. For the little girl that loved the river and for the little boy with fond memories of his birth country, our books come deep from within our hearts.

Steve Connolly is a consummate story teller. His stories display a level of detail which demonstrates his connection with humanity. This book is a great read.

Carmen Barclay Subryan,
Ph.D. Faculty Member, Howard University (ret.)
and Author

PREFACE

Seventy-five years ago, author Steve Connolly, was born of Canadian parents in Mackenzie, a bauxite company town in the colony of British Guiana. It was here that he had received his primary education and at the age of ten he had returned to Canada with his parents and brother. At the dawn of the 21st century, after four decades as a professional in the world of computer systems, he was able to retire and to reflect upon his past. In so many of these mental musings, he fondly recalled that, "... land and place of my birth ... 105 kilometres up the Demerara River".

That was the genesis of Steve's three visits back to Guyana within twelve months after an absence of sixty-three years ... just after writing his first book *Children Of Watooka: A Story Of British Guiana*. Not only were his memories as a schoolboy in Watooka rekindled, but his book "... opened a door of wonderful renewed experience ..." in the land of his birth.

The title of Steve's new book *Journey Back to Watooka: A Story Of Guyana* is something of a misnomer as the content is much more than of that enclave village. He demonstrates a great deal of knowledge about the company personnel and families who had occupied many of the houses in Watooka over a century and also about the fascinating stories of other 'houses of history' in the surrounding area. He attributes his positive attitude towards diversity as having been demonstrated by his parents and by his formative time as a youth in racially diverse British Guiana. He alludes:

> *When as a child living in Watooka, Guyanese people of colour were not permitted into our white village enclave unless they had a pass to confirm to the company Guianese constable at the small Watooka bridge that they were an approved servant/worker. Now, I am so grateful to have more friends who had been raised on the other side of the bridge than I have of my own Caucasian race.*

The author does not reserve his negative criticism only for the colonial period. He is blunt and unafraid also to denounce the policies and decisions of the PNC government under President Burnham's leadership. Consequently, Guyana lost large numbers of its middle class population to emigration. This situation is identified by the author as a core problem of the country's current third world situation. The chapter *Guyana - The*

Future is important to me for its potential to serve as a "discussion paper" for young people especially, those both in Guyana and in the diaspora.

Connolly's stories are enhanced by a 'story of stories' ... that of the history of *Le Repentir Cemetery* and of his search in this dangerous area for the remains of Kunj Beharrysingh who had died under mysterious circumstances after having been considered for the post of Police Commissioner in the mid-1960's. The real power and strength of *Journey Back to Watooka* is the storied history that is revealed. Not content with the quota provided in his first book, Steve provides a great deal more information about the physical characteristics of Guyana and its socioeconomic and political history since Independence ... not in any didactic magisterial tones but through his allusions to, and conversations with, the scores of people he meets in his travels:

> *Government and business VIPs, educators, literary gurus, bishops and other clergy, Amerindian folks, doctors, engineers, lawyers, environmentalists, conservationists, airplane pilots, artists, sports heroes, commoners and many more.*

So many of these interactions take place while based at the Rainforest B. & B. in Georgetown that three significant chapters are devoted to such.

On his returns to Watooka, Steve journeys by limo with his friend Hon. Sam Hinds, a former president and prime minister of Guyana. They observe and reflect on the changes that have taken place in the villages through which they are driven noticing also the lack of maintenance and consequent deterioration of most of the assets that the government had inherited from Demba since nationalisation during the Burnham era. Fortunately, the Watooka Clubhouse was in comparatively good shape to serve as Connolly's 'resting place' during his visit while also serving importantly as a base for meeting local folks and for researching the area's *'houses of history'* occupant stories.

Journey Back to Watooka is not simply a travel book about Guyana nor is it a history of its antecedent colony of British Guiana and the highly successful bauxite company with its mostly Canadian engineering staff at Mackenzie. Nor is it an evaluation of the ill fortunes that have befallen the country in its fifty years of transition from a colony to an independent nation. Steve Connolly's book is a powerful integrated compendium in which those important issues are addressed as a genuine, honest and well-written story of Guyana.

To my mind, there is but a single key question that cries out for an urgent collective answer by citizens of Guyana and by its huge diaspora in North America and in the U.K. ... will the peoples of Guyana be able, *as a united polity*, to find new paths to peaceful and successful human development?

I believe that the author of this Guyana Story has staked out a valid claim to be fully recognised as a loyal member of our "Guyanese diaspora" ... and my hope is that his work will be brought to the attention, not only to a full range of policy makers in Guyana, but also to the youth of Guyana everywhere who will be responsible for all of our tomorrows.

Dr. Harold Drayton,
First Deputy Vice-Chancellor, University of Guyana,
Professor and Caribbean Advisor and Author

The term underdeveloped country is based on the assumption that there exists a commonly accepted standard of development. A person or a group or a nation can only be called underdeveloped when there is general agreement what a developed or a fully developed person, nation or group ought to be like. Thus, the very category "underdeveloped" should be tested before use, since it is loaded with values and prejudices.

— Professor K. H. Pfeffer, University of Punjab

Socialism is about equality. A socialist believes that the purpose of human history is to achieve a society dominated, dominated, dominated by equality.

— Sir Arthur Lewis

In any given society, of one thousand babies born, there are so many percent near-geniuses, so many percent average, so many percent morons. I am sorry if I am constantly preoccupied with what the near-geniuses and the above-average are going to do. I am convinced that it is they who ultimately decide the shape of things to come. It is the above-average in any society who sets the pace. We want an equal society. We want to give everybody equal opportunities. But, at the back of our minds, never deceive ourselves that two human beings are ever equal in their stamina, in their drive, in their dedication, in their innate ability. And my preoccupation is with those who can really make a contribution, who can matter, given the training and the discipline.

— Lee Kuan Yew

O GUYANA!

A visitor from the north perhaps will have the most dramatic introduction to my land. When soaring among the clouds, if observant enough, he/she will notice when the blue sky is no longer mirrored by the blue Caribbean Sea. He/she will notice when that aquamarine gives way to the fertile mahogany of the Atlantic Ocean. Not long after, he/she will see life-affirming green. Now everyone may know their primary colours and be able to recognise green on a colour palette, but I assure you that you've never seen green until you've seen my green land of Guyana.

— Omari Joseph, *Explore Guyana*

O Guyana! Wow. Relaxed in my simple chair, I looked over the raw tropical foliage before me in wonder: wonder at the unique and remote beauty that lay there—every shade of green, every shape of flora, open-spaced here, yet entangled there, shining and shadowed, high and low—surrounded by humidity and quiet in the heat of the silent searing sun; and wonder at my unbelievable presence in the interior of a third-world country, only kilometres away from my World War II-time jungle birthplace, and a continent away from my current home in Quebec, Canada.

Music by Mozart played softly in the background, beautifully euphonic, reminding me of my father's love for classical music records, which he often played on a primitive machine at our home on stilts in the interior of this country, at the bauxite mining town of Mackenzie. It had been more than sixty-three years since my family had left the country, then known as British Guiana, and I had only recently returned, almost seventy-five years of age, to experience highlights of my life.

My Guyanese friend Ian Gorin, retired ER medical doctor living in Montreal, Canada, and I were being hosted at the large isolated property of our German friend, horticulturalist Hans Neher. We were eating curried rice and drinking local GT beer, while sharing our varied memories of, and stories of our pasts in, this most unique and remarkable country. I had visited Hans before, with special mutual friends, to greatly enjoy his enthusiastic and gracious hospitality. His rustic home fit perfectly into the tropical surroundings. Always capable and self-sufficient, this former engineer used lanterns again at night, given that the new overhead wiring on tall poles had been recently stolen by neighbours thus eliminating his short-lived electricity.

Just prior to this event, I had been similarly awed by my presence, one long evening, amongst seven special Guyanese friends in the old Watooka Clubhouse in Watooka, Linden, 105 kilometres up the Demerara River: four ladies and three men, all well-educated in at least four different countries, who will receive much mention as my writing proceeds. We were preparing material, awards, and gifts for the gala dinner and ceremony that would be held there the following evening to celebrate the 100th Anniversary of the Demerara Bauxite Company, Demba. (The word "bauxite" has a special meaning for each of us and will prick our ears any time it is heard.) As we enjoyed our great camaraderie, Vanessa was able to download our requested favourite songs: *Sometimes When We Touch, Bridge Over Troubled Water, Storms Never Last, Unchained Melody,* etc.

Mesmerised by the beautiful music, and by my wonderful friends, I contrasted all of this with what had been going on in this same large, and countrywide renowned, British Colonial building seven decades earlier, during World War II. At that time of supreme effort to produce local bauxite to make aluminium in Canada for the Allies, company staff and employees had to work twelve hours per day, with only every second Sunday off work. These Sundays were a time for much social revelry for the staff and wives at the Clubhouse. As not every staff member's "particular Sunday" coincided, the Clubhouse saw social events *every* Sunday. Billiards, table tennis, swimming, and playing cards were popular activities. Second World War songs were prevalent, such as Vera Lynn's *Lilli Marlene, White Cliffs of Dover,* and *Anniversary Waltz.* The Clubhouse was also where, particularly in 1942, my father hosted bauxite ship captains for supper, only to subsequently hear that one out of every three of their loaded ships had been sunk by German submarines, not long after they had proceeded to sea from the mouth of the Demerara River.

While repairs are required, the two-story building on stilts remains unchanged. The British billiard table rests dustily tarped in a corner, and the old curved bar still functions. If only they could talk! In 1942, my mother sat on one of the bar stools pregnant with the author. She would have been one of the few patrons, men or women, who did not smoke. The only aspects that were different from so long ago were the people and the songs.

Why was I so thrilled to experience these scenarios, and seemingly countless others? How did I find myself in the midst of it all? What had been the journey? "How," Guyanese university student Gabriella Cummings asked her mother, Judith, "could a white person who has lived most of his life in Canada know so much about and have so much fondness for our country?"

The purpose of this book is to answer these questions. To provide context, it is first necessary to provide a brief overview of the country's history and politics.

* * *

Indigenous people of all kinds inhabited South America long before the arrival of Europeans. Today, there are nine tribes in Guyana, all referred to as Amerindians, to distinguish them from the large population of East Indians, who form the largest race in the country.

Historians believe that the Warraus were the earliest settlers, in the northwest area of the country, more than 7,000 years ago. They are known as "water people", because they build their houses on stilts over or close to water. They have always been excellent fishermen, known for their canoe- and boat-building skills.

The Caribs (Karinya), warlike and historically known for cannibalism, may have been the next inhabitants, also settling first in the northwest.

The Arawaks were the first horticulturalists, building elevated fields to raise manioc and other vegetables, while supplementing their diet by hunting for animals.

The Wapishana emigrated from Brazil to make their lives in the southern Rupununi area of what is now Guyana. They have also been noted for being farmers more than hunters and fishers. They are excellent horse riders and perform proficiently as cowboys on the huge ranches that operate in their vast savannah area.

The Makushi natives reside in the savannah area of the northern Rupununi, and are renowned for their use of curare, or *wourali*, poison for hunting purposes, using blowpipes, with which they have phenomenal accuracy.

The Akawaios, once warlike and living mostly along the coast, are also renowned for their use of the blowpipe.

The Wai Wai Indians moved up from Brazil during the early nineteenth century. They are known for their unique skill as bead workers and weavers. The huge palm-thatch-roofed Umana Yana (Wai Wai, meaning "meeting place of the people") building in Kingston, Georgetown, near the Canadian High Commission, reflects their architecture.

The Arrecunas and Patamonas are the other two tribes within the country.

The Amerindian population of Guyana today is about 78,000 people, about 10.5 percent of the total population. Many mixed-blood Guyanese people today can trace some of their ancestry back to native roots. Sydney Allicock, cousin of my good friend Carmen Subryan, is the current Minister of Indigenous People's Affairs. He gained his admired native experience and culture by being born and raised in the Makushi thatched-roof village of Surama in the North Rupununi, in the foothills of the Pakaraima Mountains. He is a highly respected man, who is known for his desire and effort to move forward with native economic development and to keep the Amerindian culture alive.

Over much time, anthropologists have studied these tribes extensively, as they have many native communities across the borders. During the late

20th century, the Yanomamo natives were an international symbol of the last remaining "pristine" tribesmen in the world. These people live on both sides of the Brazilian and Venezuelan borders, in some fifteen to twenty villages, commencing about 300 kilometres west of Guyana's southern tri-point border with Brazil and Venezuela, on the top of Mount Roraima (which has the highest elevation in Guyana). It is interesting to refer here to the research provided by Guyanese Ivan Van Sertima, who, in 1976, published his bestseller *They Came Before Columbus*, containing claims of prehistoric African contact and diffusion of culture in Central and South America. A controversial book, it received widespread attention by African-Americans and others. Van Sertima later became an Associate Professor of African Studies at Rutgers University in New Jersey. He is renowned for his statement, "You cannot really conceive of how insulting it is to native Americans to be told that they were discovered." (Van Sertima may have been related to Joseph Van Sertima, a friend of my father who managed the Demba powerhouses for years, but I have discovered no confirmation of this.)

In 1493, Christopher Columbus made his second voyage to the West Indies, and brought sugar cane cuttings to Hispaniola, the island he had discovered the previous year. This plant flourished, and over time spread to the other Caribbean islands and to the land of Guiana. It became known as "white gold", and its production would become a huge economic engine for more than two centuries, driven by cruel slavery.

Columbus is recorded as the first European to have sighted and skirted the Atlantic northern shore of South America, on his third voyage to the West Indies in 1498. This would have included the coast of what we know as Guyana today. On that voyage he also landed on the south coast of the island he named Trinidad, after the three jungle-covered peaks located there.

In 1530, the Spaniard Diego de Ordaz sailed from the Amazon River to what is now Venezuela, and became the first European to venture up the Orinoco River. The Spanish explorer Herera would soon also journey up the Orinoco River, in 1533. Around the same time, on separate expeditions, the Germans Ehinger, Federmann, and Hohemut travelled into Venezuela, and even into Columbia, always with the prime objective of finding widely rumoured gold.

In 1535, a native related a story to Sebastian de Belalcazar of a gilded man in a golden kingdom. Belalcazar coined the name "El Dorado" for this unknown destination. For most of the rest of the 16th century, explorers with thousands of men would venture into the jungles of what are now known as Venezuela, Columbia, Ecuador, and Peru. These men, toiling in heat, struggling in rainy-season floods and muck, assaulted by snakes, alligators, jaguars, and disease, and attacked by angry natives with poisoned arrows, would die tortuous deaths…all for naught. One of the adventurers was Francisco de Orellana, who, in 1542, became the first European to descend the full length of the Amazon River.

As the undefined areas of northwestern South America generally known as "Guiana" became travelled, the fevered fascination to locate El Dorado led to the changed belief that it lay further east, over the cordillera that descended vertically south of the mouth of the Orinoco River, starting near one of its tributaries, the Caroni River. The target was now thought to lie in southeastern "Guiana", at an imaginary city, Manoa, on a large lake, Lake Parima. The dilemma then became how to gain access to it.

The Spanish had been the first Europeans to land in "Guiana", which included much of the Orinoco basin. One of their men was the Italian, Amerigo Vespucci, sailing for Spain, from whose name the word "America" was shortly derived.

The Demerara River is said to have obtained its name from the Spanish words *di mirari*, meaning "miracle" or "river of wonder". Sir Walter Raleigh named his first son "Damerei", and convinced his Queen to support his 1595 voyage to find El Dorado, "the land of gold". He found no gold, displeased the royalty, and was jailed for twelve years in the Tower of London. He was given another opportunity in 1617, when a son was killed in a battle with the Spaniards on the Orinoco River, but failed again. Raleigh, who was beheaded when he returned to England with no results, died believing that El Dorado could be reached by ascending the Essequibo River, then known as the Dessekebe River.

The area of water that included the western coast of the Gulf of Mexico (Texas and Mexico), all of Florida's coast, and the coasts of Central and South America, became known as the Spanish Main. For more than three centuries, the Spanish Main was the point of departure for enormous wealth, shipped back to Spain in the form of gold, silver, spices, hardwoods, artefacts, and other riches, including indigo.

Indigo's primary use was as a blue dye for cotton yarn. It was a major crop in Haiti, Jamaica, and the Virgin Islands, but was also produced in other areas, including what is now known as Guyana. Highly valued, it was known as "blue gold". Sir Isaac Newton used "indigo" to describe one of the two new primary colours he added to the five he had originally named. (For more than a century now, indigo has mostly been produced synthetically and is used to colour blue jeans.)

The Guyana that we know today was first colonised by Dutch settlers, its apparent lack of mineral wealth making it of little interest to the Spanish. Initially, the Dutch settled along the Pomeroon River, in the northwest, which flows into the Atlantic Ocean.

In 1627, Henry Powell was the first to bring English settlers to Barbados. They acquired various plants, such as cassava, tobacco, Indian corn, sweet potatoes, plantains, bananas, and citrus fruits, from the nearby mainland Dutch colony on the Pomeroon River. They also acquired thirty Arawak Indians to instruct them in, and help them with, growing the plants. These natives became the first slaves of Barbados, an island later denuded of trees to make way for vast fields of sugar cane.

In the second decade of the seventeenth century, the Dutch established a fort and a little colony on the high area of a small island at the confluence of the Cuyuni, Mazaruni, and Essequibo rivers, about sixty-five kilometres upstream from the mouth of the Essequibo. They called this Kyk-Over-Al, Dutch for "see over all", given its view location. The first cultivated crops there were cotton.

The Dutch West Indies Company administered the area from 1621 to 1792, granting Dutch, and later British, settlers ownership of land parcels. Many of these were expanded to become sugar plantations, thus establishing the first colonial economy there. Using methods developed in Holland, dykes, canals, and "koker" water gates were constructed to handle the below-sea-level coastal plain, where ninety percent of the population has always lived. The Treaty of Breda, signed in 1667, caused New York, then known as New Amsterdam, to be given to the British, in exchange for the British giving Suriname (Dutch Guiana) to the Dutch.

For much, if not all, of the seventeenth century, the main export of the Caribbean was not cotton, sugar, molasses, rice, or coffee; it was salt. While the salt was not produced in Guyana, it was produced on many of the islands. Even Bermuda produced salt. In return, the main imported product to the Caribbean was salt cod from the eastern coast of North America, used to feed the slaves of the Caribbean.

Within one hundred years after Sir John Hawkins became the first Englishman to capture slaves on the west coast of Africa, in 1563, and take them to the West Indies, slavery in the whole Caribbean area increased enormously, largely for the production of sugar and cotton. Almost all the slaves were obtained from the Gold Coast of West Africa. The ocean path taken from there to the West Indies was known as the Middle Passage.

Much has been written about these terrible voyages, and the resulting tragedy of slavery throughout the Caribbean. It has been estimated that almost eleven million slaves were transported from Africa to the Americas. Over ninety percent of these were imported into the Caribbean and South America. Only about six percent of enslaved Africans were sent directly to British North America, but their numbers grew relatively rapidly, due to the much higher death rate, and lower fertility rate, experienced in the tropical countries. This caused cotton production in the southern United States to rise dramatically in the early nineteenth century, causing a reduction of such in the Caribbean, and particularly in what was to become British Guiana, where the plantation production focus changed to sugar. Following emancipation in British Guiana in 1838, many former slaves left the plantations, resulting in lower production of sugar and cotton—at higher costs—than in countries that had not yet abolished slavery.

During the Atlantic slave-trade era, Brazil received more African slaves, estimated to have been 4.9 million, than any other country. The Portuguese transported many of Brazil's slaves from their bases at Luanda and Beneguela in Angola, Africa, with the last cargo of slaves arriving in Brazil in 1856. It may be surprising to know that today, with the exception of Nigeria, Brazil has the largest population of people of African descent of any country in the world. Even though Brazil gained its independence from Portugal in 1822, much earlier than other Caribbean countries achieved independence from other European countries, Brazil was the last country of the western world to abolish slavery, in 1888. It can also be noted here that slavery in South America and in the Caribbean was practiced long before the arrival of African slaves, by primitive tribes who had captured members of enemy tribes. This was proven to still be happening in the late twentieth century, at least by the Yanomamo natives, and this practice may even be continuing today to some extent.

In 1753, the Dutch established their capital on the island of Borsselen, about twenty-four kilometres up the Demerara River. By 1773 they had established the Essequibo, Demerara, and Berbice regions as separate colonies. By 1784, the capital had been moved to the east bank of the river's mouth, and named Stabroek. Cotton, coffee, and sugar were the main products. In fact, the three colonies were the largest producers of cotton in the world at the time.

Over the next several decades, these colonies would be contested regularly by Britain, Holland, France, and Spain, until they were ceded to the British in 1803 as a result of the peace settlement of the Napoleonic Wars. In 1812, the British formally renamed Stabroek to Georgetown, after King George III, and in 1831 the three colonies were united to form British Guiana.

Venezuela, which obtained full independence from Spain in 1830, bordered on the west, and has been unhappy about the location of the border almost ever since. In 1835, explorer Sir Robert Hermann Schomburgk proposed a border that formed the basis for a final boundary settlement at an arbitral tribunal in Paris in 1899.

Suriname (formerly Dutch Guiana) borders on the east, along most of the Courantyne River. This country ceased slavery in 1863, and obtained its independence from the Netherlands in 1975.

Brazil borders the south of all three of the original Guianas, including French Guiana.

In 1823, there were about 2,500 white people, mastering some 75,000 slaves, in British Guiana. The slaves revolted that year, sending a strong message to Britain, and helping to bring about the abolishment of slavery in 1834 and the emancipation of slaves in the British West Indies in 1838. A system of indenture was introduced, whereby a worker would be (poorly) remunerated for a commitment of from four to six years. Most of the slaves preferred not to continue working, even for wages, on the plantations, and moved to urban areas. To compensate for this, indentured workers were engaged from Madeira, Portugal, in 1835, and from northeast India in 1838. Indentured workers began arriving from Canton, China, in 1853.

By 1860, there were some 700 plantations in the colony. While brown sugar remained the main product, many of the plantations were abandoned. They carried the names of their British, Dutch, and French pasts: Felicity, Diamond, Good Hope, Paradise, Lust-en-Rust, Huisten, Vreed-en-Hoop, Sans Souci, and Mon Repos.

In 1880, the lumber industry was not yet developed. In fact, much of the lumber used to build the wooden structures of Georgetown was imported white and yellow pine from North America. This wood decayed easily in the tropical environment and was also attacked by the prevalent ants and termites. Over time, the colony would commence to use its own wood, primarily wallaba, mora, crabwood, and greenheart. Much of this wood would come from the tropical forests up the Demerara River.

Beginning in 1803, British Guiana was governed by British governors who, as in other British colonies, were appointed by, and reported to, England. British architecture, culture, and customs prevailed. Children were taught under the British school system. They began their day by singing "God Save The King".

The country was the first in South America to have a railway, ninety-seven kilometres in length, stretching between Georgetown and Rosignol, Berbice. Its building commenced in 1848, and was completed at the start of the 20th century. It was paid for by the Demerara Sugar Company, to transport sugar to Georgetown. (The day of the opening ceremony is remembered because a director of the company died when a locomotive accidentally ran over him!) The first three train engines, purchased in London, England, were named *Firefly*, *Mosquito*, and *Sandfly*. Later, train engines were named after governors, i.e. *Sir Gordon*, after Governor Gordon Lethem. Note that in 1854, India had only fifty-five kilometres of railway!

Bauxite, the ore necessary to make aluminium, was discovered in French Guiana in 1887, and in Dutch Guiana the following year. On December 30, 1888, Professor John Harrison and John Quelch, then a naturalist curator of the British Guiana Museum, discovered bauxite up the Demerara River at Akyma, and a few days later at nearby Christianburg. In 1913, Edwin Fickes, an Aluminum Company of America (Alcoa) engineer, arrived, and confirmed that the bauxite was of a high quality. The following year, the company sent George B. Mackenzie to acquire bauxite ore properties for the purpose to commence a mining operation. The area on the east side of the river, 105 kilometres south of Georgetown, was named Mackenzie to acknowledge his contribution. The area consisted of old, and long-overgrown, sugar plantations, such as Retrieve, Noitgedacht, and Fair's Rust.

> *One day, hunting wild orchids*
> *And wide-birthed trees for corrals,*
> *Deep in the thick, dripping forest*
> *We came across strange machinery:*
> *Cylinders, wheels, a vine-entangled mill,*
> *Giant, iron, rare, callandria*
> *Half-sunk in black and drifted soil,*
> *Rusted nearly through and broken up,*
> *A scattering of bricks that was a chimney once.*
> *Black stubs of wharf-wood, useless and forlorn,*
> *Jut out few and rotting from the river-shore.*
> *Lost, lonely relics entombed in earth and forest.*
> *And then, alerted, we found for miles around*
> *Tracings of the furrowed fields, row on row:*
> *Sugar's vanished, old plantations.*

— Ian McDonald, *A Trace Of Sugar, Essequibo*

The Demerara Bauxite Company, Demba, was formed in 1916. The first load of bauxite was shipped to the United States in early 1917. Mackenzie was planned to be divided into two sections, Cockatara for the coloured workers, and Watooka for the white staff expatriates, separated by a bridge over the Watooka Creek. Except for those who possessed a pass, such as domestic servants, gardeners, and maintenance men, coloured folks were not permitted to cross over the bridge into Watooka. British colonial practice still prevailed.

Coloured folks referred to Watooka as the "quarters", while white folks referred to it as "the camp". Cockatara was popularly called "the village". Across the river were situated the non-company, and thus less-provisioned, villages of Wismar and Christianburg.

The United States had ruled that Alcoa was too much of a monopoly and had forced it to reduce its grip. In response, it formed the Aluminum Company of Canada in 1928 to manage aluminium production operations in northern Quebec, Canada, and also to take over Demba's operations in British Guiana.

If I had to choose one word to represent the fundamental cause that puts me in a position to write this book, it would be "bauxite". From its discovery until the present, this interesting and important ore has influenced Guyana's demography, settlements, and politics, and the lives of tens of thousands of people…including mine and that of my Connolly family.

My father, Jack Connolly, arrived in Mackenzie, British Guiana, in February 1940 as a young Canadian engineer, 27 years of age and unmarried. Raised and educated in Nova Scotia, he had been working for the Northern Electric Company in Montreal. He was hired by the Aluminum Company of Canada, Alcan, to help ramp up the production of bauxite for transportation to Canada to make aluminium for the war effort. Canada would obtain all of its bauxite during World War II from British Guiana, and the aluminium produced from this would be used to make thirty-five to forty percent of the war planes for the Allies, making it a huge partnership contribution from these two countries. Most of the rest of the aluminium came from the United States, which initially obtained much of its bauxite from its mines on the Berbice River in British Guiana, and from Suriname. Later in the war, as will be detailed, most of it would come from within the United States itself. During World War II, the United States extended the small airfield at Zanderij, Suriname, and brought in 2,000 soldiers to protect its bauxite interests.

Aluminium was also important to the enemy Axis powers. It is interesting to note that during the Second World War Germany obtained most of its bauxite from Hungary and Yugoslavia. After Norway's King and government fled, when Germany took over the country, the new authorities, wanting to keep the economy going, used their own existing aluminium-producing resources with Norway's hydroelectric power to make aluminium. As the war progressed, Germany lost the ability to transport bauxite from its sources to Norway, thus greatly hindering its war effort. Mountainous Japan had sufficient hydroelectric power itself to make aluminium, and during the war obtained its bauxite mostly from the Dutch East Indies, as well as from Bintang Island near Singapore and from Manchuria. Again, as the war progressed, bauxite availability became curtailed, and Japan's ability to make war from the air was rendered hopeless.

A deep-sea bauxite "treasure"

As I was writing this chapter at our cottage in British Columbia in the summer of 2017, my neighbour, Pat Rimmer, a professional deep-sea diver, recounted an interesting related story to me.

During the last half-year of the Second World War, the US submarine *Queenfish* torpedoed and sank the Japanese ocean liner *Awa Maru* in the Taiwan Strait. First put into service in 1943, the ship had been requisitioned by the Japanese navy. Only one man, of 2,004 people on the ship, survived the sinking. (Incredibly, that was the third time he had been the only survivor of a ship's destruction!) The ship had been voyaging from Singapore to Japan, and was rumoured to be carrying much gold, platinum, diamonds, and other valuables, possibly worth up to US$1 billion.

In the late 1980s, my friend Pat was hired by friends owning a Vancouver, Canada, diving company to fulfill a contract with the Chinese government to dive on the *Awa Maru* to search for possible treasure. They used the diving ship *Stephaniturm* for this purpose. Pat and his colleagues took turns, three at a time, going down in a diving bell that could release them in their diving

> suits once on the bottom. The *Awa Maru* was found at a depth of close to seventy metres, mostly intact and lying towards its port side. It was covered in fishing nets that, over the years, had caught on it.
>
> An orange-peel grapple was used to bring up some of the contents of the six large holds. No precious goods were found. On the deck of the *Stephaniturm*, the grapple released a great many spent brass ammunition casings (intended to be melted down for the war effort), human bones, and tons of a wet, mushy, orangey-red ore: bauxite. Most likely, this ore had been mined on Bintang Island. It would have been scarce and precious for the Japanese at that time. Some uncut diamonds were also found, but no precious treasure. Five Chinese officials were present at the dive location to ensure that their objective was correctly met.

In the spring of 1941, Jack Connolly proposed marriage by blue air-mail letter to his girlfriend in Montreal, Canada, Mary Hay, who was the Head Dietitian at the Royal Victoria Hospital. She accepted by telegram. In August of that year, Mary undertook an exciting voyage from Canada on the Canadian steamship *Lady Hawkins*, stopping at Bermuda and many Caribbean islands before reaching Georgetown, British Guiana. The three-week war-time voyage was uneventful, with the ship having taken precautions to avoid German submarines, and she happily married Jack in Georgetown at St. Mary's Church on September 9, 1941, the day after her arrival.

Mary had befriended three of the officers on the *Lady Hawkins*, who attended the wedding. Sadly, they would lose their lives two voyages later, in January 1942, when their ship was torpedoed late one evening between Cape Hatteras and Bermuda. Two hundred and fifty people died, while seventy-one were rescued after five dreadful days in a single lifeboat. Those who perished included the wives of three of Jack's engineer friends in Watooka, and a family of four who were journeying to live there.

The German Navy wanted to eliminate both bauxite ore ships and oil tankers. The US east-coast cities required much oil from the port cities in the Gulf of Mexico. By January 1942, to service its war needs, Britain required four tankers of oil to arrive at its shores each day. Most of this oil was obtained from refineries on the Dutch islands of Aruba and Curacao, which obtained oil from Venezuela. At the time, the Aruba refinery was the largest in the world.

Trinidad was also a large oil source with a refinery. Hence, there existed a busy traffic of bauxite ore and oil tanker ships along the eastern US coast and between the Caribbean and Britain. Germany's Admiral Karl Doenitz commenced a submarine offensive in February 1942 that would wreak serious havoc within the Caribbean Sea, peaking that year, but mostly thwarted by the Allies by late 1943. During the Second World War, more than 400 ships were sunk in the Caribbean. I was born in the midst of all this, though my personal focus at the time was on my mother's milk and some sort of pabulum, while lying horizontal in my father-built bassinet.

Due to Mary's recurring malaria, my parents made the decision to move to Arvida, Quebec, for my father to work at the Alcan aluminium smelter, where he stayed for the remainder of the war, and for a further two years. My brother Mike was born there in October 1944. Subsequently, we moved to Texas City, Texas, for several years, where Jack supervised the maintenance of the large Texas Tinhorn Tin Smelting Company.

In December 1950, our family returned to Watooka, Mackenzie, for my father to again work for Demba. The following three years in this beautiful and unique tropical environment were wonderful for our family, and formative for me and my brother. Subsequently, all through my life in Canada, I have recalled this time with great frequency and fondness.

We left for Canada in the spring of 1953, when I was ten years of age. My father was to be an executive engineer for Alcan, helping to build the huge hydroelectric power and aluminium smelter project at Kitimat in northern British Columbia.

That was also a landmark year for British Guiana. The first ever election allowing universal adult suffrage was held. The People's Progressive Party (PPP), formed in 1950, won handily, and came to power over a Legislative Council that still took overall direction from Britain, via the governor of the colony, Sir Alfred Savage, well-known to Demba's senior managers. Leadership of the PPP was shared by its founders, Cheddi Jagan and Linden Forbes Burnham, whose later varying leadership and competition against each other would determine the political and economic destiny of the country for at least the rest of the century.

Cheddi Jagan, having been born and raised in Berbice, was an East Indian from a poor Hindu family of cane cutters. Linden Forbes Burnham was of African origin, raised in the Kitty area of Georgetown in a family led by the principal of an elementary school. Both had attended Queen's College secondary school and had performed well academically. Burnham had won the touted Guiana Scholarship in 1942, had studied law at the University of London, England, and had returned in 1949, immediately immersing himself into politics. Jagan, meanwhile, had studied to become a dentist in the United States, had married Janet Rosenburg, a white Jewish-American, had returned to British Guiana in 1943, and had practiced dentistry there for the next six years before entering politics.

The 1953 elected government lasted only 133 days before it ended in turmoil. Burnham then went on to form the People's National Congress (PNC) party, which would compete with the PPP over the long future. Each of these two parties became racially aligned, primarily East Indians versus blacks of African descent, which created a situation that further complicated the country's internal relations and overall stability.

At a British Guiana constitutional conference in London, England, in 1960, the principle of independence for the country was accepted. After years of disagreement as to how to form an independent country, a constitution was agreed to, and independence was achieved on May 26, 1966, with major celebrations held across the new Guyana. Leading his PNC party, Burnham became the prime minister. Arthur Chung became the first president. The government of Guyana was now an independent constitutional monarchy within the British Commonwealth: the twenty-third member. Four years later, the country would achieve its status as a Republic, to become formally known as the Cooperative Republic of Guyana.

Over the next twenty-five years, Linden Forbes Burnham would, sadly, lead this new country with so much potential to ruin. He was an advocate of Karl Marx and socialism. History describes him as having been bright and a great orator—but also as having been self-promoting, uncaring for people, and unable to bring his country to prosperity with his version of philosophy and government.

Major industries, such as sugar and bauxite producers, were brought under incapable government control. This included Demba, which was nationalised in 1971. Expatriates and hundreds of thousands of Guyanese people left the country, forced to leave their possessions and wealth behind, during Burnham's rule. Elections keeping him and his PNC party in power were always reported as being fraudulent. When he died in 1985, at only sixty-one years of age, the country was in far worse economic and social condition than when his leadership had commenced.

The PNC party continued to govern, under the leadership of Desmond Hoyte, for the following seven years, until 1992. At this time, former US President Jimmy Carter and his Carter Centre were present to ensure a fair election process, which resulted in a PPP government, led by President Cheddi Jagan. For the most part, citizens continued to vote by race. Sam Hinds, who had worked as an engineer for Demba for twenty-five years, rising to become the head of research there, became the prime minister.

Cheddi Jagan died in 1997, and Sam Hinds automatically became the president, serving for nine months, until the next elections were held. Janet Jagan took over the position in the latter part of 1997. Hinds had not desired to compete for the presidency, but he was chosen again as prime minister. In 1999, Jagan resigned from the leadership for health reasons; she died in 2009. Bharrat Jagdeo replaced her, followed by Donald Ramotar. The PPP remained in power until May 2015, when the election resulted in a coalition being formed between the A Partnership For National Unity (APNU) party, and the Alliance For Change (APC) party. David Granger, affiliated with the APC, is the president, and Moses Nagamootoo, also APC, is the prime minister.

* * *

A brief overview of Guyana's history and politics has now been provided. But before I relate the story of my *Journey Back to Watooka*, it is important that I provide further information about the country, and some of its contemporary aspects.

Guyana is situated at the top of South America, between one and nine degrees latitude north of the equator, and has an area of 216,000 square kilometres, about the size of the United Kingdom. While it does not front on the Caribbean Sea, it is considered a Caribbean country—the only one that is not an island. (Note that the Caribbean is made up of more than 7,000 islands.) Guyana is the largest Caribbean country, followed in size by the islands of Cuba and Hispaniola. It is the fourth-smallest country in South America after French Guiana, Suriname, and Uruguay, and is the only English-speaking country in South America.

Ninety percent of its population is found along the coast, which runs for 432 kilometres. Land along the coast falls one to two metres below sea level, and that has resulted in an elaborate system of drainage canals, and a seawall, designed by the Dutch and built by the British using prison labour, which runs for almost 300 kilometres along the coast. The capital city of Georgetown, on the east bank of the Demerara River, has been known as the "Garden City" for its beautiful flora.

"Guiana" is the Amerindian word for "land of many waters". There are four main rivers: the Essequibo, the Demerara, the Berbice, and the Courantyne. The Essequibo River is the third-longest river in South America, after the Amazon and Orinoco Rivers, at just over 1,000 kilometres in length. Its waters surround 365 islands. When its headwaters flood into the northern Brazilian rivers that empty into the Amazon River, it helps to effectively make all of northeastern South America into an island.

There are close to fifty rivers In Guyana, although some of them may really be large streams. The Pomeroon River in the northeast, more than 300 kilometres in length, which at one point runs for more than thirty kilometres parallel and close to the coast, is the most populated. It is unique in that it has no islands or sand banks. The centre of the Courantyne River forms much of the eastern border with Suriname.

Guyana has more than 275 waterfalls, which grow in number during the two rainy seasons of May-June and November-December. Kaieteur Falls is the third-highest single-drop falls in the world at 226 metres—five times higher than Niagara Falls in Canada. King Edward VIII, King George VI (Oshi), Kamarang Great, Kumerau, and Marina Falls are all more than three times the height of Niagara Falls, and are also spectacularly beautiful.

Some weekends I travel up the Essequibo River to spend time in a house set on a shore in a clearing of white sand cut from the forest. There, great beauty quiets the heart: the peace of the early morning led by a red dawn; the changing shadows on the immense river made by sun and cloud; the flights of white birds at evening, the moods of the great river changing; moonlight blazing on the white sand; the sweep of wind in the trees; and the soothing sounds of the waves of that ocean-river coming ashore.

— Ian McDonald, *A Cloud of Witnesses*

Guyana's unique and remarkable rainforest is amongst its greatest assets. It is sustainable, and so far, Guyana has been doing a good job to protect it. Various sources report that seventy-five to eighty percent of the country remains covered with rainforest—more than 160,000 square kilometres. (In comparison, it has been reported that all primary forests in Europe have been depleted, and that only five percent of virgin forest remains in the United States.) Over time, there has been little forest depletion in Guyana, and the current government strongly supports keeping things this way. Given its low population density and expansive rainforest coverage, Guyana is a world leader in carbon storage per capita.

Incredibly, there are more than 1,000 species of trees across the country. Those most sought after are greenheart, mora, baromalli, purpleheart, red cedar, crabwood, simarupa, locust, kabukalli, and wamara. Fine-grained greenheart wood, hard, heavy, and rotting/termite-resistant, is excellent for building and is used around the world for wharf piles and for other underwater purposes. Wood from this tree can weigh almost 1,000 pounds per cubic metre, heavier than the heaviest oak in North America. It does not float in water. Course-grained purpleheart wood is equally hard and, after cutting, turns from brown to a beautiful purple.

The Kanuku Mountains represent the largest protected area of rainforest in the country, four percent of the total rainforest. Largely unexplored, this pristine expanse contains hundreds of species of mammals, birds, reptiles, amphibians, and fish, and more than 1,500 species of plants.

One may contrast the above in size with Brazil's Amazon rainforest, sometimes referred to as "the lungs of the earth". In 1970, the Amazon rainforest had covered 4.1 million square kilometres. By 2015 it had been reduced by almost twenty percent, to 3.3 million square kilometres. Today, about thirty percent of the earth's land surface is covered by forest, with Brazil containing more than half of the planet's remaining rainforest.

Few countries in the world offer the abundance, uniqueness, and variety of flora and fauna of Guyana. In fact, it is a remarkable and gigantic open-aired and cage-less zoo: wild and raw, sometimes dangerous, free for its people and visitors to wonder at in awe. In an environment of more than 1,000 species of trees and more than 6,100 species of other plants, it has been recorded that there are at least 100 species of bats, 800 varieties of birds, 400 to 500 species of fish, 180 species of mammals, and 120 species of amphibians. South America has more 6,000 varieties of butterflies and even a greater variety of moths, and the Guiana Shield has more than 150 varieties of dragonflies. Guyana has its share of all of these.

Guyana has often been referred to as "the land of six peoples". Its main ethnic groups are East Indian, African, Portuguese, Amerindian, Chinese, and Caucasian. East Indians represent about thirty-eight percent of the population, with Afro-Guyanese at around twenty-eight percent. Decades of interracial marriage have led to a large mixed population, approaching twenty percent of the people. The country's population has never reached 780,000, and has recently been decreasing, to 735,000 in 2016. In 2011, Guyana ranked within the top five countries worldwide for its outmigration rate. It has a low population density of fewer than four people per square kilometre. President Burnham'sND mismanagement caused great emigration during his time that negatively affected both population and economic growth.

Today, more than three million people of Guyanese descent live outside of the country. Three hundred and fifty thousand of these people live in Canada, with about 155,000 living in Toronto alone. Large groups have also found homes in the United Kingdom, the United States, and throughout the Caribbean. Approximately 140,000 Guyanese people live as the fifth-largest immigrant group in New York City: a part of Queens is called "Little

Guyana". At least twenty-five Guyanese people lost their lives in the World Trade Center tragedy on September 11, 2001.

These expatriate Guyanese are highly interconnected, proud of their unique culture, and still very fond of their roots in Guyana. My expatriate friend in Ottawa, Sylvia Barrow, sums this up by saying, "Meh bellah button strings still lef' in de groun'". In Canada, including the Guyanese High Commission in Ottawa and Guyanese Consulate in Toronto, there are about 65 Guyanese charitable, religious, school alumni, business, literature, and other organizations in Ontario alone. The Bridge of Nations in Sudbury, Ontario, where our daughter, Julie, and family live, flies the Guyana Golden Arrowhead flag alongside those of ninety-nine other countries. Sudbury's mayor from 2006 to 2010, John Rodriguez, was Guyanese. Organisationally and individually, the Guyanese expatriates give back to their country financially, and also provide material goods, such as medical supplies, vehicles, computer equipment and school supplies, as well as donating their personal time, and much more.

More than half of Guyana's population is Christian, about a third is Hindu, and less than a quarter is Muslim. The various religious practices are widely and peacefully accepted and have helped to form popular related festivals in which everyone participates. During *Diwali*, known as the Hindu Festival of Lights, which celebrates the triumph of good over evil, small reddish-brown clay saucers containing oil are lit up by the thousands at night to decorate homes, streets, fences, beaches, and much more. *Phagwah* is another Hindu festival, where joyous revellers are doused with brightly coloured liquids and powders. The Islamic festivals of *Eid-ul-Fitr* and *Eid-ul-Aza* are also widely celebrated.

Mashramani, a native word meaning "feast after the hard work of a harvest", is the most important and largest national festival. It originated in Linden and commemorates the attainment of Guyana's Republican status on February 23, 1970. It is celebrated on this date annually and is a spectacular and colourful carnival of costume parades, blending music, art, and pageantry. Easter is another time of great festivity, with tens of thousands of kites being flown all along the coast seawall, in parks and across the land, to celebrate the resurrection of Jesus Christ.

It is interesting to note that one of Canada's largest festivals, if not *the* largest, is Caribana, held annually in Toronto. Launched by a group of West Indians in 1967 as a salute to Canada's centennial, it has been billed as North America's largest street festival, with its parade drawing more than 1.2 million people, and with an overall attendance of more than two million revellers. It is a celebration of Caribbean culture and customs, featuring steel pan, soca, and calypso music and dancing. The Guyanese community is a strong participant.

Perhaps Guyana's greatest exported contribution to world society has been its people, who mostly had to emigrate, and who then mostly took advantage of first-world universities to remarkably excel in every variety of profession conceivable: as teachers, professors, scientists, engineers, lawyers, doctors, judges, athletes, business leaders, musicians, politicians, and much more. And now, their descendants are similarly proving themselves. Vidur Dindayal's excellent book *Guyanese Achievers, USA. and Canada* outlines the outstanding contributions of dozens of Guyanese people outside of their country of birth. Yet, there are near-countless other expatriate Guyanese achievers. While you will read of many such people, including some who live in Guyana, within this book, here's a very small peek at some remarkable Guyanese folks.

The first governor of Canada's British Columbia was James Douglas, born in British Guiana in 1803. Many provincial landmarks are named in his honour, including the main street of Victoria, the province's capital city. The first two black judges in Canada, Vibert Lampkin and Maurice Charles, were Guyanese.

Edward Ricardo Braithwaite was an outstanding man who became renowned for his writing of several books, including *To Sir, With Love*, which denounced the racism that he had experienced in post-World War II Britain and in South Africa. He survived the war as a courageous Spitfire pilot, later became Guyana's first Ambassador to the United States, and accomplished much more.

Lance Gibbs, Clive Lloyd, Rohan Kanhai, Basil Butcher, Cyril Christiani, and Shivnarine Chanderpaul were outstanding world-class cricketers. Charmaine Hooper and her brother, Lyndon, played for Canada's Olympic soccer teams, with Charmaine being recognised as one of the best woman soccer players in the history of the sport. Alex Bunbury also starred in soccer for Canada and played in the US and Portugal. Percy Duncan had been a world-class track star in the mid-twentieth century, and later coached Canadian track stars, such as Guyanese Mark McCoy. Ave Mogan was the first woman elected to Canada's Cricket Hall of Fame.

Rudolph Dunbar was the first black conductor of the esteemed Berlin Symphony Orchestra. Bill Adams, born in the same small hospital as myself, grew up to own and operate the Bill Adams International Tennis Academy in Florida, which has trained many tennis stars, including Venus and Serena Williams. Maritza Correia McClendon, born in Puerto Rico to Guyanese parents, became the first black American swimmer to set an American and world swimming record. She had to overcome severe scoliosis to achieve these feats.

I am fortunate to have met Nancy Rickford, whose brother, Professor John R. Rickford of Stanford University, was elected in 2017 to the Academy of Arts and Sciences, the highest academic honour in the United States. I have met Dr. Vivian Rambihar, who is an internationally renowned cardiologist in Toronto, Canada, and whose three daughters, Sherryn, Nadira, and Vanessa, are all talented doctors.

Barbados singing star Rihanna (Robin Rihanna Fenty) has a long lineage of Guyanese family on her mother's side. Guyanese-born Baroness Valerie Amos became the first black woman to sit in the Cabinet of the United Kingdom, was Britain's High Commissioner to Australia, and also served as leader of the House of Lords.

I have enjoyed much communication and discussion with six Guyanese poets, Cyril Dabydeen, Dr. Bernard Heydorn, Peter Jailall, Dr. Ian McDonald, and brothers Petamber and Sasnarine Persaud. Most of them live outside of Guyana. Professor Cyril Dabydeen at one time was the Poet Laureate of Ottawa, Ontario. These gentlemen are also book authors, and from all of their writings one can learn a great deal about life, love, beauty, nature, history, and the country of Guyana. My wife, Carolyn, is always thrilled to see and hear Bill Newman singing calypso. With his great sense of Guyanese humour, he is one of the best such singers in Canada.

Guyana's fertility rate is 2.5 children per adult female, and life expectancy has improved to an average of sixty-eight years today (from fifty years in

1955) due to improvements in health-services delivery. The median age is a youthful twenty-five years.

Along the coast, malaria and dengue mostly do not exist, but one must be careful to avoid such when in the interior. Miners and others who work in the interior are being encouraged to use Malaria test kits and medicine for simple types of malaria; it has been proven that early detection and application of medicine can help improve recuperation. Mosquito nets for sleeping purposes are also encouraged for use in the interior. Just over 10,000 cases of malaria were reported in 2016. Guyana's 2017 cancer mortification rate of 20.1 deaths per 100,000 people is the highest of the Caribbean countries, with breast, cervix, and prostate cancers prevailing. An emphasis on vaccinations has minimised the spread of yellow fever from Brazil, where it has been prevalent.

The Gross Domestic Product (GDP) for the country is about US$3.2 billion. Gold production contributes about forty percent to the GDP, with rice at twenty-one percent, bauxite at eleven percent, and sugar at seven percent. These are followed by shrimp/fish, timber, and diamonds. While sugar production has been decreasing alarmingly, rum export is increasing rapidly. Guyana's El Dorado rum is a world-renowned product. Its flagship 15-year-old brand boasts the distinction of being the only rum to have won the title "Best Rum in The World" eight times since 1998 at the International Wine and Spirits Competition held in London, England. Judges have defined it as, "Deep bronze amber colour. Crêpe Suzette aromas waft, sprinkled with dots of barley sugar and dried pineapple, coconut and papaya. This is a sipping rum, a thinking, not drinking glass, pensive, pervasive, and ultimately satisfying".

Eco-tourism and a significant oil off-shore find, together with other possibilities, provide great positive potential for the future of Guyana, as I'll discuss in my final chapters.

With respect to "ease of doing business with", Guyana has been reportedly and recently ranked at 123 out of 189 economies. Factors such as regulations, incompetence, corruption, and credibility all contribute to this ranking. I and many of my Guyanese colleagues have had success providing help to the country, but many would agree that avoiding government involvement provides better odds for success. Working with Firefighters

Without Borders Canada in 2016/2017, I was able to obtain a commitment to provide Guyana with two used Canadian fire trucks in excellent condition, gratuitously, with transportation and training to be similarly provided. I had to give up this worthy initiative due to lack of interest and incompetence at a senior government level. Still, I feel that there is reason for great hope in the future.

Not surprisingly, Guyana has a serious crime situation. Almost all third-world countries do. Almost all Caribbean countries suffer heavily from crime, some much more so than Guyana. But overall crime statistics for countries can be misleading. For example, Guyana has been reported to have a murder rate five times that of the United States. Yet, there are areas of the United States where the murder rate is much higher than that of a third-world country. Venezuela, Guyana's neighbour, has one of the highest murder rates in the world, more than twice that of Guyana. In Guyana, handguns, knives, cutlasses, and machetes are the main weapons of choice.

Guyana has many remote airstrips, as well as remote waterways, which greatly support clandestine drug movement, for which the country is well-known. Domestic violence against women is pervasive. Most homes in the upper-class areas of Georgetown have concrete, gated walls surrounding them. Grocery and other stores have guards, and payment for goods is carefully monitored, and sometimes transacted through a caged window. Government buildings, office buildings, and some upper-class homes have guards located inside their gates.

I have visited the Police Headquarters on several occasions to speak with senior and other officers. For the most part, they are dedicated to their duties, and deserve to be proud of their work, while at the same time needing to improve their reputation for corruption. The Guyana Police Force is greatly hindered by its lack of funds and facilities. Yet, in spite of all this, and just like folks in first-world countries, Guyanese citizens go about their daily affairs normally, and with great attachment to their environment. Visitors, who are mostly Guyanese expatriates, can easily obtain safe, inexpensive taxi transportation, and can quickly learn to take safety measures so that they may enjoy their stay without concern.

The United Nations has ranked Guyana 127 out of 188 countries on its Human Development Index, determined by people's ability to make choices, to lead a long and healthy life, to be educated, to enjoy a decent standard of living, and various ingredients of self-respect. Only Haiti has a lower ranking in the Caribbean. Guyana ranks much better on the World Press Freedom index, obtaining a 2017 ranking of 60 out of 180 countries.

In 2013, the country ranked 136 out of 177 countries, near the bottom, on the perceived corruption ladder. Government concern and focus improved this position to 108 in 2016. Crimes of contraband smuggling, narcotics trafficking, people trafficking, money laundering, bribery, and fraud are all prevalent, as for many countries. In 2016 the Guyana Revenue Agency reported that eighty percent of self-employed citizens in the country, more than 70,000, were not filing tax returns. The City of Georgetown in 2016 was faced with a total of G$2 billion in unpaid property taxes, owed by delinquent property owners across the city, including 300 businesses. Few resources are available to deal with this.

Sadly, in 2017 Guyana ranked fourth in the world for its high rate of suicide. On a more positive note, it has been reported that its literacy rate of 88.5 percent is the highest of any third-world country: not surprising, given that its British-founded school system still functions well, even though funding is necessary to repair infrastructure and to modernise computer systems and equipment.

Canada's highly respected Fraser Institute gives Guyana a 2017 ranking of 136 out of 159 countries on its Economic Freedom scale (Venezuela is last). Note that Canada was ranked sixth. The World Bank ranked Guyana 124th out of 190 countries for its business environment.

All of this information confirms that Guyana is a third-world country. Naturally, it remains a major objective for the government to move things forward by overcoming many challenges, and by taking advantage of the country's many positive attributes. I strongly believe that there is much hope for this remarkable part of our planet.

* * *

After my retirement in the fall of 2000 from thirty-five years of working in the realm of computer systems, I allowed my mind to open up a part of it that had always been tucked away in sub-consciousness, and found a deserved freedom to repeatedly wander back in time to fondly recall the land and place of my birth, 105 kilometres up the Demerara River in British Guiana. Slowly, over the following years, I began to review my parents' past documents and photographs, to read voluminously about this country, and to contact all sorts of folks to help me better understand and somewhat re-live some of my past, from afar, at my home in Quebec, Canada.

The past is never dead. It is not even past.

— William Faulkner

I subsequently wrote a book, my first, *Children of Watooka: A Story of British Guiana*, which opened a door of wonderful renewed experience for me in this country now known as Guyana. Writing this book, and subsequently returning to Guyana three times within twelve months after sixty-three years of absence, was an unforgettable journey that continues to give me pleasure even now. I have been able to attend events related to my book in Guyana, and in four major Canadian cities. I have been able to meet the President of Guyana and the Prime Minister of Barbados, many senior Guyana government ministers and bureaucrats, and seemingly endless numbers of wonderful Guyanese citizens and expatriates. I have also enjoyed meeting the leaders and employees of Guyana's High Commission (Ottawa) and Consulate (Toronto), to gain a better understanding of their functions.

The purpose of this book is to relate my wonderful journey. More history of the country—storied history—will be related. The reader will encounter a great many people of Guyanese, and other, heritage, as their interesting tales and lives are related, and connected with the history, politics, economics, and society of all six races living together in Guyana. You will meet government and business VIPs, educators, literary gurus, bishops and other clergy leaders, Amerindian folks, doctors, engineers, lawyers, environmentalists, conservationists, airplane pilots, artists, sports heroes, commoners, and many more.

In my youth, I was never a fan of poetry, nor of my father's classical music. Now, I enjoyably replay his huge collection of music, first listened to in Guyana, and I also enjoy simple poetry. As I noted earlier, I am fortunate to now know at least six Guyanese poets of renown, several of whom I communicate with on a frequent basis, including Cyril Dabydeen, a current University of Ottawa professor and swimming mate of mine.

Let us remember that the artist creates his art in the crucible of his imagination, but that he lives in the society from which he draws the raw material. And the society lives in every man. Let us remember that the glory of a people is found partly in its image-makers, the authors and artists, who maintain its culture and extend it and let us remember that the living culture is one which links the elite securely with the general mass of the people, to speak to them as well as to speak for them, and in this great dialogue to forge the soul of a nation.

— A.J. Seymour, *I Live in Georgetown*

* * *

"A soft-spoken, gentle, and intelligent man"

As I write in October 2017, I have just attended the very large funeral service, held in Ottawa, Canada, of Guyanese Archdeacon William Oscar Agard, aged ninety-three years. I was so fortunate to have been with him twice over the past year. A soft-spoken, gentle, and intelligent man, he was initially a journalist for the Daily Chronicle, and then worked in Guyana's government, rising to become a Permanent Secretary before being ordained a priest in 1977. He wrote the informative book *Called to be More*, a thorough history of the Anglican Church in Guyana. Archdeacon Agard's colleague Reverend Archibald Luker won the composing competition in 1966 for his rendition of a national anthem for the new independent country, "Dear Land of Guyana". One of the judges was the renowned Arthur J. Seymour, who was then an employee of Demba, living in Watooka.

In my book you will meet Christopher Taylor, the young man who, with his partner, won an award for the design of the unique and now unforgettable jaguar logo, representing the 2016 fiftieth anniversary of Guyana's independence. More information regarding the history of bauxite mining in the country will be revealed. Unique houses, and stories of many interesting and diverse residents of Linden, covering more than a century, will be highlighted. And you will learn what it is like to write a book, and take a peek at the world of publishing.

I never imagined that things would develop for me the way that they have. When I was a child living in Watooka, Guyanese people of colour were not permitted into our white village enclave unless they had a pass to confirm to the company Guyanese guard at the small Watooka Bridge that they were an approved servant, gardener, or maintenance worker. Now I am so grateful to have more friends raised on the other side of the bridge, so to speak, than I have of my own Caucasian race. Diversity is paramount, and wonderful.

As I travel extensively every year, people respond to my mention of Guyana with, "Where is that? What about it?" The only way to answer sufficiently is with a comprehensive and interesting response. So, here it is, and it's time to proceed.

> *Strength lies in differences, not in similarities.*
>
> — Stephen R. Covey

> *Diversity: the art of thinking independently together.*
>
> — Malcolm Forbes

> *A lot of different flowers make a bouquet.*
>
> — Muslim proverb

PATHWAY TO WATOOKA—THE BOOK

If there is a book that you want to read, and it is not written yet, then you must write it

—Toni Morrison

Books have a unique way of stopping time in a particular moment and saying, "Let's not forget this".

— Dave Eggers

I had never planned to go back to Watooka. But I did go back. And it was quite a path. Quite a journey. Marvelous. Extraordinary. It had to do with a book, Children of Watooka, and, more importantly, with its contents. Here is my story.

It was February 2017, and I found myself sitting at a U-shaped bar at an American VFW (Veterans of Foreign Wars) location in downtown St. Petersburg, Florida. The ten or so men and women, black and white, sitting around the bar were enjoying lively and humorous conversation. At one point, I challenged them to determine where I had been born by posing no more than twenty questions to me. My challenge attracted their full attention and enthusiasm, but as had been the result with previous victims of this challenge, they weren't successful in providing a correct response.

Not even close. When I revealed the place of my birth, "Ross" asked a twenty-first question: "Where is Guyana?"

Going back to somewhere means that it must be a place, and Watooka was a place, and still is a place, in the Cooperative Republic of Guyana. Pretty much the same place, too. But if one were to ask someone almost anywhere in the world where Watooka is, they would not know. In fact, many people, if not most, who are not from the Caribbean do not even know where Guyana is located. A common response to its location question would be "Africa". And, in fact, I dare to say that many Guyanese folks do not know where Watooka is within Guyana. After many years of research, I have not yet been able to determine what the word "watooka" means, or how it originated. Most likely it is an Amerindian word. The Watooka Creek, the village's northern boundary, was most likely named prior to the village being named Watooka.

Just after 1910, the Aluminum Company of America, Alcoa, sent Edwin S. Fickes to search for new bauxite reserves. Although he had been aware of bauxite findings in British Guiana, he had preferred to search for such in France and in the Mediterranean. He had known engineering friends who had worked in Georgetown, British Guiana, who had died of tropical fevers, deterring him from any initial bauxite search there. Ultimately, in 1913, he did go, and voyaged in a Sproston's Company riverboat 105 kilometres up the Demerara River to Wismar. With local men using machetes, for a period of less than two weeks, he penetrated the jungle to examine bauxite potential, and determined that it would be worthwhile for Alcoa to seriously consider mining bauxite at that location. Early in 1914, Alcoa sent George B. Mackenzie to the area. He assembled derelict land that at one time had been primarily sugar plantations, such as Lucky Spot, Aurora, Coomacka, Maria Elizabeth, Three Friends, Fair's Rust, Amelia's Ward, Retrieve, and Noitgedacht. In 1759, Laurens Lodewyk van Bercheyck, a surveyor and mapmaker, produced a "Map of Demerary and Esequibo", which showed all of these plantations in operation at that time, more than 150 years prior to Alcoa's initiative.

In 1918, Edwin Fickes completed a plan for a town to be called Mackenzie, named after his friend, which would consist of two villages, Cockatara, for the Guyanese workers, and Watooka, for the white expatriate staff of the company. Mackenzie would exist along the east side of the Demerara River, across from Wismar, which would not be included as part of the company town—although, nevertheless, many workers would live there.

In 1928, Alcoa was forced to divest its operations in Canada to the Aluminum Company of Canada, Alcan, which also took over its bauxite mining operations in British Guiana, conducted through the Demerara Bauxite Company (Demba). When my unmarried Canadian engineer father, Jack Lawrence Connolly, arrived in Mackenzie in February 1940, Cockatara was building up to house about 3,000 people, to accelerate bauxite production for World War II, while Watooka was building up to about fifty houses in total along Riverside Drive, adjacent to the river. When my mother, Mary Letitia Hay, arrived to marry my father in Georgetown in September 1941, her ship narrowly escaping German submarine activity (as I described earlier), they settled down to live in Watooka together.

Easter Sunday, April 5, 1942, must have been an interesting day for my parents. My father finally had a day of rest after having worked at least twelve hours per day for thirteen consecutive days in dust, heat, and humidity (as was normal for all Demerara Bauxite Company employees at that time during the war). Unknown to them, that same day the Imperial Japanese Navy had attacked the city of Colombo, Ceylon, sinking three British warships in the process. Later that day, Jack and Mary would have attended Easter festivities at the Watooka Clubhouse. More importantly, at some quiet time on that day, or in the evening, they found the time for your author's conception.

The start of 1943 found World War II still raging overseas. Bauxite production in Mackenzie would achieve its all-time production record that year. Mary Connolly was also to prove productive, giving birth to your author on January 4 in the Mackenzie Hospital, located by the side of the Demerara River. Two coloured boys on bicycles had struggled in parallel to bring her home mattress to the hospital.

Dr. Douglas Jardine, a member of the well-known Jardine family situated in Georgetown, was my birth doctor. His grandfather had founded the *Guiana Daily Chronicle* newspaper. My mother had been struggling with bouts of malaria, and my father had been worried about her health. His contract commitment to work in British Guiana was up for renewal, and my parents decided not to risk my mother's health any further. In May of that year they left the country, somewhat saddened, to move to northern Quebec, where my father worked at Alcan's Arvida aluminium smelter. Instead of loading bauxite ships, he would be unloading them: this was where British Guiana bauxite was being shipped.

In October 1944, my brother Michael was born in Arvida. In 1945 the war ended, and in 1947 my father became a mechanical superintendent at the Longhorn Tin Smelter at Texas City, Texas. The largest tin smelter in the world, it had been commenced early in World War II to make up for the shortage of necessary tin. However, my father maintained his contacts with his engineering colleagues back at Alcan in Canada, and by the early fall of 1950, he had secured a job back in Mackenzie, British Guiana. Both he and my mother considered this move very carefully, but their remembrance of a unique and remarkable paradise in this South American country won over any hesitation that may have been present. Subsequently, our family of four lived in Watooka, Mackenzie, until May 1953, and it is this period of my young life that formed a fondness for the area of my birth forever.

Subsequently, our family moved to Kitimat, British Columbia, Canada, where my father helped lead the construction of the biggest industrial project in the world, a massive hydroelectric power facility, and an aluminium smelter that would use bauxite primarily from Jamaica. My brother, Mike, and I, completed our high school there, and went on to the University of British Columbia to become engineers. Upon graduation from university, I would move to eastern Canada and marry the great little wife of my life, and we would have two special and talented children. For thirty-five years, I would work in high-pressured computer system design and development environments.

Busy in my studies and in sports, I paid no attention to the country of my birth until May 1966, when I attended a party in Ottawa of mostly Afro-Guyanese people to celebrate the new Cooperative Republic of Guyana, which had resulted from British Guiana's attainment of independence from Britain at that time. I and my friend Dave Shanks, who had also been born in British Guiana, were the only Caucasians I noticed at the event, and we knew no one else there. I recall eating souse for the first time (and for the last time, smile).

Now and then over the years, my parents would have visiting friends who had shared experiences in British Guiana, and I would always listen intently to their fond recollections. Sometimes my father would pull out his slide projector to show coloured slide photos of Mackenzie times—people, events, and beautiful tropical scenery. A framed watercolour painting by expert artist Mary Percival, who had lived across Riverside Drive from us in Watooka, had always been displayed on a wall of my parents' home. Bamboo golf clubs and two Amerindian bows with arrows had gathered dust. Now and then, I would communicate with a friend who had also been a "child of Watooka", but these discussions rarely focused on our tropical past.

It was not until 1996 that I got somewhat back into the world of Guyana. Ned Blair, a Guyanese community leader, asked me to speak at a major Mackenzie High School Reunion that was held in Toronto, Canada, where he continues to live. About 500 people attended, and I hardly knew anyone present. I was fortunate to sit at the head table with special people such as High Commissioner Brindley Benn, Dr. Ivy Mitchell, Beryl Cummings, Virginia Echols, and others.

As the reunion continued, over a full weekend, I met new friends, such as Dr. Bernard Heydorn, creole linguistic expert, who authored the great book *Walk Good Guyana Boy*. Later, upon reading his book, I began to reflect more and more upon my past. His early past in Georgetown had been roughly concurrent with my own time in Mackenzie. I could easily relate to his stories of his youth, and they were full of great humour.

I also met Dr. Odida Quamina, and later enjoyed reading his book about union relations with the Demerara Bauxite Company, *Mineworkers of Guyana*. I also met elderly Roy and Ruth Emery, who had commenced their time in Mackenzie in 1938. He had designed the swimming pools in Cockatara and in Watooka. I began a great relationship with them that would last until their passings. And there were many others. I subsequently began to meet with Brindley Benn at his office in Ottawa.

I began to read extensively about the history of British Guiana and continued to gather a large collection of related books. This collection of books goes back to writings by Sir Walter Raleigh, and to books about early Spanish explorers and plunderers in the Caribbean and in South America. Books about the *Mayflower*'s pioneering voyage to what became the United States of America even contain ties of what became British Guiana, because it was seriously considered by the Pilgrims as a possible destination. I found the biographies of famous British sea captains such as Hawkins, Drake, Nelson, Rodney, and Somers to be fascinating, and learned that they were not exactly the heroes I might have anticipated. Canadian National Steamship Lines named their five *Lady* boats after their wives, yet those ships displayed huge framed oil paintings of these sea captains rather than those of their wives. Two of these men died at sea.

I have James Rodway's 1894 book *In the Guiana Forest* and books by Mathew French Young, Vincent Roth, and Michael Swan about British Guiana in the nineteenth century, amongst many others. Renowned scientist Dr. William Beebe spent much time researching tropical flora and fauna at the confluence of the Cuyuni and Mazaruni, rivers and wrote several detailed books on this, with prefaces written, and support given to him, by his close friend Theodore Roosevelt, who had also visited and loved the country.

Crowns of Glory, Tears of Blood, written by Emilia Viotta da Costa, is an excellent book about British Guiana slavery and the Demerara slave rebellion of 1823, and is amongst other books on the topic of slavery that I often refer to in my library. I have many of Edgar Mittelholzer's books and am very fortunate to have six autographed books by Edward Ricardo Braithwaite, who wrote directly and courageously about racial discrimination at a time when it was difficult to do so. I came to know him, and to greatly admire his integrity, forthrightness, and writing courage.

I greatly respected and learned from Father Andrew Morrison's book, *Justice*. He was another man with the huge courage to stand up to political abuse and corruption. Walter Rodney, a serious and greatly respected political activist, produced several writings, including *A History of the Guyanese Working People 1881-1905*, which are also historically instructive.

Given the time of my birth, I have been very interested in all aspects of World War II, and I have well over a hundred books on the topic. I have been somewhat more interested in the war with Japan, because much of it took place in tropical environments, similar in many aspects to my birthplace. I did not know much about the war's presence in the Caribbean, and of its effect on the countries situated there (like most folks), until I enjoyed reading *Operation Drumbeat* by Michael Gannon and *The U-Boat War in the Caribbean* by Gaylord Kelshall. Information from these and other books of similar content, together with stories of bauxite ship sinkings related to me by my father, gave me an advanced knowledge of submarine warfare in these tropical waters. Also, I was fortunate to meet in Ottawa, and interview, 84-year-old Ken Jackson, a survivor from the sinking of the Canadian ship *Lady Hawkins*, four months after my mother had voyaged on it to British Guiana. Two hundred and fifty people died in this tragedy. Ken, then a seventeen-year-old British soldier, survived in a single lifeboat with seventy others, bobbing like a cork in the water for five horrible days. His story continues to fascinate me, and he provided it to me in writing, as well.

With respect to the area of my birth, Mackenzie, a few excellent books have been written, such as *Run Softly, Demerara* by Zahra Dickson Freeth, who lived in Watooka. Another is Wendy Dathan's *Bauxite, Sugar and Mud*. Wendy was born in Mackenzie in 1934, and still has fond memories of her youth there. No book better relates the very early history of the area than Carmen Subryan's *Black Water People*. Each of these books provides an important view into British Guiana's past up the Demerara River.

On my 69th birthday in January 2012, I took down from my library shelf Rodway's book *In the Guiana Forest*, a vintage collector's item. I had read it years before but found that I had missed following up on the handwritten note on a blank front page: "Thos. Conant Oshawa Canada 1899". I immediately performed some research to discover who the owner had been.

Wow! In 1899, Thomas Conant had been about 55 years of age. He was a descendent of the Conant family, which had owned a large farm beside that of Sir Walter Raleigh in Devonshire, England, during the sixteenth century. The Conant family has had a long and distinguished history, recorded in Thomas Conants's two books, *Upper Canada Sketches* and *Life in Canada*.

Thomas was a son of Daniel Conant, who played an instrumental role in the early development of Oshawa and Whitby in Ontario, Canada. Thomas was a traveller and an author. He travelled around the world twice and may even have paid a visit to British Guiana. He was also an avid reader of history. He visited the northern armies during the United States' Civil War, and even met once with President Abraham Lincoln. His son, Gordon, became the Mayor of Oshawa, and later became the Premier of Ontario.

Now armed with a burning desire to combine my knowledge of British Guiana, and particularly of my birth place, with the additional interesting knowledge that I had absorbed, I thought that I could write some form of document that, at some future time, would at least be of interest to my children and grandchildren. I had a list of six potential titles for this endeavor, with a preference for the one that would finally prevail: *Children Of Watooka*.

Initially, the scope of my writing was to be limited to the area and history of Mackenzie, but this would change, because I ultimately wanted to combine all of the knowledge that I had gained, which include the history of the general area and the whole country. The first chapter that I wrote, commenced in the winter of 2005-2006 as a test of my ability and persistence, was not the first chapter of the book, but rather about British Guiana and bauxite. After all, this would be about the heart of why Mackenzie came to be. After I completed the draft version, I knew that I would have to, and be pleased to, widely expand the scope of the book.

I am not an author, but rather a storyteller. Every person *has* a story, and *is* a story. When I walk through a cemetery, I often stand in front of a grave and wonder about the interesting life that person must have lived. Same for an old house: if it could only talk about the people's stories lived within it! It was natural, therefore, for me to want to relate history alongside the stories of as many people as possible who had lived in it. And so I did.

By this time, many of my childhood friends and adults who had lived in Watooka had sent me information and photographs about their interesting time there. My mother's many notes and writings were invaluable, and also contributed to my writing inspiration. Of course, I also had my own memories and files.

Over the next several years, I continued to write slowly, as there was no rush. I was writing history that was unchangeable and would always be valid. I was extremely busy with many other activities and was often away from home. My research and my contacts led me to further research and to further contacts. More information came in from people who were new to me. For the most part, I had never known anyone who had been born and/or raised in the villages of Christianburg, Cockatara, and Wismar.

While this was of some concern for me, it was not going to be an obstacle. Perhaps I would have the opportunity to meet such folks for future writings.

Nevertheless, one of the greatest contributors to my book *was* raised in Cockatara, and his story is fascinating. Clarence London talked to me and sent me more than 100 pages of his writings about his family history, his time as a youth in British Guiana, and his time as an engineer working for Demba both before and after nationalisation of the company. He is a descendant of a slave, Jupiter London, and his life commenced in barefoot poverty in Georgetown. As a youngster, he came to Mackenzie to stay with his sister, Princess, and her husband, Royland Blair. He excelled at his schooling, winning a scholarship to study engineering at Howard University in the United States. Returning to work for Demba in 1960, he married Cicely, and rose through the ranks to become one of the top executives of the company. Frustrated with the country's politics and refusing President Forbes Burnham's demand that he take Development Training to correct his "bad attitude", he was forced in 1976 to leave the country with his young family. They left behind, and lost, all of their assets in Guyana, but he was able to obtain good work in Jamaica, and to happily retire in Costa Rica. Sadly, he passed away before having the chance to read the deserved story about himself and his family recorded in my book.

As the chapters began to fall into place and became robust with history and stories, I started to think about what would next be required—finding a publisher—and to consider if I might have to find an agent. I had no experience with this. I also had to think about preventing any negative legal issues from occurring. Given my unhurried writing progress, I had lots of time to do this...or so I thought.

I began with trying to find an agent, and determined that there are about thirty of them in Canada that I might consider. I tried contacting them randomly, only to learn that they are hard to contact. They do not want you to send in your manuscript, and they do not want you to talk to them on the telephone. Rather, they prefer that you send in a page or two to describe your writing, and perhaps also a chapter for them to read. There are often many people working within an agency, and if you do manage to get some writing to them, whoever gets assigned to your proposal is often random, may have no interest in your topic, and may have been splashed by the bus on her/his way to work. Indeed, they receive an enormous number of requests for their services every day and will tell you that much of it is garbage and/or won't sell. Some will tell you that once they have reviewed your proposal they may not respond…and do not.

We know that in many countries, including those in North America, the demographics are changing, and societies are aging. It is understandable that people who have had a life of interesting experiences and/or have gained knowledge would like to share this by writing a book. With today's technology, the ability to produce words and pictures on paper or electronically is amazing, and sure beats writing on tablets or using a feather with blood. So, it is not surprising that more and more people are writing manuscripts and struggling to get them published. If an agency receives hundreds of manuscripts a week, it is simply impossible for all of these to be reviewed. A screening process is absolutely necessary but never perfect. Inevitably there will be missed opportunities and some unfairness.

Agencies and publishing companies must make money to stay in business, and to do so must choose those books with a high probability of sales. They will help an author only if the author can help them, and they have to be brutal about this. Publishing companies will even pay large advances of money to proven bestselling authors who guarantee performance. In the course of my journey, I contacted about half a dozen agencies and a similar number of publishers, not even coming close to obtaining interest in my book. I had little time for all of this.

I also studied the option of making use of a self-publishing company. Almost anyone who has a manuscript can use this alternative, but one has to take all of the risk and must pay for it every step of the way. This option puts the onus on the author to market the book, and to spend much time managing a web site and handling administrative matters. This was not an option for me.

Finally, I found success.

* * *

As I entered the crowded one-bedroom apartment on the third floor of a six-story building in the old market area of downtown Ottawa, I was greeted by a frail, elderly lady of seventy-nine years. She was struggling with an illness, but welcomed my visit nonetheless. On the wall were several family photos, including a large framed oil painting of a beautiful blonde lady. This attractive and elegant visage was also framed as a large black-and-white photo by famed photographer Yousuf Karsh. I knew immediately who the beautiful lady was: my host, Inga Hessel.

I contrasted the beautiful face on the wall with the serious lady in front of me, still wearing her early-morning night robe, her salty-grey hair drawn back into a ponytail, very frail. I would learn that she was struggling with heart and cancer issues, and was distressed by the way age can destroy beauty. We sat down on antique furniture for a long and interesting chat, as she willingly revealed to me much of her incredibly remarkable past. It crossed my mind how incredible it can be to have such interesting people hiding in plain sight.

She told me of the time during World War II, when she was seven years of age and living with her mother and sibling in Hamburg, Germany, that the allies dropped a bomb on their apartment building, killing eighteen people. She and her family survived, as they would also survive a bombing at a different location. Hamburg, a major port city, was levelled. Down the street, her aunt and two small children were killed. So was her uncle, a soldier. Inga's father, a soldier, became a POW in a Russian camp.

The family survived the war, and emigrated to Ottawa, Canada, in 1953, when she was seventeen years of age. Subsequently, she obtained a degree in arts and history at Carleton University, where she had met Dieter, whom she married. Together they opened a popular bookstore in Ottawa, and later expanded their business, opening two more bookstores, employing twenty-six people altogether. She and Dieter later divorced.

Over many years, Inga became an expert on the book industry. She became a friend of all sorts of VIPs, and knew two prime ministers. Prime Minister Pearson told her, "I wish that I had had the interesting life that you have had". One time, she bought 2,500 books from Prime Minister John Diefenbaker, copies of his new biography. He did not think the books would sell well, but she set up a book-signing event at the high-end Chateau Laurier Hotel, and all the books sold. Her apartment was full of autographed books.

I thoroughly enjoyed my discussion with her about the book industry. She knew publishers across the world, and spoke directly with them rather than writing to them. She told me that she had prepared her own biography, which Doubleday was to publish, but only upon her death.

I asked her if she knew of Hansib Publishing in the UK, and she responded, "Of course!" I had only learned of this company recently from a Guyanese lady friend in Washington, DC. Inga swept her arm over the piles of literature and manuscripts piled high and everywhere in sight, remarking, "I have 490 manuscripts here now. I receive about six new ones a week to review. Now and then, I hire someone to shred them. I charge $200 to read a manuscript, and I can read very fast. I must be critical and brutal. I must decide if a book will sell, and in the rare instance when I believe such, I must then decide which publishers might be best suited for the book. I must not even be marginal in my judgement, or I will lose my good reputation".

I asked her how many, out of every hundred manuscripts she reads, she forwarded to a publisher. "Five?"

"Less than that", she responded.

We were both familiar with the annual, prestigious Man Booker Prize for nonfiction book writing. Established in 1968, it provides one of the most generous financial awards in the world. It commenced when Ian Fleming met with the Bookers Authors Division to do business, because he was not satisfied with the marketing of his James Bond books elsewhere. Canadians Margaret Atwood, Yann Martel, and Michael Ondaatje have each won an award.

> ### *The Guyana connection to the Man Booker Prizes*
>
> In 1815, a twenty-two-year-old from Britain, Josias Booker, arrived in British Guiana to manage a cotton plantation. This was at a time when cotton was becoming less profitable due to competition from the United States, where rising slavery and larger plantations had increased cotton production, creating difficult competition. Booker soon invited three of his brothers to come

> from Britain to join him to produce sugar, instead. Over time they acquired several plantations, and in 1834, when Britain abolished slavery, they received a significant sum as compensation for the release of their fifty-two slaves.
>
> In 1834, the brothers formed Booker Brothers & Company, which would immediately acquire additional sugar plantations cheaply as owners, now with no slaves, released them for sale. By the end of the eighteenth century, Bookers would own most of the sugar plantations in British Guiana.
>
> In 1880, the company began a partnership with McConnell, becoming known as Bookers McConnell. Subsequently, it acquired retail stores, real estate, transportation, insurance, radio stations, newspapers, and other businesses, to become the largest business in the country. (British Guiana, B.G., was sometimes referred to as "Booker's Guiana".) In addition, the company expanded to other world locations.
>
> When the country achieved independence in 1966, becoming known as Guyana, Bookers McConnell became a target for nationalisation by the socialist government. In 1976 its sugar operations were taken over to become part of government-owned Guysuco.
>
> In 2002, now headquartered in Britain, Bookers McConnell handed over management of the book prize to the Booker Prize Foundation, sponsored by the Man Group.

Inga spoke to me about her times with Prime Minister John Diefenbaker—they had been close friends. She had lived in upscale Rockcliffe while he had lived in nearby New Edinburgh. At that time, she had been doing considerable interior design work for many of the wealthy residents of the area, including the Firestone family, for whom she had designed an art gallery that contained many Group of Seven paintings. She had been a popular guest at Ottawa VIP receptions and at embassy/political functions.

I chuckled when she told me about the time at a boozy cocktail party when she told her friend Diefenbaker that a certain High Commissioner had been "touching her". He then approached the offending culprit to tell him to lay off his daughter.

Inga had known other famous politicians, such as Pierre and Margaret Trudeau, David Lewis, and Tommy Douglas, and many outstanding Canadian authors, such as Margaret Atwood, Peter Newman, Conrad Black, and Farley Mowat. When I mentioned people such as authors Michael Ondaatje and Austin Clarke, Canada's Minister of Finance Jim Flaherty (who had just died), and famous painters A.Y. Jackson and Daphne Odjig, she either knew of them or, more often, knew them as close friends. She had also been a friend with Bertrand Russell, the British philosopher, historian, and social/political activist. Wow. I felt that I was lucky to now know this fascinating person. I gave her the money to review my manuscript and left her, shaking my head somewhat in disbelief.

Five days later, Inga called me, in a very excited state, to tell me, "I loved it! I read it twice!" I felt so fortunate, and shortly met with her again for further enjoyable discussion, and to pay her $1,500 in advance for her work to find me a publisher. She was going to start with her friends who owned Doubleday in New York. I then left to spend the summer in British Columbia and asked her to call me if she made some good progress.

Time passed, and when I returned home that September I had not heard from her. I let a few weeks pass, and then telephoned her—only to find that her telephone had been disconnected. With an ominous fear, I Googled "Inga Hessel Ottawa obituary". Bingo. Sadly, she had died within two months of my last visit with her. Regardless of what results her help with my book might have produced, I had much more looked forward to her future friendship. We both loved books.

One of her two sons had told me that she would die with a book lying on her stomach. Perhaps she did.

* * *

It was late 2014 and time to start over again to try to find a publisher. I had little time to make progress, and my limited time was also being used to try and find endorsers for my book. I hoped to find endorsers who were a Guyanese person, a non-Guyanese Caribbean person, a Canadian author, a Guyanese bauxite engineer, and an executive from the Aluminum Company of Canada Ltd.

I was first able to find an enthusiastic Sir Dexter Hutt, who had been a "child of Watooka" after my time, and who had been knighted in England for his exemplary work in the school system. Evan Wong, whose family has played a prominent, positive role in the country's history, and who refused to accept President Forbe Burnham's offer to manage the nationalised Demba bauxite operations, also agreed to endorse the book.

I felt that Jennifer Hosten, Miss Grenada/Miss World 1970, would be an excellent representative endorser for the general Caribbean, and she graciously accepted. My special friend Margaret Fishback Powers, a prolific Canadian author of Christian books and verses, as well as author of the famous poem "Footprints in the Sand", became a fourth wholehearted supporter of my book. (Of course, all these special individuals had been provided with a manuscript copy to review prior to their agreement to endorse my writing.)

I tried to communicate with a few renowned Canadian authors, asking them to review my manuscript, but met with no success. In fact, they did not even respond, giving me the impression that some of these folks think they live on a higher plane. (After my book was published, though, I did communicate with Lawrence Hill, who wrote the best-seller *The Book of Negroes*, and found him to be quickly accessible and very personable. We ended up exchanging autographed books.)

There were some setbacks. I really wanted Dr. Robert "Bobby" Moore to endorse my book. As a well-known Guyanese educator, historian, and statesman, he was an ideal choice. For a few years, we had enjoyed discussing Guyana via telephone, though we never met. He was over eighty years of age, and usually after an hour or so of discussion he had to excuse himself, because his blood pressure would rise as we talked about the sad state of affairs in which President Burnham had left the country.

Dr. Moore formed the History Department at the University of Guyana, and was Guyana's High Commissioner to Canada in the 1970s, amongst many other achievements. After reading my manuscript, he commended me for my writing, but graciously turned down my request for him to endorse the book. He gave me thoughtfully considered reasons, the most prevalent being that he did not want to endorse my book, which related to the bauxite industry in Guyana, when he had turned down endorsement requests for the sugar and other Guyanese industries. He also did not want to appear to be a supporter of the Canadian bauxite industry in British Guiana, given that there are at least a few Guyanese people who still feel that Demba took advantage of the country's bauxite resources. I accepted his response, and still considered myself fortunate to know this exceptional and very popular man. Later, in November 2015, I had was greatly saddened by his passing in Ottawa.

Since there is much Canadian and Alcan content in the book, I needed to find an Alcan executive to endorse it. This was not as easy as I had thought it might be. Alcan had been taken over by Rio Tinto in 2007, and I wanted an executive who had worked for Alcan before it had been taken over. One previous president responded that he had never been familiar with Alcan's operations in Guyana, and another one did not respond to my letter. Another past president replied, "I am honoured to be asked to review your manuscript", but even after much prompting with his patient secretary, he did no more.

Finally, a former executive of the company recommended that I contact the last president of the company prior to take-over, Richard "Dick" Evans, who was/is now living in California, enjoying his passion for photography. He very enthusiastically read my manuscript, and agreed to write the preface for the book. Wow. His writing of it was absolutely exceptional.

I even sought support for my book by approaching a former Canadian prime minister whom I had respected, Paul Martin. Bold, for sure. I travelled to his office in Montreal, and enjoyed meeting his staff. Prior to entering politics in 1989, he had owned Canadian Steamship Lines, CSL. As my book has much content concerning shipping, particularly during World War II, I thought he might be interested. I left a copy of my manuscript for his review, along with my story of how Fred Pitre, who had replaced him at CSL, and I had been close friends. Unfortunately, Mr. Martin never responded.

I still had to find a publisher. I was still adding minor details and new stories to the book, and my bibliography had increased to more than 160 references. Years before, an acquaintance in Washington, DC, Dr. Peggy David, who had been a professor at Howard University, had recommended to me that I consider using Hansib Publications Ltd. in the UK. Of course, I had heard of major British book companies such as Penguin, Simon & Schuster, W. H. Smith, and HarperCollins, but I had never known of the UK's biggest black book publishing business, Hansib. I quickly learned that it is well known in Europe, in the Caribbean, and by expatriates of the Caribbean everywhere in the world. Excellent.

I sent my manuscript directly to the head of the company, Arif Ali. Not long after, he responded to say that he had read half of the document, and that he was enthusiastically willing to publish the book. While his company would not be able to market and distribute my book to North America, he was open for me to find some company that could work with Hansib to do so.

Mr. Ali is Guyanese and his story is quite interesting. He was born in 1935 in Danielstown, not far from Anna Regina, on the West Essequibo coast. His Muslim family, with seven children, were industrious business people, owning a rice mill, a coconut estate, and a general store, amongst other interests. Two of his grandparents had begun life in British Guiana and become indentured workers.

When he reached nine years of age, his family moved to Belfield on the Essequibo River's Leguan Island, where his father worked for the government. Then, in 1950, the family moved to Georgetown, where he continued his schooling. He went to England in 1957, and worked at many different jobs before he bought a grocery store in 1966. He came to know the British environment very well, and in particular the black community within the country.

In 1970, Arif founded Hansib Publications Limited. He named it after his parents, Haniff and Sibby. That same year, he also founded the *West Indian Digest*, his first publication, and then added *West Indian World*. Later he owned *Caribbean Times*, *Asian Times*, *African Digest*, and other publications.

By the 1980s, Hansib had become one of the longest-established third world-oriented publishing houses in Britain, and was on its way to being the largest publishing house in Europe run by and for the visible minority communities. Arif had many goals for his publications: to keep expatriate West Indians informed about news events in the Caribbean, to influence British policy makers, to support black causes and activism, such as the anti-apartheid movement in South Africa, and to strike at Caribbean leaders causing strife and dysfunction in their countries, including that taking place under the leadership of President Linden Forbes Burnham in Arif's home country of Guyana.

From the start, Arif was involved in black political organizations, such as the Indian Workers' Association. He was also Public Relations Officer for the West Indian Standing Conference, an umbrella organization of more than forty African and Caribbean groups in the UK. From 1997 to 2002 he was a member of the Caribbean Advisory Group, set up by the British government to give advice on Caribbean affairs in the UK and in the Caribbean. In 1997, the European Year Against Racism, he received the Gold Standard Individual Winner award.

Ali's close friend, Alex Pascall, has said, "I respect Arif for his business acumen and campaigning spirit: Arif is a totally Caribbean man who knows his culture. He remains Guyanese in his speech and has never tried to mimic an Englishman. Wherever Arif is, there is theatre, and you cannot miss the actor who is Arif! He tells you the truth in jokes and will tell people what he thinks of them. He is sharp, personable, forthright, cheeky, and chatty. Like a village elder, he advises people, and he has given opportunities to so many of those who have worked with him".

The famous Guyanese novelist, Jan Carew, who was a predecessor publisher and journalist in Britain, had stated, "I was a guest at his house several times on several occasions, and my first impression of him was that he is bold and fearless. His considerable gifts as a public figure are by no means fully recognised. He has been able to make a success of the multiple enterprises that he has undertaken in his lifetime, and he has done this with compassion and a generosity of spirit".

While Hansib was not a publisher at the full international level, there would be several advantages for me in working with this company. First, I would be always able to communicate with its leader, who is also Guyanese, as are others who work for him. Second, Hansib has its own website and marketing/distribution chain. Third, Hansib had been a business success for more than forty-four years and is well known in Guyana and other countries in the Caribbean. So is its leader. As well, he has a good sense of humour. Whenever I owe him money, he asks me to send him some "bauxite".

Our agreement took place in the late spring of 2015, and then I had to get serious about polishing up my manuscript. Over the next four to five months, I reviewed the document eight times, spotting only one error during the last review. This was exhausting work, but proved worth the effort, since the book would later be reviewed by thousands of scrutinising readers. Even so, I was to learn I'd missed some errors, including a few goofy and humbling ones. Jolyon King, living in Florida, an expert (in my opinion) on all aspects of Guyana, performed a thorough review of my innumerable facts, and came up with several corrections, which I greatly appreciated. (For example, I had not known that a mountain lion and a puma are the same animal). Elderly Sister Maureen Kossbiel, a talented nun friend in Houston, Texas, a former English teacher, graciously located eight grammatical errors, the only ones yet indicated to me in more than 105,000 words of writing. A few other folks also contributed corrections, all of which were incorporated into later printings of the book.

(I have since learned, during the publishing process for *this* book, that professional editing is well worth the seemingly high cost. Special software can be used to quickly identify grammar errors almost instantly. I learned during a first professional edit, for example, that the text in this book that you are reading had 660 ellipses. While there is no problem using ellipses, it is not good practice to use too many of them, as I had initially done. If you don't know what an ellipsis is, then that is a sign that you need professional help for editing!)

My publisher required that I ensure that my writing adhered to British grammar rules. This would affect quotation mark placements, spelling, and other requirements unfamiliar to me. The word "tire" had to be "tyre", "nationalization" to be "nationalisation," "aluminum" to be "aluminium," etc. I also wanted to write a poem for the start of the book, although I knew this would be a challenge, given my lack of poetic skill. However, while lying around swimming pools in Florida, I was able to create my *Watooka Moon* poem, which achieved my goal.

All that I had known about formatting my typed manuscript was that publishers wanted it to be double spaced, with the pages numbered. Hansib subsequently informed me that I would be responsible for editing the document. They also wanted me to remove all of the "hidden characters" from it. I learned that these were the typewriter commands I had used that do not show up in the writing, for things like indenting, paragraph separations, new page instructions, etc. I had no experience with this, and was fortunate to engage expert Richard Blanchard, who had helped to produce manuals for Nortel Networks Inc., to perform this task for me.

The thinking behind my book's cover design was interesting. For 15 years, my friend Paul McEwen, a former lawyer, would visit me for a week at my cottage in British Columbia. Living reclusively, he was a voracious reader, devouring about 200 books a year. I had been thinking about some images/photos of Guyana for the book cover. He told me that if he walked into a bookstore and saw such a cover it would not attract his attention in a compelling way. He suggested a solid cover. The unique word "Watooka" in the title would provide all the attraction necessary. I agreed with him, and later chose the solid colour of bright yellow, representing the Caribbean sun, to back up the title. Sadly, very sadly for me, my friend Paul died one year later, but was pleased that I was able to rush a copy of my just-published book to him prior to his passing,

I decided to have a special page at the front of the book to provide room for an autograph and a message. The leather-bound and hardcover versions of the book would have a gold ribbon. All the pages in the books would be glossy, and colour photographs would be grouped in the centre of the book. My book was to be published in 2016, coinciding with Guyana's fiftieth anniversary of independence, and I soon discovered that the government had initiated a contest to design a logo to celebrate the event. The open-mouthed jaguar design chosen as the winner had been submitted by a partnership of two young men, Christopher Taylor and Compton Babb. Upon hearing this, I found a way to communicate with Dr. James Rose within the Ministry of Culture, Youth, and Sports to seek approval to put this logo on the cover of my book. After some delay, I was very grateful for his approval. I also wanted a bookmark, designed to match the book, which would display my *Watooka Moon* poem. I contacted Christopher Taylor, the logo contest winner and a graphics design specialist in Georgetown, to seek his service. He graciously accepted and quickly created a very nice design. More importantly, this task allowed us to commence a fortunate relationship.

It was a special achievement for me. I had made it through the imposing and complex gauntlet to the finish line of publishing a robust book. *Children of Watooka* was published in the United Kingdom in March 2016.

> *A writer only begins a book. A reader finishes it.*
>
> — Samuel Johnson

THE RAINFOREST

Among the scenes that are deeply impressed on my mind, none exceed in sublimity the primeval tropical forests...temples filled with the varied productions of the God of Nature. No one can stand in these solitudes unmoved, and not feel that there is more in man than the mere breath of his body

— Charles Darwin

After sixty-three years, I was coming home to the land of my birth... Guyana. Six hours into the flight, the Boeing 767 slowly angled left, until the coast of Venezuela could be seen to the east of Trinidad.

I was excited, and so were 244 other passengers, for both similar and different reasons. It was mid-May 2016, and all of us were heading to various regions of Guyana to participate in major events to celebrate the fiftieth anniversary of independence for the country. I was also looking forward to events relating to the launch of my new book, *Children of Watooka*.

We had departed from Toronto on a direct flight. I was the only Caucasian passenger, with which I felt comfortable—I love diversity. There was a party atmosphere on the airplane. People were conversing while standing in the aisles, and there was much laughter and some singing. A pretty stewardess, in her black-and-yellow Fly Jamaica uniform, convened a game of Guyana trivia. While I felt that I knew most of the answers, I was too relaxed to raise my hand. Questions related to the country's motto, the Golden Arrowhead flag colours, the national bird, national flower, the first president, and much more. Most Guyanese people know the answers to these questions.

I was sitting near the front of the aircraft in an aisle seat, and so seated, I had the advantage of being able to talk to many folks around me—Afro-Guyanese, East Indian, and Portuguese people. I estimated that most of these passengers were middle class and well educated. Some of my seat neighbours had senior management positions in Toronto companies or owned their own businesses. Some, like myself, were retired.

I knew perhaps a dozen passengers, including Michelle Morrison and Denis Waite, who were the president and vice-president respectively of the Guyanese Cultural Association of Ottawa. Another friend, Marcia King, who worked in an Ottawa nursing home, had known resident Ainslie Gnaedinger there—a great lady who had lived at one time in Watooka, and who eventually lived to more than 100 years of age.

Within a half-hour of our landing, I could see out of the right window an immense straight waterway parting the dense green broccoli rainforest to the southern horizon: the mighty Essequibo River. We had passed the Venezuelan border and were now viewing the west coast of Guyana. We had also passed the area of Port Kaituma on the Kaituma River. The Jonestown suicide/massacre occurred only seven miles from there in November 1978.

The land was never-ending flat. I had not seen this view for more than six decades, and I was very moved by the scene. For sure, I was coming home.

I had read much about Sir Walter Raleigh, and recalled that he had sailed on two voyages in the waters below, seeking, without success, the land of gold, El Dorado, in northwestern South America. During his second voyage, he both failed to fulfill his promise to King James I to find gold, and also disobeyed the King's order to not engage the Spanish in battle. For this, upon his return to England, he was guillotined in 1618. His famous last words were, "Tis sharp medicine but it will cure all that ails you."

My extensive reading has allowed me to know much about the Essequibo River, the largest river between Venezuela's Orinoco River and Brazil's Amazon River. As a child, with my family, I had visited the river at the interior point of Rockstone, then existing only as a form of camp. Now, from the air, I could see two of the major islands at the thirty-two-kilometre-wide river mouth, Leguan and Waakenam. The even larger Hog Island sits just south of them. At sixty square kilometres, it is the largest island in Guyana, even larger than some of the very small Caribbean islands. Waakenam Island is about forty-five square kilometres in area, and is the most populated one, having about 10,000 inhabitants, mostly of East Indian and African descent. Farming is the predominant industry on these islands. (Speaking of islands, as I noted earlier, Guyana is the only Caribbean country that is not an island. It is also the only English-speaking country in South America.)

Robert Schomburgk, explorer and surveyor, wrote that the Essequibo River was named after Don Juan Essequibel, an officer for navigator/explorer Admiral Diego Columbus, the eldest son of Christopher Columbus. Admiral Diego Columbus spent much time in the West Indies. In 1537, the bones of both he and his father were sent from Spain to be interred at the cathedral in Santo Domingo, Hispaniola (now Dominican Republic). Subsequently, the bones were sent to Havana, Cuba, and then back to Seville in Spain. (Some dispute this, claiming that the remains are still in Santo Domingo.)

Standing up in the aisle to look out a window, I imagined the massive flow of water entering the ocean from the Essequibo River, which stretches just over 1,000 kilometres south, to its origin in the Acarai mountains near the Brazil-Guyana-Venezuela border. This river drains more than half the country, primarily via its tributaries: the Cayuni, Mazaruni, and Potaro Rivers empty the northwest, while the Rupununi River empties the southern savannahs. The iconic Kaieteur Falls, the third-highest single-drop waterfall in the world, is situated on the Potaro River.

I thought of some of the interesting celebrities that had been raised in the Essequibo region, such as Shakira Baksh, who came third in the Miss World Pageant in 1967. Eddie Grant, born in Plaisance on Guyana's east coast, now has a home on an island in the Essequibo. Grant formed the popular and racially integrated band *The Equals* in England in 1965. Later, he produced the 1983 hit song *Electric Avenue*, named after the Electric Avenue area in London, England, one of the first parts of the city to have electricity, and an area heavily populated with Caribbean people. In his very early youth, circa 1951, Eddie and his family lived in Wismar, now part of Linden, on the Demerara River, where his father operated a bicycle repair shop.

At the mouth of the river on the east side is the town of Parika, with a population of about 4,000 people. It is known for its ferry service to the islands and to the west side of the river, to towns such as Suddie and Anna Regina. It is a market centre and is also known for its trade in exotic pets. In 1914, the Demerara Railway Company completed a line from the capital city of Georgetown to Parika, a distance of about thirty kilometres. This same company built the first railway system in South America, a line from Georgetown to Plaisance on the east coast in 1848, to satisfy the needs of the sugar industry.

So, I knew that we were approaching the Cheddi Jagan International Airport, about forty-two kilometres south of Georgetown, and I could see the wonderful expanse of the Demerara River, alongside of which I had been born 105 kilometres further south, up the river. Everyone on board was excited, and the stewardesses had to remind folks several times to sit down. The aircraft coasted in parallel to the river, and as the wheels touched down, a huge cheer erupted. We were all back home.

I descended the stairs, and immediately felt the warm humidity. It is not a large airport, and I could see nothing but rainforest jungle across the river. I had an incredible feeling of wonder. In only six and a half hours I had been transported from one world, modern, with every facility, into another, a third-world country, unknown to me for six decades, exciting and to some extent dangerous, fighting to move forward economically, politically, and socially.

The airfield, built in the area known as Hyde Park, began life in 1941 as an American World War II base. It had been named Atkinson Field, after Major Atkinson, the base commander, who was in charge of the hundreds of American Seabees and Elmhurst Contracting Company employees responsible for its construction and operation. Working for Demba in Mackenzie at the time, my father and his engineering colleagues provided heavy equipment, operators, and maintenance men to aid in the construction of the 2,200-metre airstrip. Crushed stone for the project was obtained from the Seba Quarry, located about fifty-five kilometres south of Mackenzie on the Demerara River and owned by Walter Theophilius Roberts, a major landowner in the coastal village of Mahaica. He would also do blasting and quarrying work in Nigeria, Brazil, and Panama. ("Seba" means "stone" in the Arawak native language.)

At that time, there was no proper road from the airfield to Georgetown. Two double-decked boats, the *Batchelda* and the *Orange Nassau*, transported soldiers and goods daily to and from Georgetown. Aside from serving as a base for the airplane and blimps used to guard the country's coastal areas, the airfield was used continuously as an in-transit field for American warplanes being transported to West Africa, the Mid-East and England. One function of the blimps was to follow bauxite ships leaving the mouth of the Demerara River for Canada for some time, to provide protection from German submarines. They were also used daily to patrol the coast for submarines. In 1944, Eleanor Roosevelt arrived for a visit in the US President's airplane, guarded by four or five fighter planes.

I waited one and a half hours for my four pieces of baggage to appear, three of which contained a total of sixty heavy books. The baggage room is not air-conditioned, and everyone was a bit soaked when they finally went outside to obtain a taxi. I had been warned to be careful with taxis, because many tourists and returnees to Guyana continue to be taken advantage of, if not robbed, by fraudulent drivers. I chose a yellow cab, because they are registered with the government (although I later learned that even that is not a guarantee of safety). There are no meters in taxi cars, although there is a standard fee from the airport to downtown Georgetown. I subsequently learned, too late, that air conditioning is provided only if requested.

The next hour was quite exciting. In Canada, my driver would have been arrested for illegal driving within the first few kilometres. However, his manner of driving turned out to be perfectly normal, relative to many other drivers in the country. While he did not ever approach 100 kilometres per hour, it certainly felt like I was in the back seat of a mini Daytona racing car. Bathroom-style stainless steel handles in the back seat would have been helpful.

Almost all road vehicles are small cars, save for large army-like British/Russian trucks and mini-bus vans. I do not recall seeing any speed-limit or other traffic signs, although later trips would reveal a few. Often, the driver would move out onto the oncoming-traffic side of the road to speedily pass slower vehicles, even though many vehicles could be seen dead ahead, coming straight at us. A taxi driver would not survive without a rapid-fire car horn. Tailgating is continuous, accompanied by the squealing of brakes, seemingly weak. Sudden jerks of the car indicated that we had narrowly missed one of the prevalent pot holes, a pedestrian, or another vehicle. Through all of this, the driver was continuously talking to answer my excited questions.

For the full trip, there were houses and other buildings alongside the roughly macadamised road, together with makeshift family market stalls, loose cattle, bicycle riders, pedestrians (including uniformed school children), dogs, and other excitement. Many of the building structures are unpainted and/or unfinished. (Housing developments in Guyana are called "Schemes".) Generally, we were driving north, parallel to the river, which can vary from being near the road to a mile or so from it. Every now and then we passed over a small canal, where we could see the old rusted Dutch koker gate where the canal met the river. The canals contain overgrowth and garbage. Local folks sat on the railings of the small canal bridges, taking in the excitement of shouting, vehicle horns, and near-miss incidents..

I recalled the last time that I had travelled that road, to the airport, with my parents and brother in May 1953. Then, there had been tropical flora along both sides of the road for most of the distance. Occasionally we would have seen unpainted shacks, some on stilts, with half-naked children running about, wearing only colourful t-shirts. Some of the shacks then had palm leaf roofs. Our driver had had to watch out for donkeys, cattle, and dogs on the road.

In the early 1800s there were more than thirty plantations along this stretch of land, all fronting on the river, only a few feet above sea level. Of course, the means of transporting supplies and produce then was by boats on the river. The villages that we were driving through all seem to be joined together, and had claimed the names of the old plantations: Rome, Eccles, Providence, Golden Grove, Houston, Farm, etc. I did not know it then, but I would soon return to Farm to be hosted by a renowned former politician of Guyana. As we passed through Rome, close to Georgetown, I recalled that this was where Jan Carew had been raised. A novelist, poet, and educator, he had assisted Cheddi Jagan in bringing the country to independence.

At some unmarked point we reached Georgetown, where the traffic was very congested, with much car-swerving and horn-blowing. I was not afraid but was certainly holding on well, so to speak. It was certainly exciting. I had no idea where we were, but I did recognise tall St. George's Cathedral as we circled around it onto Church Street. We were not far from my destination: 272 Forshaw Street, Queenstown.

Georgetown has a population of about 240,000 people, who live in many wards, one of which is Queenstown. The names of the wards and streets of the city reflect the influence of the Dutch, French, and English who administered the city over time. Queenstown was purchased in 1887 by the Town Council, presided over by Mayor George Anderson Forshaw. It had been a part of a plantation named Thomas, and after acquisition was named after Queen Victoria. Forshaw also had the current City Hall building beautifully designed, and then constructed, in 1889. He had been a solicitor and businessman and, as a coloured man, had broken a tradition of white mayors. Forshaw Street is named after him. He lived on Quamina Street, in the large home now known as the Cara Lodge.

The taxi came to a stop outside of the gated entrance to a home hidden by much beautiful tropical growth. I paid the driver and followed previous advice to ensure that the number of bags retrieved from the trunk equaled the number that had entered it at the airport. Attractive Syeada Manbodh, alerted by her four dogs, met me at the gate. I had arrived at my destination, the Rainforest Bed and Breakfast guest house.

The large guest house is concrete and two-storied, with large verandas on each floor facing the tropical rainforest flora at the front. There is a second gate as one enters the lower patio, and the house entrance doors off the lower patio are barred, as are windows. Home and business security is apparent everywhere in the city. The house stretches to an eight-foot brown-painted concrete fence on both sides of the property. Ceiling fans cool the large bottom floor central area, while the four guest rooms on its sides are air conditioned during the nights.

The attachment that the hosts have for the country is demonstrated by hundreds of paintings of scenes of the native rainforest, crafts, and artefacts distributed outside and within the house, many encased in glass cabinets. One really feels that one is immersed in a rainforest environment, and with the arrival of darkness at 6:30 p.m., that feeling is reinforced by the litany of cricket and tree-frog sounds arising from the flora at the front of the house, a wonderful form of Gaussian noise that I had not heard for more than six decades. I recalled that this noise is louder on rainy nights. I had often wondered why it is rare to see any of these choristers during the day.

Introduced to my room, I immediately headed for the shower—it would be my closest friend, several times a day, for the duration of my stay. Although available, no hot water is required, and one does not really have a "shower". Water pressure in Georgetown is only half of that at my Canadian home, so one stands under a slow, but gratifying, stream of water. I did use the sink water to brush my teeth. I also took my daily malaria pill, although this is not really required unless one travels into the interior. I never slept under a sheet. We did not use mosquito netting over our beds, although this is still practiced to some extent in Georgetown. In my youth, these nets were always white, but now they can be very fancy and come in beautiful colours.

During my short stays in Georgetown I fortunately did not experience any power outages. These can be lengthy and can be a significant nuisance, especially with darkness occurring early and with air conditioning, cooling-fan, freezer and bathing requirements. For 2016, the Guyana Power and Light government-owned utility set a target of no more than seventy-five outages per household, but have already exceeded that, achieving 118 outages per household, for a total average of 125 hours of outages per residence. Citizens in North America would find this level of service totally unacceptable. On top of all this, power leakages from old equipment, combined with power theft, amount to a loss of almost thirty percent of total power distributed. Guyana Water Inc., also government-owned, hopes to have potable water available to all citizens within a few years. Only forty percent of water users in 2017 were metered, and many users are late paying their bills, or simply do not pay. Most people use bottled water for drinking purposes.

The Rainforest was to be my headquarters for my time in Georgetown. I was to find that I had made an excellent choice. Almost every accommodation in the city was full, hosting the huge influx of Guyanese folks returning to their home country for weeks of anniversary celebrations. My hosts, Syeada Manbodh and her husband, Jerry Lagra, are prominent citizens, and have much knowledge of and experience within the country. Not only was I to meet diverse and extremely interesting guests, but I would be fortunate to meet many stimulating and appealing local friends of my hosts. Many of the guests are professionals, volunteers, and students engaged in development activities in Guyana.

Many of us met on the upper veranda that evening for interesting discussion. Guests Alex and Brenda Fortune from Brooklyn, New York, would be great friends for the duration of my stay. Portuguese folks Andre and Lyn Pires were the first to buy my book from me in Guyana. Pete Oxford was a centre of attention with his interesting tales of his renowned work doing world-wide wildlife photography, his concerns for saving natural environments, and his beautiful books about these subjects. One of the first local people to visit was Sharmini Poulin, who has worked in the diplomatic world for most of her life, including in China and in Sri Lanka. She is fluent in the Mandarin language and works as a senior official in the office of Canada's High Commissioner to Guyana. She was aware of my scheduled book launch, to be held at the High Commissioner's home on the coming Friday and we shared information about some of the aspects of preparing for the event. All of us would get together several times over the coming week in the evenings.

I was up as usual at 5 a.m. the following morning, and could tell approximately what time it was by the receding night noise and by the increasing bird sing-song. I was too excited to do my usual reading at this hour. Jerry prepared breakfast for a 7:30 a.m. serving. Mango pancakes! It was interesting to see the flat pyramid-like netted covers placed over our meals as a mosquito protection—although I did not experience many mosquitoes in Georgetown at any time during my visit. Given that we were in the tropics, we enjoyed a great variety of fruit offerings. Every morning, Syeada, or the hired help, would sweep up the constantly descending litter—flower petals, twigs, seeds, and leaves—amongst the tropical foliage in the yard.

That morning, I decided to walk just over ten blocks (Guyanese say "corners") to visit the Anglican St. George's Cathedral, the tallest wooden church building in the world. As I walked along Church Street I could see men with tall boots working to clean up the parallel canal, which was overgrown with weeds and strewn with plastic garbage. At another location, I watched as a municipal worker used a weed-eater to cut masses of deep grass cluttered with cans and plastic bottles. He did not attempt to pick them up first, so all this garbage went flying around him. Every so often, I encountered a deep rectangular hole in the sidewalk that contained dirty water, within which small live fish were circulating.

What I noticed most was the humidity. My shirt was wet after only six corners of walking. I stepped into a small clothing store to buy a nice yellow shirt. When I stepped up to a counter to pay, I was politely accompanied to the back of the store, where a young woman took care of the transaction…behind bars, with the entrance to her little dark room also barred and locked. *Wow*, I thought, *this is the Georgetown that I was warned about.* Regardless, I secured a very nice shirt at a low price.

Two blocks farther, I stopped into Austin's Book Store, still on Church Street. I was greeted by the guard inside the door, who took my new shirt for safekeeping. While this store is rather small, even with two floors, it is one of the bigger and more popular bookstores in Guyana. I had communicated with proprietor Lloyd Austin on several occasions and knew that he is an astute businessman. The woman cashier behind a barred counter window somehow recognised me immediately, offering a nice a greeting. I have not often been greeted by someone behind bars!

In the centre of the first table of books that shoppers encountered, I spotted my yellow book, *Children of Watooka,* so far away from my home in Canada, waiting to be purchased. Standing beside me was a young, well-dressed man, perusing the books. I immediately struck up a conversation with him and he purchased my book. Very personable, and with a good sense of humour, he told me that he was Judge Navindra Singh. Wow. At only 43 years of age, he had risen to prominence in only a few short years. I later learned that he has gained the respect and admiration of the public for his efficiency, and for his efforts to take on high-profile criminal cases, for which he is known to hand out long sentences to those found guilty. He told me modestly that he is a member of the American Mensa Society: to be a member, one has to be in the top two percent of those who take a recognised IQ test. Given his profession, he is close to the crime situation in Guyana, and we discussed various means to maximise safety. Strangers can be easily spotted and taken advantage of, he said, using the Guyanese expression, "Strangers not know graveyard". I asked him what the best words would be for me to use to end my book autograph/message for him, an East Indian, and ever since I have used his offering for similar purchasers: "Ram! Ram!"

Lloyd Austin, the long-time owner of the store, came down the stairs to meet me, and I thanked him for his support of my book. At 77 years of age, he was a tall, intelligent man with a good sense of humour. We had a long enjoyable conversation. His store sells many books authored by Guyanese and Caribbean authors. It also specialises in school books. At the time, I was looking for a copy of Godfrey Chin's *Nostalgias*, but he did not have one for sale. I was able to help sell a few more of my own books while I was there. During a later visit to his store, Lloyd drove me around Georgetown, reciting tales and showing me some of the sights. He had once taught at St. Aidan's School in Wismar, before the area was renamed Linden.

I then left to walk a few more blocks to the steps at the side entrance of St. George's Cathedral. I was greeted inside the door by an attractive and friendly lady, Judith, who told me that she is the wife of Father Raymond Cummings, whom I was to later meet. She told me more about the church, of which I already knew some history. It was built in 1899. The church elders had decreed that it was to be constructed using the woods of the country, and none other. It has a Gothic style and is made mostly of durable greenheart wood. Hanging from the ceiling is a large chandelier that was donated by Queen Victoria.

Judith asked me why I was in Guyana, and I mentioned the fiftieth-anniversary events and events relating to my book. After some further discussion, she mentioned that her daughter, Gabriella, twenty-one, had enjoyed reading my book, and had asked her mother, "How can a white person who lives so far away in Canada know so much about our country?" I chuckled, and asked Judith if Gabriella would be at Mass the following morning. After she had responded with a smiling affirmation, I told her that I would enjoy meeting her daughter at the Mass to answer her question.

Next, at the corner of Church Street and Main Street, I encountered Guyana's National Library, a beautiful, winged, wooden two-story building built in 1909. It is also referred to as the Carnegie Building after its famous US benefactor. I had promised its Chairman, Petamber Persaud, that I would donate two books to the library.

The library is the headquarters for Guyana's library system, which includes many satellite branches. The building that I entered houses more than 400,000 books, including rare and out-of-print books written by renowned Guyanese authors, such as Edgar Mittelholzer. Having read many of his, now very expensive, books, I recalled his fascination with suicide, and that he had written in a dark and somber manner, like Edgar Allan Poe. A critic estimated that at least fifteen of his story characters had taken their own lives. In 1965, Mittelhozer poured petrol on himself in a field in Surrey, England, and immolated himself.

Petamber calls himself an oral historian and media practitioner. He is a specialist in Guyanese literature, which he promotes on his television programs and through his newspaper columns. I had come to the library hoping to meet with Petamber, should he be available. As I sat near the entrance waiting for assistance, I examined the huge interior, with its very high ceilings on both floors and expansive wooden stairs leading to the second floor. Not far from me was hung a large oil painting of Edward Ricardo Braithwaite. I was perspiring and finding it hard to believe that this archive treasury was not air-conditioned…while recalling sadly that I was now in a third-world country, where money is scarce. Mr. Persaud was out of the building and his staff were unable to contact him, but I would meet him several times in the future, and he would confirm that securing building air-conditioning is a high priority. Two copies of my book would find their way to its historic shelves and registry.

Shortly thereafter, I found myself within a few blocks of the historic Stabroek Market building. Pedestrian crossing signs do not exist—evidently, every place on every street is for pedestrians, not only for crossing, but for lengthwise movement as well. Shouting and vehicle horns make things exciting. Dozens and dozens of mini-buses prevail, adding to the hubbub. These flat-faced vans, none of them appearing to be new, are packed with up to fifteen people. Each bus has a number on its front, and there is a "money man" who sits behind the driver, extending his head and one arm full of money out of the window, yelling to attract people to use the bus. (Perhaps he is the vehicle owner!) Tourists would have difficulty using these buses, because it is never clear where they are going, and the fast natural creole language of the local folks is tough to understand. I took a bus only once, but got off after only a few blocks, before I got lost. I had been the only passenger in the packed van who had not been talking.

In the blazing heat, I made it to the roofed Stabroek Market building itself, which was surrounded with vendor booths. After entering the building's dark interior, I did not wander far before a foot-long rat tore across the old dirty cement floor. And, incredibly, not much further along, I heard, "Hi, Steve!" Sitting on a stool outside the counter of a meat-vendor's booth was a grinning Lorna Jessemy, a Guyanese friend of mine who lives in Ottawa, Canada. She had arrived on the same airplane as myself, and was visiting her brother, who owned the butcher shop. Meat hung everywhere, and several employees were busy cutting and preparing the produce.

Guyana has more than 1,800 species of fish, and all sorts of these are sold at Georgetown markets: red/grey snapper, sea trout, lukanani, churi churi, queriman, basha, four-eye, cuirass, bangamary, hassar, gilbaka, tilabi, and many more. Fish-head soup is a Guyanese specialty: the whole heads are the main ingredients and sucking on the spicy stuff is delightful...for some. A non-Caribbean tourist would also have difficulty knowing what to do with the great variety of fruit that is available: sapodilla, locust, whitey, star apple, mamee, tamarind, cookerite, somatoo, pomegranate, corio, owara, soursop, guava, papaw, five fingers, custard apple, sourie, and much more. On several corners, I encountered a man with a machete cutting off the tops of coconuts, then putting a straws in them for buyers to quench thirst. Makeshift booths everywhere were selling leather goods, music CDs, soft drinks, clothes, mosquito nets, carved coconuts, crafts, and baked goods.

Construction of the iron-and-steel Stabroek Market building was completed in 1881. It may be the oldest building in the city that is still in use. The area is easily the busiest in Georgetown and is a high-crime area. Indeed, I was excited all the time that I was there.

Exiting the market, I walked for several blocks, taking in the excitement, then arrived at a very busy intersection where two sets of vendors sat on chairs on the sidewalk, selling soft drinks from large tubs of ice. Given the heat, their business was brisk. I struck up a conversation with a woman named Lyneth, who was sitting on a small bench with both large and small Golden Arrowhead flags in her hands. When I had asked her what she was doing, she smiled and responded, "I tryin' to catch meh hand". This meant that she was trying to make some money by selling the flags. I asked her if I could take a photo of her, attractive and with her colourful flags. "Oh sir, you make me blush!"

I then humorously posed the question, "How, ma'am, can a black lady blush? That would be like me, a white guy, seeing a ghost and turning white!"

She shrieked with laughter. Oh, well. I bought her a drink, and sat with her for a half hour, helping her sell flags.

On Regent Street, I entered Matt's Record bar, one of the oldest music stores still operating in Georgetown. "Matt" is a lady with short red hair. She met me at the door, smiling and extending a nice welcome. We talked for some time. I learned it was her 86th birthday, and I initiated several clients and myself singing "Happy Birthday" to her. Eventually, we came to talk about my book. She was particularly interested in its World War II content. She told me she had been raised on the west side of the Demerara River. She recalled that as a little girl she had been frightened by a huge monster floating in the sky above and had run into a nearby cane field to escape from it. She later learned that the "monster" had been a blimp from Atkinson Field across the river, being used by the Americans to look for German submarines in the ocean. This event had probably occurred in 1942, when the menacing submarine presence was at a peak. On one occasion that same year, a blimp observing the ocean off the British Guiana coast spotted a slow-moving sailboat containing three sun-roasted men. A fast torpedo boat was dispatched from Atkinson Field to rescue the men—one of whom was Henri Charriere, later to become known as "Papillon". All three men had escaped from the Devil's Island prison in French Guiana. Charriere lived in the country for two years before moving on to Venezuela.

It was on this day that I learned Guyana's money system...somewhat. G$200 will buy US$1. G$5,000 will buy US$25. So, one has to carry around one of these two currencies, or both. If you carry mostly Guyana dollars, you will have fistfuls of paper bills. I preferred to use the Guyana paper bills, and so I had to find a way to minimise bulge and maximise security. On future excursions, I did not carry my wallet, just a credit card and three wads of Guyana bills in three different pockets. The smallest Guyana paper bill, which I infrequently encountered, was G$20—five cents US. I got rid of them by adding them to service tips.

 I also learned that hiring a taxi for any distance over five or more corners made sense. They are very economical: I could taxi from downtown Georgetown to the Rainforest for only G$400. The vehicles were mostly air-conditioned, and the drivers in every case were clean and well-dressed. I was pleased that most were talkative, which permitted me to enhance my knowledge of local whereabouts, news, and politics. I would mention the names of former/current politicians and would get the taxi driver's opinion as to which of them were honest and contributors to advancing the country's fortune…or not. The taxis have no meters, and tipping is optional. Independent taxi drivers are called "barefoot cowboys". On one taxi I noticed a bumper sticker that read, "Who God bless, no man curse".

 Early in the evening at the Rainforest, several friends and the house guests gathered on the upper veranda for diverse discussion before five of us headed east of Georgetown for a big fiftieth-anniversary "Concert of the Legends" at Providence Stadium. This 16,000-seat facility has replaced the old Bourda grounds as the National Stadium for Guyana, and was built, with financial help from India, for world-class cricket test matches. Guyana has the only major Test Level cricket team in South America.

 The next morning, I was up early and reading (as usual) when Syeada came down the stairs to ask me if I wanted to come with her on her regular stray-dog feeding round at 6 a.m. She had several stainless-steel bowls of homemade dog food, meat and rice, mixed and covered. I had plenty of time to do this before going downtown to Sunday Mass at St. George's Cathedral at 7:30 a.m., so I readily agreed. I did not know it then, but I was to make this salvation run with a lady renowned in the country for her affection and care for stray animals and birds. This particular early-morning objective was to feed dogs at three locations.

 Our first stop was on Republic Avenue at the very large wooden High Court building, dull yellow in colour, with interesting architecture, and not particularly well maintained. Two dogs, Pumpkin and Lulu, came trotting up to the high open gates to meet Syeada, who led them to their regular eating place. Pumpkin was missing most of a hind leg but hopped around unconcerned. Syeada told me with disgust that a previous angry owner had chopped the dog's leg off with a machete. As I waited, I checked out a body that was lying on the sidewalk to verify that his chest was still moving up and down, and guessed that he was there as a result of a previous evening not unassociated with alcohol. The High Court is the third-highest court in Guyana with respect to power and responsibility, behind the Court of Appeal and the Full Court. It functions above the Magistrate's Court.

More dogs hungrily appeared for Syeada's treat at the renowned Castellani House, at the corner of Vlissingen Road and Homestretch Avenue, designed by Cesar Castellani, one of the most prominent and prolific architects of British Colonial buildings in British Guiana. Erected between 1877 and 1882, the building served government officials initially, until country leader Linden Forbes Sampson Burnham and his wife, First Lady Viola Burnham, moved in during 1965. They resided in this luxurious home, which during his Burnham's time was referred to as "The Residence", until his death in 1985. This is where the President enjoyed his Chivas Regal and Royal Salute whiskey. It is still in remarkable condition, and is now Guyana's National Art Gallery. The dogs were happy to see Syeada again.

While I had never seen Castellani House, I had always tried to envisage it, given a story related to me by a woman friend. When she had been a young woman working in the field of education, she had one morning been waiting for a bus near the front of the house. Burnham had come by mounted on a horse, together with other men, also mounted. He had whistled at her rather rudely. A woman of courage, she had told him off… and from then on, on any morning that they had met, he had removed his hat to salute her. We are proud of you, Norma De Haarte!

Our final stop was at an elementary school. Given the day being a Sunday, all was quiet as Syeada fed the dogs. She knows all their names. I saw no movement at the guardhouse, and Syeada murmured that the guards are often asleep in the mornings, sleeping off the effects of Guyana rum. Oh, well.

* * *

> *I always tell those willing to listen that if they love and are kind to their animals they will be loved and protected in return.*
>
> — Syeada Manbodh

Syeada, then fifty-five, is an engaging, dark-skinned, black-haired East Indian lady, full of energy and enthusiasm. After enjoying many personal/group discussions, attending special events, visiting with close and interesting friends, cleaning up beach garbage, watching her cook and paint, and feeding stray animals with her, I have come to know her as an exceptional, caring, and special person/friend. It is no wonder that she is so popular, and that guests, thanks also to Jerry, continue to return to the Rainforest. She is naturally attached to the fauna of the country. One evening, we were up on the second-floor veranda when she used a small noisemaker to attract some of her flying friends—bats who were eating mangoes high up in her yard tree.

Syeada Manbodh was born in Bartica, where her father operated a sawmill and a store. They lived in a wooden home with a beautiful view of the Essequibo River. Her Muslim upbringing did not permit her to touch or own a dog.

Subsequently, the family moved to Georgetown. She lived there until she and her family moved to Toronto in the 1980s. There she studied marketing and accounting, and worked using these skills until she moved back to Guyana in 1993. Over the years, she became deeply involved with the Guyana Red Cross, helping abused young children, and subsequently became involved with the Guyana Society for the Prevention of Cruelty to Animals. She has won awards from both of these organisations for her work. She related to me how a wealthy woman from South Africa who had come to live in Georgetown had demonstrated great skill at taking care of abused and stray animals. It was from this mentor that Syeada developed her care and love for animals.

One of her main passions is to have dogs spayed and neutered. This greatly reduces the number of dogs that have to be put down whether they are healthy or not. She has helped arrange for foreign veterinarians to come to do spay and vaccination work in Guyana, particularly in the lower-income areas, such as Sophia and Bartica.

Her reputation for care and kindness for animals causes her to constantly receive calls to help animals in distress, often from the police. On one occasion, on the eve of Mashramani, she received a call from a lady to help rescue a dog that had been thrown into a caiman-infested canal at Ogle with a chain around its neck. The woman had tried to rescue the dog, named Carliza, but had been unsuccessful. Syeada arrived to complete the rescue of Carliza, using a boat, and the two women had befriended each other. The lady who had called her had been First Lady Deolatchmee Ramotar, wife of then-President Donald Ramotar. Syeada has been grateful ever since for the help that the Ramotars have provided for her animal-rescue endeavours.

I have been on a few animal rescues with this "voice of the homeless animals" and "the dog lady", as she is affectionately known. Not all of her rescues, though, relate to dogs. On one occasion, she took me along in her vehicle to rescue a wounded white egret. The call was for her to go to a certain place on Vlissingen Road that we would recognise because we would find a large dead dog at the edge of the road. We found the dog quickly, recently killed but already bloated by the tropical heat. The dog was lying by a canal parallel to the road. No water could be seen in the canal, because it was full of lily pads, with huge beautiful flowers rising on high stems—hundreds of them. We searched up and down both sides of the road but, alas, without success. Syeada does not give up easily, and was naturally disappointed.

At times, she has been called to the Ogle airport to remove stray dogs from the runways. Once she took two abused monkeys into her home, one of them named Bully. Syeada showed me a photo of this bushy brown-haired animal in one of wildlife photographer Pete Oxford's books, and smiled with so much deep affection at her Bully that I was very moved to see her face light up so. Another time, she and volunteer friends greatly improved the conditions for the horses and other animals that end up in the police pound. She has always been grateful to the friends who have donated their time and money to help her cause. I have often seen her wince at the shoulder pain that has accrued over the years, due, she says, to the many dog kennels that she has had to lift.

On one occasion in February 2012, the *Kaieteur News* reported, "Many of our sons and daughters of the soil are recognised for their sterling contributions to their country and countrymen in various ways, but Syeada is one who deserves a National Award for the monumental contribution that she has made for Guyana's pets and other animals, particularly those in distress". It was no wonder that subsequently Guyana recognised her by giving her a Woman of the Year award.

Abused cows, horses, and donkeys also receive her attention. One lady wrote about the time when Syeada took her to visit a donkey that had been abandoned on the East Coast. "We spotted 'Bruck Up' lying down in the grass under the hot noonday sun. This in itself is unusual for such animals that would normally seek the shade of a tree or just graze. When water was offered it was readily accepted by the thirsty donkey, which did not even attempt to get up. Eventually, after some encouragement, the poor animal struggled to its feet, and the few steps it took were obviously painful. Indeed, the hoofs were overgrown and the right front hoof was twisted at right angles. Its knee joints appeared swollen and arthritic. The laceration on its back, although not open, was still oozing, and the big growth hanging down between its front legs looked very unpleasant. Were it not for the kind persons who fed and watered this poor animal each day, its suffering would be unimaginable". It is no wonder that many people have recommended that Syeada be made the head of the Guyana Society for the Prevention of Cruelty for Animals.

One Sunday morning, I noticed an interesting letter to the editor in the *Stabroek News*. A woman walking in the Botanical Gardens with two of her dogs, Ange and Coco, had discovered a huge amount of smoke blanketing the back section of the gardens. She had called the fire department, and while they were fighting the fire, had discovered a homeless man setting a second fire not far away. When the woman demanded an explanation, the man said that the place where he sleeps under the tree was strewn with garbage, and he wanted to get rid of it. The woman had written to the newspaper encouraging all citizens to be the eyes and ears of taking care of their environment. This caring person was Syeada Manbodh.

Even as far back as the mid-1850s, villages and towns had established fenced animal pounds for the keeping of stray animals, such as cows, horses, donkeys, dogs, and others. These were administered by a pound master, working under the authority of the local authorities. To recover a stray animal from the pound, the owner had to pay a fine, and the costs for the care and feeding of the animal. Being a pound master was a thankless but necessary job.

One evening while I was alone at the Rainforest, I received a call from a man who wanted to talk to Syeada. As she was not present, I asked the man if his call was an emergency, and he responded in the affirmative—something about a dog. Syeada later returned to deal with the situation. She chuckled when she asked me if I had known who the man on the telephone was, which I hadn't—he had just left his name as "Dave".

It turned out to have been Dave Martins, a Guyanese music legend who has written more than 100 songs and was a leader of the popular Caribbean musical group Tradewinds. Of course, I had heard of him and I was aware of many of his songs, such as *Not A Blade Of Grass,* written, but not directly relating to such, about the continuing border dispute between Guyana and Venezuela. His hilarious song *Mr. Rooster* relates to sixteen sexy chickens chasing a rooster. He now prefers to sing alone, mixing comedy with his songs. He had performed at some of the fiftieth-anniversary events. Obviously, both he and Syeada know each other well.

A Victoria Regia plaque in the Rainforest, presented to Syeada by the Caribbean Voice organization, pays this tribute to her:

> *A life characterised by a unique focus on humanitarianism and/or protection, advocacy and activism.*

* * *

Syeada dropped me off at St. George's Cathedral just in time for the 7:30 a.m. Mass. The large interior of the church was far from being full, and I was provided with two Mass books at the entrance by a pretty lady. I took my pew about three quarters up to the left of the centre aisle and sat close to a few ladies on my left. All the women wore colourful dresses, and the men were neat and clean in short-sleeved shirts and pressed pants. A heavily perspiring Father Andrew Carto would preside over the Mass, with much assistance, including from Father Raymond Cummings and from Deacon Andrew Hoyte.

Once I had completed my initial prayers, I sat to admire the wonderful structure, an icon of Guyana. The humidity was noticeable, and ladies were using hand fans to cool themselves. Many of the tall columns hosted electric fans, and I was grateful to be sitting directly in front of one of these. Over two dozen Golden Arrowhead flags, to celebrate the fiftieth anniversary, also hung from the columns. The whole wooden structure was very solid, attesting to the strength and durability of greenheart wood. A few pigeons cooed up in the netherworld of the very high ceilings. All the side window jalousies were open, and were only closed, I surmised in the event of a rare serious storm.

Just before the Mass commenced, I noticed a very distinguished tall man, suited, walking up the isle past me, with two also distinguished ladies. I could not take my eyes off them: they were simple in their manner, but somehow singular. Noticing my glances, the lady beside me told me that the distinguished folks were President David Granger, his wife, Sandra, and one of his sisters. Wow.

I was amazed at the simplicity of these people. There was no entourage, at least in the church, and to see them genuflect humbly and in public was very positive for me, and a contrast to the negative manner of Donald Trump, who was running for President in the United States, and to that of Guyana's previous President Burnham, who everywhere I went had a negative reputation. This gave me a sense of hope for the country, now led by a man with a reputation for honesty and intelligence, and somewhat indifferent to power and status.

After communion, I headed straight for the front doors of the church, to be in a position to take photos of the President and First Lady leaving the church. Exciting for me. Undercover policemen presided over the sweeping front stairs, while police in uniform guarded the black limousines and patrolled the streets. The young policemen on the steps were interested to talk to me about the "kit" issued to Royal Canadian Mounted Police, and about their rank structure. Once the country's leader and ladies had been given a proper farewell, they entered the vehicles and their cavalcade slowly pulled away, with sirens blaring. This is the custom in Guyana—continuous sirens always accompany the President's movement.

I immediately proceeded to briefly speak with the Very Reverend Andrew Carto on the front steps. He then wished for me to take care, using the Guyanese expression, "Walk in de corna!" Before I stepped down the high and expansive steps, I looked out upon the city scene displayed before me, now vacated by the president's entourage. It had been upon these steps that a wide-eyed seven-year-old Godfrey Chin, now renowned for his Guyana stories in his book *Nostalgias*, had looked out upon The Great Fire that had consumed the heart of the city on February 23, 1945. This conflagration commenced on the second floor of Booker's Drug Store on Main Street, when escaped alcohol vapour was negligently enflamed. Many historical buildings and precious artefacts, books, and papers had been destroyed over several blocks.

Back inside the church, I again met a smiling and attractive Judith Cummings, who introduced me to her daughter, Gabriella, and to her daughter's friend, Brigid, from Nigeria. Both were pretty, polite, and very well-dressed. "Gabby" is studying to become a lawyer, while Brigid is hoping to become a medical doctor. One of Gabby's brothers wants to follow in his father's footsteps to become a priest. I hope that I satisfied their desire to understand how I was able to write my book all about the history of their country… rather, our country. Guyana needs wonderful young people like these young women to lead it into the future.

Early that afternoon, back at the Rainforest, I was extremely fortunate to meet an esteemed and bearded eighty-year-old visitor to the guest house. A good friend of Syeada and Jerry, he had come to purchase a book from me. Stanley Greaves. Wow. Guyanese, he is one of the most distinguished artists in the Caribbean—a painter, sculptor, and writer. I greatly enjoyed my discussion with him, as we took turns sharing our backgrounds. He has been quoted as saying:

> *Ideas and concepts, to a certain degree, determine the materials and techniques required to give them form. I still don't talk about myself as making art. Other people do that. I am a maker of things. In the early days I found matchboxes, cigarette boxes, bits of string, wire, empty boot-polish tins, whatever, and made things. Drawing was just another activity and still is. My favourite medium is still wood, of course. My hitherto*

secret occupation of writing poems, which has now come to light, is another form of making. My first tool was a penknife, which was used to carve boats, guns and knives and a figure which, when shown to (Edward Rupert) Burrowes, made him present me with some carving tools from under his bed They were a bit rusty, but with loving care were brightened up and sharpened. I still have a few of them.

My inspiration for pottery came from the marabuntas... the wasps that make tiny spherical clay pots in which to lay eggs. I was about ten and thought that if creatures without brains and fingers could make pots what about me? My experiments came to an abrupt end when my newly made wet pots were put to be baked in my mother's coal-pot. I felt that just as she used to put soft dough in an oven to get hard, the same would happen to my pots. They exploded and my experiments were banned, much to my annoyance. It was about thirty-five years later at Howard University that I made a fresh start...

There is so much to this artist that it would fill a book. He has won many awards, including Guyana's Golden Arrowhead Medallion. Other guests at the Rainforest were also fortunate to meet him. His mentor had been Edward Rupert Burrowes, a Barbadian, who is acclaimed as the "Father of Guyanese Art". Stanley's work is displayed at Castellani House.

One of our guest mates was a most interesting man whom Syeada and Jerry have known well for many years: internationally renowned wildlife photographer and conservationist Pete Oxford. When in Guyana, the Rainforest is his home away from his home in Quito, Ecuador, where he has lived with his wife, Renee Bish, for more than thirty years. Syeada had let me know in advance that Pete would be back as a guest, and I had very much looked forward to meeting him. Over the week, several of us would have the pleasure of hearing him speak to us of his exciting and interesting adventures into the wild in many countries. Our first thorough insight into his work was to be that very Sunday afternoon at the Herdmanston Lodge, only five blocks away, also in Queenstown. We were all invited to attend a launch for his latest book *Undiscovered Guyana*, a coffee-table book with photos of Guyana's scenery, people, flora, and fauna. We already knew much about the book, since he had already shown us a privileged copy.

A comfortable crowd of well-dressed invitees was present under a set of large open tents to keep off the heat of the sun. Three government Ministers were present, including David Patterson, Minister of Public Infrastructure, and I was also able to meet Pierre Giroux, Canada's High Commissioner to Guyana, for the first time, although we had previously exchanged messages. Members of the Diplomatic Corps, special invitees, and representatives of organizations that are working to protect and preserve Guyana's rich diversity were present. I enjoyed the hors d'oeuvres, and especially the fifteen-year-old El Dorado rum.

President David Granger had challenged the country's head of the World Wildlife fund, Aeisha Williams, to produce a book to educate the people of Guyana, and the world, about the incredible biodiversity in the country, and to do so in coordination with Guyana's fiftieth anniversary of independence. Pete Oxford was engaged by the Ministry of Natural Resources and the World Wildlife Fund to produce the book. The book launch had been scheduled for this particular day, May 22, because it was the United Nations-sanctioned International Day of Biodiversity across Guyana.

Pete did an excellent job presenting all aspects of his book, and referring to many of the beautiful photographs. One of the photographs was that of the brown capuchin monkey, Bully, that I mentioned earlier. These monkeys are common in Guyana, and are very intelligent, capable of using complicated tools. Pete had earlier told us that the Guyana Defence Force had provided a helicopter with pilots for twenty days for him to take the, mostly aerial, photos for the book. That had been very beneficial and exciting for him. A video was also shown, and one of its beautiful scenes was that of two pretty native-looking women, one dark brown and the other black—Syeada and Sharmini Poulin!

According to Pete, "The objective is the most basic form of conservation, and that is to create a sense of pride in the country. And until you've got a sense of pride for your country and your resources, there is no empathy towards conserving those resources. So, the first building block that I see with this book is to develop that sense of pride and unity in the country".

Pete presented a copy of his book to Hon. Sydney Allicock, Minister of Indigenous Peoples' Affairs, whose contribution to the development of the Makushi people of the Rupununi has been enormous. He continues to be a leading advocate for the protection of Amerindian rights, and for the sustainable use of natural resources. Allicock is a pioneer of community tourism in Guyana and is a director of the company that operates the renowned Iwokrama Canopy Walkway. I was also able to briefly meet Hon. Raphael Trotman, Minister of Natural Resources. I would come to know him much better later in my travels.

That evening, many of us sat down with Pete again at the Rainforest to reflect on his book launch event and on his work. Ever since his childhood, he had wanted to work in nature and to travel. He has accomplished all of this, and has travelled to many of the world's most pristine and remote corners of the world to do his photography work. He continues to search for images of wildlife and native cultures, with the understanding that the conservation of one is inextricably linked to that of the other. Amongst many other achievements, he is a Fellow Founder of the International League of Conservation Photographers and a Fellow of the Royal Geographical Society, and has published in *Time Magazine, International Wildlife, National Geographic*, and other publications. He and his wife, Renee, have published more than a dozen books. He has been a tourist guide in the Galapagos Islands and in the Ecuador jungle. He and his wife are currently working to produce a book about venomous snakes in Ecuador.

One of Pete's specialties is having the ability, technique, and courage to enter a dangerous jungle environment to set up high-end camera and video equipment in order to photograph unique animals in the dark. He has done this to capture exceptional photographs of, for example, jaguars in the Guyana interior. (In my tongue-in-cheek opinion, a good penalty for an obnoxious juvenile delinquent would be to drop him/her from a helicopter for a full night in the Guyana jungle.) Pete told us about the three months it had taken him to finally capture on camera an Iberian lynx on the Iberian Peninsula in Spain. According to Pete, "Rainforests...have to be one of the most challenging photographic environments on earth, especially the way humidity destroys expensive camera gear. Usually everything is either cryptic or very backlit, which is a problem in pursuit of my passion.

I have spent many hours dangling from ropes in the canopy, atop makeshift platforms, and in remote blinds deep in the forest. My rewards have been many. I am, for example, probably the first photographer to photograph directly a black panther in the rainforest...it was an incredible experience to be with the cat for about one hour at 6.8 metres distance!"

In our discussions, Pete emphasised that he is much more of a conservationist than a photographer. While he is mostly pleased about the forest preservation policies in Guyana, he is also aware of some of the shortcomings. He is far more concerned with other parts of the world, where he has seen atrocious human treatment of the environment. The world's oceans are full of plastic. During the last several years he has been doing more and more underwater photography in South East Asia, where he is seeing pollution everywhere. He asked us if we could guess what he sees as the most prevalent throw-away plastic in his ocean travels. The answer? Plastic spoons.

Pete told us about the overfishing situation at Lake Malawi, also known as Lake Nyasa, in Tanzania and Mozambique in Africa. The lake, at 575 kilometres in length, is the third-biggest in the world, and has more species of fish in it than any other lake, more than 1,000 species of cichlid alone. About twenty years ago, the governments, given the aid by international organisations, distributed countless mosquito nets free to people to counter malaria. The poor populations began immediately to use the nets for fishing, putting huge stress on the fish stocks. The tiny holes in the nets also caught the fish fry and fingerlings that are the future for fish life. Over twenty years, the fish stock in the lake has diminished by more than ninety percent.

Human indifference to environmental sustainability motivates Pete to produce his photography. Handsome and athletic looking, his good health, skill, and motivation will continue to serve him well to serve the world.

At some time around 9 p.m. that evening, I received a stimulating telephone call.

JOURNEY BACK TO WATOOKA

*Responding to a sun still shining,
a river still running, a jungle still growing,
to diverse friends waiting and to a
distant drum drumming... indeed
that is a Demerara homecoming.*

—Steve Connolly

Eh, Steve ...

Eh eh maan, ah glad glad, fuh see yuh back 'ome!

— Dr. Bernard Heydorn, Author, *Walk Good, Guyana Boy*

A beige limousine pulled up to the gate at the Rainforest...the four dogs were barking...and two plainclothes East Indian men opened both back doors of the vehicle. A bearded man stepped out on the far side, came around the back of the car, smiled, and greeted me warmly. *How fortunate I am*, I gratefully thought. Of course, I recognised him—who wouldn't in this country, and elsewhere—as Samuel "Sam" Hinds, former president and prime minister of Guyana.

It had been he who had called the previous evening. We had not seen each other since 1997 in Ottawa, Canada. Since then, we had communicated several times as he had provided me with information for my book, but we had never had any extensive quiet time together to discuss so much that we had in common. Now we would have that time, at least for the one-and-a-half-hour ride that lay ahead of us.

We were off to Watooka.

I had not planned for this—I had expected to take a taxi to the area of my birth.

The two men in the front of the car were referred to as the chauffeur and the "close man". Both were trained security men, and armed. This service is provided for life to any living past president of the country, twenty-four hours a day, seven days a week—shift work. They loaded two of my suitcases, holding forty heavy books, into the trunk. Our purpose was to attend a double event in Watooka, Linden: the kick-off for celebrating the 100th anniversary of the Demerara Bauxite Company, Demba, and the coincidental launching of my book. Including much more, my book relates the history of Demba in British Guiana until it was nationalised in 1971.

We would soon pass close to Alexander Village in West Demerara, where Sam was born in December 1943. Mostly, though, he was raised in Mahaicony, on the East Coast of Demerara. His father had worked for Booker's Cooperage. An even more renowned person who was born and raised in Mahaica (not Mahaicony) was Sir James Douglas, born in 1803. By the time he was sixteen, Douglas was in Canada, working for the North West Company. Later he joined the Hudson's Bay Company. He would rise to become the first governor of Vancouver Island and the mainland of British Columbia. Many people are not aware of this, nor are they aware that this Guyanese man is known as the Father of British Columbia. There is a statue of him in Mahaica, and an identical one in Fort Langley, British Columbia. This was accomplished by our mutual friend, Clyde Duncan, in Vancouver, British Columbia, who is Douglas's greatest fan. Then-Prime Minister Hinds participated in all of this.

We were now passing through Rome, and even while talking to my host my thoughts turned to Jan Carew, born there. (At one time, his absent father worked as a porter on trains in Canada.)

I had read Carew's *Episodes in My Life*, and I continue to have some strong disagreements with his thinking—at least, his thinking as a young man. I recalled reading that once, while in Russia, he heard a young Russian tell him that Harriet Beecher Stowe's *Uncle Tom's Cabin* was a fine book. Carew responded that such a statement would not endear him to Afro-Americans. What? Stowe and the other members of her large, high-achieving family were all leading abolitionists. Her book was acclaimed all around the world and, next to the Bible, became the bestselling book of all time. President Abraham Lincoln, upon meeting her in 1862, said, "So, you are the little woman who started the great war".

Carew, a Marxist, pushed hard against British colonialism, and rightly so, but his socialist idealism and his demand for immediate independence, rather than a longer term, phased approach, would later prove to be a failure.

Sam told me of his youth in Mahaicony, and of his schooling. He is very grateful to his parents and grandparents for the effort they made to help finance his way and to encourage him to study. He went to school barefoot in primary school. He did very well at Bishop's High School. One of his teachers was the hugely respected Dr. Robert "Bobby" Moore, who would later establish the Department of History at the University of Guyana, and subsequently became Guyana's High Commissioner to Canada.

At school one day, Sam was attracted to a notice, posted by Demba, looking for bright student applicants for scholarships to university. Given the poverty of his family, this appealed to him. He told me how he applied, and then flew to Mackenzie for interviews. It was during this application process that he met Jim G. Campbell, Demba's managing director in Georgetown, as well as the plant operations manager in Mackenzie, Norm Fraser. Both men had been close friends of my father in Mackenzie during and after World War II. All three men had arrived in Guyana in 1940. Norm Fraser and my father were raised as neighbours together in Sydney, Nova Scotia.

While I already knew most of his story, Sam related to me how he won a scholarship, and chose the University of New Brunswick in Canada to study for a chemical engineering degree, which he commenced in 1962 in Fredericton, New Brunswick. There he would discover the meaning of snow, hard study, and being a long, lonely distance from home.

During the summer of 1964, he earned money to support his studies by working in Alcan's chemical laboratories in Arvida, Quebec. At the same time, I was earning university expense money for my electrical engineering studies at the University of British Columbia by working in Alcan's electrical engineering department in Kitimat, B.C. Given my family's past residency in Arvida, I was able to recognise several of the engineers that Sam worked with that summer. So, he and I had a lot in common. While I had graduated two years ahead of him, we both received Canada's engineering iron ring upon graduation, symbolising our moral, ethical, and professional commitment to our future careers.

As we talked non-stop in the back seat, I noticed that Sam was still wearing his iron ring. Mine had recently been lost while cutting wood at my farm in Quebec, and I was in the process of replacing it. Sam Hinds is probably the only past president and prime minister of a country who has worn the Canadian engineering iron ring. How many people can you think of who have been both a president and a prime minister? How many engineers have ever achieved either of these political positions?

Sam commenced work for the Demerara Bauxite Company in 1967, in the Quality Control function. Over the years, he rose to become the Engineering Head of Research. At one time, he discovered a means to use the starch in cassava roots to eliminate certain impurities in bauxite. During the latter part of his engineering career, he became interested in the country's politics, with ties to Cheddi Jagan and the People's Progressive Party (PPP). In 1992, not long after he became involved in politics, demonstrating his calm demeanour, personableness, and leadership qualities, Sam became prime minister.

I did not want to talk politics with him, and we did not, except for one question that had always remained in my mind. President Cheddi Jagan died in March 1997, at the Walter Reed Military Medical Centre in Washington, DC. The Americans gave his coffin a 21-gun salute as his family and his remains left Andrews Air Force Base for Guyana. The honour the Americans had shown for Jagan had been somewhat ironic, given that they had worked against him during his bid for power in the 1950s and 1960s given his then-reputation for having affection for communism. All along the route that Sam and I were now travelling, tens of thousands of people had stood to watch the procession of Jagan's remains from the airport to Georgetown. His state funeral was probably the biggest that will ever be held in the country. After two days of huge line-ups to view his body at State House, his remains were taken for viewing in Corentyne, East Berbice, where he had been born as the son of indentured a sugar plantation working couple in Port Mourant. Guyana's Police Chief, Laurie Lewis, estimated that more than 100,000 people viewed Jagan's Hindu cremation, in a simple rural burial site, on an open pyre made of layers of "Long John" wood and coconut husks. His daughter, Nadira, and son, Joey, together with his wife, Janet, subsequently dropped his ashes over the Berbice, Demerara, and Essequibo rivers from a helicopter. I was interested to hear from Sam how the citizens of Guyana had come to love this man so much.

Sam, who had then still been the prime minister, immediately succeeded Jagan as president. His first duty was to declare six days of mourning. He was quoted as saying, "He was the greatest son and patriot to have walked this land".

Nine months then elapsed before Guyana held an election, which Jagan's American wife, Janet, won to become the next president. My question to Sam was, "Had you wished to run for the presidency?"

He responded in the negative and told me that he had supported Janet to represent the PPP. Knowing Sam somewhat, this response did not surprise me. (At least he had been president for nine months, otherwise he and I would not be being chauffeured to Watooka!) Almost two years after her election, Janet Jagan had to resign due to health reasons and was replaced by Bharrat Jagdeo. Sam Hinds continued as prime minister. Janet Jagan died in 2009, and was cremated like her husband. Her children, Nadira and Joey, also spread her ashes onto the three major rivers of the country.

Sam had always signed his letters to me in the past with the word "Comrade". I wondered as to the origin of this expression, one that is not generally used in the western world, to my knowledge. Sam's reply was simple. "It is a sign of friendship". However, it nevertheless may have originated with the attachment that Guyanese socialist leaders had in the 1950s and 1960s to Russia and Cuba.

At election time in May 2015, Sam decided he would not stay any longer in politics and retired as the longest-serving prime minister in the history of the Caribbean. Moses Nagamootoo, born in Berbice and of Tamil ethnicity, has taken his place.

During his time in politics, Sam won many accolades, including an honorary doctorate from the University of New Brunswick. He has always had a reputation for being very personable, and for being incorruptible. He has also been criticised for not having moved his country forward more during his time in office.

It is difficult for me to judge this, as an outsider, but I will say that most would agree it would take decades under any leadership for the country to recover from the condition in which Linden Forbes Burnham left it. Imagine the bleak situation of a country that loses a majority of its middle-class and educated people. Burnham caused all of this to happen, to the extent that tens of thousands of people were forced to leave the country with nothing, people who then excelled in professions and leadership in the Western World, as have their children. There are now about 735,000 people who live in Guyana—and more than three million Guyanese people and descendants who live outside of the country. It took decades to get into this situation, so it is no wonder that it is taking just as long to exit from it. There is much hope for the country, though, and I will comment on this in a later chapter.

As I sat with Sam, President David Granger had been in power for a year, as head of a political coalition. He graduated from Queens College, and after a short period joined the Guyana Defence Force. He performed well, helping to put down the Rupununi uprising in 1969. He obtained military training in Britain, Brazil, and Nigeria, and rose to become Commander of the Guyana Defence Force, being promoted to Brigadier General. My publisher, Arif Ali, had recently travelled from the UK to Guyana to arrange for the president, and other VIPs, to obtain a copy of my book.

We had been driving south on the road from Georgetown to the airport. Near the airport, we turned left to commence travelling on the Soesdyke-Linden Highway, with about seventy-three kilometres yet to drive. This road was built and opened in 1968. It put several river transport ships and boats out of business, such as the renowned *R.H. Carr* passenger ship, on which our family had often travelled in the past. It had made the nine-hour voyage from Georgetown to Mackenzie three times a week.

The two-lane north-south Soesdyke-Linden Highway is mostly straight, with minor undulations, is paved, and is quite isolated for its duration. Low-lying tropical growth is found on both sides, growing mostly in laterite and/or white sand. There is no marking line down its centre. After more than thirty years, it was given a general repair from 1997 to 1999. Asphaltic concrete was used from Soesdyke to Kuru Kuru, and the rest of the road was covered with a thin coat of asphalt and fine aggregate. The old greenheart wood bridges were also improved with reinforced concrete. Sam had never been able to understand the priority given to this highway, given its relatively rare use compared to much busier routes along the coast. He had only commenced to work in Mackenzie when it had been built. We rarely saw a vehicle during our trip.

One would not want to have a vehicle breakdown on the road, given its isolation and the potential of being robbed. The road also has a reputation for accidents. Sometimes the glare of the sun can be detrimental and often, when a heavy rainfall is encountered, hydroplaning can occur if one is driving too fast. Not too far from the commencement of the highway, Sam pointed out to me the place on the road where John Cummings had died in an accident in November 1971. He had been the principal at Linden's Mackenzie High School. In 1996, at a very large Mackenzie High School Reunion event held in Toronto, Canada, I was fortunate to sit at the head table with Beryl Cummings, who told me about the tragic loss of her husband. She was then living in Jamaica, as she is now, and had been so proud of her four children, who were all going to get through university.

In 1985, the year he became the country's president after Burnham's death, Desmond Hoyte's family set out to Linden from Georgetown to attend a function. While Hoyte was traveling separately, his family met with a terrible traffic accident on the highway. Sadly and tragically, his two daughters and a sister-in-law were killed.

Although our times in Mackenzie were separated by almost fifteen years, Sam and I know many people in common, and talked considerably of them: Morrisette, Idaman, Nascimento, Rosane, Percival, Jomini, Campbell, Chan, London, Blair, Wilson, Haynes, Wong, Fletcher, Senecal-Tremblay, Whicher, Seymour, Hiscocks, Parris, Thompson, Forbes, Johnson, and many more.

We talked about Edward Ricardo Braithwaite. This is the Guyanese man I mentioned earlier who wrote several books against racial discrimination, the most renowned one having been *To Sir, With Love,* published in 1959, with the popular movie adaptation produced in 1967. Braithwaite also wrote at least five other books, all of which I have, all autographed. Following heavy losses during the early part of World War II, Britain's Royal Air Force hired about 500 aircrew from the Caribbean. Braithwaite was one of these, and performed bravely as a Spitfire fighter pilot. Incredibly, on June 27, 2012, living in Washington, DC, he turned 100 years of age.

I related to Sam some details about Braithwaite's book, *Honorary White*, published in 1975, about his visit to South Africa in 1973. South Africa had recently lifted the ban on his book *To Sir, With Love,* and he had thought the occasion was cause for a visit, to see if in fact the apartheid government was improving its treatment of black people. His visit had given the government a dilemma: what kind of visa to give him? If they gave this renowned man a no-privilege visa, as for blacks, then the world would be upset; but providing him with an all-privilege white visa was not an option for them. So, they ended up giving him an "honourary white visa", which allowed him some privileges; i.e., he could find accommodation at restricted hotels, etc. His book had revealed the sordid and unjust racial discrimination that was still being fully practiced and that had rightfully disgusted him. Incredibly, the country was still banning the famous book *Black Beauty*.

Decades of bauxite mining have left huge open pits in the vast area around Linden, some of which are filled with beautiful emerald-blue water. At some time around 2005, Sam engaged Guyanese Dr. Bert Allsopp, a renowned expert on fish, to determine if fish could be grown in the bauxite ponds as an industry. While the acidity of the water prevented this, Sam still feels that this idea may yet prove viable, with a species of tilapia, common in Brazil, that can thrive in acidic water. I had met Dr. Allsopp at the celebration of the fortieth anniversary of Guyana's Independence celebration in Vancouver, British Columbia, sharing a table with him. He had worked in many countries as a fish consultant, had started the shrimp industry in Guyana, and later modestly gave me a long list of his achievements and awards. A brother, Dr. Richard Allsopp, is renowned for having developed the *Dictionary of Caribbean English Usage*. Both are now deceased.

Sam had brought along a book entitled *From Third World To First*, written by the former Prime Minister of Singapore, Lee Kuan Yew, LKY, whose thirty-one years in office made him the world's longest-serving prime minister. I could easily understand why this book would be of significant interest to my back-seat host, particularly in relation to Guyana. British Prime Minister Tony Blair once referred to LKY as "the smartest leader that I have ever known". With meritocracy, religious tolerance, racial harmony, and technology, Yew transformed Singapore into a modern, trendsetting city, gaining the title "Garden City", once the description for Georgetown, Guyana. "Kuan Yew" stands for "light and brightness", with an alternate meaning of "bringing great glory to one's ancestors". Yew was certainly a man deserving of these descriptions.

Shortly after World War II, Yew attended the prestigious London School of Economics in England, with some very bright scholars from other countries: Errol Barrow (Barbados), Linden Forbes Burnham (British Guiana), Michael Manley (Jamaica), and Pierre Trudeau (Canada). Together, they were taught democratic socialism by the fiery and brilliant professor Harold Laski. India's Jawaharlal Nehru had been a previous student. Barrow had been a navigator for Britain's RAF during World War II. Nehru, Yew, Burnham, and Barrow would lead their countries later to political and economic independence. All, except for Burnham, would leave a positive legacy of leadership. As the first prime minister of Barbados, Barrow issued the following quotes of renown:

> *We diminish ourselves if we do not see the good in others.*
>
> *Government will not be found lingering on Colonial premises after closing time.*
>
> *Friends to all, satellite to none.*

We were getting closer to Linden. It had been a year since Sam had last visited the town. We had passed over several creeks whose names, such as Kairuni, Moblissa, and Bamia, I did not recognise. As a child, I had always travelled on the river in the *R. H. Carr*, so I had only known of a few creeks near Mackenzie. We passed by Amelia's Ward, a housing area that did not exist during my family's time in Guyana. I easily recalled Kara Kara

Creek, however, and when we crossed over it, I knew that we were near our destination. In our time, our family had sometimes taken a small boat up that once dark creek in the rainforest to fish and to catch butterflies. I quietly thought of a later time, during the 1964 Wismar Massacre, when East Indians hid in the creek to escape the violence.

Our vehicle passed by the road entrance to the little village of Rainbow City, which, according to my memory, may not have existed during our time. This village and that of Kara Kara had been severely flooded during heavy rains the previous month, causing much damage. Hymara Creek had been so full of garbage and growth that it could not function to move the water, hence the flood.

My Ottawa, Canada, friend, Malcolm Lovell, apprenticed with the bauxite company in his early days, and lived in Rainbow City. He is unaware how this name came to be, however, so let me propose the following. In 1967, England's BBC produced the TV series *Rainbow City*, about a multi-ethnic part of Birmingham. This was the first time the BBC featured a black actor (a Trinidadian) in such a series. Well-known Guyanese actress Carmen Monroe had also played a significant role. Perhaps the little village through which we were passing had obtained its name from the TV series.

With Sam as my guide, we passed by the plant operations area and the main gate, the same gate that tens of thousands of workers had entered and exited over 100 years, including my father on his little red motor-scooter bike during the mid-twentieth century and before. Sam pointed to some of the houses that had not existed in Cockatara during my time, while telling me about their previous tenants, many of whom I was familiar with. I noticed that the name of the main street, Arvida Road, had been changed decades ago to Republic Avenue. I was still having difficulty understanding where we were, until suddenly we were parallel with the old railway tracks to the mines and the beautiful old British colonial Watooka Clubhouse came into sight. Our limousine slowly entered its long entrance as I looked around in absolute wonder at a sight I had not seen for sixty-three years... one that I had often taken for granted as a child. While not looking exactly as before, the wide expanse of grounds appeared reasonably well-kept, and the old building also seemed to say, "Welcome back!"

When onlookers and staff saw our vehicle's doors opened by Sam's two "close men", they knew someone important had arrived. They must have thought that I was a third "close man", although, at seventy-three years of age, I may not have looked as capable as our real protectors. After the greetings, we commenced our slow walk to the celebration tents that had been set up on the grounds about two hundred metres in front of the Clubhouse, near the old railway tracks and in an open-air museum of ancient heavy equipment. In front of the Clubhouse, I stood in awe not far from the end of the old Watooka swimming pool, which had been like a second home for me and my little friends as a child. Fond memories flooded my mind. There it was. Was I really here again? Was this a dream?

Walking another thirty metres, we came adjacent to the place where the small bridge used to be to cross the Watooka Creek. When our family left Guyana in 1953, this bridge was the entrance to the village of Watooka. A black Demba policeman had presided at a guardhouse there, to ensure that people of colour did not enter the white village unless they had a pass permitting them to do so (i.e. servants, gardeners, labourers, etc.). This practice was discontinued a year or two later. The bridge stood about 100 metres from the Demerara River. The company launches, the *Dorabece* and *Polaris*, had been docked in the creek near the bridge, and the bridge had been used to draw the launches up vertically so that their bottoms could be cleaned. I was saddened and disappointed to not be able to see the bridge due to the jungle growth that was now present. In fact, the road going to the bridge was no longer there...and neither was the bridge. The creek was still there, but you could see no water because of the fallen growth that pervaded it.

As a child, I was permitted to cross this bridge with my family to get to church on Sundays, but rarely otherwise. At one time, my parents tried to have my younger brother, Mike, and I join the Cub Scout troop in the black community. This had not been permitted by Demba, and had angered my parents. Mike and I were not concerned, because we were confined to our own little world and did not know what we were going to miss.

I had to exit my musings, because we had to move on and we did. Photographs were taken of us together, and we soon arrived at the tented area, which was packed with folks. This area is the Old Railway Yard, the former transport hub for workers heading to and from the mines. It will be the future site for an expanded open-air heavy-equipment museum. After more greetings by many officials, and photograph taking, we were seated at the front of the full crowd, at a table facing the assembly and close to the podium. It was hot—thank goodness for the cold bottled water that was prevalent! We were to be there for four hours of speeches. Interestingly, no washroom was necessary for me. As I would find at future times, in the humid heat one can drink copious water and lose it via perspiration.

The tented area was close to decades-old massive mining equipment, such as two old dragline buckets that are so large you can drive a vehicle into them. They had been used by giant machines to remove bauxite overburden. There were also some giant Turnapull earth-removing vehicle tires. (As children, we used tubes from these in the Watooka swimming pool, floating them on the water so we could dive through them from the high diving board.) There were also small sided rail scooters that had been used for many purposes. In times long past, after the miners had taken the train to the mines to work for the day, their wives made their lunches, which were transported to the men by scooters. Decades of mining operations left tons of derelict metal equipment lying under the burning sun all over the mined areas. Voracious scrap metal dealers seized this metal, even the old railway rails—even those across the river, along the line from Wismar to Rockstone.

The many seats were full. The audience included schoolchildren wearing black-and-yellow uniforms, local folks, and, in the front seats, dignitaries. Our "close men" had brought the boxes of my books up to a special table reserved for their display next to Sam and me. I had never met a single person in the crowd, although I did know of several of them. I had been so quickly introduced to many of them individually that it had been very hard for me to remember their names. Sam, of course, knew them all. No one could fail to identify me, since I was the only white person there. All of this greatly excited me, and I could hardly wait to speak…several hours further into the program.

Horace James, a very kind and personable man, gave the opening remarks, highlighting the importance of the 100th anniversary. In the past, he was the CEO of the bauxite Linmine Secretariat, and spoke about the local bauxite history, in which he had played a long and integral role. A mining engineer, he is currently the head of government-owned National Industrial and Commercial Investments Ltd. and, because of his extensive knowledge and enthusiastic interest in the Guyana bauxite industry, was a leader in the establishment of the Linden Museum in 2006 in the building that, commencing in 1925, had been Cockatara's Recreation Hall.

One of the speakers was Pastor Renis Morian. I learned later that he had been raised in Campbellville, a tough section of Georgetown. In his youth, he was a leader of the "No Collar Gang", which was into all sorts of vices and serious crime. Many of its members did not live long. Thanks to a mentor, Renis removed himself from this influence, obtained an education, and developed his faith in God. Amongst many other achievements, he is known for his work to help youth. At this event, he spoke as the chairman of the Region Ten Democratic Council. (For government purposes, Guyana is divided into ten regions. Each region is governed by a Regional Democratic Council, RDC, with its eighteen members, including chairman, elected every three years. Within a region, towns and villages are governed by Neighbourhood Democratic Councils, such as the one governing Linden.)

I met and listened to tall (almost 6'4"), solid Orrin Gordon speak about past bauxite mining history. Until Mayor Holland was elected, for twelve years Gordon was the head of the Interim Management Committee that had managed Linden. He had been a star cricket player, a bowler, in the country during his youth.

Two senior officials of the Chinese Bosai Minerals Group company were present, Acting General Manager Eric Yu, and Secretary Norman McLean. Attractive Vanessa Mitchell-Davis handled public relations activities for Bosai. Superintendent Orin Barnwell represented the Russian RUSAL Bauxite Guyana Company. Yu and Barnwell talked about Guyana's bauxite history, with Yu emphasising some of the environmental improvements that Bosai had implemented since it had commenced its operations ten years earlier. Barnwell related the chronological sequence in which companies had managed the bauxite operations on the Demerara River: Alcoa, Alcan, Demerara Bauxite Company, Guybau, Guymine, Linmine, Omai, and Bosai.

I found Norman McLean an interesting individual. A policeman as a young man, he rose up to become a Major General, and Chief of Staff, of the Guyana Defence Force, GDF. Since his retirement from the GDF, he has functioned in many posts, including human resources manager for the Omai mining company. He has a fine sense of humour and says that he has so many metal nuts and bolts in him from accidents that he goes to see a mechanic for a check-up rather than a doctor. Once, when a journalist asked him what he would like folks to say about him when he dies and they're standing around his open coffin, he replied, "Look, he moved!" Born in Georgetown, he was brought to Mackenzie by his nurse mother in 1944.

After I had been given the opportunity to speak briefly about my past and my book's journey, the next speaker was Carwyn Holland, the new mayor of Linden. Until 1970, Demba managed and controlled Mackenzie: for sure, it was a company town. Subsequently, a formal Town Council was established to manage everything. Its first mayor, in 1970, was Egbert Benjamin, who had been a welder/fabricator for Demba. Gloria Layne became the first woman mayor of Linden, and of any town in Guyana, in 1974. For twenty-two years prior to late 2015, an Interim Town Council was undemocratically in place. Democratic elections were finally held, and now Linden has sixteen councillors. These councillors choose a mayor and a deputy mayor from amongst themselves: Carwyn Holland and Waneka Arrindell. Within the period until the next election, the councillors review these two prominent positions each year, and can vote for a change if so desired. Elected officials are not paid for their work.

As the tenth mayor, and the youngest, at thirty-eight years, Carwyn Holland is full of vim and vigour. He's passionate, progressive, and impatient to improve the economy and social situation in Linden. He is the only mayor who was born in Linden. He impressed me, acknowledging his youth/inexperience and emphasising he is open for advice and support. He believes that there is great hope for the town, and he wants it to have the status of a city. He wants to make it a gateway to Brazil by improving the current rough road south to the border. Job creation and jobs for youth are paramount and can be achieved via infrastructure projects. Garbage disposal is a high priority, as are necessary improvements to the roads, which are full of potholes and washouts and are in a constant state of disrepair. Heavy rains are hell. He has led the successful re-initiation of the toll charge for use of the Kara Kara bridge to bring in much needed revenue for the community. He feels that Linden has great potential as a tourism destination, and he would like to see a branch of the University of Guyana situated in Linden. "We must treat our town as the jewel of our nation that it is", he said.

During my presentation, I had stated that British Guiana helped to win World War II by producing bauxite at record levels for shipment to Canada, to make aluminium used in almost forty percent of the warplanes for the Allies. More than 400 ships were torpedoed by German submarines in the Caribbean during the war, many of them bauxite ships. The Guyanese people and management worked twelve hours per day for thirteen out of every fourteen days for Demba, in hot, dirty, and very trying conditions. All this story and much more is covered in my book *Children of Watooka*. Based on my talk, the quick-thinking and well-meaning mayor stated that the world owes compensation to Linden for their World War II achievement. I cringed, quietly disagreeing with this statement.

At a later function in Georgetown, I was able to speak to Mayor Holland alone, and offered some humble advice: the world does not owe Linden or Guyana any compensation for its wonderful contribution to winning World War II. Other countries also made wonderful contributions. For fifty-five years of its existence, Demba contributed significantly to the welfare of Mackenzie and the country. Thousands of houses were built by the company, as well as roads, social and recreation facilities, churches, schools, trade-school facilities, a police force, and much more. It was the major contributing industry in the country. People from all over Guyana came to work in Mackenzie, to obtain the best jobs in the country and in most of the Caribbean. It had the greatest concentration of engineering talent in the Caribbean. A union was permitted. Over time, racial discrimination was greatly diminished, and many of the top engineers, who became Guyanese, had been gifted educations by Demba. Cockatara and Watooka, the two villages making up Mackenzie, were pristinely cared for by gardeners and company workers. Almost all folks who were a part of this often-called-paradise situation recall it with great fondness, especially compared with the current depressed situation, which has endured for decades. Mayor Holland is on a rapid learning curve and cherishes good advice, and I am his biggest cheerleader. As I am writing at the end of 2016, his councillor colleagues have just re-appointed him as mayor again. He has the potential to be a fine leader.

* * *

I must interrupt my writing at this point, December 13, 2016, for some sad news. I have just heard that Edward Ricardo Braithwaite died in Washington, DC today. He had turned 104 years last June 27. He was a great man. I wrote about him in my book *Children of Watooka*, so here I will offer only a few words. As I mentioned previously, he was the Guyanese gentleman who wrote the book *To Sir, With Love* in 1958, which was made into a popular movie in 1967. He was a man of great integrity and courage. I will always remember his words to me: "I am not an exceptional man, but rather I am a man who has had an exceptional life".

One story. Just prior to Guyana obtaining its independence from Britain in 1966, Linden Forbes Burnham called for Braithwaite to visit him from his home in France. When he arrived, Burnham asked him to become Guyana's first ambassador to the United Nations. Two conditions were requested: first, he must become a member of Burnham's political party, the PNC, and second, he must be knighted by England. Full of his usual integrity, Braitewaite replied that if he was to be an ambassador for the country, then he must represent all the people, not just those of a political party...and he did could not understand why he must be knighted by a country from which they would separate. Burnham then withdrew his requests, after which Braithwaite had accepted the position.

I once asked Braithwaite if he had ever been married. He replied, "No, but I had two close calls!"

Thanks to previous Watooka residents Meigan Chan and Dr. Peggy David, I was introduced to E. R. Braithwaite more than a decade ago. I was fortunate to have several discussions with him, to obtain his story and to discuss various matters. In 2011, I wrote to Prime Minister Sam Hinds to inform him that Braithwaite would turn 100 years the following year, and that it would be nice if Guyana could find a means to celebrate this event. This was accomplished, and he was royally hosted for his special milestone birthday. Afterwards, he expressed his joy to me at having been hosted in Guyana, with a highlight having been sitting in the front seat of a theatre to watch a re-enactment of *To Sir, With Love*. President Donald Ramotar presented him with the Cacique Crown of Honour, Guyana's second-highest award.

Dr. Peggy David and her husband, Dr. Wilfred David, had both been Guyanese professors at Howard University. She was particularly close to her friend "Ted" Braithwaite and has had his biography prepared for a long time. He did not want it to be published before his death. The world can now look forward to some captivating reading. An educator, a World War II Spitfire pilot, a fighter for social justice, a statesman, a man of integrity—a great man—has passed away.

> ### *"One of Guyana's greatest gifts to the world"*
>
> In January 2017, thinking of my conversations with E. R. Braithwaite, I remembered I still had his telephone number, and decided to call his partner of many decades, Jeanette Ast. I was pleasantly surprised when she had answered, and we had a nice conversation. For much of her career, she worked as a journalist in New York for the Canadian Broadcasting Corporation, CBC. She is a Caucasian who had come from France and had met Braithwaite in New York. She told me that her partner had never been interested in having his biography written. He had felt that his own published books were sufficient. His passing had been sudden: he had been outside in the morning, had returned looking fine, and then later had expired.
>
> A memorial service was held in March 2017 to celebrate the life of Eustace Edward Ricardo Braithwaite at the Washington, DC, National Cathedral. Guyana's UN Ambassador, Dr. Riyad Insanally, eulogised, "Ted Braithwaite was not just a son of Guyana, he was one of Guyana's greatest gifts to the world as scholar, educator, writer, diplomat and humanist".

* * *

Paula Walcott-Quintin, visiting from New Jersey in the United States, in her role as President of Linden Fund USA, spoke about the upcoming Bauxite Century events planned for the fall of 2016. I had known and communicated many times with this talented and attractive lady, but met her at this event for the first time. We would attend several events together over the coming year, including another of my book-launching events later that week in Georgetown. The Linden Fund USA was formed in the northeastern US in 2005 to provide aid to the Linden area in Guyana, after the country experienced severe flooding that year. Since then, the Fund has continued to provide aid to the schoolchildren of Linden, as well as to fund community projects. Paula is a highly respected administrator at Rutgers University.

At intervals within the program, schoolchildren entertained the crowd with singing and recitals. Most of the speakers focused on the past mining history of the area, but Sam Hinds, while eminently speaking of such, also pointed out that a successful future economy would require industrial diversification, to lessen the dependence on diminishing bauxite production opportunities. Raphael Trotman, Minister of Natural Resources, closed the event with a final talk about the hopeful mining potential for the future.

My table of books was then surrounded with interested and interesting purchasers, so many that all the books disappeared quickly. This was great fun, but I regretted that I could not remember everyone's names and had too little time to be as personable as I had wished. I did donate and present a book to Sandra Adams for the Linden Library.

One woman brought up a very elderly man, shuffling with a cane, and introduced me to herself and to her father, James Simon. He was ninety-nine years of age and had known my father. I sat down with him, and tears came to my eyes as he shakily stated, "Your father always gave me encouragement". Sadly, James would not survive until his 100th birthday.

This wonderful event closed at 2 p.m., and then two dozen of us were hosted for lunch in the Watooka Clubhouse. As I climbed up the outdoor stairs, for the first time in sixty-three years, with other guests, I looked over the tropical-lawn landscape surrounding the swimming pool in wonder, and then stepped into the first floor of the historic building.

Wow. Almost nothing had changed. All greenheart wood, high ceilings, and stained walls and floors, and one could look outside in many areas via expansive screened windows to see the massive mango trees. I was seated to the right of Sam Hinds, who was at the head of our long table, and we were waited on by an excellent staff, whom I would become much more acquainted with in the future. After some great discussion with all of these special folks, we had to move on.

I was to be interviewed about my book at radio station 104.1 Power FM Guyana in nearby Richmond Hill. When we arrived at the entrance to this housing area, Sam could not recall where the ratio station was, so he asked the driver to move the car over to the front yard of an aged house, where a lady was at the front door. She came hurrying out, having seen that the bearded man in the back seat had rolled down his window to speak. As she got close to the car, she shrieked in excitement, "It's Mr. Hinds! Mr. Hinds! It's the Prime Minister!" At least, it was the *former* prime minister. Sam took all this in stride and had a chat with her before getting directions to the nearby location of our destination. This was yet another example, many of which I had already seen, of his natural personableness with the ordinary folk.

After my radio interview, for which I was very grateful, I donated a book to the station for a program they wanted to prepare.

We headed back to Georgetown, enjoying non-stop discussion all the way. At the village of Farm, we entered the gated entrance to Sam and Yvonne's home and property, which fronted to the airport road, behind a white concrete wall. The guardhouse guard was on the spot; there was also another, but unmanned, guardhouse on stilts at the side of the house. Sam showed me around the expansive tropical yard, with the white house on stilts at the centre of it. The day was waning into twilight, and the security lights were on all around the place, lighting it up like day time. While most middle-class folks would envy this nice place of residence, it is a step down from the Prime Minister's Residence they enjoyed on Main Street in Georgetown for more than two decades, and a far cry from their old home at 116 Riverside Drive, far in the past in old Watooka. Ever grateful for the wonderful day and companionship, I thanked my host as I climbed back into the limousine to be driven to nearby Georgetown.

The "close man" had expressed polite regret that he had not been able to hear my radio interview in Linden, so he was delighted when I repeated it for him and his partner. Rather than go directly to the Rainforest, I asked them to take me to the Tower Suites, the old Tower Hotel on Main Street. The hotel is reputed to be the oldest in Georgetown, if not the country, built in 1866 at another location. It was moved to its current location in 1910, and has changed hands several times. I did not recognise it: it had recently undergone a complete change and was now orange/brown painted concrete, in contrast to the white wooden jalousie-windowed structure of the past. Our family had often stayed at the old premises; my mother always remembered waking up in the morning to hear the tropical birds doing choir work outside her window. The last time I had seen the hotel, when our family left the country in 1953, it had been colourfully decorated with flags, pennants, and bunting to celebrate the coronation of Queen Elizabeth II.

My purpose for this visit was to meet Guyanese Vibert "Alex" Miller who, with his wife, Beverley, and other friends, was also visiting Guyana to participate in the fiftieth-anniversary celebrations. Alex and I had befriended each other via email after he read my book. He and Beverley had been living in Brooklyn, New York, for some time, very close there to Alex and Brenda Fortune, who were staying with me at the Rainforest. Alex and I had much in common, given our separate pasts in Guyana. He was also an inveterate reader, was charismatic and witty, and liked to modestly share his knowledge.

We met in the lobby and proceeded to the Tiki Bar, by the modern swimming pool, and enjoyed some wine and beer. At eighty years of age, he was moustached and handsome, with a good sense of humour. While we enjoyed our lively talk, I surveyed the balconies overlooking the pool under a starlit sky, and thanked God for this experience of being with a good friend in the country of our birth, near the finish line of our lives. Alex obtained his first university degree in England, and then had obtained an MBA in the United States, where he later worked for IBM. In 1972 he moved back to Guyana, where he met Beverley, and after some time became responsible for overseeing several government-owned corporations. Later, he worked for the Guyana Timber Export Board, handling major contracts.

One of them was to provide lumber for the Coney Island Boardwalk and park benches in New York City. He also taught at the University of Guyana.

Sadly, it was too close to the finish line for Alex. I would meet him twice again for short discussions over the week, during which he suffered a stroke and spent two nights in the Public Hospital before being released. Beverley worked hard on the telephone, trying to arrange for a fast return back home for expert medical treatment.

I would never see him again: he passed away that September. My friend. I still keep in touch with Beverley.

* * *

Almost a week later, at 8 a.m. on Sunday morning, a jovial Hon. Sam Hinds and his limousine appeared at the front gate of the Rainforest. I invited him in to the guesthouse veranda, where an excited Syeada and some of her guests were able to meet him and take photos. Of course, he already knew of Syeada and her outstanding work to help animals. I had already been to 6 a.m. Mass at the Brickdam Cathedral, another historical edifice of Georgetown. Bishop Francis Alleyne had presided. I had met him earlier that week at his home across the street from the Cathedral and met him again at my book launch at the home of the Canadian High Commissioner. Another priest had given the sermon—a loud one, with constant finger-pointing at those of us attending, done in a manner that I had not appreciated.

We settled into the back seat of the car, looking forward to sharing the full day together touring the bauxite plant and mines and old Watooka. Sam knew that I was anxious to be free from being formally hosted, in order to be free to walk down old Watooka's Riverside Drive and to swim in the Watooka pool after sixty-three years. We would, however, be hosted for the first half of the day by Bosai Minerals Group Guyana Inc., which owns and manage the bauxite operations. We were off to Linden.

So, how did Linden become the name for the second-biggest town in the country, after Georgetown? It is an interesting story, a political one, which relates to the history of the country over several decades, and to the unfortunate demise of its economy and social welfare.

Born in 1923, Linden Forbes Burnham excelled at Queen's College in academics and in debating. In his graduation year, he was the top student in the country, and won the prestigious British Guiana Scholar award/scholarship in 1942. Unable to go to England to study because of the war, he taught in Georgetown, and commenced courses as an external student with the University of London. In 1945, he was able to move to England to finish his studies, and passed his bar exams as a lawyer in 1948. He returned to British Guiana in 1949 to commence a law practice, and to immediately immerse himself into politics. To say that he was ambitious and self-centred would be an understatement.

Managed by the British, a general election was held in December 1964. This is considered the last fair and free election held in the country until 1992. The two main competing political parties were Cheddi Jagan's People's Progressive Party (PPP), and the People's National Congress (PNC), led by Burnham. By forming a coalition, Burnham won, and became prime minister.

Prior to the election, his sister, Jessie, had written a booklet to warn the country of her sibling, "BEWARE MY BROTHER FORBES". In it, she described him as brilliant, a plotter, a manipulator, selfish, and power-loving, with a certain dark strain of cruelty. She wrote:

> *There are two Burnhams; the charming and the cruel. I say BEWARE of both.*
>
> *I have watched this brilliant brother use his brain to scheme, to plot, to put friend against friend, neighbour against neighbour and relative against relative. I have watched him with his wit and charms manipulate people like puppets on a string.*
>
> *The world can tolerate such men as individuals. But our beloved country cannot tolerate such men as LEADERS.*
>
> *For today I fear for my country and my people should my brother become PREMIER or PRIME MINISTER. It is from this fear, this concern that I speak. BEWARE, I say, of my brother Forbes. His motto is that personal ends justify ANY means used to achieve them.*

Jessie Burnham's warning went unheeded but would prove to be entirely prophetic. Until her brother's death in the poorly equipped Public Hospital in 1985, the country sank into ruin and despair. Within ten years of the country's independence in 1966, the State owned eighty percent of the economy. Businesses, army, police, schools, and other organizations had all been politicised, and subjected to Burnham's socialist approach. Skilled and educated people were replaced by those holding the PNC party card, whether qualified for jobs or not. Mostly, people of Burnham's own ethnicity were given key leadership posts. All of this and more led to food and commodity shortages, corruption, huge emigration, inflation, and a lack of respect in the western world for his leadership, which caused a drought of external investment and financial support.

> *He was devoted to causes; but he was his greatest cause.*
>
> — Ashton Chase

In the 1964 election and afterwards, voters were polarised by ethnicity. East Indians comprised about thirty-eight percent of the population, while Afro-Guyanese amounted to about thirty-three percent. The town of Mackenzie was mostly inhabited by Afro-Guyanese, who had mostly supported Burnham. For them, he was a rising star. In 1970, Burnham commenced his move to nationalise industry, commencing with the bauxite businesses owned by Canada on the Demerara River and by the United States on the Berbice River. He served notice to Demba that the company must be turned over to Guyana's government in the following year, 1971. Most of the company's workers, and some of the Guyanese management staff in Mackenzie, supported this move. They had been so enamoured with Burnham that they had changed the town's name to Linden in 1970, after their leader, replacing Mackenzie, which had been the name for more than fifty years. It is not clear how the process of the name changing occurred, but it would not be surprising if Burnham himself initiated the change. Wismar Main Road, across the river, was renamed Burnham Drive. Arvida Road in Cockatara became Republic Avenue.

The town had been originally named after George B. Mackenzie, who had been a Scottish-American working for Alcoa in the United States. He was the person who accumulated the bauxite lands for the company and the country to benefit from in the future.

The fifty-five years of Demba's bauxite operations were very prosperous. Commencing with nationalisation in 1966, the next forty-five years for the most part have been very unfavourable. People today who recall the past prosperous time treasure it hugely, while correctly blaming the subsequent economic decline on Linden Forbes Burnham. It is difficult for me to understand that the paradise that I lived in as a child continues to be named after a cruel tyrant who brought the country to ruin. To my mind, there exists strong reason to change the name back to Mackenzie, or to some other name acceptable to the town's citizens.

When Burnham died in 1985 at only 62 years of age, Desmond Hoyte of the PNC became the leader. It was not until 1992 that a properly conducted election was held. The Jimmy Carter Center out of the United States presided over the process, even though it had had difficulty obtaining Hoyte's approval to use standard and proper procedures. Carter himself was there, and in 2007 stated, "The most personal danger that I have felt since leaving the White House was in Guyana in 1992". Two of his representatives were placed at every polling station, and in Georgetown, at the election centre, Carter found himself in the midst of serious rioting. Cheddi Jagan's PPP won, and as noted earlier, Sam Hinds thus became a Member of Parliament and prime minister. This was when he left his senior engineering post with the bauxite industry in Linden, and began his long career in politics.

In early 1971, Sam was called to Georgetown to meet with Burnham, who knew that Sam was in favour of bauxite company nationalisation. Most likely, Sam had voted for Burnham, along with the majority of his community. Sam confirmed to Burnham that a substantial number of Guyanese managers in the bauxite operation were in favour of nationalisation, and agreed to assemble them, with Demba's permission, for a meeting with Burnham. This meeting was held on February 22, 1971, with no Canadian expatriates invited. The following day, Republic Day, Burnham announced to the country that Demba would be taken over by the government. Sam was not yet thirty years old, so it was unusual that the country's leader called upon him, less than four years out of university, for assistance. It may have been helpful that an uncle of Sam's had been a close friend of Burnham but by this time Sam had already developed his own positive reputation.

Sam and a few associates then drew up a proposed organisation chart, given that almost all the expatriates would be leaving, as well as some Guyanese staff members. There was no question that less experienced people would have to be promoted into positions that had been filled by more experienced/skilled staff...such as Evan Wong. Evan, whose Chinese family's lineage was entwined with the history of British Guiana and who had been asked by Burnham to lead Guybau, the name given to the nationalised company. He rightly turned down this offer, stating that the new enterprise would fail (for all the reasons that it eventually did). Burnham by then had realised that this was a real possibility, but told Evan that he was already politically committed. Politics had ruled over practicality, expert advice, and common sense.

My father had retired in 1971 in Canada after thirty-five years working for Alcan. He and his many Alcan engineer colleagues across the country watched with deep disbelief and disappointment what was happening to Demba, and to Guyana in general. Like Evan Wong, they all correctly predicted the inevitable outcome of ruin.

* * *

Still on our drive to Linden, we talked of Sam's retirement. He had been out of politics for one year and was in limbo. He was taking some courses on typing and computer use. He is in a great position to write his biography, as well as about the bauxite industry and politics. Any book he would publish would have high sales potential. His wife, Yvonne, born in Bartica, is well known, and keeps busy with many activities, one of which is serving as head of the Guyana Relief Council.

Sam and his PPP colleagues had hit the headlines only four days earlier, and we discussed this interesting event. Thousands of people had gathered at D'Urban Park in Georgetown for the midnight Flag Raising Ceremony to celebrate the fiftieth anniversary of independence, celebrated on May 26. The Ministry of Culture, Youth and Sports had organised the event, and had reserved seats for the three previous presidents of the country—Sam Hinds, Bharrat Jagdeo, and Donald Ramotar—but had failed to reserve seats for other MPs of the opposition PPP. This had been an unforgivable error, to the extent that Sam and all members of the PPP, greatly offended, had departed together just before the flag-raising.

The flagpole is the tallest in the country, sixty metres in total, with almost six metres of it buried in the ground. The huge Golden Arrowhead flag, roughly nineteen metres by ten metres and weighing seventy pounds, briefly stalled during its raising. One woman yelled, "Everyone blow!" The large crowd echoed her call, and when the flag released and reached the top of the staff, there was a thunderous roar of pride and approval. Minister Nicolette Henry subsequently released an apology to the PPP via the news media that, to my mind, was weak and not credible.

Of note, the Golden Arrowhead flag, then new, raised for the Independence ceremony at midnight on May 25, 1966, at National Park was much smaller. It was raised by a young army Second Lieutenant, Desmond Roberts, without a mechanical device—unlike in 2016. Looking back at that year, the *Guyana Chronicle* reported Roberts as saying:

> I was nervous about getting it right. The flag started to go up slowly but then when it was nearly at the top the wind did the trick and it flew beautifully. It was really a beautiful flag. Nobody had ever seen it. People were gasping, and some were even crying. Then, Prime Minister Burnham called up Dr. Cheddi Jagan and the two embraced. It was really a remarkable event. It set in motion all kinds of ideas that the whole nation will come together. At the time it looked hopeful. We have to change this nonsense about race and ethnicity for this country to develop. We have no reason to be poor. I hope that one day everyone would be wealthy in Guyana… and by that I mean able to lead a comfortable life. We have everything to make it possible.

Chosen from among a large number of proposals submitted to an international competition, the five-coloured flag had been designed by American Whitney Smith.

Having entered Linden, we were driven into the Constabulary Compound in old Cockatara, to find several vehicles and officials waiting for us outside of the dull-yellow Constabulary Hall. Sam had graciously agreed to help me with several personal objectives I had had in mind for the day, the first being to find and take some photos of the old Blair home in the compound, at 52 Constabulary Road. For decades, the compound had housed the families of Mackenzie policemen: Archibald, Langevine, Graham, Rose, Elber, Ward, Blanchard, Hamid, etc. John and Olivia Blair had raised nine children in Mackenzie, including my great friend, Ned, their eldest son. John was the first black man to become a member of Demba's staff, as head of the Constabulary. The Blair family will be highlighted in a later chapter.

Bosai's acting general manager, Eric Yu, introduced us to several Bosai officials and to others, including Horace James, who was to become a good host and friend for me on later visits. There must have been a dozen of us, and we had only started our group walk down the dirt road when a big lady, followed by a small group of children, came running up to Sam. "Mr. Hinds! Gimmee money! Prime Minister, you got lots of money. I need money! Gimmee money, Mr. Hinds!" Personable as ever, "Mr. Hinds" did an exceptional job of handling the situation, and we moved on.

Only a few houses further, we found the old Blair home. Bosai's Head of Security was amazed that I had picked this house to stop at, exclaiming, "My family used to live in this house!" Well-maintained when occupied by the Blair family, it now reflected neglect. The corrugated metal roof was rusted, and the house needed a paint job. It was originally built on stilts, but the bottom part was now sided. We had a photo shoot, and then returned to several vehicles for a tour of the plant and mine operations. The neighbours must have wondered what was going on.

For the next five hours, we were going to focus on bauxite. Aluminium is the most abundant metal element, forming about eight percent of the earth's crust. Unlike gold and silver, it is not found in its pure form, and is usually bonded to oxygen. In 1821, P. Berthier, a French chemist, analysed a hard, reddish, claylike material he had found near the village of Les Baux in Provence, France. It contained a high percentage of alumina. He named the ore bauxite, after the village. Around 1825, European scientists found a way to extract aluminium metal from bauxite's alum powder, at a very high cost. With its attractive surface sheen, aluminium, for the next sixty years, was the world's most precious metal.

Charles Martin Hall discovered an efficient oxygen separation process to produce aluminium from bauxite in the United States in 1886, as did Paul Touissant-Heroult in France that same year. In the Guianas, bauxite was first discovered in French Guiana in 1887 and in Dutch Guiana the following year. On December 30, 1888, Professor John Harrison and John Quelch, then a naturalist curator at the British Guiana Museum, discovered bauxite up the Demerara River at Akyma and, a few days later, at nearby Christianburg. These discoveries launched a series of activities that led to the formation of the Demerara Bauxite Company, Demba, in 1916, owned by Alcoa in the United States. Alcoa created Alcan in Canada in 1928 and transferred Demba ownership to it.

The bauxite seams vary in depth from a metre to more than twelve metres and can extend horizontally for a thousand or more metres. Geologists believe that the bauxite deposits were formed by laterisation, or tropical weathering, where the original rocks were decomposed and the soluble components carried away, leaving behind a combination of silica, ferrous, and aluminium oxides. The alumina content of the aluminium oxides is the content desired. The principal bauxite deposits in the country have been on the Berbice and Demerara rivers to date, but exploration is determining other promising sites.

We were driven through the main gate, and could see the old metal corrugated buildings everywhere, with numerous big conveyor belt structures joining them. The old wooden office buildings were still functional but were ancient in appearance. We were toured over to the dock, where the Danish ship *Thorco Liva* was being loaded. One of our Chinese hosts pointed to an old blue metal loader, still functioning, and told me it had been built under my father's direction in the 1940s. We were also shown the two expensive dust-collector towers that had been recently constructed to minimise the dust that had plagued the whole area for almost a century.

Coming in from the Highway

The towering uneven chimneys of Mackenzie
Pulsing out heavy pink banners
In a confused monogram
Swirling its umbrella across the river
The dusty inverted basis of the industry
Not in water but in dust
Invisible rain comes down
Covering tables, clothes
Penetrating carburetors
Flowing into the Demerara with the rains.

— A.J. Seymour, *Miniatures from Mackenzie*

Bosai is very conscious of its environmental responsibility. Sam could have led the tour: he was the most knowledgeable person in the whole group.

A guide led us through the old chemical laboratory where Sam had spent a good part of his working life. The ground floor of the wooden building is not the pristine white-coat laboratory that one might expect. We were given samples and explanations of the four types of bauxite products produced by the company. The major product is Refractory "A" Grade Super Calcined (RASC) bauxite. The calcination of bauxite is done in monstrous rotary kilns almost one hundred metres in length, which are lined with refractory brick and inclined at a slight angle to the ground. Washed bauxite is fed into the higher end of the slowly rotating kiln, which is heated to a very high degree until all surface moisture and chemically combined water is removed. The resulting material is used by refractory industries throughout the world to make brick, castings, and monolithic for steel, aluminium, and other high-temperature industries where refractory linings are required to protect furnace walls. RASC bauxite is also used to make electrical porcelain, welding electrodes, and anti-skid surfaces for roads. Super chemical-grade bauxite, cement-grade bauxite, and abrasive-grade bauxite are three other company products.

The old and weary but still-functional office building was pointed out to me. I wondered how my father and his colleagues could have stood up to the heat and humidity in these buildings, especially during World War

II, without air-conditioning. It was here at the end of January 1942 when one afternoon my father returned to the office from the plant yard to be shocked, together with all of the office staff, at the news that three of his colleague's wives had died voyaging from Canada to British Guiana when their ship, the *Lady Hawkins*, had been torpedoed. The country, although then somewhat isolated from the war, was still being regularly affected by it.

A dozen of us in several vehicles were next driven fifty to sixty kilometres through old and new bauxite mine territory, interspersed with low rainforest. At times we could see moonscapes of bare beige to red-brown laterite, at times flat and level with us, in other places huge cavities, even deep valleys, of open-pit mine works. The roadways were of the same coloured earth as that which surrounded us, pounded out by massive trucks hauling ore. One could see how sudden heavy rains had caused washouts and depressions, which ensured slow vehicle travel. In many places, we saw ancient heavy equipment and parts, such as old shovel buckets, discarded and rusting.

On one occasion, helmeted and under a hot tropical sun, we all clambered out of our vehicles to stand in wonder on the edge of a seemingly Grand Canyon-like valley, more than two kilometres in length and up to 100 metres in depth. On the far side, we could see the layers of white sand and laterite earth, the overburden that had been dug out to get at the bauxite seam far below. Nearby, I encountered my first cashew tree, and was amazed to see the reddish-yellow fruit hanging like Christmas-tree bulbs, each one suspending a cashew nut.

We also stopped at a very large building used for heavy-equipment maintenance. After the bauxite becomes exposed, hydraulic backhoes are used to fill eighty-five-ton Caterpillar trucks for hauling to the washing plant. During my father's time, during the mid-twentieth century and after, overburden and bauxite were removed using huge electric draglines and transported to the plant by train. This practice has long been discontinued.

The maintenance shop foreman halted work so Sam and I could speak with the men. All of them were dressed neatly in khaki pants and short-sleeved shirts and were athletic-looking. We were all happy to share bottles of cold water. This was a fun event, and we were able to keep the men laughing with our stories. I told them that when I had left the country as a child sixty-three years previously I had been of their beautiful ebony black colour, but after all that time living in the cold of Canada (I spreading my arms out), "Look what happened to me!" Oh, well.

On our route back to Linden, we suddenly exited a rainforest area to arrive at the old Mackenzie airstrip. Wow. Still no buildings. The arched corrugated metal hangar erected in 1962 to house Demba's new airplane at the top end of the airstrip has long since gone. About two kilometres long and very wide, the unique tarmac is perfectly flat and in excellent shape. What used to be an area of red-brown earth on three sides of the facility was now covered by tropical growth right up to the tarmac edges. The western end of the airstrip, yielding a spectacular view over the Demerara River far below, was where airplanes usually took off from. Like Atkinson Field south of Georgetown, this airstrip was built by the Americans in 1941-42 as an emergency facility for use in World War II. Again, Demba had provided heavy equipment and operators to help with its construction. Isolated, with no security, it is ideal for small airplanes to take advantage of for smuggling drugs and other illegal goods.

Perhaps no pilot, not even his close friend Harry Wendt, has made more takeoffs and landings on this airstrip than Tom Wilson, who flew Demba's eleven-seater De Havilland Otter DCH-3 amphibian commencing in 1962. He flew almost every day for almost seven years, transporting company executives, employees, country politicians, visiting VIPs, and goods of all kinds. He survived a crash landing when the Otter's engine had, in his words, "blown a jug!" Tom flew the Otter all over the country, landing on water or on hard surfaces (eight airstrips existed around the country during his time, including one at Port Kaituma, where the Jonestown shootings occurred). The aircraft could not land on soft ground due to the small circumference of the nose wheel.

While Demba celebrated its 100th anniversary in 2016, Tom simultaneously celebrated his eightieth birthday in British Columbia, Canada. Let me be the first to suggest that the everlasting runway facility be named "Wilson's Airstrip". Many readers of this book will recall flying with this capable and personable pilot...my good friend.

Folks may wonder whatever happened to the old faithful De Havilland Otter amphibian, which Tom watched being built in Montreal before flying it to British Guiana. It went much the same way as the renowned river steamer *R.H. Carr*, which finished its life as an iron skeleton at Skull Point on the Cuyuni River. The Otter was sold to Bradley Air Services in Carp, Ontario, Canada, and crashed near Gagnon, Quebec, in 1974. No one died.

Acting General Manager Eric Yu and some of his management staff hosted us for a late lunch at the Watooka Clubhouse. We were served by an enthusiastic staff, and I continued to find it hard to believe that after all the years, I was back at the place of my birth, with such a diverse group of interesting and special people. We continued to talk about Bosai and bauxite.

Bosai Minerals Group is headquartered in Chongoing Municipality in southwest China. It employs 3,500 people and sells its mining products in twenty countries. It acquired the Demerara River bauxite operations at the end of 2006, and employs 550 workers, with fourteen Chinese men on staff. Guyanese Orrin Barnwell is the superintendent in charge of mining operations.

The bauxite commodity market is very competitive, and mining companies need to be very efficient to be successful. On the positive side, Bosai's bauxite deposits are of the highest quality in the world. This is because of the high alumina and low iron content, ideal for RASC production. This is offset by the fact that all the low-overburdened bauxite has been mined out during the past century. On average, sixty-one metres of overburden must now be removed to reach a bauxite seam. While other countries with bauxite deposits may have a lower-quality product, they nevertheless have less overburden to remove. Tunnelling for bauxite is not an option due to the soft laterite earth. Eric Yu also informed me that the area still has 100 years of proven bauxite reserves. Given that the operations once employed more than 6,000 men, high employment now prevails. I got the sense that Bosai sincerely wants to improve on its success to date, to improve its care of the environment, and to do even more to support and to be part of the community.

The most exciting part of our day's journey was now to begin, in the heat of the mid-afternoon under rain-threatening clouds. We thanked our hosts for their hospitality, then were driven along the old road by the railway tracks down to the south end of Riverside Drive, where Sam, myself, and a bodyguard exited the car. During our time there had been about sixty houses, almost all on stilts, along both sides of the road. Five additional houses were built not long after at the south end. The old narrow road is parallel to the river and is mostly in bad shape, full of large potholes and narrowed almost to a wide path at the north end. Ditches on both sides of the road can still carry water, but they are in poor shape.

We commenced our walk where the home of the Hutt family still stands, but soon had to take shelter from heavy rain under the front-door overhead of a non-stilted concrete home that had once been lived in by Mr. and Mrs. Campbell. He had been the keeper of the nearby golf club, which in our time had six holes, and where folks had used bamboo golf clubs. Margaret had been an assistant of J.G. Campbell in Georgetown and had commuted back to her home every weekend. Sam related all of this to me until the rain abated, after about ten minutes, and we continued our walk.

In spite of the rain, it was hot, and especially humid. The limousine followed us within thirty metres and our armed "close man" walked halfway between us and the car. All was quiet; no one was in sight. It seemed like High Noon in Hadleyville in New Mexico Territory, before the shoot-out.

I had known many of the residents in the houses during my childhood, and Sam had later known mostly different residents during his time. Having great reminiscing fun, we shared our knowledge of old times as we stopped beside most of the houses. Sam referred to it as "a walk down memory lane". Many of the houses seemed vacant, and many were in disrepair. Unlike in the past, many properties were not well maintained, including the expansive yards. Raw tropical growth prevails. Also unlike in the past, we could not see the river behind the homes on the west side of the road. Tall growth now triumphs, including much relatively young bamboo greenery. During all my time in Guyana, I did not see any lawnmowers. Lawns are mostly cut using weed eaters.

I had related a World War II story to Sam as we had strolled slowly along the pot-holed road. In one of these houses, a man had been noticed to have two fridges, which had caused some quiet discussion of suspicion. Subsequently, Demba's constables had checked things out, and found that one of the fridges contained a radio transmitter. They had discovered a German spy.

Even during Sam's time, in fact at the time of his arrival from university, there were spies in the community of Mackenzie—CIA spies. From the early 1950s, the United States was concerned about Cheddi Jagan's political leadership. Jagan had obtained, even throughout the Caribbean, a label as an anti-colonial communist. Neither Britain nor the US wanted him to succeed in leading the country. Jagan had established ties with communist Cuba, and the US did not want two communist footholds in the Caribbean. Hence, the US established the CIA in British Guiana, to sabotage Jagan's chances for success and to support Burnham. By the early 1960s the CIA was well-established, and US President John F. Kennedy remained very concerned, to the extent that he even agreed to meet with Jagan at the White House in late 1961. Jagan was refused any support. Later, at the time of Guyana's achievement of independence under Burnham's leadership, a Guyanese engineer who arrived in Mackenzie to work for Demba was, unknown to anyone in the area, a senior CIA agent coordinating covert activities with other agents. His wife recently confirmed to me that even she had not known of her husband's clandestine work.

As we approached a yellow house backing onto the river, civic #116, Sam commented that this had been his family's home during his early years as an engineer. I would be welcomed into this home later in the year. At times, people waved to us from the top of their outdoor stairs. On a few occasions, residents rushed out to greet Sam at their fence gates, where we greatly enjoyed meeting and talking to them. (No Canadian prime ministers have ever showed up at the entrance to *our* home!)

About halfway up the road, I shouted to my colleague that our old Connolly home, dull yellow, with a red corrugated-metal roof, was to our left, backing onto the river. Wow. The creek to its right was plug-full of green growth, making it impossible to see water. A low, gated fence enclosed the property, and all seemed neat and tidy, with the large yards, front and back, well-maintained. The right-hand side of the bottom of the stilted house had been closed in since our time there. Unfortunately, no one was home, but nevertheless, we toured the property and took photos. The even grass was soaked and spongy from the rain. A chain-link fence bordered the backyard, about five metres in from the river, which could be seen through a small boat-launching space in the tall growth. In olden times, the grass had extended to the river, except where there had been a giant bamboo tree.

I recalled the many times our family had encountered snakes, both large and small, there. *Every time I remember ole time story, water come a meh eyes.*

With some reluctance from me, we moved on up the road, until we approached the area on the right where the old wooden, stilted Watooka Day School building, which included a small cinema, had been located. A small yellow concrete school building now takes up half of the vacant area. The houses on the sides of the school and across the road all once contained interesting residents, whom I recalled from my youth. Only three houses from the end of our trek, we encountered the old white Grimes-Graeme home, for which I highly recommend some serious renovations and a paint job. Just then, a pretty young blonde in sandals came running out of the house shouting "Steve! Steve!" Sam must have been impressed, or at least amused, to see this reunion, given my sixty-three-year absence versus her youth. Caucasian Rachel Ivancie. I suspect her excitement related more to encountering Sam than myself.

The three of us enjoyed an excited chat. I had met Rachel only days before, when she and her Linden doctor boyfriend, Richie, had guested at the Rainforest in Georgetown for an evening. She was an American Peace Corps nurse working in Linden and loving her work. Incredibly, there are now about thirty doctors working in Linden, compared to three or four in our time. The American Peace Corps has been active in Guyana ever since Independence in 1966. Currently, there were about seventy members working in Guyana. We parted, and two houses later Sam and I stood in front of the old Manager's House—a real sad story of neglect. Interesting and very capable managers and their families had lived there. Many, since the very early days, had been close friends of our Connolly family. This great property will get much attention later in my writing.

We walked across the road to the Watooka Clubhouse, where I was to achieve another major objective, well-known to a chuckling Sam Hinds and to those new friends in Linden that I had encountered: to swim in the old Watooka swimming pool. I changed in the old change room under the Clubhouse. There was no bench, and the few wall pegs for clothes were crowded with apparel. At the poolside in my bathing suit, hot and perspiring, I encountered about a dozen adults—and thirty-five beautiful black children cavorting in the pool and paying no attention to me.

As a child, living in Watooka for three years, I had spent most days in the pool with my brother, Mike, and our little white friends. We could swim like fish, and some of our pool mates went on to become champion swimmers in North America. The high and low diving boards had been removed but, amazingly, the pool was, after almost seventy-five years, still functioning well. It was designed by Roy Emery, an amazing engineer inventor and friend of my father, and later, of myself. He also designed and supervised the construction of the swimming pool in Cockatara.

So, I slipped into the pool totally unnoticed by the playful children. As children, we had been able to swim two lengths of the 18-metre pool twice underwater with ease. I thought about trying to do so for one length of the pool, but then reasoned that such would be foolish without practice. Also, the water was opaque for some reason…and it was full of kids. Nor was the warm water refreshing. In my past, the water had been clear but bluish, due to heavy doses of chlorine, which had always resulted in bloodshot eyes. I finally got the children's attention, and they circled around to hear me relate an interesting story while Sam took photographs of us. I pointed to the one-inch-square smooth ceramic tiles that were lined about a foot wide around the water's edge. Emery had placed those there so that years of lapping surface water would not erode the cement that would otherwise be there. I told the children that the pool had opened in April 1942 during World War II, and had been delayed because it had taken three ship voyages from Canada to bring the tiles. The first two ships, returning for bauxite loads, had been torpedoed by German submarines.

It was time to part. Knowing my penchant for storytelling and for listening to storytellers, Sam proposed that we head up to Richmond Hill to visit the home of a long-time raconteur friend of his, James "Jimmy" Kranenburg. Seeing our small entourage at his gate, Jimmy strode down his long driveway to open the large gate and to greet us warmly. Tall, gangly, and talkative, he led us up the outdoor steps and into his home, where we met Bonnie, his Chinese wife. (She was to later tell me that labaria snakes are prevalent on the large grounds around the house.) For over an hour, Jim regaled us with his stories of working in the area. He had known Maurice Nascimento well—they had worked together surveying—and he had often flown in the Otter with Tom Wilson. We enjoyed copious quantities of Brazilian

Malt Whiskey with ice, while Jim's waving long arms added emphasis to his interesting tales. In 1981, their son, James, became the second student out of the Mackenzie High School to become a Guyana Scholar. (Alfie Collins was the first to do so, in 1974.)

We arrived at Sam's home in the early dark. He signed some anniversary books for me while I gratefully thanked him for his accompaniment and friendship for the wonderful day. I was then chauffeured to the Tower Suites, where I met some friends for us to *fire one* at the Tiki Bar. My journey back to Watooka had been a highlight of my life...but it was not finished yet.

THE RAINFOREST I

I said it before and I'll reiterate—our country
is poetically blessed with some of the most awesome
primordial and pristine landscapes on earth in spite,
or because, of the ruggedness and impenetrability
of our forested and mountainous regions.
And if Guyana is a poem, then I will be an eagle,
a Harpy, soaring against cathedrals
of green, tumbling cataracts
and mist shrouded peaks.

— Dennis Nichols, *Kaieteur News*

It was almost six a.m. on a Tuesday morning as I walked from the Rainforest to the Herdmanston Lodge about five blocks away, still in Queenstown. I was greeted by the security guard who was opening the gates, and I proceeded into the lobby for an early coffee, to read the newspapers, and to meet folks if possible. The newspapers were full of the exciting events that were occurring that week to celebrate the fiftieth anniversary. Georgetown has five major newspapers, and they are produced very colourfully. Many pages usually contain criminal happenings, including murders, vehicle carnage, government oversights, and various forms of corruption/fraud. As

I was short for time in Guyana, the newspapers allowed me to understand what events were going on so that I could plan to make the most of my time. Over the week, I got to know most of the staff of the Lodge on a first-name basis, as I would appear here early every morning. This heritage lodge is one of the few hotels that has maintained its colonial appearance.

I returned to the Rainforest in time to shower and, together with the other guests, to be seated for the 7:30 a.m. breakfast, prepared by Jerry Lagra under a turning ceiling fan. It is time now to write about some of Jerry's interesting achievements. A major one has to do with...peanuts.

For the most part, southern Guyana is uniquely different from the rest of the country. Known as the Rupununi, and representing more than twenty-five percent of Guyana's area, it is considered the largest open-range savannah in the world. It is separated north from south by the Kanuku mountains, home to much unique flora and fauna. (Kanuku in the native tongue means "rich forest".) This area is one of the most biologically diverse regions in Guyana. About half of the country's bird species and eighty percent of the country's species of mammals can be found here. In early times, Makushi tribes inhabited the north Rupununi, while the Wapishana tended to be in the south Rupununi. The very primitive Wai Wai natives were found in the tropical jungle south of these savannah areas. Most of the population is indigenous, living on a subsistence diet. One of the few cash crops in the region is peanuts.

Over decades, Jerry Lagra has worked to develop countries in the Caribbean, primarily in Guyana. In 2002, as Executive Director for Societies for Sustainable Operational Strategies, with help from the Universities of Georgia and Florida and working with Banks DIH and Demerara Distillers Ltd., he led a project to industrialise peanut production in the Rupununi. Research to determine the best types of peanuts for growing, fertilisation practices, planting and harvesting equipment, and peanut-plant processing was conducted over several years. With respect to the goal of building a sustainable market, the Ministry of Education was also involved and supportive.

Today, more than 400 peanut farmers produce peanuts for a factory operation in Aranaputa, North Rupununi. Set between the Pakaraima Mountains and the gently flowing Rupununi River, between thick forests and open savannah, the factory employs 100 workers to produce peanut butter for lunches for more than 4,000 students in forty or more schools. The student lunches also contain cassava bread and juice, which are also produced locally. Student attendance at schools has also increased/improved. Coastal schools are also starting to benefit from this program, and new markets are being sought.

Jerry told me that, as a Rural Development Facilitator, he had worked on numerous other development projects, many of which were not successful, but, for sure, the peanut endeavour has been remarkably flourishing—and he deserves great merit, given his from-the-heart desire, like Syeada's, to help others. He has also worked successfully to install solar electricity capability, for lighting and radio systems, in the primitive hinterland village of Wayalayeng. At the time of my writing, the government had taken over management of the southern peanut industry, and results have been diminishing. Time will tell.

After the usual enjoyable and varied breakfast discussion, I took a taxi to the Brickdam Cathedral downtown. The fortress-like dark concrete building was closed. Its old wooden predecessor burned down in 1913, and it took until 1927 to be re-built, completely fireproof.

Since the cathedral was closed, I walked to Main Street, to the old colonial building housing the Ministry of Culture, Youth and Sports. I wanted to meet well-known Dr. James Rose, a former vice-chancellor of the University of Guyana, to thank him for the favour he had done me by giving me permission to put the government-owned Fiftieth Jubilee logo on the cover of my book. With a brief explanation, I was able to quickly obtain a pass, and proceeded into the historic building, surprisingly, alone. Reaching the second floor, in a really cramped hallway and series of rooms, I encountered Dr. Rose rushing out of his large office for a meeting. So, I was able to extend my thanks and accept his apology for not being available for my unscheduled meeting, totally my fault. Thus ended my shortest meeting in Guyana!

A short walk later, still on Main Street, I stood in front of the re-built Sacred Heart Church. Wow. This church is special for me. It was built to cater to the Portuguese people in 1861, and opened on Christmas Day. In

2004, 141 years later, it burned down— on Christmas Day. Photos of the fire are spectacular.

This is the church in which my parents were married on September 9, 1941, during World War II. My mother had arrived on the *Lady Hawkins* the previous day, and three of the ship's officers that my mother had befriended had attended. As I recounted earlier, four months later, on January 19, 1942, these men died when the *Lady Hawkins* was torpedoed by the German submarine U-66.

My parents enjoyed a short honeymoon at the Hope Guest House on the beach at Belfield, east of Georgetown, prior to taking the *R.H. Carr* to Mackenzie. The church has been re-built to exactly look like the old one— except for its different white-with-red trim, which is a bit gaudy for me.

Not far along, on the other side of the street, is the huge old American embassy building. Four stories high, it is worn and derelict, an unpainted wooden structure, in stark contrast to Prime Minister's Residence up ahead, on the south side of the street. As I walked past the Residence, I thought that, after more than two decades in this large home, Sam and Yvonne Hinds must have found it difficult to move out last year.

Even more prestigious is the President's home next door. Looking through the wrought-iron gates, one can see a very expansive lawn, with the home set far back down the straight and paved entrance lane. The high concrete and wrought-iron fences of both properties were variously decorated with Guyana's flag and fiftieth-anniversary colours. Both, of course, had guardhouses up front, near the gates.

I next arranged for a taxi to take me to King's Jewellery World, headquartered on Quamina Street. I wear my father's gold wedding ring, which he obtained in British Guiana so long ago, and its small ruby had gone missing. King's was formed in 1970 by Looknauth Persaud, who had been known as "King", and is owned and managed by his family. The company is the originator of the wrist jewellery band worn by cricket players internationally. The company employs about 100 employees in eight locations and is a strong community contributor. It offers a wide variety of unique and beautiful jewelry made from Guyana gold and diamonds.

I met a guard at the door, and there appeared to be a few undercover security men on the two floors of the store. I was able to have the missing ruby in my ring replaced with a nice inexpensive diamond. A bottle of Fiftieth Jubilee fifty-year-old El Dorado rum was on display in a glass cabinet, on sale for US$2,500. I met Harrinand Ralph Persaud, the Chief Financial and Marketing Officer, who is one of Looknauth's three sons. He is well-educated, with an MBA degree, and he explained to me various aspects of the company's design techniques and operations.

Guyana's main export commodity, approaching US$800 million annually, is gold. It represents more than half of the value of all goods exported. In 2010, it was estimated that there were 11,000 miners employed by the industry. This did not tally the number of "artisanal miners", otherwise known as "pork-knockers", working on small illegal operations. It was estimated that the total number of freelance miners was 25,000, working in more than 3,000 locations. Obviously it has been difficult for the government to obtain accurate production figures. Illegally mined gold cannot be sold directly to the Gold Board, but the unlicensed pork-knockers can sell their gold to permitted gold dealers at a discount, and the dealers can sell the gold to the government for its full value. As long as the treasury receives the gold, it has been mostly content with this, although efforts are being made to minimise freelance mining.

Much gold gets to the various jewellers in the vast, dim-lit indoor Stabroek Market building. One industrious janitor who sweeps the floor daily has reported that every day he takes the swept dirt from the floor home, to use a gold pan in his bathtub to find gold for extra pocket money.

My next stop was the Bank of Nova Scotia, a relatively new building, on Robb Street, not far from 44 Robb Street, where the old home of my good friends the Beharrysingh family had been. The Bank of Nova Scotia commenced operations in Georgetown in 1968, and has five branches in the country. Under the hot sun, a long line of perspiring people ran from an ATM machine inside the front door to some distance down the block. I joined a long S-shaped line inside the bank, since I required a teller to obtain funds. The air conditioning was ineffective, due to the open front door, and the air had a tinge of human body odour. Fortunately, there were interesting folks to talk to—and incredibly, the two women in front of me, from Ottawa, Canada, recognised me. After one hour, I reached a pleasant teller, who informed me that I would require my passport to obtain funds. Oh, well.

I dared to walk in the hot sun to the Rainforest, and on the way came across the Bourda Market area, where I strolled past stalls mostly selling all sorts of food, vegetable, and fruit produce. I encountered a lady selling bird peppers. Wow, I hadn't tried one of those for more than six decades. Not much more than a thumbnail in length, these glossy all-bright-colours-of-the-rainbow carrot-shaped peppers are very enticing. However, I recalled the heat given off by these little beasts and asked the lady if I could buy one. She must have thought that I was joking, but I asked her how many G$100 could buy, and she gave me a dozen in some plastic wrap. These peppers are not in the top group of the world's hottest peppers, but they are very hot. That night, I would cut three of them up to put in my curried rice and chicken...which required two glasses of cold water to accompany the meal. Guyana's heat, rain, and silty soil are ideal for growing peppers.

We had a great evening on the veranda.

The next day was the day before Fiftieth Anniversary Day. At 5:30 a.m., I stood before an interesting large old white house in excellent condition, just down Forshaw Street, about half a block away. It is the office for the Russian RUSAL Bauxite Company of Guyana Inc., BCGI. Years ago, until nationalisation in 1971, it was the office of the Demerara Bauxite Company, then headed by Jim G. Campbell. *Wow*, I thought. *There has been a lot of history experienced in that building.* RUSAL took control of bauxite operations at Kwakwani and at Araima on the Berbice River in 2006. With more than 500 employees, it produces about seventy percent of Guyana's bauxite, compared to thirty percent produced by Bosai. Bauxite mining on the Berbice River commenced with the Berbice Bauxite Company in 1942. The US Reynolds Co. took over the operations in 1952, and continued until it, too, was nationalised by Burnham's government in 1975. For several mornings, very early, I enjoyed chats with the lady guards at the guardhouse just inside the tall white wrought-iron fence.

Not far away, also on Forshaw Street, is the home of "Mr. Coconut", according to Syeada. He has made his living all his life selling coconuts on his bicycle or at street corners in downtown Georgetown. Chop the top off the coconut with a sharp machete, shove a straw in, and a customer has a coconut drink. All his four children now participate in the business.

After some time at the Herdmanston Lodge, and then breakfast at the Rainforest, I hired a taxi and headed for Duke Lodge in the Kingston area of Georgetown. Located on Duke Street, it offers guests only a short walk to the seawall and ocean. Our family had stayed here in the old days, and brother Mike and I had enjoyed swims in the pool. I was given a tour of the premises by Amanda, the pleasant manager. She explained to me that the wooden structure, made entirely of greenheart wood, has been carefully preserved to keep its colonial architecture. On one wall in a dining room was a large mural painting, showing owner and pilot Captain Gerry Gouveia flying one of his Roraima Airways small airplanes. His wife, Captain Debra Gouveia, is also a pilot.

The Gouveias are hardworking entrepreneurs owning many businesses in Guyana. Visitors to Guyana first encounter a Gouveia business when they arrive at the Cheddi Jagan International Airport and see signs for the Roraima Executive Lounge Services, one of the plushest VIP lounges in the Caribbean. Aside from the Roraima Duke Lodge, they own the Roraima Residence Inn, Roraima Airways, a travel agency, Arrowpoint Nature Resort, and other businesses, which together employ about 270 people. Gerry has flown for more thirty years in Guyana and in other areas of South America and the Caribbean. He was a Major in the Guyana Defence Force, and Chief Pilot of the Army Air Corps. He is one of five owners of the Ogle Airport. His small reliable airplanes provide tourist services to interior resorts, and medical emergency service to bring patients in to Georgetown from remote parts of the country. He received the Tourism Entrepreneur award for 2016. I did not get an opportunity to meet Mr. Gouveia, but on a later visit, I was able to enjoy some brief discussion with Debbie at the bar.

Alex and Brenda Fortune, who were guest colleagues at the Rainforest, greatly enjoyed their one-day tour to the Arrowpoint Nature Resort. Arriving very early in the morning at Duke Lodge, they were taken by bus to the Roraima Boat Launch facility on the east side of the Demerara River and taken by speedboat for just less than an hour up the river to the west side, and then up the glassy dark tributary, Kamuni Creek. Through a jungle environment with captivating flora lining the creek, the boat passes by the Santa Mission, to shortly arrive at the resort. Tourists are given excellent meals, and can kayak, canoe, swim, hike in the forest, go caiman spotting, bird watch, fish, watch nocturnal wildlife, and visit the nearby Amerindian Santa Mission, which Roraima has adopted and where the company has established a library and other facilities. There are about 200 natives of Arawak descent living in the village, which has existed for almost 160 years. A giant silk-cotton tree exists there that the natives call "Kamaka", meaning "mother of all trees", which has roots, it is said, spreading throughout the village.

At the Duke Lodge, I sat down for coffee on the covered deck, reminiscing about swimming in the pool below while talking to a couple seated nearby. Subsequently, after he overheard me telling stories, I was invited to sit down at a table with a young man, Shawn Hart, who was enjoying a breakfast of fruit. Guyanese, he was living in England, and was now vacationing in Georgetown. He let me know that he is the grandson of Robert Hart, who he said had been a political force in the 1950s and '60s. In fact, he had been the leader of the People's National Party. Shawn was very proud that his grandfather had fought politically against Burnham and his Marxist approach.

Early that afternoon, Francis Ferreira came to the Rainforest to talk to Jerry about an artwork project and to purchase a book from me. He had a small walrus tusk that Jerry wanted to have mounted. At the time, I did not know who Francis was, but was later informed about him by Jerry. Francis is a renowned Guyanese sculptor, whose work is known all over Guyana and in the Caribbean. At a future exhibition of his work at the Pegasus Hotel, I was able to see the beautiful free-form wood sculptures that he is known for. One of his mentors was the "incomparable" Phillip Moore, who has used all sorts of media for his art: wood, canvas, calabashes, soda corks, wire mesh, seeds, and used barrels, amongst other things.

> *I am an ancient soul in a modern body...a spirit bathed in an African body in the country of Guyana and the universe. I often feel as a timeless being ever existed and deathless though my body will change through the earth and reappear in other forms of vegetation, etc.*
>
> — Phillip Moore

During the late afternoon, I walked in the heat to the not-too-distant Guyana Zoological Park. It was a far cry from the wonderful place that I had known as a child. In fact, I was shocked to find it in very bad shape. I paid US$1 for an entrance fee, and that was too much. The few animals and birds were certainly not in environments that simulated their natural habitat. They looked worn, sad, and lonely. I met the lady zoo manager, who told me that plans are being made to improve everything. As for most initiatives in Guyana, money is lacking. I asked her if she could open the closed gift shop for me and, once inside, was shocked to find it bare of goods, and having the look of a garage or storage shed. From somewhere in the dust, she found a paper bag containing small bird figurines, carved out of balata and hand-painted. I bought a few for my grandchildren.

The renowned manatee pond is still there, more linear than round. It is mostly covered in small lily pads and some plastic garbage. I was told that one or more large anaconda snakes(s) live in the pond. Syeada Manbodh has, at times, led schoolchildren to the pond to clean out the garbage. One time, she and Jerry were willed US$2,000 to help animals, and they used it to restore and paint a monkey cage. The historical "kissing bridge", built in 1885 over the pond, is surprisingly still present. Constructed of solid iron and painted white, it remains in popular use for taking photographs. My parents did so on their honeymoon in 1941. In 1916, former US President Theodore Roosevelt and his naturalist friend, Dr. William Beebe, stood on this bridge, where Roosevelt remarked, "I would willingly stand for two days to catch a good glimpse of a wild manatee". The bridge was a highlight of my visit. The other highlight was when about fifty big wild white egrets landed in a very tall tree. They were beautiful...but I made sure that I did not wander under the tree.

The Botanical Gardens was established around 1880 from part of the old Vlissingen plantation. The Zoological Park was formed as part of it in 1952, only a year before our family left British Guiana.

That evening was a quiet, sociable one at the Rainforest. None of us planned to attend the midnight fiftieth anniversary flag-raising ceremony at the nearby D'Urban Park. A Dutch couple from Holland, Brian and Jolanda, and their twenty-three-year-old son, formed an interesting part of our discussion group. The young man had just returned from a six-day interior trek to the top of Mount Roraima, a giant flat-topped mountain in the Pakaraima Mountains of the Guiana Highlands. It is the source of many rivers in Guyana and in the Amazon and Orinoco basins. About 2,800 metres in height, and fourteen kilometres long, having 400-metre cliffs on all sides, it has a point on top that is where the borders of southwest Guyana, Brazil, and Venezuela meet. Although it is not the highest point in Brazil, nor in Venezuela, it is for Guyana. Three quarters of the tabletop lies in Venezuela, and the forested path to the top is accessed in Venezuela. Otherwise, one has to be a rock-climbing expert.

The young Dutchman's group trek had taken him across Guyana's savannah for the first day, through rising high-tropical growth on the second day, and through rising rainforest to the tabletop on the third day. Trekkers must be physically fit. Venomous rattlesnakes may be encountered and, to respect the environment, one must poop into plastic bags that are carried by a guide. It rains almost every day on the top and this, together with regular winds, allows for almost no growth on the mountain's sandstone surface. On the top, the young man recalled walking on pure quartz gravel, which it is forbidden to remove. Tents are not used at the top; instead, the group sleeps in a cave, where he remembered seeing some type of gold in the ceiling. It would take another day to reach the point where the three country borders meet.

My Guyanese/Portuguese friend, Welesley "Wes" Arthur (his wife's name is Valerie), who worked as an accountant for the Demerara Bauxite Company, wrote the following song/poem decades ago. The subject is a monument that is on the top of Mount Roraima:

The Monument

There's a column standing there my boy, and it's made of sand and stone,
Cemented into one mass, and it stands there all alone.
Triangular they've made it, that's the only way they could.
Each side's a different country, each edge points where it should.

When I was much younger I met an old man then
Who had been around our country, through every nook and bend.

He said he worked in mighty forest, he toiled in steaming swamp
With the Boundary Commission, thorough heat and chill and damp.

Their mission was to draw lines, to mark what's ours, what's theirs.
You see the treaty had been settled after long and bitter years.
At the point from where they started, when they came full circle round,
That's where they built the monument, on a height of rocky ground.

He said, "This side, that's Venezuela, only Spanish spoken there.
On the other side lies Brazil, where Portuguese you'd hear.
The third side, well that's ours, and English is our tongue,
But from our man-made monument, you know, you'd never hear a sound."

Now many years later this thought has come to me,
What if we took the monument down and dumped it far at sea,
All the grass and trees and rocks there, would they notice any change?
And the birds and snakes and creeping moss, would they sense an altered range?

Happy Fiftieth Anniversary Day! I awoke at 5:00 a.m. There was still celebration noise coming from D'Urban Park, but by now it was rather subdued. I was glad that I had foregone the event and was fresh and ready for another interesting day. At 6:30 a.m., I found myself again at the Herdmanston Lodge. As I walked into the lobby, I was greeted warmly by a smiling dreadlocked gentleman sitting on a couch, dealing with his smartphone: Selwyn Pieters, Barrister and Solicitor in Toronto, Canada, Attorney-at-law in Guyana and Trinidad, and legal advisor to Guyana's government. We gave each other a fist-shake, and immediately became befriended. He was in Guyana to help the government investigate a riot that had occurred almost two months previously at the Camp Street Prison in Georgetown. Seventeen prisoners, including "Fungus", "Cruel", and "Bad Boy", had perished in a fire set by themselves. Reportedly, most of them had been charged with murders. Apparently they had been upset because remand processing was taking too long and because illicit cellphones had been taken from them. Selwyn was to look into all this.

Every year, several hundreds of criminals are deported to Guyana from the US, Canada, Britain, and other countries. Even in these countries the prisons are overcrowded, and the court systems are backlogged. Since the terrorist attack on the World Trade Center in 2001, the US has deported some 3,500 Guyanese back to Guyana, ninety-five percent being criminals. Guyana cannot afford or adequately handle this situation. One can imagine the prison conditions in third-world Guyana. There are five prisons in the country, containing more than 2,100 prisoners, many of them waiting long periods for hearings performed by a court system that cannot handle the workload efficiently. At the start of 2017, more than 10,000 cases were backlogged with the High Court. Unlike the US and many other first-world countries, Guyana mediates only about ten percent of its cases. The rest remain seriously plugged up in the courts. Selwyn knows Judge Navrinda Singh and can't understand why this judge hands out sentences that are extraordinarily long—fifty years or more in some cases.

The newspapers around us were full of photos of the celebrations of the previous night, and of the situation where the government had not provided seats for the government opposition VIPs, who (as I mentioned earlier) had walked out as a large group just prior to the raising of the huge flag.

Naomi, one of the gracious staff, then invited us to help ourselves to the smorgasbord breakfast, mentioning that for me, a non-guest, breakfast would be on the house. While doing so, we were joined by a smiling, well-dressed man who had a religious cross hanging from his necklace. Selwyn introduced me to the Bishop of Guyana, Anglican Charles Davidson, and we shook hands while chuckling at our manner of meeting. I had only recently been introduced to the bishop via telephone by my Toronto friend Ned Blair. The bishop had been provided with a copy of my book by Ned's sister, Cheryl Kijewski, who lives in Virginia in the US. He and his wife, Maureen, had been visiting the Lodge for breakfast, and had been sitting in a corner, probably watching the friendship between myself and Selwyn develop. I would be seeing them the following day.

The day was cloudy, with a prediction of some heavy rain. It was also the day for the Fiftieth Jubilee Parade. Like all Guyanese parades, this one would be showing off much cultural diversity, and would be bright and colourful. Pete Oxford had all of his high-end camera equipment prepared for the event and had chosen an advantageous location for his work. As I do not like crowds, and four hours standing in the heat and heavy rain did not appeal to me (not even counting guaranteed parade delays), I chose other interesting activities with which to occupy myself. And, the clouds were starting to darken...

Over Guiana clouds

Little curled feathers on the back of the sky
— White, chicken-downy on the soft sweet blue —
In slow reluctant patterns for the world to see.
Then frisky lambs that gambol and bowl along
Shepherded by the brave Trade Wind.
And glittering in the sun come great grave battleships
Ploughing an even keel across the sky.
In their own time, their bowels full of rain
The angry clouds that rage with lightning
Emitting sullen bulldog growls
And then they spirit themselves away in mist
and rain.

— Arthur J. Seymour

Early the following afternoon, a Friday, my taxi drove up to a large gate in Bel Air Gardens, which opened onto the curved entrance driveway leading to the residence of Canada's High Commissioner to Guyana (and Suriname)—the home of Pierre and Blanca Giroux. I was purposely early for my Guyana book launch, so that I might have some quiet time with the host. I was thankful for the air-conditioning and was interested to see the Canadian artwork that surrounded me on the walls and on the coffee tables.

The High Commissioner and I enjoyed an hour's discussion, and I learned that he has worked in the Caribbean region for more than thirty years. He is fluent in French and Spanish. His organization performs a great variety of functions relating to Canadian companies and citizens in Guyana: visa processing, expedition of goods, government relationships, Canadian aid to Guyana, and much more. He is very supportive of Guyana in its defence against Venezuela's continuing border dispute/aggression. His residence is in an affluent area, with the British High Commissioner's residence being next door. He had graciously offered to host a garden reception to welcome and introduce my book, for which I was extremely grateful. His residence property is high-walled, with extensive lawns and tropical flora. A large swimming pool with sky-blue water lies invitingly at some distance from the house.

As we heard the first guests begin to arrive, we walked out onto the large covered patio, where a podium, microphone, and flags had been installed, together with drinks and hors d'oeuvres. My books had been set up on nicely covered tables. While I knew of a few folks who would be attending, I really did not know who would be there. I was so very fortunate I didn't need to worry about it. I stood near the patio entrance to welcome wonderful guests.

The High Commissioner opened the event with some nice introductory remarks, and was followed by Dr. Rupert Roopnaraine, Minister of Education. I had not met him before and was not aware of his interesting background. In his youth, he excelled at cricket for Queen's College and in 1962, like Linden Forbes Burnham twenty years before him, was the Guyana Scholar. This permitted him to study at Cambridge in England, where he was also the captain of the university's cricket team. Perhaps the most interesting information revealed in his talk was that he, former Prime Minister Sam Hinds (who was also present), and I were all born in the same year: 1943.

Minister Roopnaraine began working with Walter Rodney as one of the leaders of the Working People's Alliance (WPA) in 1977, together with Eusi Kwayana and Clive Thomas. At one time he was arrested for burning down the PNC headquarters, although somehow, he got removed from the charge; some of his colleagues, however, were later murdered. He himself barely escaped murder by PNC thugs, escaping their pursuit through sugar cane fields with the help of sugar cane workers. When the leader of the WPA, Walter Rodney, was assassinated in 1980, Roopnaraine became the WPA leader. He has been reported to be "inhumanly honest", and has devoted himself to bettering his country.

In the 1992 book *Guyana at the Crossroads*, edited by Christine Craig and Dennis Watson, Roopnaraine is quoted as saying:

Justice will become a reality. The joint pursuit of making a decent living through jobs, self-employment, or business while sinking the roots of democracy deep into our society is crucial if Guyanese are to begin treating Guyana as their permanent home.

Of course, I was given the opportunity to speak about my book, and to underline that my purpose for writing it had been to help record some of the country's history, particularly that of the Linden area. After my talk, I enjoyed mingling with the exceptional people who had attended. One of these was the Catholic Bishop of Georgetown, Francis Alleyne. Born in Trinidad, he was appointed to his current post in 2003. The Anglican Bishop of Guyana, Charles Davidson, and his wife, Maureen, were also present, as was their good friend Paula Walcott-Quintin, who was staying with them at Austin House, and whom I mentioned earlier.

Since then, Paula, who lives in New Jersey, has become an exceptional friend to me, and she will be mentioned further in my writing. Her presence in Guyana at this time would be the second of three visits for 2016. (Paula likes to say, "I always lose weight when I visit Guyana. I am never hungry here". The heat and humidity are pervasive, for sure!) Bishop Davidson is also the Bishop of Suriname and Cayenne. He is yet another fine and successful product of Cockatara, Mackenzie, where he was born and raised.

Austin House is a beautiful building that was renovated in 2012. This is the home of the Davidsons. Facing High Street in Kingston, it was named after Anglican Bishop William Austin (1807-1892), who had resided in the original house, known as Kingston House, until his passing. Kingston House was demolished in 1894 to build the current house on the spacious grounds. I would later pass by this house, and wonder at its beauty. Its sloping top-hung shutters (known as Demerara windows), six-paned windows, steep roofing, yellow paint, and beautifully fenced and gated and very well-maintained grounds combine to force attention.

Former tennis star, businessman, and journalist/author/poet, Ian McDonald, Caucasian, was present. I had not known much about him prior to this day. Wow. He was born in Trinidad in 1933 and became its tennis champion as a teenager. At twenty-two years of age, he moved to British Guiana to work in the sugar industry for Bookers. He immediately became Guiana's tennis champion, and is the only player from the Caribbean to have played at Wimbledon, representing two countries, Trinidad and Tobago, and Guyana. He was Guyana's tennis champion for more than fifteen years. In his more than fifty years in the sugar business, he rose to become an executive with Bookers, and was also the CEO of the Caribbean Sugar Association. His athletic awards and those for literature seem endless, and describe an exceptional achiever. His love for poetry is unsurpassed, and he has also produced several of his own poetry books. He has expressed his genuine love for the reading of poetry as follows:

> *But at the end of the day what I get most out of good poetry is pleasure, pure enjoyment in what Coleridge called "The best words in the best order", a feeling of intense contentment and lasting satisfaction that I have discovered a perfect expression in words of some fact about the world or feeling or thought which once I have experienced it there seems to be no other way it could have been written or said, an inevitable achievement of the human imagination to be savoured and remembered.*

McDonald wrote a weekly column for the *Stabroek News* newspaper for more than twenty years and his book *A Cloud of Witnesses*, which showcases 100 of these works, gives an excellent review of a wide variety of interesting topics, and even more interesting information about the author himself.

Like Dr. Roopnaraine, Ian McDonald studied at Cambridge University in England, where he captained the tennis team. His uncle, Arthur McDonald, was a test pilot for Britain prior to World War II, and rose to become Air Marshall Sir Arthur McDonald, one of Britain's top air force commanders. When Pakistan gained its independence in 1947, he was seconded to become Commander-In-Chief of the Pakistan Air Force. In addition, he later become one of the world's top yachtsmen.

There were many other interesting guests, including Carwyn Holland, the mayor of Linden. I met Nirvana Persaud, CEO of Guyana National Trust, a government organisation that has a mandate to identify important historical monuments and sites in Guyana and find ways to maintain and improve them. Forty-two of these have been identified in Linden, including the old Watooka Clubhouse. All my books were sold. I regret that I did not have time to swim in the pool and wave the Canadian and Guyana flags.

The following morning, I took a taxi to the government's National Communications Network (NCN) radio and TV station on Homestretch Avenue near D'Urban Park to be interviewed about my book. Although we had communicated several times across the ocean, this would be the first time that I would meet the very congenial interviewer, Petamber Persaud. We would be appearing on his weekly programme *Oral Tradition*. He also hosts a bi-weekly programme, *Between the Lines*, and writes a weekly column in the *Guyana Chronicle*. Thusly, he is one of the best-known literary advocates in Guyana. His brother, Sasenarine Persaud, is an author and poet who spent much time in Toronto, Canada, but now lives in Tampa, Florida, where we had met. As children, they lived in Campbellville, where their father earned his living as a cane cutter, while their mother worked as a rice cutter. Though relatively poor, the two sons were never denied the fare to visit the National Library in their youth. When he got married, this literature guru gifted three of Edgar Mittelholzer's rare books to his wife: *A Swarthy Boy*, *Corentyne Thunder*, and *The Life and Death of Sylvia*. In 2016, Petamber rose to become the Chairman of the National Library. I have proposed to Petamber that the next time I visit Guyana, he must let *me* interview *him* on his program.

My next endeavour was also most interesting. I hosted twenty-year-old Christopher Taylor for a long lunch at the Pegasus Hotel, on the seawall in Kingston. I had very much looked forward to meeting this bright, well-dressed, and handsome young man. All of Georgetown was decorated everywhere for the Fiftieth Jubilee: colourful, colourful, colourful. Much of this vibrancy came from banners depicting the beautiful Fiftieth Jubilee logo that Chris and his partner, Compton Babb, had designed to win a contest. Decals of the design were on car bumpers and windows. Souvenirs of all kinds portrayed the open-mouthed jaguar. As the government had clearly stated at the announcement of the competition, the winners received only a nominal amount of money, and had to hand over copyright to the government.

Chris was doing graphics design for a small company and, like most young people, was being very pensive re his plans for the future. I suggested to him that he take photographs of his design displayed everywhere in the country, to create an album that he could use as a testament of his capability to any potential employer, such as Walt Disney World.

That afternoon, at the same hotel, New Era Books was to have a book sale event with several authors, including myself, present for signing. Karen Bacchus-Hinds owns two New Era Books stores, one in Georgetown, and the other at the Cheddi Jagan International Airport. Chris, who is also a photographer, brought his excellent camera along for the event. As we walked through the hotel lobby, I could not miss noticing an attractive afro-Guyanese lady with long orange hair. Wow.

Signs had been set up at the hotel entrance directing folks to a special room reserved for the book sale. We met Karen and her staff, who had set up all sorts of books about Guyana and the Caribbean for display. My yellow-covered book stood out, as per my original strategy. I recognised many of the other books as ones I either had or have heard of. Many of them are still selling well a decade or more after having been published, and I hope that such will be the case for *Children of Watooka*

Incredibly, the first person to enter the room was the lady with the orange hair. We exchanged pleasantries, and she then found out that I had been born in Mackenzie, just like herself. When she introduced herself as Margaret Haynes, I asked her if her father had been Peter Haynes, whom I had talked to just prior to his passing in 2014. Margaret broke into tears and gave me a big hug, and I shook hands with her brother Terry. Peter *had* been their father. Margaret and Terry are two of ten siblings—Margaret is "Number Five". Peter had a most interesting career with Demba, to be related in a later chapter.

Many interesting folks, mostly well-educated young and old, including doctors and professors, perused the books, and I tried to talk to all of them. It was impossible for me to remember all their names, unfortunately. I did meet Peter Ramrayka, author of *Recycling a Son of the British Raj*, which is about his life in the cultures of Guyana, Britain, and India. On my way back to the Rainforest, I asked the taxi driver to take Chris Taylor to his home in East Ruimveldt first.

Two days later, I felt both saddened and exhilarated: saddened because it was my last day in the country of my birth, exhilarated because of the incredible experience that I had enjoyed. That afternoon, I casually toured the

Marriott and Pegasus hotels at the seawall, and then appeared at the nearby Police Officer's Mess, located at the Guyana Police Force Headquarters at Eve Leary on Young Street, hoping to meet some officers with whom to share some stories. I had known Police Commissioner Laurie Lewis during the late 1990s but had never met him. I helped acquire some used Royal Canadian Mounted Police (RCMP) laboratory equipment as a donation to Guyana's police force. He had been a good athlete at Queen's College, and eventually became a Director. He was known for his high professionalism and for his dedication to, and empathy for, youth. He died in 2012, and was given a 21-gun salute: he was the second-longest serving police commissioner, and the only one to have served under two governments.

I immediately met two police officers in the large Mess, and offered to buy them cold beers, which they readily accepted. We then retired to some comfortable sofas on the expansive second-floor veranda. We had an enjoyable discussion, and the beers were downed gratefully, given the day's heat. There was a large water-filled ditch across the road below us, and I was informed that a large anaconda, about six metres long, had been found there recently.

Based on what I read in the newspapers each day, policing in Guyana is a real challenge. Not only is the crime level extremely high, only third-world facilities and equipment are available to the police. That very week, pirates carrying cutlasses had boarded a fishing boat near the Courentyne River. The five fishermen had been tied up, doused with gas, threatened to be burned, and thrown overboard. Four of them had died. There is lots of room for new police recruits, and it can be a rewarding career for courageous men and women.

I enjoyed an early evening drink at the Tower Suites Hotel's Tiki bar, and hoped that my friends Alex and Beverley Miller had been able to find an early flight back to Brooklyn, New York, where he could find good medical care.

After my fond farewells to Syeada, Jerry, and the Rainforest, I climbed into my taxi for a final ride of excitement to the airport…though it was not too bad, really, due to the early hour. The Fly Jamaica flight was delayed for four hours, permitting me to spend much time at the New Era Books store, helping to productively sell and autograph my books. I greatly enjoyed this, and the store employees were grateful for my unplanned appearance. At the duty-free shop, I also bought some of that Guyana golden syrup, fifteen-year-old El Dorado rum.

As the airplane rose in the sky, once again I could see out the window as it crossed the Demerara and turned west along the coast. It all felt like a dream. So much had happened in only eleven days—a highlight of my life.

Little did I know that I would be returning in less than five months.

RETURN TO THE RAINFOREST

A man searches the world over for what he needs and returns home to find it.

— George Moore

Seated in an aisle seat, I settled in for the almost seven-hour flight from Toronto, Ontario, Canada, to Georgetown, Guyana. It was October 2016, and this would be my second visit to this destination for the year. There was an empty seat between myself and the relatively young East Indian woman seated at the window, Pauline Rodrigues. The flight would seem much shorter with this attractive Guyanese seat partner, and I was finding that we had much in common, and that we were both storytellers.

Although she lived with her family in Toronto, she was returning to Guyana to visit her elderly parents in West Bank Demerara. Other family siblings were returning for a short vacation also. We talked about many topics, but one was of particular interest to us: Venezuela and Guyana.

Venezuela is currently in dire straits with its socialist government. People are close to starving, and inflation is out of control. Crime and corruption are prevalent. Fishermen, normally satisfied with their industry, have suffered as much as other citizens, and some have resorted to piracy, attacking and robbing other fishermen. This is also happening off the coasts of

Guyana and Suriname, but to a much lesser extent. Also, Venezuela has been unsatisfied with the location of the border between itself and Guyana for more 175 years. This struggle has had its highs and lows, always simmering away, and has risen again. Venezuela has always claimed that their eastern border should be the Essequibo River, and therefore all land west of the river should be theirs. This represents about sixty percent of Guyana's territory, and the loss of it would probably wipe out any economic future for the country. (As well, it is certain that Venezuela is incapable of properly governing the land between its current borders, although that is a separate issue.) In May 2015, Exxon Mobil discovered substantial oil deposits in the ocean about 160 kilometres off of the contested territory. This has caused Venezuela to raise the issue again.

The ocean off of Venezuela, and anywhere along the north coast of South America, can get very rough, and over time there has been no end of ship and boat tragedies. Also, as I've mentioned earlier, few people know that during World War II German submarines sank more 400 ships, many of which were oil tankers and bauxite ore ships, in the Caribbean Sea, along the northwest South American coast. As a result, the bottom of the ocean there is littered with the hulks of sunken ships and boats. The distance between Trinidad and Georgetown, Guyana, is about 700 kilometres. Many ships have sunk in this area. Trinidad, at its closest, lies only eleven kilometres off the coast of Venezuela.

In the early 1980s, one of Pauline's sisters lived in Venezuela. Pauline has also lived there. Her sister, her brother, Joseph, and an uncle boarded a boat in Venezuela to visit their parents in West Bank Demerara. In the dark of night, a ship hit their boat, turning it over and leaving everyone in the water. Joseph had told her about the tragedy, saying that their uncle waved for him to swim to shore. He could hear people screaming all over the surface of the water, and he could not find his sister, so he began a long swim to shore, where he was found by members of Venezuela's army. Pauline and Joseph lost their twenty-six-year-old sister, and a few days later, the body of their uncle was recovered, missing one leg and covered with piranha bites. The sinking had occurred near the mouth of a river where there is always "sweet" fresh water, permitting piranha, caiman, and other freshwater life to exist.

The previous evening, I had dined at a high-end restaurant near the Toronto airport, as arranged by Ned Blair, to meet with him, Tony McWatt, and Ken Singh. Tony is a great fan of Guyana and is the editor of *Caribbean Graphic*, a newspaper published twice a month, full of interesting news and articles for Caribbean folks in Canada and in the Caribbean. Our purpose was to discuss the possibility of gathering successful Toronto Guyanese businessmen, of whom there are hundreds, into some form of Council, to find ways to fund and benefit Guyana.

Tony was leading this idea, although it was not foreign to our minds. Ken's Atlas International Freight Forwarding Inc. business could be of great help to ship goods cheaply/gratuitously to Guyana. He has done so many times. Tony was to fly on the same flight as myself to Guyana the following morning, as he had scheduled himself to visit a government minister to discuss ways expatriates can further help the country. It should be noted that for decades, great numbers of expatriate Guyanese, individually and within organisations, have found ways to help the country, through donations of technology, medical equipment and supplies, school equipment and books, consulting, finance, clothing, and much more.

While claiming our baggage, I bade Pauline farewell, and then joined Tony to share a taxi to Georgetown. This was a wild ride to remember. The brakes on the vehicle groaned often, and the car swung from side to side as it ducked in and out to pass. I asked the driver if the brakes needed repair and he replied that they were fine.

I unloaded my bags, mostly full of books, at the Rainforest, and was happy to find Syeada waiting for me...as were all four of her dogs. I learned from her that Jerry had been in Miami since June, being tested for a stomach ailment. I could see that she was worried about this, and that she might have been reluctant to give me all the details. She introduced me to Florence Sibler, a pretty and physically fit lady like Syeada. Florence is a Guyanese East Indian in her fifties, with a delightful voice, who loves to travel. Her husband is a scientist, and they live in Switzerland. She is a nurse, having worked in the world of psychiatry, and speaks five languages.

The following morning, I hosted Petamber Persaud for breakfast after he drove me to the Oasis Cafe on Carmichael Street. This simple restaurant provides a different house coffee every day and is a popular place for foreigners. He had asked Russell Lancaster, renowned for acting, singing, and love for the arts, to join us but Russell wasn't available. Petamber related the details of his family to me. He is is very grateful for his mixed-race marriage. With respect to the National Library, he told me that the need for air-conditioning was a priority, without a funding solution as yet. Petamber also gave me a long write-up that he had written about *Children of Watooka* in the *Sunday Guyana Times*. He stated that my book would do very well in Trinidad's 2016 Bocas Literary Festival, with results to be known in the spring of 2017. Given his renown in the Caribbean world of literature, he made me feel cautiously optimistic.

As we were enjoying our discussion, I heard two young ladies speaking French at a nearby table. and after paying for our breakfast, I went to their table and spoke French with them. Emilie Montpetit-Meilleure and Melodie Gendreau, are both from Quebec, Canada. Emilie lives very close to my home. She has just recently joined the staff of the Canadian High Commission. Melodie, a nurse, told me that fifteen American Peace Corps medical staff had just been summoned to Georgetown from Linden because of terrorist threats. I learned later that this turned out to be harmless threats by a mentally disturbed person well-known in Linden.

When the young ladies heard about my book, they expressed enthusiasm for buying it, and I told them they could do so at Austin's Book Store... where I was heading next, and where Petamber drove me before parting. The staff recognised me when I entered the store and called for Lloyd Austin to come down from his upstairs office. We then exchanged greetings and pleasantries. He still did not have copies of Godfrey Chin's *Nostalgius*, but he did purchase more books from me, since he had sold out and copies ordered from England had not yet arrived.

Soon, we had a group of people talking excitedly in a circle. Some were from Canada, organisers for the Canada-Guyana Outreach Mission, which provides medical services and supplies to Guyana. They are based in Strathroy, Ontario, as is one of the leaders, Yvonne Joseph Triesman, who has often been to nearby Watford, Ontario, where my parents are buried. And then in walked Emilie and Melodie, two pretty and smiling ladies. Lloyd was chuckling. A bunch of Canadians had found themselves in his store, and all were happy to be in Guyana!

A handsome man was also smiling nearby as he overheard us enthusiastically telling stories. He recognised me and introduced himself to all of us as Robeson Benn. We invited him into our circle for continuing lively discussion.

I had met Robeson Benn in Linden the previous May. Up until the May 2015 elections, he was the Minister of Public Works for the PPP government. He had had homes in both Linden and in Georgetown, but the one in Linden had burned down earlier that year. He is a certified geologist and does consulting work in that field. I am fortunate to know him. I had also known his father in Canada, Brindley Horatio Benn, who at the time (1993 to 1998) was Guyana's High Commissioner to Canada in Ottawa. In fact, it had been Brindley who had introduced me to Sam Hinds in 1997 upon Sam's visit to Canada at that time. Renowned in Guyana, Brindley Benn is known to have coined the country's motto, "One People, One Nation, One Destiny". He entered politics in the 1950s, and over time became a leader within the PPP and the WPA, always fighting hard against the PNC dictatorship. He died in 2012 at 86 years of age. I would meet up again with Robeson in Linden later in the week.

Later in the day, I visited King's Jewellers to purchase jewellery for my wife and friends back in Canada. A lot of the beautiful silver and gold necklaces, earrings, pendants, bracelets, lapel pins, broaches, etc., related to the Fiftieth Jubilee. I walked to St. George's Cathedral to have my new accessories blessed. I was fortunate to again meet Judith Cummings, two sons, and Gabriella there, who greeted me with smiles and introduced me to Deacon Andrew Hoyte. He has a degree in theology from McGill University in Montreal, Canada, and enthusiastically agreed to bless my jewellery at a side altar. Judith told me he was a powerful speaker and that I should attend one of his Masses to hear his sermon. During the blessing, we had one thing in common—perspiration.

That evening, Syeada chauffeured Florence and me to the city's first Coconut Festival, at the Arthur Chung Convention Centre at Liliendaal in Georgetown, not too far from the Rainforest. Arthur Chung was Guyana's first president, from 1966 until 1980. His function had largely been ceremonial. This situation changed in 1980 when Linden Forbes Burnham, the prime minister who had all the power, had the constitution changed to give full power to the president...and then caused himself to become the president. Chung was the first ethnic Chinese head of state in a non-Asian country. He lived to be ninety years of age, died in 2008, and was buried near the tomb of Sir David Rose at Seven Ponds in Georgetown's Botanical Gardens.

Within the building, we toured interesting craft booths and an area where the innumerable products and uses of coconut were being displayed. A coconut-husk shredding machine was chomping away on coconut shells, providing clean, light strings of material that would have many uses. Coconut material is used for making fibre board, coco peat, coco husk, coco crush, moss substitute, hydroponics, coir fibre, craftwork, potting medium, fertiliser, padding and much more, and is used for soil stabilisation, as well. Coconut oil has dozens of uses, from moisturising creams to cooking to shoe polish. I also met Donald Sinclair, who is the Ministry of Tourism's Director General, and his close friend from Bishop's College days, lawyer Mayo Robertson. Since then, I have always found Donald to be responsive to any request for information about Guyana.

Subsequently, we walked outside to watch the modelling show and to listen to music, but the sound was annoyingly loud, hurting our ears with its high-decibel drumming and shrieking, so much so that we soon departed for the Herdmanston Lodge for cool coconut-water drinks.

Early the following morning, I was again back at the Herdmanston Lodge, mostly talking to the staff. After a later breakfast at the Rainforest, I took a taxi to the Anglican Christ Church on Waterloo Street. This heritage 1830s building is said to have been erected on "cockpit" ground, where regular cockfighting and betting had occurred. I went there because I knew it was the church where Bishop Charles Davidson presided, and I wanted to hear his sermon.

It was bright and hot within the church. I noticed eleven idle tin-pan drums up in the balcony. The pews were not full. Those folks who were attending were very neatly dressed in colourful shirts and dresses—neater than I am used to in North America.

Bishop Charles is a large-chested man who does not need a microphone to speak. He spoke eloquently about the need for money to keep the church and its properties, including Austin House, properly maintained.

He mentioned as to how he and his wife, Maureen, who lived in the elegant and historical Austin House, had replaced the electric stove with a gas stove to save money. They had also traded in a big car for a small one.

As I listened to his passionate plea, I could not help but wonder how the parishioners would be able to afford what is required. Months later, via telephone, the bishop explained to me that most people have sufficient money to give to the church, but they need to review and change their spending priorities to do so. Everywhere one turns to in Guyana there is a legitimate need for money.

Near the end of the Mass, a deacon asked for the few visitors in the church to stand up and tell everyone who they were. Sitting in the middle pew about three quarters of the way back, I saw everyone turn to look my way...then I turned around and everyone there was looking forward at me. I was the only white person at Mass. So, I enthusiastically spoke briefly, even if somewhat surprised.

Bishop Davidson's oration had caused me to chuckle, because I had thought of a related story I had read in my friend Wendy Whalley Dathan's book, *Bauxite, Sugar and Mud*. Her family had recalled the very small ants that at times had invaded their Watooka home—they'd called them "fine ants". Then one time, a woman who had been to Georgetown complained about a church sermon, saying that all the priest had talked about was "fine ants!"

I left the church on foot, and just around the block on Middle Street, I saw an entrance into Promenade Gardens. It is still a beautiful place and does not look like it has deteriorated much.

The Promenade Gardens, which had their beginning in 1851, are on the site of the old militia Parade Ground, where many slaves who took part in the 1823 uprising were executed. At that time, more than 10,000 slaves rioted, primarily due to their masters having not permitted them to practice religion—because religion would teach them right from wrong, and thus educate the slaves about the wrongs their masters were exercising upon them, thereby amplifying unrest and creating more problems for their masters.

The leader of the uprising was a slave named Quamina Gladstone, who was executed and gibbeted during the insurgence. Hundreds of slaves died during the uprising, and many others were subsequently executed, their heads spiked on poles erected along colony roads and at the Parade Ground. Executions also occurred on many of the fifty-five plantations that sourced the rioting slaves along the East Coast. Quamina Street in Georgetown is named after the slave hero. A statue of Mohandas Gandhi, who advocated peaceful resistance, is in the park. The park bandstand was built in 1897 to commemorate Queen Victoria's Diamond Jubilee.

As I exited the gardens, I looked up and across Middle Street to see a young shirtless man shooting a basketball on an outside court. Even with an hour to go before noon, I was very warm, but I wandered over to challenge the young man to a basketball-shooting game of H-O-R-S-E. There are many things that I cannot do well, but even at my age I can still shoot a basketball well, even though I have rarely practiced in the past several years. I felt confident when he accepted my fun contest. He was not a good shooter, but I shot even worse…and lost. Oh, well. At one time, I was chasing a missed-shot rebound towards high grass near a ditch when my opponent shouted for me to watch out for a snake. I let him retrieve the ball.

That afternoon, Sharmini Poulin, her husband, John, Maureen Mondonza, Syeada, Florence, and I boarded two vehicles and headed for the twenty-acre plant-growing property of horticulturalist Hans Neher. The property is not far south of the beginning of the Soesdyke-Linden Highway, where a sandy dirt road proceeds bumpily for about one mile before reaching the tropical plant farm. Hans is a good friend of Jerry and Syeada, and often visits them when in Georgetown. I had met this interesting man on my previous visit, and he had been one of the first to purchase my book. He and his lady friend, Martina, were waiting to greet us outside of his old rustic bungalow amid what appeared to be lush, low jungle growth. We were soon all seated around a table on the back patio enjoying a picnic lunch, including beer and coconut water, while Hans told us about his amazing enterprise.

In his seventies, Hans is a self-taught expert in tropical horticulture, although he's a mechanical engineer by education and experience. Originally from Frankfurt, Germany, Hans worked in Africa, but has now been in Guyana for more than twenty-seven years. He sells his plant products everywhere, but particularly in Georgetown. The large Princess Hotel property there is furnished extensively with his plant products. His landscaping skill has also helped to enhance the Promenade Gardens, Buddy's International Hotel at Providence, the Brickdam Cathedral, and the Cheddi Jagan International Airport. Two of his daughters work in Georgetown marketing plants and trees. He has built up a large inventory "for the beautification of Georgetown", which he feels will take place as the country's economy improves. He has fifteen dogs, and one of our colleagues remarked that it must be a major task to clean up their droppings. Hans responded with a chuckle that he does not have to do anything. Scarab beetles tunnelling underground rise up to the poop and pull it down into the earth. So there. There were no dog droppings to be seen. He has one cat that gets rid of snakes. "Cats", he said, "are faster than snakes".

We were given a tour through the whole area. No greenhouses are required, just netting to shade certain plants. (Guyana *is* a greenhouse.) A huge wallaba tree grew near the house patio. Hans said that its branches moved at night because colonies of bats land on it to eat its flowers. Wallaba trees are a prevalent hardwood in Guyana, used for many purposes, including power poles.

Hans grows more than 280 different types of plants and bushes, and about thirty types of palm trees. His knowledge and skill allow him to overcome many challenges. Large rhinoceros beetles, for example, dig into the ground to devour the roots of small palm trees. He showed us one-inch diameter holes: by inserting his finger next to them he could force out beetles. He pours diesel oil into the holes to deal with these pests.

The variety and colours of all the tropical growth was raw, and beautiful to take in. The water table is not far below ground level, and Hans showed us his homemade swimming pool, surrounded by tall shade trees and an open-sided shed for respite from the sun. Wondering what might be lurking in the black water, I did not find it inviting, even though it had a certain beauty. Hans bathes in it frequently.

Guyana has many interesting tropical plants. Hans has grown *syngonium podophyllum*, also known as the "arrowhead plant", listed among the top ten of the United States National Aeronautics and Space Administration (NASA)'s list of plants which reduce airborne microbes, increase humidity, and induce positive psychological effects on the planter. The leaves begin with an arrowhead shape, and then change into three to five finger-like sections as the plant matures. The plant is useful for purifying the air in the home and in the office.

Our host has eight employees, who in terms of productivity, he says, could be replaced with only two or three hard-working ones. Only two of them can read and write. Recently he had been away to one of the Caribbean islands for a week, and when he had returned, no work had been done. He had no electricity, and he and Martina were using lanterns at night, because some neighbours had stolen his recently installed wiring off his poles. I will return to this beautiful raw jungle garden.

The following afternoon, I found myself back at the Duke Lodge bar for a drink. I got to know the young neatly dressed bartenders, Shawn and Shawnie, and they verified to me that the same type of daily liquor-usage audit is performed at their bar as I had seen performed at the Tower Suites Hotel. Incredibly, each morning, each liquor bottle on the shelf is carefully weighed, and compared to a computer-managed system that compares what quantity is left in each bottle to what should be left according to sales over the past twenty-four hours.

For a while I was the only one at the bar, and being a storyteller, I told them one. The huge three-story American embassy building across the street had been renovated in 2014. It is made of Virginia pine, which does not stand up well in Guyana, where most wooden structures are made of the long-lasting greenheart wood. One morning, after enjoying coffee at Duke Lodge, I had ventured across the street to ask one of the many soldiers guarding the Embassy if I could go into the building to use the washroom. This was not to be, but it did cause several bored soldier colleagues to saunter over to hear me tell some of my US Marine stories. What fun. (Usually, US embassies are guarded by US Marines, but they would not be present at this location until later in the year.)

I was joined briefly at the bar by Debbie Gouveia, who owns the Lodge along with her husband, Gerry. We talked mostly about their well-known support for the Santa Mission on the west side of the Demerara River, and their associated Arrowpoint Tour business. She is rightly very proud of the help they have given to this Amerindian village, including the creation and support of a library.

That evening, Syeada, Florence, and I walked down the street to Maureen Mondonza's home, where she looks after her elderly mother, who has lived there for more than fifty years. Their house is directly across the street from the RUSAL office. We entered the backyard, which looked like a jungle environment. A high concrete wall surrounded the large area, which had sandy ground everywhere, amongst several large tropical trees growing buck mangoes, Buxton spicy mangoes, golden apples, malacca apples, breadfruit, and other fruit. Bats were flying around and feeding on the fruit. In the centre of the yard, under the trees, was a huge teepee gazebo, with bamboo poles holding up black netting. Lanterns hanging in the trees gave a mysterious but comfortable soft light to the dark environment. Of course, the frogs, crickets, and lizards were in wondrous chorus.

Maureen told me that her father had been an accountant working in Mackenzie/Linden at one time and had been one of the first to drive a vehicle on the initial rough road built from Wismar to Lethem. She had lost her husband when he was in an accident in Georgetown while riding his bicycle. She has a master's degree in economics and has studied at McMaster University in Canada and at Stanford University in the United States. Her sister, Fay, also graduated from prestigious Stanford University, with a Ph.D. in physics.

Maureen worked in the Diplomatic Corps most of her career and is now a relatively young retiree. She produced a bottle of "Pulse" wine, which is supposed to be an aphrodisiac. After a few sips, chuckling, they asked me if I was feeling its effects. It is made from bark indigenous to Guyana and to the Amazon basin. After some great discussion, we walked the short distance back to the Rainforest. We passed one large, beautiful, walled home, reputed to be owned by a drug dealer. Syeada knew the name of every dog that barked at us along the way.

Very early the next morning, I commenced my walk to the Herdmanston Lodge, hoping to meet up with some interesting people or event. I walked by three garbage trucks parked on a small vacant sandy property—they looked dirtier than the garbage that they hauled. There was always plastic garbage in this area on my walks. Less than a corner from my destination, on the opposite side of Peter Rose Street, I passed a large and impressive well-maintained wooden colonial building, the Brazilian ambassador's residence.

Malcolm, the head of security for the Lodge, was just opening the front gates, right on time at 6 a.m. Across the street, security guard employees were arriving at the headquarters of the Integrated Security and Federal Management System company. This company provides security guards for houses and businesses in Georgetown. While the guards, mostly women, were rather elderly, and did not appear to be in good physical shape, they did seem to be enthusiastic to commence their day of work, and greeted arriving colleagues cheerfully. Uniformed, neat, tidy, and disciplined, they lined up on an outdoor patio in rows while their leader, Bharrat, addressed them with the morning's instructions. He had informed me that the average salary is about G$2,500 (US$12.50) per day. They do not carry arms; they have telephones in their guardhouses to call for help. The guards all climbed into old minibuses to be delivered to their posts.

Arriving early as usual at the Herdmanston Lodge, I enjoyed greeting the staff (Malcolm, Susanna, Keon, and others), and read the latest news in the colourful newspapers. I enjoyed meeting a distinguished-looking elderly couple who were departing for their home in Grenada. I determined that they are mutual friends of Jennifer Hosten, who was Miss Grenada/Miss World in 1970, and who is an endorser of my book. I regret not having had the opportunity to better know them. On my return walk to the Rainforest, I passed a small parked minibus for the "Keep Smiling" Bus Service. A young boy, red t-shirted on his bicycle, stopped beside me to ask for some money for food. He was on his way to school, and I was pleased to meet his request.

I got back to the Rainforest in time for a shower and for breakfast with Syeada and Florence. It was going to be a busy day for all of us, and it would also be Florence's last day as a guest. When I told them that I was scheduled to meet acting Police Commissioner David Ramnarine that morning, Syeada told me to tell him that she, the "dog lady", has great respect for him. "He is a hard-working, honest man who takes action and who is trying to make a positive difference with little resources to do so". She knows, or knows about, most of the politicians and government leaders, and many times I would enjoy giving her a name to get her quick, short judgement.

My taxi pulled up by the Police Headquarters gates and large guardhouse on Young Street at Eve Leary, where I was met and greeted by a smiling young officer, Tony Passad. We knew of each other because his mother does housework for the Rainforest. It was going to pour rain, and I entered the Commissioner's building just in time.

I was ushered up to the top floor, to a small hot waiting room. I knew that the Commissioner was an extremely busy person, and I was very grateful for the ten minutes or so that I would have with him. I had given him only short notice of my wish to meet with him. I had been fortunate to have been an Assistant Commissioner for the RCMP in charge of informatics, and I had known Laurie Lewis, a previous Police Commissioner of Guyana, so I would have something in common with David Ramnarine.

After half an hour of watching the downpour outside the window, I was accompanied down the hall to meet the moustached Commissioner, who warmly reciprocated my greeting. Thankfully, his small office was air-conditioned. Framed photos of the country's president and prime minister were mounted on the wall. A mountain of paperwork covered his desk. Given the daily newspaper crime reports, I do not envy his work. Some police corruption also exists, and he is known for dealing with it summarily.

We spoke of our pasts briefly, and he asked where he could get a copy of my book. Graciously, he closed a side door to change into his tanned shirt jac uniform for a photo shoot with me. He called upon Superintendent Thomas, who is in charge of informatics, to join us, and asked him to give me a tour of his facilities downstairs. The Commissioner apologised for his workload and gave me his home telephone for me to call him on the following Sunday.

Superintendent Thomas then introduced me to his full staff of eleven dedicated workers, who showed me some of their equipment. For the whole country, they have only forty-seven computers, hooked up to a central database, although they hope to double that in the near term. I purposely did not do any comparisons with the RCMP's extensive modern facilities. There is no comparison possible. Greatly saddened, I had to remind myself that Guyana is a third-world country, decades behind our first world in technology and funding. Nevertheless, I greatly admired their enthusiasm and hope for the future. I wished that I was younger and could help them.

Upon leaving at the gates, I surveyed the dull yellow buildings making up the compound, noticing the many dated vehicles, some of them discarded. I chatted briefly with Tony and congratulated him for being a policeman.

Not far up the street, I encountered the large guardhouse of the high-walled Canadian High Commission. Perhaps the High Commissioner would be free for a chat?

It wasn't long before his office called back to the guardhouse to have me cleared to enter. There are four to five people working at the guardhouse, and once cleared, I was met by Sharmini Poulin, who welcomed me and escorted me upstairs to see a smiling Pierre Giroux. He only had ten minutes, as visitors were expected, but he graciously welcomed me to sit on a comfortable sofa. We talked of several things, and I told him about my project to have a used Canadian fire truck donated to Linden. I had been working with Fire Fighters Without Borders Canada in Vancouver, British Columbia, to commence this initiative. This unique and caring organisation had already arranged for more than sixty used fire trucks to be donated to third-world countries, including Peru, Chile, and Mexico. They were anxious to do so with me for Guyana, and the process would be easier, since Guyana is an English-speaking country. The High Commissioner offered to help with this endeavour whenever required. Guyana forgives customs duties for charitable goods. I knew that my short visit was finished when four well-dressed people from Grenada were announced at the door, and I soon found myself on the ground outside the guardhouse waiting for a taxi.

A slim and not unattractive young woman came walking along on the road, seemingly talking to herself. She came over to me, shook my hand, and knelt to say a few Muslim prayers…or so I thought. I enjoy talking to people of all kinds, including street people, and this one turned out to be interesting. I wish that I could have recorded the mostly one-way conversation. For the most part, she spoke gibberish. Then she reached a point where she wanted me to come with her. Rubbing her tummy, she said, "I'm in plume…and ready to bloom. You can put your seed in my tummy and we can make a baby. I won't give you any problems…you can come back every now and then to see me and the baby".

The lady security guard standing nearby, outside of the guardhouse, was a serious listener. My new friend started to become aggressive when I kept resisting her repeated offer. The lady guard called for a big male guard to come out, and he commenced to earn his pay. She "cut her eyes" at him and gave him a mouthful. Finally, she started to walk away, muttering loudly.

And then my taxi arrived. Pierre's guests may have been wondering why he was smiling as he looked out of his window.

At 5 p.m., Syeada drove Florence and me to the seawall, close to the Pegasus Hotel in Kingston, to an area where there is a bandstand and where the public likes to use the steps up to the seawall to sit on benches and to walk along its seemingly endless length. It is a great place to get somewhat cooler from the ocean breeze, and it is renowned as a place where Guyanese folks like to fly kites, particularly at Easter.

At high tide the Guyana coastland is mostly below sea level. In 1855, a significant flood did much damage, and destroyed Camp House, the manor where governors resided. Construction began that year on a seawall that by 1882 had reached its present length of over 400 kilometres. Much of it was built by prisoners, and granite was used from a quarry near the Mazaruni Prison on the Mazaruni River. The seawall has served a great purpose, protecting towns and villages all along much of the country's coast and preventing erosion. (In the late 1700s, the estates of Kierfield and Sandy Point existed north of Georgetown, but they had disappeared into the sea by 1804.)

Always community-minded and environmentally concerned, Syeada had brought us here to join a dozen other folks to clean up a small portion of the beach before darkness arrived. It was low tide and we could see garbage everywhere. This was a regular Tuesday late-afternoon event. Syeada has at times also worked with schoolchildren to help clean the beaches. We were assigned gloves and bags, and within an hour and a half, the group had collected forty-five bags of "stuff" within about a single acre of beach sand.

Plastic was prevalent everywhere. People in Guyana are encouraged not to drink tap water, and it is a hot and humid country. Therefore, plastic bottles are used on a much higher per capita basis than in first-world countries. Recycling has not been implemented in Guyana and waste-management systems and procedures are primitive. The current government and the City of Georgetown are concerned about this, but must yet demonstrate action to deal with the mess. Again, funds to do so are scarce. A recycling capability would create jobs and could be mostly paid for by charging extra for bottled drinks, etc.

Caribbean countries are amongst the worst for creating solid waste. The country of Trinidad and Tobago is the worst of them, creating 14.4 kg of solid waste per capita per day, while Guyana is not far behind at 5.33 kg per capita per day, according to World Bank data. The world average is 1.2 kg per capita per day.

We found many small red-clay diyas, used by the Hindu people for special events and for praying. These miniature flat bowl-shaped containers can have a cotton wick in them, floating in ghee or vegetable oil, which can be lit to hold a flame.

Upon darkness, we handed in our gloves and were treated to some cold drinks and goodies. It was a good thing that it was dark, because we could not see the garbage that remained, stretching kilometres to the east. Nevertheless, we felt good to have helped out. We then headed to nearby Duke Lodge for some more cold drinks and fun discussion on the patio near the pool. *How fortunate I am to be with these two active, vibrant, pretty, and caring ladies,* I thought to myself.

That evening, at 10 p.m., we were going to say goodbye to one of them—Florence. This brave little lady was going to leave at this unruly hour to commence a drive through the Guyana jungle south to Brazil, and then on to Manaus, where she would head for northeast Brazil. She would be making stops along the way and planned to be home in Switzerland for Christmas. Wow. Promptly at the appointed hour, Frank Singh from Rainforest Tours appeared in his solid SUV, to greet us and to put Florence's belongings into the back of the vehicle. She was to be the only passenger. I was pleased that Frank seemed to be a very confident and personable man. We gave Florence a big hug, and watched the vehicle disappear into the dark. They had to leave at that hour to catch a ferry in the morning, deep in the heart of the jungle. Amazed at this wonderful and capable woman, I told myself that I would not be able to emulate her.

In the future, I was to learn that she had been in very capable hands. Frank and Sabita Singh started their successful Rainforest Tours business out of their home in Georgetown in 1995. From his previous business work, Frank had come to know the interior of the country intimately. His father had been a farmer in Golden Grove, until he put wood around the frame of an old truck to make a bus and commenced the Buxton Pride bus service. Frank has developed a working relationship with natives in many Amerindian villages and is a strong advocate for preserving the rainforest environment.

The first part of Florence's drive would be easy, all the way south to Linden, because the road is paved. There they would cross the Demerara River and continue south, but now on mostly sandy road, for 124 kilometres, to the poor village of Mabura Hill, where facilities of any kind are scarce. Heavy logs are extracted from this area, and the trucks can make the primitive roads even more difficult for driving. Frank would be carrying a chain saw to clear any possible fallen trees. Most likely he was also carrying a gun.

For the next eighty-four kilometres, the road narrows, with close green jungle on both sides. The road is mostly dirt, with some sand, and can be very difficult to drive along, with deep mud and water-filled depressions during and after heavy tropical rainfall. The village of Kurupukari is then reached on the east bank of the Essequibo River, and a ferry must be taken to Iwokrama on the far side. Florence and her host would reach this point the following morning. The Iwokrama area, representing two percent of Guyana's rainforest, 371,000 hectares, has a name that in the native tongue means "place of refuge".

They would spend one or two days here while Florence enjoyed some spectacular time on the renowned Iwokrama Canopy Walkway. This is found at Corkwood, about seventy-two kilometres further south from Iwokrama. With aluminium platforms and steel cabling on four levels up to thirty-three metres high, one can experience a myriad of flora and fauna. Birdwatching is spectacular. In the very early mornings, one can hear and see the birds begin their cheerful day, all sorts of varieties: pompadour cotingas, green aracari, macaws, parrots, orange-breasted falcons, red-billed toucans, oropendolas, and many more. Canopies in Guyana's jungle can exist at three levels, with different flora and fauna at each level. The very large blue morpho butterflies, for example, prefer to settle and feed on the top canopies. The walkway is also used for research purposes. Down on the ground, jaguar sightings are prevalent in this area.

The canopy walkway was funded by the Canadian International Development Agency and built by the Canadian Greenheart Construction

Company (GCC). It is the only canopy walkway in the Guiana Shield. GCC built a similar canopy walkway at the Botanical Gardens at the University of British Columbia in Vancouver, Canada.

During the next stretch of the route south, Florence and Frank would reach the Amerindian village of Annai, at the northern part of the Rupununi savannah. It is a well-established village of mud-brick huts with palm thatch roofs, which are scattered over a wide area and shaded with coconut palms and mango trees. The next leg of the journey would be a final run to Lethem on the Brazilian border, where they would have a layover of another night or two. The heavy driving would be over at this point. In 2009, Brazil built a bridge here over the Takutu River to Bon Fin on the Brazilian side, with paved driving thereafter all the way to Manaus.

In the late 1920s, when Henry Ford undertook the building of Fordlandia on the Tapajos River near Santarem on the Amazon River, he dreamed of a modern road straight north of Manaus, reaching the ocean at Georgetown, British Guiana. This would have greatly reduced the distance to Fordlandia's rubber had to travel to the United States from the existing method, which required transporting it east down the Amazon River and north all around the top of South America. Slowly but surely, his dream, which may have been shared much earlier with his close friend Theodore Roosevelt, is taking place. Manaus is six degrees latitude below the equator, while Georgetown is six degrees above the equator.

Florence, courageous and adventurous, reminded me of the final stanza of Robert Frost's renowned poem "The Road Not Taken":

> *I shall be telling this with a sigh*
> *Somewhere ages and ages hence:*
> *Two roads diverged in a wood and —*
> *I took the road less travelled by,*
> *And that has made all the difference.*

In 1972, Mathew French Young, born in 1905 in British Guiana, led the building of the jungle road from Wismar to Mabura Hill for the government, so the Forestry Department could penetrate this greenheart-forest area. By 1974, he and his men had completed the road even further south, to Kurupukari on the east side of the Essequibo River.

While building the Wismar-Mabura Hill-Kurupukari dirt road, Young had to overcome many physical obstacles, as well as encounters with snakes and jaguars. It was not unusual for him and his men to encounter anaconda snakes with a length of more than ten metres. "These snakes are harmless as long as they do not have an anchor for the tail", he wrote. "They cannot wrap around anything and constrict it". They also encountered a variety of poisonous snakes, including small white-tailed labarias, carpet labarias, and haimaralli water snakes. The larger of these snakes can bite through a rubber boot, delivering a bite that, if not immediately treated, can lead to a painful death within forty-eight hours.

As a surveyor and road builder, the adventurous and capable Young had come to know the country thoroughly as a diamond and gold prospector, plantation manager, explorer, and hunter. His work in the jungles and savannahs of his native country for more than fifty years are wonderfully revealed in his in his book *Guyana: The Lost El Dorado*, with a foreword written by his friend Brigadier Joseph Singh. Both of these men were involved with helping the Americans clean up the aftermath of the Jonestown Massacre in 1978. More than 900 people had died, with their bodies rapidly decomposing in the hot tropical environment. Even respirators could not prevent the terrible body stench from nauseating the recovery operation soldiers, who had to use helicopters to carry the body-bagged corpses to the Timerhi Airport for large airplane transport to the United States.

On two different occasions, I would meet with two other adventurous and very bright, young attractive ladies, Rainforest B. & B. house guests, each a marine biologist and explorer, each focused on the conservation of the *arapaima* fish via separate projects. Dr. Cynthia Watson, born and raised in Mahaicony, East Coast Demerara, Guyana, obtained her doctorate at the State University of New York, while Brazilian-born Dr. Lesley de Souza did so at Auburn University in Alabama. *Arapaima* are amongst the world's largest freshwater fish and are the largest in South America. They can exceed 300 kilograms, with a length of up to three metres. In Guyana they occur primarily in the Branco and Essequibo River basins, being found in about 200 lakes and ponds. They are obligate air breathers and surface every five to fifteen minutes to do so.

The requirement for the *arapaima* fish to breathe air has made them vulnerable to intensive harvesting. Prior to the 1960s, the Amerindian population treated these fish with great respect, catching them for food infrequently. Since then, harvesting these fish for revenue has greatly depleted their populations, hence driving the important need for conservation, which commenced with studies and action around the year 2000. At that time, Guyana's *arapaima* fish population had been estimated to have diminished to about 800 fish with a length of one metre or more. Since then, conservation efforts have increased the population more than seven-fold, determined by tagging and monitoring these fish.

As a child in British Guiana during the early 1950s, I admired a huge stuffed *arapaima* in the Georgetown Museum. Recently, I have seen separate photos of Cynthia and Lesley frolicking and holding these large, seemingly tame, fish in various waters of the Rupununi. Lesley has tagged many of these for her tracking study, and has been the first person to track them from a small bush airplane. On my last encounter with her at the Rainforest B&B, she was heading off with a party of ten explorers for a hike into the Guyana interior, led by Pete Oxford. Our discussions had been most interesting. Otherwise, for example, I would not have learned about the chemistry of firefly bioluminescence. I could not help but admire the thrill that these biology and conservationist experts get from their interesting, exciting, and contributing lives.

> *Our connectedness to each other and all that surrounds us cannot be overlooked and should be relentlessly explored.*
>
> — Dr. Lesley de Souza

PHOTOS

Rainforest B&B (Florence)

Syeada and Jerry with special guest Hon. Sam Hinds

PHOTOS

Pretty lady friends

Hans Neher, Horticulturalist

RUSAL HQ (former Demba HQ)

Steve, Selwyn, and Bishop Charles

PHOTOS

Two renowned achievers, Rupert and Ian

Melodie and Emilie

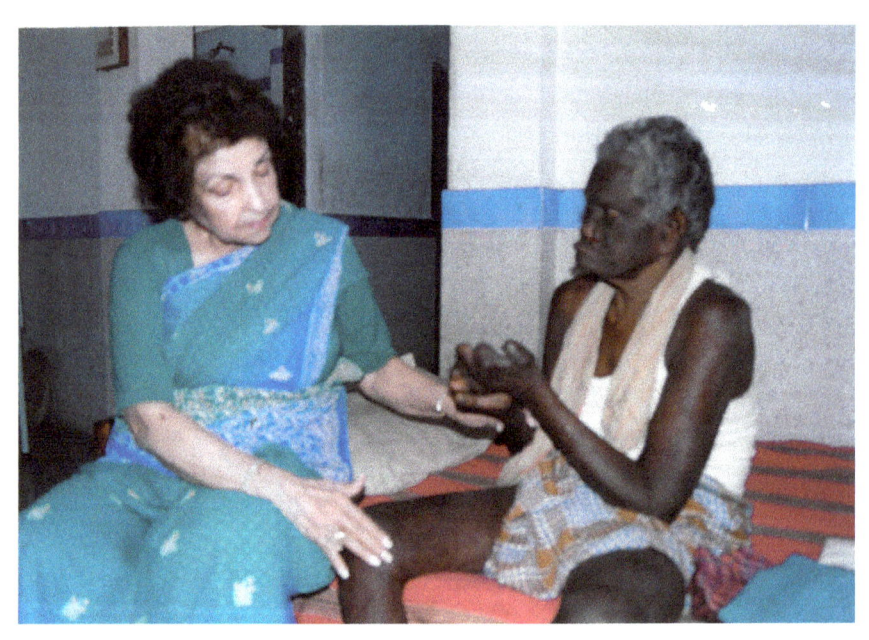

Mother Indrani and Leper

With Freundel Stuart, Prime Minister of Barbados, and Ned Blair

Mother Olive and her Blair family

Bauxite Century and book-launch event at Linden

Steve and Hon. Sam Hinds at Watooka

PHOTOS

Old bauxite mine

Paula and the engineers

Bauxite friendship at Watooka Clubhouse

Three beautiful friends at Old Three Friends Mine

PHOTOS

Watooka Clubhouse

Watooka swimming pool

Nancy, Paula, Steve, Carmen, and Maureen

Horace and Carmen, two achievers

PHOTOS

Steve and Hon. Sam Hinds, friends by bauxite

Kunj and Eileen Beharrysingh with family

With former First Lady Yvonne Hinds

Kunj's Tomb

PHOTOS

We found it!

MY SEARCH FOR KUNJ

EVEN such is Time, that takes in trust
Our youth, our joys, our all we have,
And pays us but with earth and dust;
Who in the dark and silent grave,
When we have wander'd all our ways,
Shuts up the story of our days;
But from this earth, this grave, this dust,
My God shall rise me up I trust.

— Sir Walter Raleigh, *The Conclusion*

Scary. Exciting. I was standing on the cement corner of a broken tomb base, for safety, at the head of a wiggly trail deep in Le Repentir Cemetery. Two also-excited black men stood on the crushed green-growth ground at the other end of the raised tomb, carrying the machetes they had used to hack our way through seven-foot-high tropical Guyana growth to reach our goal. Hundreds of other raised tombs lay around us, but we could not see them because of the dense, overgrown tropical foliage. Confined to this small hacked-out enclosure, we were entombed ourselves in the huge, dangerous, and renowned Le Repentir. We did not want to stay long…just long enough for me to pray. We had found Kunj at last…or, at least, his remains.

Kunj Beharrysingh.

* * *

Le Repentir Cemetery, found in the heart of Georgetown, Guyana, is amongst the largest in the Caribbean—and probably the most dangerous. It has a storied past that deserves attention, as does its future.

European settlements began in British Guiana during the middle of the eighteenth century. The Dutch came first, then the French and the British. These settlements were primarily founded in the Essequibo and Berbice regions, at the mouths of their major rivers. At the turn of the eighteenth century, settlements were also being established at the mouth of the Demerara River, and along the west and east coasts of the country. At that time the population of the Essequibo and Demerara areas was about 80,000 people, including some 75,000 slaves, mostly of African origin. There were only 2,500 whites in the whole colony. Plantation crop production was primarily cotton, sugarcane, coffee, indigo, and rubber. As slavery and cotton were established in southern North America in the early nineteenth century, cotton prices were driven downwards, causing British Guiana plantations to exchange cotton for rice production.

Hundreds and hundreds of plantations were established, bearing names relating to the language of their past occupying countries. Dutch: Groenveldt, Vryheid's Lust, and Vreed-en-Hoop. British: Perseverance, Hope, and Providence. French: Mon Repos, Non Pareil, La Bonne Intention… and La Penitence and Le Repentir.

The plantations La Penitence and Le Repentir had an interesting beginning. Frenchman Pierre Louis De Saffon, born in 1724, had killed his brother in a duel over a woman. As dueling in France at the time was illegal, he had fled, exiling himself to the colony of Demerara, in what is now Guyana. His diligent work ultimately allowed him to acquire two sugar estates, which he called La Penitence (the penitent; remorse) and Le Repentir (the repentant; regret), testaments to his lifelong mental pain for having committed fratricide.

De Saffon died in 1784 at sixty years of age, after a successful career as an owner of plantations. His will requested a trust fund be established, after all debts had been paid, to pay for the maintenance of orphans until they reached the age of sixteen. Decades later, this requirement was met. Pierre Louis De Saffon was buried at what is now the corner of Saffon and Broad streets, in the churchyard of St. Saviour's Church in Charlestown. The granite Saffon Monument stands over his grave and is often discerned by those who pass by on their way to the La Penitence Market.

Up to 1781, the Dutch had a capital for the Essequibo-Demerara region on the island of Borsselen, up from the mouth of the Demerara River. When the British took over that year, a town was established on the east side of the Demerara River. The following year, the French took over and named this town as their capital city, La Nouvelle Ville. The same year that De Saffon died, 1784, the Dutch again took over the colony, and named the town Stabroek after Nicolaas Geelvinck, Lord of Stabroek. In 1803, during the Napoleonic wars, the British captured the colony again, and in 1812 named the capital city Georgetown after King George III. In 1831, the regions of Essequibo, Demerara, and Berbice were combined to form British Guiana.

In 1823, as described earlier, the Demerara colony experienced a major slave uprising, led by cooper Jack Gladstone, son of carpenter Quamina, both slaves on the plantation Success. Hundreds of slaves were executed, including Quamina, and Gladstone was deported to St. Lucia. As was common in those days, Gladstone had obtained his surname from Sir John Gladstone, who had owned but never visited plantation Success. Sir John's son William later became the prime minister of Britain, in 1868. It is not clear to what extent the slaves of La Penitence and Le Repentir participated in the uprising. This event helped greatly to lead to the abolishment of slavery in the country in 1834.

In 1829, the Protector of Slaves was assigned to rule on a case of cruelty to women slaves who belonged to plantation Le Repentir, but who at the time were working on plantation La Penitence. Both plantations were still producing sugar. The women had been required to remove megass, the fibrous product left after sugar has been removed from sugarcane, from the sugar factory. The plantation owner was fined for having forced the women slaves to perform their work under conditions that were unacceptable. This was one of the hardest sugar-work tasks, and required leniency, yet in this case, the megass production rate exceeded the ability of the women to remove the megass, slowing down overall production. This maltreatment by the owner, although serious, was rather minor compared to the atrocities often experienced by slaves in those decades.

A large part of Le Repentir first became a cemetery in 1861. The first person entombed there was Antonio Gonzales, originally from Madeira, on March 15, 1861. One month later, American Confederate forces attacked Fort Sumter in Charleston, starting the Civil War, which led to the end of slavery in America.

As Georgetown expanded over the years, it grew south to swallow the plantations of La Penitence and Le Repentir. The west end of Le Repentir developed into the area of Georgetown known as Charlestown. The huge twenty-two-acre east-end cemetery is bordered on the south by Albouystown and West/East La Penitence, on the north by Wortmanville and Lodge, on the west by Charleston, and on the east by Plum Park.

It is not clear how the first cemetery tenant, Antonio Gonzales, was buried. Georgetown is from one to two metres, below sea level and must be protected from the ocean and from the Demerara River by dykes and a seawall. Most of the tombs are above ground, with a flat rectangular cement slab, about one and one half metres by three metres, upon which sits a wooden coffin, enclosed by walls and a roof of cement (when new). Often, they are painted blue, pink, white, and other colours. Some are surrounded by a flat-topped railing, supported by posts, all made of cement. Some tombs have open-paged porcelain Bibles attached to the head.

Areas of the cemetery were set aside for the deceased from the various religions of the country: Hindu, Muslim, Anglican, Presbyterian, Roman Catholic, Chinese, and Baha'i. Up until the country obtained its independence in 1966, the British maintained the cemetery as well as one would expect today in North America and in Europe.

> *On the same side of the town as the Botanical Gardens lies a large area of palm-covered land which forms one of the largest cemeteries in the world, a place of considerable beauty where the ornate tombstones of planters who died in their prime—the death rate among the English in the old days was high—stand*

beside those of humble soldiers, but always some distance from the simple crosses or the unmarked graves of the Negroes.

— Michael Swan, *British Guiana, The Land of Six Peoples*

My friend Ron Medas was raised on Broad Street, to the west of the cemetery, and recalls it well. His father was a policeman (and a drum major). At the time, during the 1940s and part of the 1950s, the cemetery was maintained very well, with palm trees soaring tall in places, with bridges over small waterways, and with grass cut for easy passage amongst the tombs. Unlike other children, he preferred to fly his kite up at the sea wall rather than in the cemetery. In the mid-1950s, he was taken to see the burial site of his four-year-old brother in Le Repentir. A cement slab had been laid over the site where the coffin had been buried in the ground. This slab would later be removed, and a raised tomb built in which his mother was interred. And, years later, his father's cement tomb was placed upon that of his mother.

Medas recalls, "The cemetery contained the tombs or graves of people from all levels of society. One of the most touching burial sites was the large tomb containing the remains of Catholic Arthur Abraham and seven of his nine children, who had tragically died when their house was fire-bombed during a period of unrest in 1964. Mr. Abraham, Portuguese, had been a highly respected senior civil servant in Cheddi Jagan's government. The hugely attended funeral service, with the eight coffins, had been held at the Brickdam Cathedral.

"As children, we stayed well clear of the cemetery, out of fear of possibly encountering ghosts ('jumbies' in the local terminology). One thing that comes to mind was the grand funeral processions, complete with marching and music, which took place when a member of a Lodge (like Masonic) was to be interred."

My friend Paula Walcott Wharton Litt's family lived on QQ Bent Street in Wortmanville, only three corners from the cemetery. When her mother had died in 1947, Paula was less than two years old, and part of the farewell ceremony was to pass Paula's little self back and forth over her mother's coffin. Folks then held the belief that this ritual would prevent the mother from taking Paula with her.

On one occasion, during an afternoon, I was driven past the cemetery, and noticed a long line of vehicles parked along the road at its unkempt edge. Apparently, this is the case when burials are performed, and often loud music and partying takes place late into the night, causing friction with nearby residents. Paul Gonzales, who I was to later meet and who was an admirer of the Beharrysingh girls in his youth, and a good friend of their youngest brother, Derek, recalled when a flurry of grave robbing occurred over a period of time, and the stench of fresh bodies greatly annoyed residents on Princess Street. Some thieves didn't even wait until the bodies had been entombed. They extracted the gold from teeth while the bodies lay in the coffins, stuffing the mouths to make the faces appear normal. Paul noted, "Body mining for gold in Le Repentir sure beat searching for it in the far reaches of the Cuyuni!" In early 2005, severe flooding along Guyana's coast caused bodies to surface and float in the cemetery.

Note that none of the more than 900 persons who died in the renowned Jonestown mass suicide were buried in Le Repentir, or in Guyana. All the bodies were flown by the US Army to Dover Air Base in Delaware, US, for identification and distribution for burial. Almost half of them were buried at Evergreen Cemetery in Oakland, California, near San Francisco, where the cult had functioned prior to Guyana. Jim Jones was cremated in Dover, and his ashes distributed over the Atlantic Ocean.

* * *

It was a humid warm Monday morning in October 2016 when my taxi pulled up to a small yellow building raised on enclosed stilts. Several men were quietly resting outside on the ground, some beside their horizontal bicycles. Except for a large modern one-story crematorium building within sight some distance away, the area was rather isolated. I paid my taxi driver, somewhat reluctant to be left alone in this area of ill repute.

I climbed up the stairs to find a man and two women seated at desks. This was the Office of the Sexton, responsible for keeping the records of all those interred in the Le Repentir Cemetery, records that are available all the way back to 1861 in spite of the heat and humidity. The small interior is not air-conditioned, nor were there any circulating fans.

I told one of the women that I wanted to find the tomb of Kunj Beharrysingh, who I thought had died in 1967. She brought out two very large light-brown record books, and commenced looking through the records for 1967. No luck. She then reviewed the records for 1968 with no results. Some of the pages had been torn, but mostly they were in good shape, given that almost fifty years had passed.

> *The Supervisor's office is a simple place:*
> *A chair, a desk, a concrete vault*
> *Where archives of all burials are kept;*
> *The leather covered volumes stretch centuries back.*
> *It sets things in perspective right away:*
> *The record is equal in these careful books,*
> *Inscribed for all an austere common fate.*
> *No space for high or space for low:*
> *The line of written detail does not change,*
> *All are put down here the same,*
> *Bare, unblemished soul-mates, row on row.*
> *In the field you do not get to see*
> *The part of burial that does not show*
> *Obscurity or utmost fame:*
> *The scene below is much the same.*
>
> — Ian McDonald, *The Place We Go, Mercy Ward*

I was then permitted to sit down, and I reviewed all the records from 1967 until March 1970. The handwriting was beautiful and was the same for all these years. I did not find any record for Kunj Beharrysingh, and began to wonder if he had been recorded in some special register, given that he had been renowned at the time of his death. I then decided that I would have to obtain the exact date of his death via communication back to Canada with his family, and return to the records in a week or more later.

However, I had been very excited when reading the records to encounter the details and site locations of a few men I had known of as a child in

Watooka. The first was Major James W. Hiscocks, who had died in a fall in September 1967. He and his family had lived across Riverside Road from our family back in the early 1950s. He had been a well-known manager in the Demerara Bauxite Company (Demba)'s personnel department, and had also been responsible for managing the popular Watooka Clubhouse. His wife, Sheila, was the daughter of A. George King, who had been a lawyer associated with Demba for more than fifty years. His father, Joseph A. King, had done the legal work to create Demba's land holdings and to incorporate the company in 1928, and was the first chairman of its Board of Directors. Sheila's great-grandfather had been an adjutant in the Georgetown Militia in the 1870s. All three of Major Hiscocks's children, David, Gillian, and Phillip, were born in British Guiana.

A second name I had recognised immediately was that of Joseph Van Sertima, who also had died in September 1967. My father had known him well. Van Sertima was of Dutch, aboriginal Indian, and African ancestry. He had been a stalwart Demba employee, working in the powerhouse for many years.

Maurice Nascimento had been entombed in *Le Repentir* in April 1970. He had had an interesting career in the country. He had prospected for gold and diamonds, and gained a great skill working in the tropical rainforest, with all its wonders and dangers. At one time, he accompanied British Guiana's well-known Vincent Roth, who was in the northwest of the country doing magistrate work and handing out mining licenses, amongst other government duties. Our family came to know him after he joined Demba; he lived at the southern end of Riverside Road in Watooka. He had worked much time in the rainforest for Demba on geological surveys. Demba's pilot, Tom Wilson, often flew Maurice into forest waterways for him to carry out river gauging work.

A very nice well-educated elderly woman came up the stairs and into the office with her son and his wife. We had an interesting discussion, and they were able to determine the area of the cemetery where their loved one's tomb was located. We then all walked down the stairs, where I found two men sleeping under a tree beside their bicycles and weed-eaters. I took a photo of them while others sat by chuckling. They awoke, and I asked them if they had partaken of too much El Dorado rum the previous evening.

Grinning, they introduced themselves as Aubrey and Shawn. They agreed to guide me through Le Repentir for a fee.

I had been warned by many folks about the dangers of the cemetery. With the country's demise over many decades under the leadership of Linden Forbes Burnham, it had fallen into deep disrepair. In the tropical open-air greenhouse-like conditions of heat, humidity, and fast, heavy rain, the undergrowth had become overgrowth, and the tombs had fallen out of sight within massive entanglements of high greenery, impossible to pass through in most places. Small waterway canals had become over-silted, full of wild lilies, and small bridges had become rotten and collapsed. Metal entrance gates have greatly deteriorated, and garbage can be found at them and in many other places that the overgrowth was not hiding.

Poisonous labaria and carpet labaria snakes are common in Guyana, and in Le Repentir. They can reach a length of three feet or so. Their two fangs retract to the tops of their mouths when they closed. The venomous Guyana parrot snake is also prevalent there. Unlike other non-poisonous emerald-green parrot snakes, this snake is a viper, appearing in darker green, with peppered black spots and a creamy yellow stripe lengthwise. Aubrey also told me about the "black-back" coral snakes that one must look out for. This is one of six varieties of coral snake found in Guyana. It is red in colour, with black bands bordered with white (or yellow)—tricoloured. Compared to other coral snakes, it has small eyes, and its poison is highly neurotoxic. If one gets bitten by one of these snakes in Le Repentir, one does not head for the Office of the Sexton, where there is no anti-snake bite medicine—one heads straight and fast to the emergency ward of the hospital!

I had asked one of the onlookers at the office whether one might encounter the deadly bushmaster snake, recognised by its wide head, and could one outrun this aggressive serpent. His answer had been, "' E gonna catch you fas', ma-an! 'E gonna stand up like stick, 'e mad, eyes like fire!" Fortunately, this snake is not found in Le Repentir, but is certainly feared in the interior of the country.

Aubrey showed me his still swollen face, stung by a red marabunta wasp in the cemetery the previous day. He and Shawn also spoke of prevalent

Africanised bees, of which one must be aware. They attack in swarms, and many Guyanese folks, and animals, have been killed by such an attack.

Africanised bees were introduced from Africa to Brazil in 1956 to increase honey production. Found to be unmanageable, they escaped into the wild, and gradually found their way north into Guyana by the mid-1970s. With five times as many guards as "normal" honeybees, they are ferocious defenders when their colony is disturbed by humans or animals. They can attack with little provocation and can stay agitated for many hours.

Carrying large weed-eaters and pushing their bicycles, Aubrey and Shawn led me to a rusted gate, and we proceeded to walk down the long central road-path through Le Repentir. This wide dirt access way can still accommodate a vehicle moving slowly. A few of these road-paths cross at right angles as one proceeds; they lead to gates at the edges of the cemetery, but are hardly passable by a vehicle. For much of the first part of our traverse, there were no tombs in sight, due to the wall of growth on both sides of us. My guides assured me that we were nevertheless passing by hundreds of above-ground tombs.

Caiman and criminal activity are also present. Some of the slum housing areas surrounding the cemetery are not the kind one would chance to walk through even in daylight. Shawn described to me the time a man on a bicycle had passed them on this road path, with a dead seven-foot-long caiman pointing straight ahead over the front handle bars of his bike. Le Repentir has also been a perfect place for criminals to do away with an enemy or victim, either killed on the spot, or killed elsewhere and brought here for disposal. Incredibly, funeral homes have, at times, disposed of bodies simply by leaving them exposed where convenient. The corpses of these disposals decompose rapidly, and soon become evident due to their horrible odour. Same for animal bodies. When Aubrey and Shawn discover a human corpse, they call the police, who come for investigation purposes. Ultimately the body is disposed of at the new crematorium. In some cases, bodies are buried in the cemetery without authority to escape expenses. At times, vagrants have taken over, charging a toll for visitors to enter the cemetery.

Suicides in the cemetery are not uncommon. My author friend Dr. Bernard Heydorn recalls the time in the 1950s when a relative of his and a friend sat on a tomb, engaged in a suicide pact. They started to drink a poison, but Bernard's relative stopped, and so lived. His friend died frothing at the mouth.

As we stood nearby to a cow and two tethered horses, munching grass on the road path, my guides explained to me their occupation. They work for themselves, offering to find tombs for people looking for their deceased loved ones. They do this using the coordinates obtained from the Office of the Sexton. Wearing high rubber boots and using weed-eaters and machetes, they will hack, cut, and clear a path to the target tomb. They charge about US$25 for this service. They will build a new tomb for US$400 to US$700. This they do by building the cement forms and hand-mixing cement with the white sand that is prevalent in the country and perfectly granular for this purpose. They can work with plaster, will paint the tombs if required, and will restore tombs. Most importantly, they will engrave the location identification into the cement at the end of the tomb.

The cemetery is now more than eighty percent full, and ways have been found to conserve space. Tombs can be built on top of a previous tomb for a family. Sometimes, Aubrey and Shawn will bust open the end of a tomb and, using a hoe, carefully draw out the bones of a deceased occupant—this is permitted to be done only after ten years. These bones will then be put in a bag, while a new coffin/body is slid into the opened end. The bag is then placed in the tomb, which is then sealed with cement.

As we slowly walked to the far end of the cemetery, the tombs began to be visible, a sea of above-ground rectangular blocks on pads, many coloured pink, blue, and white, others greyed or blackened by age. As I mentioned earlier, some have porcelain open-page Bibles mounted on the top at one end. Many of these are stolen by the grave robbers who also break into tombs for profit. Some tombs were noticeably broken in on portions of their tops. A quick glance into these apertures revealed only dark empty space.

In his 1898 book, *Twenty-five Years in British Guiana,* Henry Kirke wrote:

> When the vaults were opened, in one case the inside was absolutely empty, although a person had been buried there within the memory of many persons then present; in the other, which had held two coffins, two or three well-polished bones were in one corner and nothing else. Damp, ants, rats and land crabs

> must be accountable for the disappearance of body, coffin and everything...not even the metal fittings of the coffins being found.

As I looked across the huge expanse of the cemetery, only a few trees, and these only tall palms, could be seen. For more than a century and a half, a whole cross-section of society has been entombed in this cemetery: celebrities, soldiers, policemen, athletes, politicians, clergy, government officials, businessmen, murderers, expatriates, poor folks, unknowns, and more.

My guides took me to the accessible tomb of Dr. Walter Rodney, whom I had read much about in my past. His tomb was distinct from the others surrounding it, because of its cement post railing and a plaque on a post denoting his renown. We sat on the flat railing top to discuss tomb building, while I also reflected on Rodney. He had graduated from Queen's College, and had been an outstanding high-jumper in athletics. He grew to become a socialist and a political activist, and the leader of the Working People's Alliance (WPA) a party that had opposed Linden Forbes Burnham's People's National Congress (PNC) government. Rodney had openly taunted and denigrated Burnham. At thirty-eight years of age, in 1980, he was assassinated in a car bombing. A Commission of Inquiry had later found that the assassination was carried out by Burnham's government. More than 35,000 people attended his funeral service. Rodney was also renowned as a historian.

> *A culture is a total way of life. It embraces what people ate and what they wore; the way they walked and the way they talked; the manner in which they treated death and greeted the newborn.*
>
> — *Walter Rodney*

I would later meet and talk with his brother Eddie Rodney, a former PPP Member of Parliament, at the National Library, where he is a member of the Library Board.

Catholic Jesuit priest Father Andrew Morrison was another renowned individual, and certainly a hero, entombed in Le Repentir, in January 2004 at eighty-four years of age. A tall, humble man, he had been a political activist who was not afraid to speak up. He had taken over editorship of the *Catholic Standard* from Father Francis Fenn, S.J., who had been a friend of my parents, and who had baptised me in January 1943. Both priests had had the highest level of integrity and had used their newspaper to speak out harshly against the governments of both Jagan and Burnham. They fearlessly raised issues relating to human rights violations, election frauds, violence, and other serious matters detrimental to the country. Under Burnham's oppressive rule, the newspaper was denied access to necessary equipment and materials and had to overcome several libel lawsuits and attempts by the government to shut it down. Father Morrison used to walk around the Stabroek Market selling his newspaper. He survived several attempts to take his life. His friend, Father Bernard Darke, mistaken for him, was murdered in 1979.

At the end of his life, Father Andrew Morrison was the priest at St. Joseph The Worker's Church in Linden, which opened in June 1951, and for which my father led the building project. When Father Morrison died, his funeral Mass was held at Sacred Heart Church in Georgetown (where my parents were married in September 1941). Father Joseph Chira was the lead celebrant while the President of Guyana and other dignitaries of all kinds were present. The night before he died, it was later reported, he had asked for his shoes: he was going home.

Home, for a while anyway, was to be a tomb in Le Repentir cemetery. The Society of Jesus, involving Catholic Jesuit priests, first commenced in the country in 1857, four years prior to the start of Le Repentir being used as a cemetery. Jesuit priests have been buried in the cemetery ever since. Regional Superior, Father Paul Martin, S.J., told me in 2016 that the Jesuits have a large cement vault structure, with room for about twelve entombed coffins. It is now the case that when a Jesuit priest dies, the tomb with the oldest "tenant" is opened, and the remains are scraped into a pillow case. The new corpse is then placed in the tomb together with the pillow case and its contents. Amen. Father Morrison may not yet have a tomb mate.

In 2015, to prepare for the coming 2016 Fiftieth Anniversary of Independence Jubilee, the City of Georgetown attempted to clear the cemetery of debris and growth, using contractors, heavy equipment, prisoner labour, and other services, such as a beekeeper organisation to remove bee colonies. Labourers wore high boots, protective clothing, masks, and hats. However, it all appears to have been for naught: Aubrey and Shawn told me that by the time the clean-up operation reached the far end of the cemetery, the first-cleared end had mostly grown back again. This was what confronted us upon our walk in the furnace of the sun. I later read that ten men would be required, with equipment, on a permanent basis to maintain the cemetery, but the city had not yet found the means to do so.

A week or more later, I returned to the Office of the Sexton with an agreement for my taxi driver, Ricky, to be with us with his car for safety... if we could determine the tomb location with the information that I now possessed, that Kunj Beharrysingh had died on November 20, 1967. I mounted the stairs of the office building again, waving to Aubrey and Shawn, who were sitting under their favourite tree, grinning and talking to others. They wished me luck. The lady officer once again produced the 1967 book register and within minutes, I hit pay dirt. Wow! Somehow, we had previously missed the clear and neatly written information—perhaps Kunj had not wanted to have his tomb detected. After all, he had not wanted to be entombed in Le Repentir. His first name in the records was spelled "Kungh", and he had been entombed on November 22, 1967. He had died young, at 58 years of age.

With thanks to the officers, I headed down the outdoor stairs and with excitement presented the coordinates of the tomb to my guides: 17-C28. I don't think that Ricky was particularly excited. No weed-eaters would be required, because the growth in the target area would be far too dense and too high. Shawn started down the road path on his bike. I climbed into the taxi with Aubrey, who had two machetes. We were driven to the halfway point along the perimeter road, then turned onto Cemetery Road. We entered through the old gate there, and travelled down the dirt road path until we met Shawn. We could not proceed with the taxi any farther due to a large depression on the road path.

With Shawn leading the way, the two guides faced a wall of high entanglement that only solid machetes could penetrate. Tall razor grass was first encountered. Its saw-toothed edges face downwards, so that one had to be careful withdrawing a leg to take a further step forward. Slowly, hacking their way under the hot sun, Shawn and Aubrey proceeded, until they disappeared. The two horses were tethered nearby. Both Ricky and I were uncomfortable waiting in plain sight, looking up and down the long road path, hoping that no criminals were looking for easy prey.

After twenty minutes, the guides reappeared, walked down a further 30 metres, and started to hack into the greenery again. Ricky and I sauntered down to hear them talking and hacking. Now and then I would shout to ask if they were getting closer, obtaining only a negative response. They seemed to know what they were doing, with determined confidence. I told Ricky again that I was uneasy, and he responded, "I was born in Guyana and I have lived here all my life…yet I am very uneasy in this place also".

Just at that moment, we saw a lone man walking towards us in the distance.

I decided that I would choose the worst of two possible evils, and started to enter the twisting trail being carved out of the growth, to be with the guys with the machetes! I possessed a six-foot-long palm branch stick that Aubrey had carved up for me, removing the saw teeth along much of its edging. I walked on top of about a foot of cut greenery, and I did not want my feet to penetrate it through to the ground, where I might step on a snake. Suddenly, the searchers shouted that they had found the tomb!

Aubrey balanced himself carefully back to me to guide and help me forward, encouraging me not to step on other tombs barely visible below the green cuttings. For a while, we could not see Shawn at the site, given the twisty trail, along which they had stopped now and then to inspect tomb identifications. Then we turned a corner, and there was the tomb, with Shawn beside it holding up his machete as a sign of victory.

They had chopped out the enclosure, but we could not see other surrounding tombs: we could only see for a few feet down the twisting trail that had been cut. The tomb gave the appearance of blackened cement, though it had once been white, and one end had been crushed in at the top. Only blackness could be seen through the opening. I thanked my friends for their success and, standing on the cement base, I quietly prayed for/to Kunj, telling him how grateful I was for my friendship with his family, and for the good values that he had instilled in them. I reminded him that his wife, Eileen, had also been just as responsible for this.

Feeling uncomfortable in that scary place, I took one last look downwards, then signalled to my guides to move out. Aubrey reached back several times to help me find my balance. Half way back, my left leg fell through the top of a tomb to above my knee. Wow. Scary. Dark. Aubrey hauled me up. My shoe and pant leg were covered in a black soot-like dust or mould. The tomb had felt empty.

Ricky was happy to see us back on the road path. The lone man had simply passed him by silently, continuing his walk. Back at the Office of the Sexton property, we used a water standpipe to wash off most of the black, while a few close cattle watched quietly. Later, I had to dispose of my socks and pants due to the blackness that had pervaded my clothing, right to the skin. A shower had never felt better.

* * *

So, who was Kunj Beharrysingh?

In the mid-1970s, I was managing a systems design and testing group at the Bank of Montreal in Montreal, Quebec, Canada. I began working with a pretty, young East Indian woman, Judy Beharrysingh, who was a perfect working partner. Her enthusiasm for her work, her professional dress and manner and, in particular, her natural sense of courteousness and proper Christian values impressed me. Both of us concentrated on our work, and it was not for some time, I believe, that we came to understand that each of us had been born in British Guiana. Even so, we spent little time discussing our pasts. Elinor, one of her older sisters, also worked in our Division, and I came to know her as well. It was not until decades later that Judy and I met again, and she became a close friend of my family. I have met most of her five sisters and two brothers, all of whom live now in Toronto. Here is some of their family story…and that of their father, Kunj.

Kunj Beharrysingh was born in Berbice in northeast British Guiana, now Guyana, in 1909. He was a descendant of East Indians who had come to British Guiana from the area of Bihar in the province of Uttar Pradesh in northeastern India, probably as indentured workers. In 1838, five years after emancipation in British Guiana, the first ships, the *Whitby* and the *Hesperus*, arrived from India bearing workers to be indentured. These workers were needed to replace plantation slaves, who had refused to go back to work, even to be paid, in the trying conditions.

Kunj grew up wanting to be a policeman and had succeeded at doing so. He married Hasanara "Eileen" Ishmael. Kunj chose "Joseph", or "Joe", for his English name.

Like most police families, the Beharrysinghs lived in many locations. One of these was Suddie, Essequibo. Daughter Elinor recalls how, at only seven years of age, she enjoyed regularly polishing her father's belt, boots, hat, buttons, and shoes. While the family was able to live in a large house, there was no electricity—they used oil lamps for lighting and reading.

By 1952, the family had reached its final total of eight children: Barbara, Elinor, Rosemary, Desiree, Valerie, Rudy, Judy, and Derek. Kunj was sent by his Guyana Police Force to England, to the prestigious Hendon Police Training School southeast of London. He made his country proud when he became the top policeman in his class, for which he was awarded the distinguished Baton of Honour. Upon his return to British Guiana, he established and became the head of the Police Training School in Georgetown.

His children describe their father as a "tall, dark, and handsome man" whose manner and bearing were impressive. At home, he was revered as a father and as a strict disciplinarian, ensuring with his finger-rapping ruler that his children well learned their "shilling arithmetic". Three of his children later went on to win Police Scholarships. Several of them became colony experts in the sports of tennis and table tennis. At sixteen years of age in 1956, Elinor had been proposed to by a young Scottish soldier who was in the country with his mates to quell unrest. He had had to meet with Kunj to ask permission for the marriage but had quickly been dismissed. With six young, attractive and athletic ladies in his family, Kunj had had his hands full.

It is to be noted that just prior to Beharrysingh's training in London, his older police colleague and good friend, David Rose, had also attended and had also excelled in his class. Both men then rose to the senior ranks of the police force. David Rose became the Godfather for Beharrysingh's two youngest children, Judy and Derek. In 1964, he was chosen to be the Administrator of Antigua.

Meanwhile, Kunj Beharrysingh was dealing with troubled and violent political times in Guyana, particularly from 1962 until Independence in 1966. His family members recall him coming home in Georgetown exhausted from dealing with the Wismar Massacre in 1964 and with other riots. Peter Owen was the Police Commissioner at the time. On one occasion, Beharrysingh was taken by a police vehicle to a riot area to relieve a police officer on horse. As the vehicle stopped beside the horse and rider, the policeman was shot off his horse, and fell at the feet of Beharrysingh, who then suffered a heart attack. He summoned another policeman to take care of the fallen horseman, and then climbed back into the vehicle to be taken to the hospital. Nevertheless, he donned his uniform the following day to report for duty.

The politics and violence were drawn along racial lines: the blacks versus the East Indians. An International Commission of Jurists (IJI) was invited to investigate the country's racial violence, and one of the recommendations was for the police force to more align itself with the demographics of the country. At the time, the East Indian population was not proportionally represented within the police organization. Kunj Beharrysingh was an anomaly in that he was East Indian and had advanced upwards with respect and admiration within a mostly black organisation. President Burnham reluctantly accepted the IJI recommendation... but then never acted.

In 1964, recruitment of a Special Services Unit (SSU) was initiated by the government. The British Guiana Police Force was assigned the responsibility for administration, discipline, and training of the SSU. The composition of the unit was fifty percent East Indians and fifty percent other races. Kunj Beharrysingh would have had much to do with this. In 1965, the government decided to form a National Army and disbanded the SSU, with most of its members serving as the first soldiers in what was to become the Guyana Defence Force. Some of these members will get attention later in my writing.

Police Commissioner Peter Owen left in 1965, and was replaced by Ian Pollock, the last British Police Commissioner prior to Independence on May 26, 1966. It was at this time that Kunj Beharrysingh may have acted in the position of Police Commissioner, until Prime Minister Linden Forbes Burnham appointed Felix Austin to the post on January 1, 1967 (although I have no evidence to prove that Beharrysingh acted in the top post). Burnham did not want an East Indian, nor a man who was not afraid to speak up, to lead the Force. PPP leader Cheddi Jagan, according to the

Beharrysingh family, had not particularly liked Beharrysingh, because of his lack of fear of speaking out. Yet he recommended to Burnham that Beharrysingh be appointed to Police Commissioner. This did not occur. According to his family, Beharrysingh retired in early 1967.

With the family still living at 44 Robb Street, Kunj Beharrysingh was also busy operating a small trucking business, together with cattle raising and other interests. From time to time, on Saturday afternoons, he would visit the Police Officer's Mess to socialise with his colleagues. In mid-November 1967, he met a British cardiologist at the Officer's Mess, who was in Georgetown performing staff training at the Public Hospital. After discussing Beharrysingh's angina, the doctor invited Beharrysingh to visit the hospital the following day for an examination.

Kunj Beharrysingh was then examined and admitted to the hospital. He soon suffered a heart attack, with a doctor presiding. Oxygen was required, but the hospital was short of many supplies, and this was one of them. He was then wheeled in a stretcher to another hospital area to obtain the oxygen, but before it could be administered, he expired. The hospital did not notify the family before sending Beharrysingh's body to the morgue (sometimes in those days referred to as the "dead house").

A member of the family, after being notified, contacted Elinor, the second-eldest daughter, who was working at Barclay's Bank. She immediately fled to the morgue. There, she frantically pulled back sheets covering deceased bodies until, shocked, she had found that of her father. She immediately commenced a form of artificial respiration, without success. Devastated and outspoken, she then visited the hospital to blast them for the loss of her father who, except for mild angina, had been in good health. Given the violent events of the time, the family have always wondered whether their father was assassinated. No proof of this has ever surfaced, but there is a family feeling that a doctor may have administered an injection of poisonous fluid to silence their father.

Two days later, a very large funeral procession proceeded from their Robb Street home to the Le Repentir Cemetery. Many businesses closed for the event. Large crowds lined the streets. The police were present in great numbers, with many mounted on horses. At the cemetery, then still well-maintained, a white above-ground tomb had been prepared, not too far in from the road down through the middle of the grounds. The casket was hefty, perhaps made of heavy wallaby wood. It was difficult to slide the coffin into the tomb from one end.

The family members had always known that their father did not want to be buried in Le Repentir, but rather to be buried with his parents in Berbice. His police colleagues preferred otherwise.

> *Live an exemplary life as a leader. When you are gone, you will still lead from the grave because your influence, impacts and inspirations will become information for the living.*
>
> — Israelmor Ayivor, *Leader's Ladder*

Over the next several years, the Beharrysingh family moved to Canada, mostly to Montreal at first. The last to leave was the mother, Eileen, and her youngest son, Derek. Not long after, young Judy joined her sister Elinor to work at the Bank of Montreal, where I first came to know them.

In 1966, David Rose was knighted, and became Guyana's governor general. His wife, Lady Patricia Rose, was a medical doctor, known for her work with lepers at the hospital in Mahaica. The Beharrysingh family remembers both as very kind, personable, and capable individuals. During the rehearsal drills for the induction ceremony for Guyana's first governor general, His Excellency Sir David Rose, Private Jerome Brutus died accidentally when a cannon fired while being loaded. He was buried in *Le Repentir* with military honours.

In 1969, while Sir David was visiting London, England, scaffolding fell on the car he was riding in, causing his death. He is buried at Seven Ponds, also known as the Place of Heroes, in Georgetown's Botanical Gardens, as are three past presidents and national poet Martin Carter. He was posthumously awarded Guyana's highest award, the Order of Excellence.

Ian McDonald recalled the State Funeral held for Governor General Rose. "It was the time of Diwali and it was night when they bore him into town from Timerhi Airport. What I remember best were the thousands of kindled earthen lamps and lighted candles which everywhere people held in their hands in his honour, golden flowers in the dark". The bauxite ship *Sunrose* was named after him.

Four days prior to Kunj Beharrysingh's death, a young neighbour of the family made Guyana very proud. Shakira Baksh, Miss Guyana, came third in the Miss World contest in London, England, on November 16, 1967. She was born in Maryville on Leguan Island in the mouth of the Essequibo River in 1947. My Hansib publisher, Arif Ali, recalls her as a child often visiting his Aunt Zedica Jabbar's store, separated by a small canal from the Baksh residence. Ali's Uncle Abdul Jabbar had been the manager of the Maryville Estate. Shakira's mother, Saab, an accomplished dressmaker, raised Shakira and her two brothers on her own. Sometime later, the family moved to Georgetown to live in a "bottom house" close by to the Beharrysingh home. In 1964, a time of violence, Shakira worked in the J. F. Kennedy Library at the American Embassy on Main Street in Georgetown. Violent protesters wounded three employees, including Shakira, who recovered well.

According to Indrani Gayadeen, who knew the Baksh family well, Shakira's mother made the dress that had helped Shakira look so beautiful in the Miss World Pageant. Shakira subsequently commenced a modelling career based in London, England. At some time during the very early 1970s, actor Michael Caine was watching TV, and jumped when he saw the beautiful woman, Shakira Baksh, starring in an advertisement for Maxwell House coffee. Within a short time, he had contacted her, then not living far from him, and they were married in 1973. Their marriage continues to endure.

Guyana first entered a candidate into the Miss World Pageant in 1966, just after gaining independence. Umblita Sluytman, Miss Guyana, came in eleventh that year. Judy Beharrysingh entered the Miss Guyana competition in 1968 and did well, coming in runner-up to Alexis Harris, who went on to rank sixth in that year's Miss World Pageant. Judy's sisters recall her, at seventeen years, preparing for the event. Judy was sponsored by the Davson Sugar Company, yet her mother was still required to sew a competition dress for her. Judy learned how to wear high heels and to present herself on stage. She had long black hair almost down to her waist. During the competition, she answered nine of the ten skill testing questions correctly, but AlexisHarris gave correct answers for all of them.

Alexis Harris's dress had been made by Walter Greene, who went on to become a sought-after fashion designer. Her father, Wilson Harris, had initially been a government surveyor, spending seventeen years in the country's wild, tropical interior. He later became renowned, and was knighted, for his work in literature. Her uncle was Jan Carew, novelist, anti-colonist activist, advisor to Caribbean and African Heads of State, and much more.

One of the judges for the 1968 event was Ian McDonald, who, as mentioned earlier, had been a tennis star for Trinidad and then for Guyana, the first person from either country to play at Wimbledon. Since then, he has become much awarded as a writer, author and poet. He recalled for me, "I do remember how very attractive and active the Beharrysingh girls were. In those days, I can assure you, it was very difficult to choose between the extraordinary number of very beautiful Guyanese girls. Our record in the Miss World contests tells the story!" Another judge that year was Indrani Persaud Gayadeen, who is a good friend of the Beharrysingh siblings and of whom you will read later in this book.

Pamela Lord became Miss Guyana in 1969, and came fourth in the Miss World Pageant. Runner-up to her in Guyana was Marguerite Pooran, a school mate of Judy Beharrysingh, who would later marry Chris Jardim.

In 1970, Jenny Wong from Watooka, Mackenzie, won the competition for Miss Guyana. Later that year, she befriended Jennifer Hosten from Grenada, and convinced her to compete for Miss Grenada. Hosten did so, and became Miss Grenada 1970. Both young women then competed in the Miss World Pageant in London, England, that November, with Bob Hope presiding. Glen Campbell and Joan Collins were some of the judges. Jennifer Hosten, presenting herself as a "nutmeg princess" won the contest. Jenny Wong, with her long black waist-length hair, was a semi-finalist, coming in eleventh.

Jennifer Hosten was the first black woman to ever win the event. Also, Miss South Africa had been runner-up. *Two* black women. This result upset many racists, who protested. Sadly, at that time, even the famous book *Black Beauty* was still being banned in South Africa. Jennifer Hosten went on to entertain with Bob Hope in Vietnam during the following year, and to accomplish many other achievements. She was a radio host and Grenada's High Commissioner to Canada and worked overseas for Canada's International Development Agency. My wife, Carolyn, and I, are fortunate to know her, and enjoyed hosting her and her husband, Jim

O'Hare, at Guyana's Fiftieth Anniversary Gala Event in Toronto in October 2016. She is much more than a beautiful woman.

It is interesting to note that for the first six years following Guyana's entry into the Miss World Pageant in 1966, their contestants averaged seventh amongst more than fifty world competitors each year. In May 2016, I attended the colourful and exciting Miss Guyana World event at Parc Rayne Hall in Georgetown. Wow. The lady competitors were strikingly beautiful in their fancy dresses, and each of the seven finalists spoke well within the limited time allowed. Dancers from each of the ten regions in the country performed in their native dress, with colourful accoutrements. Just as interesting was the high-class dress of the people, both men and women, in the audience: diverse-race and mixed-race Guyanese folks look outstanding when they dress up. Actress and radio personality Nuriyyih Gerrard had won the competition taking over from last year's winner, singer Lisa Punch. I was fortunate to meet and talk to Reesa Sooklall, the most recent girl to have won the competition for Miss Guyana Talented Teen.

One hot morning, I was walking along Main Street, trying to find Demba's old Bauxite House, a large building that had been used for various company purposes in the old days. I finally determined that it is now the headquarters for the Ministry of Culture, Youth and Sports on Main Street, very close to Sacred Heart Church. On my walk to there, I stopped at the gate of the old large De Freitas mansion, which looked somewhat in disrepair. A seemingly elderly and frail East Indian woman, long past her beauty peak, came to the gate, and subsequently invited me to sit with her in the cramped guard house. Her sister sat on the windowsill, totally silent, resting her head upon her pulled-up knees while staring straight ahead. My welcoming host introduced herself as Joan De Groote, a name that surprised me given her race. During a relaxed and enjoyable chat she informed me that she had been a contestant in the 1970 Miss Guyana Pageant, and proved it to me by answering many of my questions, for which I already knew the answers. Wow. She told me that her mother had been Esther Chung, who had been a Miss British Guiana Pageant winner, and who had later worked at Chung's General store in Mackenzie.

In October 2016, I also had the opportunity to meet with Guyana's acting Police Commissioner, David Ramnarine. I asked him if he, also raised in Berbice, had ever heard of Kunj Beharrysingh. His response was, "Sure, he was famous".

Kunj's youngest son, Derek, guards his father's Baton of Honour with great pride. His second-eldest daughter, Elinor, told me that her father, through the spirits, had told her in 1996 that he had finally made it to heaven."

Kunj...

Baton of Honour... wow.
You surely made your mark...
Time has long pass'd and now
Your hollow'd tomb is dark.
In Heaven you now rest,
'Twas God who sent you here...
You truly now are bless'd,
Long gone from Repentir.

RETURN TO WATOOKA

I soon realised that no journey carries one far unless, as it extends into the world around us, it goes an equal distance into the world within.

— Lillian Smith

It was time to journey back to Watooka again. Sam Hinds had sent his chauffeur and "close man" to pick me up at the Rainforest. I had sold most of my books, so I did not have a lot left to carry.

I enjoyed the ride to Sam's house while talking to my front-seat caretakers. At one time, they had performed this duty for former President Bhagdat Jagdeo. I chuckled to myself, imagining they were wondering who the not-famous person in their back seat was. They listened to East Indian music on the radio until we reached our destination.

When we entered the front gate of Sam's property, he was there to greet me, and I was invited upstairs into the house. Yvonne was away on travel. Prior to entering the door, I passed a large fish tank that reminded me, with its colourful moving content, that I was indeed in the tropics.

This particular week was a focus for celebrations relating to the 100th Anniversary of the Demerara Bauxite Company, even though it was taken over by the government in 1971. Disappointingly, there would be no representation from the Aluminum Company of Canada, Alcan. This company was taken over in Canada by Rio Tinto in 2007, which paid a huge sum of $38.1 billion in a competition with Vale and Alcoa. Dick Evans, Alcan's CEO at the time, was reported in the Wall Street Journal as stating that it was the biggest mining industry takeover in history... and the worst in terms of making business sense. (Dick Evans, you'll recall, graciously wrote an exceptional preface for my book *Children of Watooka*.) Rio Tinto was given an opportunity to participate in this special Guyana event, but declined.

Our drive was uneventful but, as before, our discussion was non-stop. Sam told me that he was reading a good book, *From Third World to First: The Singapore Story*, by Lee Kuan Yew, and I made a note to obtain a copy. Maybe Guyana could learn from this success story. We were to participate in an all-afternoon Bauxite Century Symposium. Sam would be on a panel of bauxite industry experts. Each panelist would speak about the current status of this industry in Guyana, and would also provide a synopsis and ideas for the future. While important government, regional, and local VIPs would be present, the venue would also be open to the public. Given the unemployment in the one-industry town, and the associated poverty, this event would be of great interest to the local population. Everyone would be hopeful that their experienced leaders would be able to direct and lead them into a bright and robust economic future. Sam and I talked at some length on this topic, with me being a student, learning from his bauxite industry experience and unsurpassed knowledge of all aspects of the country. The event was to be held at the large Constabulary Hall in old Cockatara.

When we exited the limousine at the front door of the hall, we were warmly greeted by numerous folks. I was able to meet Robeson Benn again, as well as Orrin Gordon, who would be the moderator for the event. It was very special for me to again meet Horace James and Paula Walcott-Quintin, two of the main event organisers. Robert Shang and Eric Yu, the two top officials for the Chinese Bosai Minerals Group Guyana company, enthusiastically welcomed me, and asked me to take a front seat with them. It was then that I again met Raphael Trotman, the young impressive Minister of Natural Resources, who sat beside us. A former lawyer, he has had a prolific political career, and at one time was Speaker of the National Assembly. He asked me where he could get a copy of my book.

Earlier in the week, school-event organisers Nancy Butcher, Lauren Parris, and Paula Walcott-Quintin, had presided over school spelling bee and debate contests. Two copies of my book had been presented to students of the Christianburg Wismar Secondary and Wisroc Secondary schools for prizes. In her youth, Paula was a Guyana net-ball star for Mackenzie High School. She was born and raised at Lot 34 Half Mile in Wismar.

After the opening address by Mayor Carwyn Holland, all of the panelists spoke: Newell Dennison, Acting Commissioner, Guyana Geology and Mines Commission; Dr. Samuel Hinds; Sylvester Carmichael, former marketing manager, Bauxite Industry Development Company (BIDCO); Major General Norman McLean (Ret.); Secretary Bosai; and Victor Wright, Board Member, SET Foundation. Some of the presentations, of course, referred to past bauxite history, and to the current situation of high-quality bauxite with reserves for another hundred years, and how these advantages were offset by heavy overburden challenges.

Victor Wright, representing a group of scientists, engineers, and technical experts in the United States, outlined their proposal to develop bauxite mining operations in the Pakaraima area in the country's interior. The aluminious laterite bauxite reserves there have been determined to be enormous. They have invented a process to concurrently extract aluminium, iron, and other metals from this laterite, and to do so using recently discovered natural gas and peat to power the process. (Guyana has enormous quantities of peat along its western coast.) All of this would require new transportation, harbour, and other infrastructure facilities. This major undertaking would require a private consortium of industry and financial partners, with the SET Foundation serving as a technology provider. My friend Irvin Davis, former bauxite operations engineer at Linden and now living in the US, is helping to lead this unique initiative.

First Bauxite, a Canadian company, is also planning to develop their fifty-year lease to bauxite deposits in the Bonasika area in northwest Guyana. The recent discovery of oil off Guyana's coast may enhance the ability of the country to provide the necessary power to facilitate future industry. Sam Hinds cautioned listeners that the country, and Linden, must diversify its industry in the future to minimise risk and to maximise opportunities for an improved economy and social environment. For example, there are possibilities in Linden for future iron production, steel fabrication, cement production, furniture manufacturing, and much more. (Much of this will be presented in detail in a later chapter of this book.)

A question/discussion period followed and became disturbing at one point when an angry man near the back of the room shouted his concern that bauxite was leaving in ships for other countries without Guyana's authorities knowing what other valuable metals and minerals were also in the ore. He felt strongly that Guyana is getting ripped off. Whereas I could understand that most people are not educated in the science of bauxite and aluminium, it was hard for me to understand the man's anger. Orrin Gordon, the moderator, did the smart thing and called on bauxite expert and economist Sylvester Carmichael to respond to the man's concern in layman's terms. He did such a great job that after the meeting, I went up to introduce myself and to congratulate him.

It was very hot in the packed hall, and I was grateful for the cold bottled water that was available. Minister of Natural Resources Raphael Trotman closed the event with his thoughts about future opportunities, while also identifying current projects in progress. He announced the formation of an expert Bauxite Sectorial Review Committee, which will assess the industry and offer recommendations on the feasibility of building an alumina plant. Of course, I was happy to hear that Sylvester Carmichael would be one of the two leaders, together with E. Lance Carberry, an economist who has had a renowned past in the public service and who is very knowledgeable about the bauxite industry.

At the end of the symposium I think that most of the attendees thought that this event was not a requiem for 100 years of the bauxite industry, but rather about the generation of real hope for a bauxite future, in tandem with new, diverse industries.

A Mrs. "Babs" Gittens approached me after the meeting to tell me that her father, a mechanical engineer, had known my father. This would have been in the very middle of the twentieth century. Wow. So long ago. She had her photo taken with Sam and myself. Subsequently, event organisers, panelists, and others retired for a late and relaxed lunch at the Watooka

Clubhouse. At times I paused to be grateful for being with all these interesting and capable people.

I was sitting near Mortimer Mingo, a previous Region Ten Chairman. He had also been a policeman earlier in his career, and offered me a story that is hard for me to forget: one time, a police horse broke its leg and had to be put down. Mortimer and his colleagues took a leg and prepared it for a unique feast, "Gallup Curry". Mortimer is currently the Chairman of the Linden Hospital Board.

I had some time to walk around the grounds and to relax alone in the Clubhouse. The Demerara Bauxite Company had commenced operations 100 years ago. I tried to think about what was happening back in 1916. Houses in Mackenzie had not even been built. The whole area would have been very primitive, with old plantation growth swallowed up by tropical rainforest. Much more had been happening in the outside world, even aside from a raging World War I. Britain enforced conscription that year. Enrico Caruso recorded *O Solo Mio* for the Victoria Talking Machine Company. Singers Dinah Shore and Martha Raye were born. So were future bandleaders Ray Ellington and Harry James, actress Betty Grable, and jazz musician Buddy Cole. Canada's original parliament buildings burned down. Women in the US were allowed to attend a boxing match. So long ago.

I retired early to my room, #23, on the top floor near the head of the stairs. It was to be a busy tomorrow, and a hot, humid one again. There are only nine guest rooms in the old Clubhouse, and they are all on the top floor. (There must be a reason for the high number on my door.) All of the rooms are situated off the long/wide enclosed veranda that overlooks the expansive yard and the river, except for the last two rooms, which are larger and find themselves at the north end of the veranda: "The President's Room" and "The Prime Minister's Room". My room was next to them.

Most presidents and prime ministers of Guyana have occupied these rooms, although I doubt that included Cheddi Jagan or his wife. I chuckled to myself, wondering if, when the prime minister visits, is he permitted to sleep in The President's Room. Sam Hinds had been both president and prime minister, and I chuckled again to myself, wondering which room he had chosen at different times in his political life. I wondered in which room Fidel Castro had slumbered during his state visit to Guyana and to

Linden in 1973. I opened a few bureau drawers to see if I could find any Cuban cigars, but to no avail. If only the walls could talk.

When I first entered my room, I looked around in awe. All nine rooms are intact from the past. There were two double beds, and at the far, spacious end was a sitting room with sofas, tables, and other old but comfortable furniture. I could look out the windows for a great view of the swimming pool and surrounding greenery. My bed had sheets trimmed with old-time lace. The high walls were vertical boards of greenheart wood, painted white. There was no easily available hot water, but that certainly was not an issue. The shower, which would become my dear friend, did not shower, but was more of a stream with its gravity drop. All fine with me. I was grateful for the air-conditioning, which is only provided in the guest rooms. I slept well.

Breakfasting alone in the morning, I was treated royally by the staff. The early view, between the historic and massive mango trees, of the dark, softly flowing river was extraordinary. Everything was bright and green along the river banks. This was heaven…made more wondrous by my memories, flooding back to me, of my youth here so long ago, and of being so grateful for this journey back to my roots. Truly, a dream come true. I was anxious for the day to proceed, with a special event planned out in the rainforest at a historic, still-isolated location.

It was not long before I had a nice surprise. As I was descending the outside stairs to walk around on the grounds, I heard, "Steve!" Unmistakably, it was a special friend whom I had never met: Carmen Barclay Subryan. We hugged. She had come directly from the airport to see me before heading for her sister Irene Adam's home across the river in Wismar. She had not slept for almost two days.

It was so special to see her. She had retired from Howard University as an English faculty member earlier in the year and was coming back to the place of her birth to offer her services to helping children. She had authored three excellent books, *Black-Water People*, *Black-Water Women*, and *Black-Water Children*, all relating to the area of her birth, the area in which we now found ourselves together. On several occasions in the past, I had communicated with her for professorial advice while writing my book. She was a descendant of Robert Allicock, one of the first European settlers in the area. The reader will learn much more about her in a later chapter.

Guyana's government, to commemorate the Bauxite Century celebrations, had created four special Bauxite Centennial postage stamps, and they were to be unveiled. The stamps had resulted from a collaboration between the Guyana Post Office Corporation, the Bauxite Centennial Committee, headed by Horace James, and the Russian bauxite company RUSAL. For sure, these stamps will be collector's items. British Guiana/Guyana has always produced beautiful and valuable postage stamps. Currently, the world's most valuable postage stamp, which sold for US$9.5 million in 2014, is the British Guiana One-Cent Magenta, produced in 1856. These new centennial stamps colourfully depict various aspects of bauxite mining operations.

The big event would be held at the Three Friends mine, the first bauxite mine in the country, situated about nineteen kilometres south of Linden, and accessible via road and by the Demerara River. In 1810, Major John D. Paterson, a Scotsman, arrived to buy plantation Christianburg on the west side of the Demerara River, about 105 kilometres from the coast. He was joined by his two friends, John Spencer and John Blount, who also bought old plantation land in the area. Spencer also bought land at Akyma across the river on the east side and further south. Akyma is an Amerindian word meaning "surprised wonder", as in "Oh, my!" Sugar had been the main product in the area, but Paterson recognised a huge potential for logging and mill work. He built a mill and commenced to become wealthy. His two friends also entered into the business of producing logs and sending them to Paterson's mill.

As recounted earlier, in 1914 the Aluminum Company of America sent George B. Mackenzie to the area to assemble old plantation property for the eventually unveiled purpose of mining bauxite (although the stated purpose was to produce oranges). Not long after, Alcoa commenced to mine bauxite at the Three Friends property in 1916. The overburden then had been minimal, fortunately so, because the primitive mining method had been for men to pick and shovel the revealed bauxite into mule carts, which took the ore to be loaded onto punts at the nearby river for transport north to its mouth, where the ore was transferred onto ships. The first shipload was transported on the *S.S. Fagersand* in early 1917. A staff house, an office, and a laboratory of considerable size were established at Akyma, to be used until Mackenzie was developed.

By 1939, the world was preparing for World War II, and so was Alcan. By that time, another mine, Trewern, had opened near to the Three Friends mine, and a single-track railroad had been constructed to take the ore by train to Mackenzie, to be loaded onto ships after processing there. At the start of the war, these two mines were close to exhaustion, and a new mine was required to supply the aluminium needed for the war. Thus, the Hope mine was opened, directly across the river from the Three Friends mine, and would earn the right to be called the mine that helped win the war. Perhaps its name was given to represent the wish for the Allies to achieve victory.

The overburden for this mine was also minor. Prior to the commencement of mining, however, a bridge, fitted with railroad tracks, had to be constructed across the river to meet the east-side railroad track. This project, led by Philip H. Morgan, was no easy task. Morgan, assisted by another highly competent man, Harry Hamilton, was known as one of the best construction men that ever wore an Alcan helmet. My father had been fortunate to have known and worked with him. It is interesting to note that a significant amount of Hope mine bauxite ended up in Davy Jones's locker at the bottom of the sea, due to the sinking of bauxite ships by German submarines.

In 1943, Demba opened the Maria Elizabeth mine less than two kilometres south of the Three Friends mine. This mine was named after a daughter of Nancy Allicock, who was married to John Spencer. The following year, the Topira mine was opened further south, at a bush clearing known as Ituni, and a small village was established there, together with a railroad to join the one ending further north.

By the end of the war, the *Hope* mine was exhausted: it had served the Allies with great merit. In 1967 a much-needed bridge was built from Mackenzie to Wismar. The old Hope mine bridge was taken down, with the centre of it being barged downriver to become the centre of the new bridge. That new one-lane bridge, which was also used for large trucks to haul bauxite, is now fifty years old and is still used by large logging trucks. It needs to be replaced. Certain metal pieces of the old Hope mine bridge had been left in place for historical purposes, but scrap-metal dealers have removed those.

I had various options to be driven to the Three Friends mine. I chose to go in one of the elementary school busses with the children. The bus was packed with well-mannered and uniformed children, and with no air-conditioning, it was hot. All the children had lunches and cold drink bottles. Very soon we were on the dirt road, with dense tropical growth on both sides. From time to time, the vehicle had to slowly wind its way around water-filled depressions caused by recent rain. Our average speed may have been less than sixty kilometres per hour.

At last we arrived. I had not known what to expect. The road ended about sixty metres from the river, where there was an open space with a large tent set up for shade purposes, full of simple chairs. Except for an old house up on stilts, surrounded by a raw tropical shrub yard and various trees, we were enclosed within high rainforest. It had been seventy-five years since the ground had been cleared for mining purposes. Several more school busses arrived, as well as many other vehicles.

It was hot and humid...and we experienced a three-hour delay. Government officials being driven from Georgetown were late, and we had no idea where they were, until we were finally informed that they had taken a wrong fork in the road and were far off in the rainforest. Meanwhile, we were grateful for the coolers full of ice and bottled water. Many of us lined up on a bluff by the river for photo taking, where one end of the old Hope mine bridge had been. The silent river moved quietly below, fully surrounded by jungle on both sides, except for the small opening where we stood. My father would have stood at this place seventy-five years ago, not knowing that he would have a son who would also stand here so far into the future.

The many school children at the event were all uniformed, in different uniforms for different schools, and were extremely well behaved. To pass the time, I was given the green light to tell them stories from the podium. I told them also that I was so grateful that I had a grandchild that looked just like all of them, a beautiful little African girl with dreadlocks and a beautiful smile, who is full of music and dance. Subsequently, I had to relieve myself, and went back towards the bridge and up to a small clearing where a group of men were sitting in the shade. I walked past them to the top of the clearing, intending to go over it and into the dense jungle: there was a gully down below that I had no intention of investigating. It was then that the men shouted for me not to go further. There was a big boa constrictor down below, near the water. Thank you, gentlemen. These snakes cannot move as fast as a person can walk, but if you get too close they can strike faster than the eye can see. When young, a boa constrictor eats rats, mice, and squirrels, whereas when large they go for monkeys, wild boar, and deer.

Finally, the government officials arrived to speak and to unveil the stamps. Paula Walcott-Quintin did her usual superb job of organising things and of being the emcee. Enrico Woolford from the Ministry of Telecommunications unveiled the stamps, while both Horace James and Post Master General Karen Brown spoke. I sat beside them enjoying my cold water. I enjoyed meeting Linden's Deputy Mayor, Waneka Arindell, later. She had also endured the long wait in the heat of the day. Similarly, I met Baybert Winslow Parris, who is a proud Lindener, and who has faithfully recorded some of the town's history. At the conclusion, after things were tidied up, I was fortunate to be chauffeured back to the Watooka Clubhouse by Horace James, whom I would come to know and to immensely like.

Horace has been a huge contributor to Guyana and to Linden for all his adult career. He was trained as a mining engineer at the Humboldt School of Mining in England, and worked in various capacities in the bauxite industry at Linden, rising to become the Linmine Secretariat CEO. He worked to have the government-owned Linmine bauxite company privatised in 2004 when Bosai took over. At one time, around 1980, he was the Regional Ten Chairman. At the start of 2016, he was appointed to head troubled National Industrial and Commercial Investments Ltd., NICIL, a government holding company responsible for managing the privatisation of selected state-owned enterprises (SOEs), and for managing/monitoring contracts related to resulting undertakings. One of these many projects was to ensure the viability of the relatively new five-star Marriott Hotel with Marriott International.

NICIL is also responsible for managing all government shares, stocks, and securities of SOEs until they become fully privatised. The Linmine Secretariat reports to NICIL under the leadership of Emmett Alves. It is responsible for properties that used to belong to the Linmine bauxite operation and were not sold to Bosai, such as the Watooka Clubhouse, the Mackenzie-Wismar bridge, and other properties. It is also responsible for looking after the security of, and working with potential investors to find uses for, more than 8,000 hectares of depleted bauxite mines.

Devoted to the community of Linden, Horace also manages, with a strong desire to improve, the Linden Museum, situated in the old Mackenzie Recreation Hall. Now and then on our drive through the narrow dirt road surrounded by rainforest, the vehicle would come to a clearing, usually close to the river, where we could see one or more small unpainted shacks up on stilts, with outside stairs. They had a certain beauty, and I wondered what an average day was like for the residents.

It was a pleasure for me to have some personal time with this personable, capable, and humble man. No wonder he had been awarded the government's Golden Arrowhead Medal of Achievement earlier in the year. For the remainder of my time in Guyana, I would keep bothering Horace to loan me his medal...without success.

That evening was very special for me, one of the best, with a very interesting and special group of new friends. I will always treasure it. First, we all sat together for an early warm supper at the Clubhouse. Then we settled into a large room next to the very spacious bar and entertainment room. Our room was yellow-painted, with vertical greenheart wood boards rising to a high ceiling. We sat around a huge table, close to three metres square and covered with a nice table cloth. Our duty for the evening was to prepare gift and certificate awards for the Bauxite Centennial dinner and dance the next evening at the Clubhouse.

Vanessa Mitchell-Davis, Community Relations Officer for Bosai, is a camera expert, and is very efficient with her iPhone and iPad, as is Emmett Alves, head of the Linmine Secretariat, with his. Emmett received his mining-engineer education in Moscow, Russia. Vanessa, a twenty-five-year bauxite operation veteran, attended the Linden Technical Institute, where she learned electrical installation and instrumentation. She then worked in various functions relating to electrical aspects of heavy-duty earthmoving equipment, and various other vehicles. She played a major role in wiring up the panels for the new bauxite power plant. Subsequent to all of this, her presentable manner and photography/writing skills gained her her present occupation, in which she prepares press releases, handles company communication, and leads bauxite operation tours.

I have mentioned Paula Walcott-Quintin before, a former radio broadcaster, often called upon in Linden and in the eastern United States (she lives in New Jersey) for her exceptional organisation and emcee skill. Lauren Parris was the manager of the Watooka Clubhouse and of its wonderful staff, while Nancy Butcher was the former Head Teacher at the Regma Primary School. And then there was Horace James and myself. Four very capable and attractive ladies, and three engineers.

Lauren's parents had produced six daughters and a son, George, Jr. Her father, George "Sonny" Parris, began work as an apprentice with Demba at only fifteen years of age, and later became known for his longevity working for the company, and for his outstanding personality. Lauren's mother, Vivienne, was respected so much for her head nursing skills that the Vivienne Parris Health Centre is named after her.

Emmett and Paula worked together to design coloured certificates relating to the commemorative stamps for awards. while Nancy and I packaged gift bags. All of us enjoyed varied discussion, with interesting storytelling and good humour. Lauren's father worked for fifty years or so in the bauxite industry, and she is related to the brilliant Haslyn Parris, who was the manager of the Guybau bauxite operations when Demba was nationalised in 1971. Nancy is the niece of Basil Butcher, now living in old Watooka, who was a Guyana cricket star in international competition.

I started off the music by asking Vanessa to download and play Dan Hill's beautiful song *Sometimes When We Touch*. He became renowned when he put out this song in 1977. Dan Hill has been a Canadian singing star for decades. He published a great book, *I Am My Father's Son*. He comes from a remarkable family. His father, Daniel Hill, a black man raised in the United States, was the first head of Ontario's Human Right's Commission. His mother is white. His brother Lawrence is a renowned writer who wrote the international best seller, *The Book of Negroes*. Amongst others, Lawrence also wrote *Black Berry, Sweet Juice,* about racial identity. I had found both books to be exceptional reading. Sadly, their younger sister, Karen, died at 56 years of age just after completing her book, *Cafe Babanussa*. I found Lawrence Hill to be very approachable when he readily agreed to trade autographed books with me. I would consider myself to be very fortunate to meet these two talented brothers.

Vanessa downloaded many other great old songs for us. including: *Bridge Over Troubled Water* by Simon & Garfunkel, *I'm Not Me Without You* by Lorrie Morgan, *Storms Never Last* by Jessie Coulter, *Honky Tonk Angel* by Kitty Wells, and many more. How amazing all of this was for me, listening to Guyana stories and western-world music, almost within walking distance to tropical jungle...and with Guyanese colleagues who knew and enjoyed these songs as much as I did. Incredibly, I thought to myself, the last song I had heard in this room, 64 years ago, had been Bing Crosby singing *White Christmas* played on a Bakelite 78-rpm record on a gramophone. At nine years of age, I had attended a children's Christmas party with about fifteen little friends, all living in the Watooka village.

At one time, we discussed Donald Trump and Hillary Clinton, who were in the running for the election of a new US president. Then we briefly discussed Obama and previous presidents. When we got to Bill Clinton, one of the ladies chanted, "Wee-na! Wee-na!" Wiener. Oh, well.

I was still unable to convince Horace to loan me his Golden Arrow of Achievement Medal.

I arose bright and early the next morning to enjoy a walk around the Clubhouse grounds. From time to time during my stay, I had been talking to Johnnie and Andrew, the two handymen. I had been challenging Johnnie to locate a labaria snake for me, dead or alive. I would pay him G$1,000 if he could do so. He told me that they can be found at times between the river and the building, because, "Dey like to come t'ards the big house for de heat!" I did not understand this, but accepted that these poisonous snakes were around, and I was always careful with my wanderings and steps. Johnnie told me that if I found myself close to a labaria snake, had a stick, and needed to deal with it, that I should come at it straight on rather than at its side—it likes to strike sideways.

For most of the day, I planned to walk down Riverside Drive to photograph some of the houses to be included in this book. My plan was to match these historical, intriguing, and somewhat mysterious houses with the families that had lived in them, in order to tell their stories. There are about sixty old houses, almost all on stilts and constructed of greenheart wood, on both sides of Riverside Drive, which is close and parallel to the Demerara River. In my family's time, the most prestigious house had been the first one at the north end of the Drive, close to the Watooka Clubhouse. It had been the Manager's House, and was the largest of the homes, with the largest property. Sadly, the house is in great disrepair. Some of the corrugated metal roof is turned up and damaged, and the wooden building needs a serious painting both inside and out. Fortunately, it is entirely repairable, and so it may still have the opportunity for a long future. Unlike most of the other homes, it is owned by NICIL, as is the Watooka Clubhouse. The front yard, bordering the road, is impassable with overgrowth. The extensive back yard, once a tropical garden with a well-maintained lawn, is no longer such. It is now dense tropical growth all the way, about sixty-five metres, to the river.

I entered the property by the side gate, hearing the voices of many children emanating from the interior of the house, and talked briefly to a very young girl coming down the wide stairs. At the same time, I met a young woman whom I knew of but had never met: Carmen Barclay Small, a niece of Carmen Subryan. I enjoyed my chat with her, and to learn that she and her family live in the green house next door. She is the principal of St. Aidan's Elementary School across the river and is a central figure at old St. Aidan's Anglican Church. Later in the year, I would learn that she won the Teacher of the Year Award for Linden in 2016. Extremely community-minded, she was helping to supervise visiting children who were camping in the house for sporting activities being held in the area. They lived in Kwakwani on the Berbice River, 100 kilometres to the east of Linden, accessible via a dirt road. Normally this is a two-hour drive, but it can take twice as long after a good rainfall. I have been fortunate to have known members of many families that had lived in that old house, up to 1971, when Demba was nationalised. Sometime around 1951, I attended the birthday party of little Virginia Echols, which took place in the large area underneath the home, as well as out in the expansive lawn and garden. I will always recall dancing with her to Patti Page's song *Tennessee Waltz*.

I have always found the name "Riverside Drive" to be misleading. "Drive" implies motor vehicles. Yet, in my youth, there were only seven motor vehicles in Mackenzie. and our family had been fortunate to have one of them: a small, green, very-much-used Singer convertible. Usually, though, my father had driven a small red motor scooter, while my mother, brother, and I had used bicycles. "Road" would have been a more appropriate description. Now, as I commenced my walk, I saw that the start of the road at the Manager's House has posts and some minimal metal work to prevent passage by motor vehicles. They must now enter/exit Riverside Drive by a few side roads that exist along its length.

For the first five to six houses, the road was more or less a path, with grass covering the edges of it, extending from the unkempt ditches on both sides. Septic waste appeared in the ditch at the start of my walk. Horse droppings were at my feet, and a telephone wire crossed the road just above head height. By using a notepad, I was able to match/record my photos with the house civic numbers, many of which were not indicated on a house.

It was hot, and very humid. Dark rain clouds seemed to be approaching. Most of the houses were in need of painting, and while the old corrugated metal roofs still seemed to function, they probably needed to be replaced after seventy-five or more years of service. Certainly, the very large, mostly low-fenced, yards of the homes were nothing as compared to our past. Of course, some of the properties are well-maintained, but many of them have been badly neglected. In our time, a full-time gardener was assigned to every four houses. Every lawn had been perfectly cut, using well-sharpened scythes with expert ability. Flowered bushes were prevalent and well-manicured, use of flowered trellises was prevalent, tree branches were trimmed, and fruits and nuts were gathered. It had been a paradise—and it still can be.

I came to the place where the Watooka Day School, our little elementary school that never had more than fifteen students, once stood. It had been a long wooden structure that had included a small cinema. We had played out in its large playground and underneath it during rainy periods. We would chase small lizards and step on their tails, whereby they would release them for our souvenirs. This structure no longer exists, replaced with a smaller two-story school building, made of concrete blocks and painted yellow. I mounted the outside stairs and was able to talk to a young school teacher. The beautiful little children were all in uniform.

I next came to a yellow home on the east side of the road, hidden somewhat by a huge breadfruit tree. A tall man with a canister on his back was spraying the sandy front yard. "Jack" gave me permission to take a photo of himself with the house in the background. He was spraying the ground to prevent grass from growing. He told me that the owners of the house were away, and then informed me that it was the home of Basil Butcher. Wow. In his eighties, this renowned athlete was still living, and doing so in old Watooka! He had been a superb cricket player for Guyana long ago. The large breadfruits, six time bigger than a cricket ball, looked ripe enough for picking.

A few houses further, on the same side of the road, I saw a family of several adults and children under the house and on the outdoor steps and entered the gate to talk with them—the Muslim Kadir family. Next to their home, separated by a green growth-filled creek, was a blue home owned by the Luckhoo family, the old home of Major James "Jimmy" Hiscocks, whose wife, Sheila, had been a member of the well-known King lawyer family in Georgetown during the first half of the twentieth century. Their children had been Gill, Pip, and David. Across the road from this home was our old Connolly home, now a dull yellow colour, and owned by Grant and Sauda Kadir, who unfortunately were not home. The road had become less of a path and more of a road, although there were large potholes here and there.

Next door to the old Hiscocks' home is the Percivals' old home. It is in quite acceptable shape, its yard now surrounded by a wire fence, and it has lots of nice flowering trees and bushes. (I should note that in our time I cannot recall any yard fences.) An elderly lady just outside of this yard fence was raking leaves from under a sourie tree. She smiled and waved to me, so we began a discussion, and I related some details about the Percival family to her. It turned out that she was helping to maintain this property in the absence of the owner. Introducing herself as Norma Howard, she invited me across the road to her home, a blue wooden house that in our time had been inhabited by the Theo Hunte family. We sat in the spacious area under the house and talked at length. She has lived there for about fifty years, and was interested to know that our family had lived just two houses north of her, well before her time. We had much in common, and as we talked, I looked at the view of her backyard and that of what had been the Krellers' back yard so long ago, between her home and that which had been ours. We could see the dark river in between some of the high growth at the back of her yard. To exemplify the raw and wonderful variety of tropical growth, I asked her to identify for me the flora that was within our view: hibiscus, mango, breadfruit, guava, paw paw, plum. lemon, lime, malacca apple (also known as red cashew), pomegranate, avocado pear, soursop, gooseberry, bamboo, surinam cherry, sourie, and genip. The yard ground was a mix of sand and rough grass. Norma offered me some spicy channa that she was cooking upstairs, but I declined, given the excellent nourishment provided to me at the Clubhouse. She told me that the average house in Watooka would sell for approximately G$1 million, or US$50,000. For a North American, this would be very cheap and good value, given that the greenheart structure of these buildings is still very solid, the houses are very spacious, with wide verandas offering beautiful tropical views, and they sit on expansive grounds.

I was very grateful to Norma for her offering of coconut water. It was a hot and sticky day. I continued my walking journey until I reached a yellow house within a fenced property. I could easily see the river at its back, since the whole yard was quite open. A woman at the top of the stairs was watching me, and she came down to meet me at the front gate. She very kindly invited me up into her house for some respite, as she could see that I was sunburned and perspiring. Her name was Zallina Jabar. She introduced me to her sister, and together they fetched some cold coconut water and two tall fans to direct at me. From their inside veranda, I had a beautiful view of the yard below, and of the river. Incredibly, this had been the home of Sam and Yvonne Hinds during their early time in Mackenzie. Two more sisters, of a total of eight, were to arrive for a reunion on the weekend. A brother made up the baseball-nine siblings. Their father had been Abdool Jabar, who had worked in the Milling Department of Demba for much of his career, until as he had aged and taken on more lighter work, such as maintenance of the Watooka Clubhouse.

As I continued down the road, I was reaching the far end as I had known it. I passed a concrete-block single-story house that I had not known, marked "Kara Kara Masonic Hall", the old home of the golf course keeper, Campbell...and where Sam Hinds and I had briefly taken refuge, under its front door eave, when rain clouds had passed earlier in the year. The next home, at an angle to the river, had been the old home of the Walter Hutt family. A son, Dexter, continues to spend his adult life in England, where he was knighted for his outstanding work in the school system. Dexter is one of the gracious endorsers of my book *Children of Watooka*.

After our family left Watooka, five additional houses were built at the end of the road. I knew that at various times many families I had not known had lived in them: Chan, Wong, Gill, Cole, Alvarez, and Godette amongst them. By this time, I was labouring under the heat and humidity, and was ready to turn back when I heard the engine of a motor vehicle start, and walked to the gate of the fenced house to be welcomed by Steve Bovell, whom I had met earlier in the year when he had purchased two books from me. He offered to drive me back to the Clubhouse, while at the same time I met his wife Verona. They were on their way to their bakery in Wismar. I was fortunate as well because a short but strong rainfall was about to commence. Children were having great fun in the swimming pool. I enjoyed a warm lunch, and then had a shower and a brief nap before I performed another walk down and back Riverside Drive again to continue my work, this time without meeting anyone except uniformed school children.

I took a taxi over to Wismar, my first time across this one-way bridge, soon to have a toll booth. It was my first time in Wismar since 1953, when our mother took my brother and I over there with others, in the company launch *Dorabece*, to walk along the river on Wismar Main Road. We watched the active market activity on the roadside, with vendors having tables or blankets on the ground to sell their goods, mostly fruit, meat, and vegetables. (Our mother never bought the meat, since it was not protected and often covered with flies.) Women in colourful garb balanced huge baskets of goods on their heads as they walked, chatting to one another. Others knelt at the riverside, washing clothes and batting them with a small paddle. I recall a barber set up under a tree, with chickens running around him and his customer. It had always been exciting for us to make this visit, and it was exciting for me now.

The taxi took me partway up a hill in Half Mile for me to photograph the house where my friend Paula Walcott-Quintin was born and raised. Next, I paid a short visit to Carmen Subryan and her sister, Irene Adams, at Irene's home, also in Half Mile. We then went back to the road along the river, now known as Burnham Drive, and drove north for a short distance to Katabulli Creek. Just after crossing the bridge, I asked the driver to stop while I took some photos of a former home of a new friend of mine now living in Brooklyn, New York—Vashti Hinds, a former nurse. She is a good friend of Carmen Subryan, and later in this book, I will relate how her faith allowed her to overcome childhood tragedies and make a success of herself. There are several towns and villages on this side of the river, and I was unable to orientate myself. I returned to the Clubhouse to prepare for the Bauxite Century Gala Evening.

The Watooka Clubhouse has been the centre of countless celebrations, festivities, and parties, starting in early World War II. During the war, my parents and their friends used these events to relax, at a time when wartime conditions caused the men to work endless long days in tough dust and heat conditions, without much rest. *White Cliffs of Dover* and *Lili Marlene* were Vera Lynn songs that emanated from the crowded bar and banquet room, while the billiard balls knocked together under a long overhead light, struggling to pierce clouds of American Camel and Chesterfield cigarette smoke. Almost everyone smoked cigarettes then (my mother had been one of the exceptions.) Men with a British background tended to prefer pipes. Men always wore tropical suits, while the ladies wore dresses or skirts. The bartenders were busy serving hard-liquor drinks, which were more popular than beer, and they were expert with the mixing of popular bitters. The old historic British billiard table is still present, covered and tucked away in a dark corner of the banquet room. It needs work. If it could only talk.

About 100 folks attended the Gala Evening event. I had jokingly offered to serve behind the bar, allowing the only white person in the room to be serving the black attendees, thus completely reversing the situation of so long ago. How times have changed and, for sure, for the better. Lauren Parris's staff had done a marvellous job decorating the room with balloons and bunting.

Most of the people were very well-educated and were still contributing strongly to their society in many ways. Maureen Davidson, Bishop Charles Davidson's wife and a close friend of Paula Walcott-Quintin, was present. Paula, of course, attractive and professional as usual, did a remarkable job as emcee. Minister of Housing Valerie Patterson was present; she is a Lindener, and prior to becoming a Member of Parliament for Region Ten, she was CEO of the Linden Enterprise Network, a government-owned organisation dedicated to creating new and diverse businesses in the area. Carmen Subryan and her sister, Irene Adams, enjoyed the evening, as did Horace James, who deservedly wore his Golden Arrow of Achievement Award medal and was presented with a plaque for his Bauxite Century Committee leadership. Statuesque and attractive Sonia Graham, head of the local radio station, appeared in a beautiful red outfit, adding to the showcase of Linden's society. The hardworking lady staff members in their white uniforms were finally able to rest on the veranda. The best entertainment of the evening for me was watching Nicky, one of the staff members, dance hilariously. She is a gifted dancer for sure.

"Ras Como" provided superb tin-pan music for the evening. His real name is Compton Narine, and this icon is distinguished by his height and by his very long grey dreadlocks. I had a long conversation with him as he had been setting up his beautiful chromed steel drum pans. He is Guyana's leading steel-pan entertainer and is known as the country's "ambassador of the steel pan". Using his laptop computer together with his tin pans, he provides a virtuoso performance that is exceptional. He was the founder of the National Steel Orchestra and is a mentor to amateur steel-pan musicians in the country. He is often called upon to perform at major country events and when celebrities visit Guyana. On this evening, we were very fortunate to enjoy his music.

After a peaceful breakfast with Horace James, overlooking the beautiful view of the grounds and the river, I went downstairs to have a last walk on the grounds and around the extremes of the property. I met Yonette Wilson, the tall and young security guard, at her desk under the Clubhouse. Looking very trim in her tanned uniform, she invited me to walk with her around the grounds. There is now a low chain-link fence along the river for the full length of the property, about 100 metres, with a small aperture near where the old stelling used to be. This area now consists of short, rough tropical growth. We also walked on an old cement walkway in parallel with Watooka Creek, with about ten metres of tall growth, bamboo mostly, separating us from the green growth-filled creek—we could see no water. At one point she pointed out a salapenta to me in the dark shade of bamboo growth, calling it "an overgrown lizard". I was pleased that it was not a salapenter.

a snake that is not large but is poisonous. At some distance in front of the Clubhouse, on the far side of the swimming pool, Yonette invited me to pick sourie fruit that was growing abundantly on a four-metre-high tree. These are light green, soft, and about the size and shape of a small cucumber. To me they were tasteless, but she later showed me how to dip them in hot sauce for eating enjoyment. I collected enough to fill a jar full of vinegar, provided to me by the Clubhouse, to take home with me to Canada. Yonette has been army-trained and is competent with the use of pistols, rifles, and the AK-47. Later, I joined her out by the fence at the river, watching her fish. She would take some bait to place on a hook, then whirl the line around for a long cast into the river. She had two lines, and had caught two fish. All I could tell was that the fish, although about the same size, were not perai (piranha). Johnnie confirmed that he had not yet found a labaria for me.

An SUV backed up to the Clubhouse under-area, and fifteen boxes of my books were unloaded for storage in an air-conditioned room in the building. Horace James would use these to sell at various events in the future, and for sales at the Clubhouse and at the Linden Museum. Johnnie had to stop his labaria hunt to haul all the boxes upstairs. Horace then drove me to old Cockatara, near the river at a small market area, where he opened the Museum to show me around.

The assets of the Museum are owned by the Linden Town Council. Many interesting mining artefacts and documents were on display, while others remained in boxes. The large room did not appear to be visited often, and one could tell that, as for most small-town museums, even in North America, funding is scarce. Together, we reviewed a large file of old *Mackenzie Miner* newspapers, some of which I have at my home. They had all turned to an orange colour, and many issues were missing. These newspapers give an excellent view into the social and economic life that existed in this bauxite community as far back as the times of my family there. My father and his colleagues had often been profiled, quoted, and written about in the content. Later, we walked around the corner to the busy edge of the river, where food vendors were at work. Personable Horace was often greeted by many who know him.

Back at the Clubhouse, I packed my bags, said farewell to Lauren and her staff, and looked around for one last time. *Farewell, Watooka. I will be back.*

Paula and I would be driven by her godson, Kenneth Charles, who would drop her off at the airport, then take me further into Georgetown. I greatly enjoyed talking sports with Kenneth, an enthusiastic young man who is a heavy-duty equipment operator for the RUSAL bauxite operation in Aroaima. He was particularly happy that Minister Raphael Trotman had announced that bauxite workers would not now be taxed on overtime pay. Paula would return to Linden from her home in New Jersey in less than a month to help organise and to emcee the major Bauxite Century Anniversary Arch Ceremony, which would be well attended, with President David Granger present. I have not met many Guyanese expatriates who have demonstrated their love for Guyana like this special lady. She certainly deserves a medal for this.

I returned to my Georgetown lodgings, the Rainforest, to prepare for a special event the following day. It was good to see Syeada again, and this time there were three young American Peace Corps ladies staying with us. All of them are working in the health arena in Guyana, and it was of great interest to me to talk to them about their work around the country, and to discover they were friends with Rachel Ivancie, who had been removed from Linden by the Peace Corps because of a threat. I learned that, according to them, the relatively new infected-mosquito-caused Zika-virus disease is much more prevalent than the figures being reported. Some of Guyana's hospitals are so crowded that pregnant women are sleeping two to a bed, feet to head. All of these young women were enthusiastic about their work, and I could tell that their time in Guyana was very special for them.

The next morning, I attended Mass again at St. George's Cathedral, to hear Deacon Andrew Hoyte deliver his usual thunderous sermon that ensured the focused attention of everyone. Even the pigeons high up in the rafters were standing at attention, and the two horses outside on the lawn stopped munching grass! Later that morning, when I heard a steady sound of sirens, I knew that President Granger and his ladies were heading either to or from church somewhere.

Dressed in my new beige shirt jac, I appeared at the Pegasus Hotel promptly at one p.m. Sam Hinds had invited me to the annual Guyana Relief Council (GRC) luncheon, and I was looking forward to meeting some interesting people and to better understand the functions of the organisation. I was invited to sit at a front table just in front of the long head table, and sat beside George James, a friend of friends of mine who had read my book. I immediately felt comfortable in a room of distinguished scholars and businesspeople.

I was approached by a very attractive lady, wearing a white full-length dress, who introduced herself as Yvonne Hinds. Wow! I had never met her. She is the attractive head of the GRC.

One purpose of the luncheon was to raise funds for the GRC. The GRC owns and manages the Yvonne Hinds House of Hope, which takes in families who have experienced difficulty or distress, such as losing a house by fire. It has operated as a charitable function for twenty-two years and is supported by elite volunteers and by community-minded businesses such as King's Jewellers and China Trading and Manufacturing Company.

My last evening at the Rainforest was quiet and enjoyable, as Petamber Persaud dropped by for a discussion about literature and authors. He presented me with a recent small book, *Made in Guyana*, that he had written, relating to the wonders of Guyana, and also gave me a recording of his NCN-TV interview with me, as well as an interview that he had written up in the *Guyana Sunday Times*. He is a pleasant and personable man whom I value as a special friend. It was from him that I learned about another interesting Guyanese person, John Edmonston. He was a freed African slave, born in British Guiana, who taught taxidermy to Charles Darwin, and who had excited the naturalist with stories of magnificent flora and fauna in the tropical rainforest of South America, influencing Darwin to famously voyage on the *H.M.S. Beagle*. Edmonston had learned his taxidermy from Charles Waterton, an English naturalist and explorer who had written *Waterton's Wanderings in South America*, a book that also inspired Charles Darwin. Waterton spent much time in British Guiana.

Very early the following morning, I gave Syeada a farewell hug, and told her that I would continue to pray for her Jerry, who was still in Miami struggling with cancer. He can be very proud of his courageous and hardworking lady, who dearly loves and cares for him.

On the flight home, I was most fortunate to sit beside Dr. Julian Amsterdam, who is a medical director in Guyana's government, and who struck up an interesting discussion with me. A specialist in infectious diseases and in tropical medicine, he was heading for a medical conference in Toronto. I imagined how busy this man must be, given that he also has a family of five children. He was a perfect target for my questions about health in Guyana, and he listened intently to a medical story about my father, who retired in northern British Columbia in 1971 after thirty-five years with Alcan.

That winter, he and my mother travelled to California for sun, golf, and touring. My father had become seriously ill, to the extent that my pregnant wife and I were summoned to California for his impending death. At the last minute, a young doctor, experienced in tropical medicine, learned of my father's past in British Guiana, and had immediately operated to verify his theory and to save my father's life. A tropical amoeba of some kind, which had been dormant for decades in his liver, had revived to cause the illness. He and my mother lived to enjoy twenty-five wonderful years of retirement together.

Dr. Amsterdam nodded knowingly, and I was pleased that Guyana has this man and others like him to give of their knowledge and skill to help their people. We spoke about Guyana and hope for its future, perhaps represented by the following inspirational expression:

> *There is no medicine like hope, no incentive so great and no tonic so powerful as expectation of something tomorrow.*
>
> — Dr. Orison Swett Marden

HOUSES OF HISTORY—WATOOKA

Houses of history,
Houses of lore,
Speak to me,
Come to the fore.
With all of your glories,
Reveal them to me.
Tell me your stories
Hiding in thee.

As I had walked slowly down old Riverside Drive, after sixty-three years of absence, I could see the general deterioration, though certainly not total, of the old stilted houses along the pot-holed road, bordered by the aged cement drainage ditches. Many of the corrugated metal roofs were rusted and/or dirty looking, almost all the yards were fenced, with old-looking gates, and many of the houses needed painting. The large yards, for the most part, were not perfectly manicured, as I had known them as a child, and the small creeks, not really running, that passed under the road were filled with green growth, so that any contained water was hard to see.

However, the variously coloured houses surrounded by raw and widely diverse tropical growth had a certain mystical beauty that formed a compelling attraction for me. Walking along in the furnace of the day's heat, I felt alone, as residents were scarce to be seen, giving me a mistaken feeling that this was a ghost village. I thought of life there as I had known it, and wondered as to who else might have lived, strangers to me, in these simple wooden structures over the past six decades. Each of these houses has so many stories to tell. What fun it would be to sit down with each one to listen to and to discuss these stories...if the houses could only talk!

Prior to relating stories of these houses, it is important to tell the fascinating story of their beginning. In December 1913, the Aluminum Company of America, Alcoa, sent their chief engineer, Edwin Stanton Fickes, to British Guiana to examine the quantity and quality of bauxite that had been discovered there. Despite concerns about disease, particularly malaria, Fickes recommended the company seriously commence mining operations there, some 105 kilometres up the Demerara River.

In 1914, Alcoa sent George Baines Mackenzie to the area to complete further exploration, and to acquire lands containing bauxite. Alcoa formed the Demerara Bauxite Company in 1916, and also acquired Sproston's Limited, a dry goods, construction, and shipping company, to support related mining operations. By the end of 1918, Fickes completed planning the design for the town of Mackenzie on the east side of the river, named after George Mackenzie, who had recently died. The town would be composed of the bauxite plant operations, the village of Cockatara for the workers, and Watooka, in the south, for the management staff.

To ensure well-designed houses for the tropical communities, Fickes engaged the United Fruit Company, headquartered in Boston, Massachusetts, which was also doing business in British Guiana and in other Caribbean locations. Morris Knowles was the renowned planning engineer chosen from this company to design the houses.

The main reason for building the houses on tall stilts was to deter termite activity and to allow for good air flow. Each stilt was to stand upon a cement base, containing a small surrounding moat of Bunker-C oil. The houses would have extended eaves and screened windows and doors, requiring no glass. (Today the oil moats no longer exist, having been cemented over or replaced. My brother Mike recalled to me the times when we would watch ants successfully cross over the Bunker-C oil moat, martyr ants first dying in the oil to form a bridge for the rest to cross.)

Walls would consist of only one layer of wood, which was covered with an inside coat of glossy paint to inhibit insects from climbing. Fickes and Knowles would also become involved with the house planning and designs for Alcoa's bauxite operations in Moengo, Suriname, which commenced bauxite shipments in 1922. Some of the tropical housing designs for Henry Ford's rubber-producing town of Fordlandia, Brazil, which would begin building in 1927, were influenced by Knowles's work. His design of the Mackenzie houses would be cited in *Canadian Geographic Magazine*.

Much of the wood used to build the houses originated from Garvey's Mill, located not far from where the worker's homes were built on the old plantation Retrieve, in what became known as Cockatara. George Garvan Allicock, a.k.a. "Garvey", was a descendant of Robert F. Allicock, one of the first European settlers in the area, and Ann Mansfield, a free coloured woman. After the historic Paterson wood mill closed at Christianburg across the river, Garvey's grandfather opened his own mill, and ownership had been passed down to his father, and then to himself. Garvey and his men would cut giant greenheart logs from the rainforest upriver and transport them downriver to the mill. Greenheart, as I've mentioned before, is known for its resistance to rot and for its weathering capability. For this reason, the houses of Watooka have successfully endured almost a century of life. The houses in both Cockatara and in Watooka would be company-owned.

In 1914, when George B. Mackenzie, a Scotsman and geologist, arrived in the area by canoe with an Amerindian guide, he was met by Garvey's father, George Allicock. In his seventies, Mackenzie had been working for Alcoa at the mining town of Bauxite in Arkansas and was an expert on bauxite ore. The towns of Bauxite, first, and then Mackenzie, named after the Scotsman, would grow to have extraordinarily similar industrial experiences.

United States bauxite ore was first discovered in Bauxite, Arkansas, in 1887, a year prior to its discovery in British Guiana. George Baines Mackenzie was responsible for exploring and assembling the bauxite lands in this area of Arkansas, prior to 1900, well before he was assigned to do so in British Guiana. Bauxite became a mining town around 1903, when it employed more than 400 workers. As in Mackenzie later, the ore was first mined using picks and shovels.

The first shipment of bauxite ore from Mackenzie, British Guiana, was delivered in 1918 by the *S.S. Fagersand* to East St. Louis, Missouri, for processing there by Alcoa. By then, this was also the destination of bauxite ore from Bauxite, Arkansas. During World War II, more than ninety percent of the aluminium used to make Allied war planes came from these two towns. While Alcoa was importing bauxite ore from the Guianas, almost all of its own country's supply was being produced in Arkansas. Workers were Mexican, Italian, and Afro-Americans, who were segregated into three housing camps by race. For a long time, bauxite operations at Bauxite were managed by C. Lawton Rucker (1893 - 1957).

Bauxite, Arkansas, is now just a small town with a population of fewer than 500 citizens, reduced considerably from its population of over 20,000 during World War II. While bauxite ore is still mined in Arkansas, this town's history in bauxite mining is now long over. It is proud to show off the only historic house in the world made of bauxite, built in 1893 for the local doctor, and its museum, which contains a dress made of aluminium. The historic two-story wooden Rucker House can also be found there. Built in 1905, it was the home of Walter A. Rucker, the plant supervisor.

The US Sherman Anti-Trust Act, a competition law, required that Alcoa give up some of its holdings, so in 1928, the Aluminum Company of Canada, Alcan, was formed, and also given responsibility for the Demerara Bauxite Company in British Guiana. Britain then required that all bauxite ore from British Guiana be processed within its Commonwealth, so bauxite from British Guiana began to be shipped to Alcan's new aluminium smelter in northern Quebec, Canada, but not until 1936, when the alumina plant became available there.

All the houses in Mackenzie were owned by the company, and residents were assigned to them as employment required. The company also provided all the furnishings, including cane and crabwood furniture, straw mats, the kitchen woodstove and icebox, beds, linen, and much more. Residents would come and go, with some simply moving to a different house for various reasons. As decades passed, and the Guyanese population became more educated and advanced to higher positions in the bauxite mining business, the houses developed histories as homes to people representing all six races peculiar to the country.

The thought had occurred to me that, given my study, knowledge, friends, and contacts related to Watooka's past, I might be able to bring to life at least some of the stories of these houses, and of some of the interesting people who had lived in them—including of some who still do. Subsequently, I also accomplished some enjoyable research, and I hope that the reader will find the following results of interest. The photos of the houses are mostly recent, even though their condition generally has deteriorated.

#138 Riverside Drive

The Manager's House. Most likely, this is still the largest house in old Watooka, and may have been the first home constructed. It is the closest house to the Watooka Clubhouse, and is now in a state of disrepair, although it is still functional, often being used for visiting youngsters to camp in while touring, learning, or at sports competitions. Its once gardened yard, extending sixty metres to the river, is entangled with tropical growth, making it impossible to approach the riverside any more. On a positive note, the building is still capable of being restored—and should be. It is owned and managed by NICIL. Of all the homes in Watooka, it was the most prestigious, always reserved for the local Demba manager's family. This manager reported to Demba's managing director, who resided in Georgetown. Over the decades, it was also a centre for hosting prestigious guests, and for holding special tea parties, rum parties, anniversaries, and holiday and other celebrations. It could easily accommodate more than 100 guests, and double that if the area under the house was used. As mentioned earlier, as a youngster, I recall having attended the birthday party of Virginia Echols underneath the house in 1950, and having my first dance, at seven years of age, waltzing with her to Patti Page's song, *The Tennessee Waltz*.

In 1918, Vincent Roth, a surveyor and magistrate, arrived in the area that had then been known as Watuka Rocks, and noticed men constructing the original Watooka Clubhouse (not referred to as such then) for use as a bachelor's residence. Even today, at low tide, one can see rocks appearing in one area on the river off the bank near the Clubhouse. River traffic has always had to watch for these obstacles.

In 1921, Ralph Hamilton Carr, an Englishman, was appointed to be the managing director of Demba, residing in Georgetown. At that time, there would have been a plant supervisor/manager located in Mackenzie as well, but I have been unable to determine who this was. A recession for aluminium in 1921 and 1922 caused the bauxite operations to be shut down until the spring of 1923. By that time, Alcoa had sent John Samuel "Sam" Rucker, from Bauxite, Arkansas, to manage the bauxite mining and plant operations in Mackenzie. A Mr. Crabtree was the chief engineer.

Rucker and his wife, Leona, had been staff writers for the *Bauxite News* newspaper in Bauxite. In Mackenzie, they became popular central figures, who contributed strongly to the communities of Cockatara and Watooka. Leona would establish the first Girl Guide and Brownie troops in Cockatara. This couple may have been the first to have lived in the Manager's House.

In February 1932, Vincent Roth again appeared in the area, and met Rucker, Crabtree, and Fung-A-Ling, who explained the bauxite operations to him. He had seen a huge barge, *Klondyke*, at the wharf that, with a tall crane on it. It was being used to bring bauxite downriver from the mines, and then to ships that could not reach the wharf, the river having not yet been surveyed. They were anchored several miles further downriver, to be loaded from the barge. By then also, since 1928, the *R.H. Carr* steamer was being used to transport passengers and goods to and from Georgetown. This large boat had been preceded by several other steamers, such as the *Mazaruni, Puruni,* and *New Amsterdam,* and the paddle steamer *Sproston Wood.*

The Ruckers returned to Bauxite, Arkansas, in 1932, where Sam became a sheriff and would pass away in 1936. Leona would later, in 1944, commence the well-read iconic Bauxite *Pick and Shovel* newspaper there. It is interesting to note that government surveyor Vincent Roth had met Sam Rucker in Mackenzie in 1932 and, in his book *A Life In Guyana, Volume II,* referred to the workers' housing area of Mackenzie as Kokataru. At that time, he had been assigned to survey more than 160,000 hectares of land between Mackenzie and the Berbice River.

The year 1932 was a year of retrenchment for the bauxite company. Perhaps that is why the Ruckers returned to the United States. It was certainly why the Chief Medical Officer for the company, Dr. George Giglioli, was terminated after ten years' employment. He proudly presided at the opening of the Mackenzie Hospital in 1925, and his research there had set him on the road to determining that the *anopheles darlingi* mosquito carried malaria. He also determined that these mosquitoes could not survive on the brown acidic waters of the Demerara River and on its blackwater creeks... until the dust from the bauxite operations mixed with it to reduce the acidity. Giglioli and his family had lived in one of the large houses just north of the Watooka Creek, near the hospital. After his time in Mackenzie, he became the Chief Medical Officer for Davson Sugar Estates, and later was appointed to be the Chief Malariologist for the country.

Ralph Hamilton Carr died suddenly in 1926, possibly the victim of malaria and ptomaine poisoning. A blackwater fever breakout was occurring at that time. Englishman Frank B. Henderson was appointed Demba's chairman and managing director. Blakeslee Barnes, a chemical engineer expert, may have briefly followed Sam Rucker as manager of the operations at Mackenzie, but this is not clear. Certainly he was there and had been responsible for studying the possibility of establishing an alumina plant. Major R. J. Kinsey and H. J. Hendra, two Englishmen, followed as Mackenzie bauxite operation managers and would have lived in the Manager's House in sequence. Hendra would leave in 1938 to play a significant role in Alcan securing cryolite from Greenland in 1940. During that year of World War II, the Germans took over Denmark, leaving Denmark's Greenland threatened. The free world's only supply of cryolite, a necessity for the process of producing aluminium, was located at Ivigtut, Greenland. Canada and the United States worked together to rapidly protect this important commodity.

In 1938, F. Leslie Parsons became the manager at Mackenzie. He was a civil engineer (a graduate of McGill University in Montreal), had bridge-construction experience in the United States, and had led the construction of the alumina plant in Arvida, Quebec. He had been a football, rowing, and swimming star at university, and was a no-nonsense, yet considerate, man, just what was necessary to preside over the coming war-time bauxite production. At the time of his family's arrival via the *Lady Drake* (which would be torpedoed and sunk in May 1942) there were only about sixteen staff members, and in preparation for about fifty or more staff members to come for the war effort, the majority of the Watooka houses began to be built at this time. Parson's family, consisting of his wife, Kay, and children, Barbara and Jimmy, had lots of room to enjoy in the Manager's House. It had a large master bedroom and a large guest bedroom, both with en suites, and bedrooms for each of the children. Barbara, at eighty-five years, related to me many details of living in the big house, shared with their dog, Pug, and a pet turtle and armadillo. They rarely ventured out on the huge expanse of manicured lawn extending down to the river, due to the bete rouge insects and snakes prevalent there. By this time, the houses in Watooka had refrigerators. Oxley, the cook, still using an ice box at her home in Cockatara, always put her hat on to open the "cold" fridge.

Parsons was my father's boss when he had arrived in February 1940, together, later that year, with Jim G. Campbell and Norm Fraser, who would both subsequently rise to become the top executives for Demba, through to it being taken over by the government in 1971. He often rode a horse to work, while the others used motor scooters and bicycles. As a reward for his excellent results, Les Parsons was transferred to Alcan's operations in northern Quebec in 1943, to manage Saguenay Terminals Limited. This, too, was a major challenge, due to the responsibility for managing more than 100 ships used for bauxite shipping in the wartime conditions, with frequent loss of them due to German submarine activity.

H. Vance Echols was the next Demba manager to arrive, an American mining engineer who graduated from the University of New Mexico. He and his wife, Kay, contributed enormously to the community, and Echols High School, now known as Mackenzie High School, was named after the family. Two parrots, named Robert and Laura, were housed in a large cage in the expansive yard, which was maintained by Rahoman the gardener. Daughter Lisa would grow up to marry a member of the renowned Tijuana Brass Band, and Ginnie would marry an engineer, while forever retaining a particular fondness for the country of her birth. In 1950, the Echols family moved to Georgetown, where Vance took over from Frank B. Henderson as Demba's managing director. His wife, Kay, became the Girl Guide Commissioner for British Guiana.

In 1938, Harriet Jomini voyaged on the *Lady Drake* to join her husband, Harry, in Watooka. Harry was the deputy manager, reporting to Les Parsons. They left in 1946 to work at Alcan's operations in Quebec, and then returned in 1950 for a brief period when Harry took over as Demba's manager. He and his family, by then including two children, Ellen Louise and Henri, resided in the Manager's House. After a few years, the family was transferred to British Columbia, where Jomini engineered the building of hydroelectric facilities for the Kitimat Aluminum Smelter, which commenced production in 1954.

Prior to 1953, Roy Johnson took over the manager's post, and lived in the Manager's House with his second wife. (His first wife had died in the tragic torpedo sinking of the *Lady Hawkins* in January 1942, in which two other wives of Watooka engineers had also perished.) Johnson was a pioneer Canadian engineer in Mackenzie, along with my father. After a few years, he returned to Canada, and was succeeded by Norman Fraser. Jim G. Campbell assumed the managing-director position in Georgetown. Fraser and his wife, Betty, would live in the Manager's House the longest time of all its residents, until forced to move out in 1971 with the nationalisation of the company. You'll recall Fraser and my father had grown up together in Sydney, Nova Scotia, as neighbours.

The Manager's House received its first Guyanese tenants in 1971 when the dramatic business change I've mentioned several times occurred: the socialist government nationalised the Demerara Bauxite Company, after changing the area's name from Mackenzie to Linden, and replaced its Canadian-engineer leadership with two bright Guyanese PNC Party socialists. The company would be called Guybau, and Paterson A. Thompson would become the managing director, or president, in Georgetown. Reporting to him would be William Haslyn Parris, who would be the new operations manager in Linden, and who moved into the Manager's House with his wife, Cosmos, replacing Norm and Betty Fraser, who left sadly for Canada.

Parris was born on March 2, 1941, in Buxton, East Coast Demerara. Buxton still has a reputation for being a rough place to be raised in. The area had been the plantation New Orange Nassau until 1840, when it was purchased by 128 slaves who had been emancipated in 1838. They then named it after Thomas Powell Buxton, a British parliamentarian and fervent abolitionist. At that time some of the emancipated slaves were employed as indentured workers, earning very little. Accordingly, to pay the $50,000 (I'm not sure in which country's currency) cost of the plantation, they gathered their meagre savings, which consisted of a great load of coins, and used a wheelbarrow to bring the payment to the land seller.

Parris first came to be known as "brilliant" in secondary school at Queen's College, where, in 1959, he graduated as the top student in the country, winning the prestigious British Guiana Scholar Award. He graduated from the London School of Economics and commenced to teach at Queen's College in 1962. He rose rapidly to become the Chief Economist at the Bank of Guyana in 1969. As 1971 approached, President Burnham sought the advice of Parris for the best way to gain control of Demba, resulting in its nationalisation on July 15, 1971. Burnham first asked Evan Wong, Demba's most senior Guyanese engineer, to manage Guybau, but Wong declined and left the country, accurately predicting the future demise of the bauxite industry due to its takeover by the government. Parris later played a key role in nationalising the Reynold's Bauxite Company on the Berbice River, which become Bermine, and later he became the head of both companies when they were consolidated to become Guymine in 1975.

Under Parris's leadership, bauxite and alumina production reached record highs—until the latter 1970s, when results began to spiral downwards. The alumina plant in Linden was forced to close in 1981. At this time, Parris took over from Paterson Thompson as head of BIDCO, the Bauxite Industrial Development Company, which did not succeed in enhancing the industry. He became Deputy Prime Minister in 1984, responsible for planning and development, but stepped down in 1991 to become a consultant and author. At President Burnham's huge and long funeral service in 1985, Parris moved the huge attendance by playing *Goodbye My Love* on his trumpet.

Haslyn Parris died at seventy-five years of age in 2016. He had led constitutional reform, and had authored essays on his personal thoughts and on economic development. He had expressed his good sense of humour by writing two volumes of short stories, entitled *Ribald Tales of Guyana*. He was awarded the Cacique's Crown of Honour, one of the country's highest awards. Eulogies referred to him as being elevated in his meticulous work ethics, and as being humble, modest, and brilliant. *'E eat bulb!* One of these eulogies was delivered by Tommy Payne, a friend of many of us now living in Ottawa, Canada, who had grown up in Buxton with Haslyn. Tommy later became the Chief Archivist for Guyana.

I have not been able to determine with confidence who may have lived in the Manager's House, if anyone, after Parris and his family. Subsequently, though, the house was used for bauxite company meetings, and, as I've mentioned, for children from surrounding areas to camp in during sporting events.

Paterson Thompson became Guyana's representative to the United Nations for two years, 1969 to 1971. He went on to become a board member of many organisations before retiring in Barbados.

#135 Riverside Drive

When our family arrived in Watooka in 1950, this very large home was occupied by the Grimes-Graeme family. Dr. Rod Grimes-Graeme, with wife, Muriel, had arrived in 1945, a Canadian graduate of McGill University, to become Demba's chief geologist. Their son, Roddy, was a popular boy in the village and a good playmate of mine. He had a favourite guava tree near his home that he frequented. He found that if he climbed high enough, and if the timing was right, he could find enough guavas without worms (which could make one "wonderfully sick"). One time, he showed me the results of his bowel movement, revealing a mass of wriggling worms. I could only imagine as to what was going on inside his stomach, and I can still recall the look on his face when his mother administered the carbon-tetrachloride remedy.

Roddy's family moved to Montreal, Canada, where he completed his schooling before returning to Guyana. At some time around 1966 he obtained his airplane pilot's license, and in 1969 formed a partnership with Demba's former Otter pilot, Tom Wilson, to start Inair, a small charter-airplane company flying out of Ogle airport. They used a Cessna

205 until in 1970, Roddy wiped out the airplane in a crash that he survived without injury, on the very wet Ekereku dirt airstrip. They recommenced operations with a Cessna 206. Roddy continued operating this business alone after 1972, when Tom and his wife, Maureen, moved to British Columbia, Canada.

In 1969, Roddy married Elaine Maria Jardim, a daughter of a most interesting family.

Elaine Maria was born in 1945 in Antigua. Her father, John Jardim, managed Antigua Distillery Limited for eight years, and introduced the renowned Cavalier brand of rum, made from fermented molasses, in the early 1950s. Prior to Antigua, John and Olive Jardim had lived in British Guiana, where he had been prominent, working as a chartered accountant for Sproston's Limited. In 1926, he bought a large piece of land on the west bank of the Essequibo River, about thirteen kilometres south of Bartica, which he called Goldmine. This property was very close to the Wolga Estate, owned by his friend Jocelyn Matthews. Whenever they had free time, they would travel from Georgetown to their properties for enjoyment. In 1952, the Jardim family, including six children, moved back to British Guiana, where John became head of the J.P. Santos Company, a prosperous property and investment firm established much earlier by Portuguese businessman Joao Pedro Santos.

In the early 1960s, Jardim helped Peter D'Aguiar form the United Force political party with about fifty Portuguese businessmen. This party was formed to prevent Jagan's PPP from achieving power, while at the same time disagreeing with the approach being taken by Burnham's PNC. Between 1963 and 1965, while President of Georgetown's Chamber of Commerce, John Jardim submitted a proposal to the government to build a 310-kilometre road from Ituni to Lethem. He wrote, "A very important reason for the highway to Lethem is to promote the expansion of trade with Brazil... and Georgetown could serve as a free port for goods in and out of the Rio Branco and Amazonas regions of Brazil".

After her marriage to Roddy, Elaine Maria and her Jardim family would be taken by Roddy in his airplane to the Goldmine property, where Roddy and John had developed an airstrip. Like John and his family, Roddy rapidly developed a love for the area. But as time moved on, Burnham's socialist movement broke the back of private enterprise. John retired from J.P. Santos Company in 1974, and in 1977 moved with Olive to Antigua, where, according to Elaine Maria, he died of a broken heart the following year, because he was so frustrated by, and discouraged with, Burnham and his hurtful government. The riots of the early 1960s had burned down J.P. Santos Company buildings.

In 1977, Roddy and Elaine Maria sold Inair, three Cessna 206s, to Air Services Limited, and moved to Antigua. There, Roddy commenced his Yamaha sales business, with branches in St. Kitts and Nevis and in Monserrat. Elaine Maria established her popular Best of Books bookstore in St. John's. Roddy, Jr., who has the same love for the water as had his father (which began in the Watooka swimming pool), owns Aquafilms, which offers water tourism and amazing photography around Antigua. Brother John lives in England with his family. Sadly, Roddy passed away in early 2016.

Elaine Maria's oldest sister, Anne Jardim, has also had a remarkable career. Born in 1936 in British Guiana, she attended the London School of Economics before returning to her birth country. In the early 1960s, she became a political activist, and almost had her house burned down in 1964 during Georgetown rioting. In 1967, she became one of the first three women earn doctorates from the Harvard University Business School. In 1970, in Burnham's government, she became the new country's first ambassador to Venezuela, subsequently also performing this duty in Brazil and Chile. In 1973, with Margaret Hennig, she founded the School of Management at Simmons College for women in Boston, where she remained as dean with Margaret until 1997. Together, they wrote the pioneering bestseller *The Managerial Woman.*

#94 Riverside Drive

As I climbed up the front outdoor stairs to this house, I imagined the rising roar of more than 110,000 cricket fans in Karachi, Pakistan, cheering as big Basil Butcher, a Guyanese man representing the talented West Indian team, strode confidently and impressively, in his all-white uniform and protective padded armour, to the crease batting area. While he starred for the opposition offence, he nevertheless commanded huge respect from the knowledgeable crowd and from cricket followers around the world. In this event, he would score his first Test century, more than 100 runs, for the West Indies.

In wonder and amazement, I continued up the stairs to meet this renowned athlete and his gentle wife, Pamela. I had met Pamela on an earlier visit, but Basil, in the twilight of his life, had been sleeping. She and I had settled into nice conversation in the shade under the stilted house. Their expansive yard is free of grass due to the regular chemical spraying of the ground by Jack, their handyman. She had pointed to the area where she had last seen a labaria snake. A large mango tree and a large breadfruit tree were positioned at the corners of the front yard.

Now I was to meet this couple, who had been together for over fifty-five years. While age has slowed him down, of course, Basil is still big, of Amerindian and black races, handsome and impressive—the first person with aboriginal blood to don "whites" for the West Indies cricket team. Everywhere in Guyana, at the major hotels, in bars, and in homes, the sport of cricket is being watched.

Basil Fitzherbert Butcher was born in 1933 at Port Mourant in Berbice, where he was raised and learned to play cricket. Cheddi Jagan, who rose to become president of the country, was also born there. Renowned West Indies Test cricket players Joe Solomon, Roy Fredericks, John Trim, and Rohan Kanhai all came from the Berbice area. Butcher played with other Guyanese cricket superstars, such as for Clive Lloyd, Shivnarine Chanderpaul, and Lance Gibbs. Several streets in the country are named after these heroes.

Coached by former Test cricketers Clyde Walcott and Robert Christiani, and captained by Sir Frank Worrell and Sir Garfield Sobers, also former cricket stars, Butcher and Kanhai made an awesome duo of batters on the British Guiana/Guyana and West Indian teams. Rohan Kanhai became, arguably, the best cricket player in the world, being compared with Bradford and Ponsford of Australia, Hammond and Hobbs of England, Sunil Gavaskar of India, Sobers, Walcott, Weekes, and Worrell from the Caribbean islands, and Clive Lloyd of Kanhai's own country. Competing within the Caribbean from 1954 to 1972, Butcher collected 11,628 runs, averaging 49.99, including thirty-one first-class centuries, while capturing forty wickets. While playing for the West Indies, he amassed seven Test centuries, recording 3,104 runs for an average of 43.11, with 209 not out being his highest score.

Barbadian Sir Garfield "Garry" Sobers is considered to be amongst the top five cricketers in the history of the sport. Butcher and Sobers were competitors, representing their countries and teammates, when playing for the renowned West Indies teams of the 1960s. Of interest, Sobers's father, Shamont Sobers, had been a merchant seaman, a "general servant", aboard the Canadian steamship *Lady Hawkins*, the ship my mother voyaged on to marry my father in British Guiana. Four months later, on January 19, 1942, when the ship was torpedoed by German submarine U-66, seaman Sobers, thirty-four, died along with 249 others. His son, Garry, one of six children, was only five years of age. Most likely, my mother, Mary, who befriended all whom she met, had known Shamont.

Wes Arthur, who lived down the road from the Butchers, recalls the time he went to Barbados to visit a cousin who knew Garry Sobers well. Sobers was a gifted golf player, and the two cousins had been invited to follow Sobers on a round of golf. Sobers, knighted by then, had been the only person permitted to drive his golf cart onto the tee grass. One of the golf holes had been named "The Sir Garfield Sobers Hole", and was, and probably still is, 365 yards long.

In 1958, Sobers scored his maiden Test century, progressing to 365 runs, a new world record for the highest individual score in an innings. This record held until 1994, when Trinidad and Tobago's cricket star Brian Lara reached a high of 395 runs. Today, the Sir Garfield Sobers Golf Championship in Barbados is the premier amateur golf tournament in the Caribbean.

Sometime around 1962, Basil Butcher married Pamela Liverpool, who had also been born and raised in Berbice. She had been in the same class at Berbice High School as the author's close friend, Ned Blair. In 1963, Pamela suffered a miscarriage with her first pregnancy, while Basil was on tour in England with the West Indies cricket team. He received the news in the midst of a match, which caused him, deeply upset, to bat for a century of 133 runs, permitting his team to win. Subsequently, Pamela produced four healthy children.

In 1965, the Demerara Bauxite Company, Demba, hired Basil to teach cricket to the children of Mackenzie, so Basil and Pamela moved to Watooka. Around 1970, they opened a sports store in Cockatara, and Basil went on to remarkably develop cricket in the area, producing expert Guyanese cricket players. Both he and Rohan Kanhai were entered into the Berbice Cricket Hall of Fame. His son, Basil, Jr., has been a fitness coach for the US Cricket Women's team.

On one occasion, I had the opportunity to attend a Sunday Mass at the Anglican Christ The King Church with Pamela. Because my father's good friend Gordon Johnson had led the building of this church, which opened in June 1951, I had been given an opportunity to speak from the podium at the end of the service. Parishioner Gloria Britton, who had been the principal of the Mackenzie High School, then graciously drove Pamela and me over to the St. Joseph The Worker Catholic Church to meet Deacon Berchmans and some of the parishioners. My father had led the building of this church, which also opened in June 1951. Both churches face the Demerara River and are simple in design. They have floors made of large ceramic tiles, and the walls are openly louvered to the outside air, permitting some form of cooling in the tropical heat.

By far, the biggest celebration across the country is the annual Mashramani carnival, also known as "Mash". It began in Linden in 1970 to coincide with Republic Day on February 23. Two years later, in 1972, it had become so popular that it had spread to the capital city of Georgetown, and it subsequently spread to the rest of the country. Basil Butcher was chosen to be chairman of the committee in Linden that first organised the carnival. He suggested that the name of the festival be an Amerindian word, and with research help from Demba employee Allan Fiedtkou, the name Mashramani, meaning "celebration after a day's hard work", was chosen. Other members of the committee included Demba employees Jim Blackman, A.J. Seymour, Wordsworth McAndrew, and Adrian Thompson. The preliminary and main festivities include massive colourful float parades, calypso contests, steel-pan "Panarama" contests, spectacular costume competitions, masquerade bands and dancers, street dancing, and much more. Tens of thousands of Guyanese, Caribbean folks, and tourists participate in this huge event.

Just like at Mashramani, whenever Basil Butcher stepped into the crease, one could expect fireworks.

#97 Riverside Drive

This was the home of Keith and Mary Percival, two high-achieving people who lived long and remarkable lives. They arrived in Watooka in 1951 with their very young daughters Karyn and Heather. Mary was the daughter of Dr. Walter Kendall, Chief Physician of the Gravenhurst Hospital in Ontario, Canada, which specialised in tuberculosis, except while it served as a POW camp for German prisoners during World War II. Keith had been a star athlete and football player for Queen's University in Kingston, Canada. His father, Dr. Walter Percival, a Deputy Minister in Quebec, authored several technical and Quebec-history books.

During World War II, Keith was a first lieutenant aboard the Canadian minesweeper *Caraquet*, which performed duty in the dangerous North Atlantic Ocean and was present during the invasion of Normandy in 1944. Keith and Mary met on a blind date in New York City, where he was attending Columbia University studying business. Mary was there to study art, and in her later life would become one of Canada's most renowned watercolour painters. Our family still has the treasured painting she did of our Watooka home, situated across Riverside Drive from their home. Prior to meeting Keith, Mary had lost her fiancé, who died on his 23rd mission as a navigator when his bomber was destroyed over Europe.

Keith Percival became Demba's personnel manager, with 600 employees reporting to him. He oversaw many functions, including operations of the Mackenzie Constabulary, the Mackenzie Hospital, and Watooka Clubhouse. Labour relations was also a major responsibility: Keith had to personally intervene to settle the strike of 1953 by standing atop a flat railway car to speak to and pacify a large crowd of strikers. He would negotiate often with union leaders Carter and Lovell.

Mary recalled to me their wonderful time in Watooka. She had been busy with her two young children, as well as in many community activities. She was an avid golfer and enjoyed using her bamboo golf clubs to play on the primitive six-hole course. She recalled that everyone in the village knew not to put their hands on the outdoor stair railings at night to avoid small snakes. Keith told me that every month he had had to provide a stool sample to the hospital, and that his only wonder about the test result was as to what *type* of worm he had.

In 1952, a third daughter, Sandra, was born in the Mackenzie Hospital. She would grow up to establish, with her husband, Walter Kaczmarek, Canada's Mark's Work Wearhouse clothing franchise. Keith and Mary would retire early and travel extensively before settling down in the Muskoka area of Ontario, Canada.

#132 Riverside Drive

In 1928, a young man named Joshua "Jos" Whalley voyaged on a freighter ship from England to British Guiana to commence work as the accountant for the Demerara Bauxite Company at Mackenzie. His wife, Gladys, would soon follow him, in 1929, to this new and intriguing part of the world, although she took a passenger ship. They would take up residence at #132 Riverside Drive, on the river side of the road.

At that time, there were only 16 residents of Watooka, including four wives. Many of the current Watooka houses had not been built, and the Watooka Clubhouse had not been expanded. Most likely, their house did not have a civic number at that time. It would have been freshly painted.

Gladys recorded that, unlike in Georgetown, the spacious verandas were fitted with screens to keep out the mosquitoes, moths, and flying beetles that often at night could be heard banging against the screens, attracted by the light inside. Mosquito nets for beds were obligatory, and the two-inch-thick mattresses were of lumpy flock or horsehair, placed on very rusty and squeaky cup springs. The furniture was also provided by the bauxite company—English-style, but made of local crabwood. They had a maid, cook, and washerwoman, all three of whom wore prim cotton uniforms and white starched caps. There was an enormous wood stove in the kitchen that smoked, and an ice box that leaked. Ice arrived from Georgetown on the *R.H. Carr* steamer three times a week, and was delivered by "Old Foxy" using his donkey cart. Experiences relating to snakes, scorpions, perai, ants, howler monkeys, spiders, and large frogs were prevalent. The four legs of the ice box were each in a tin can containing water, to prevent ants from being mischievous. Jos had a parrot named Laura that would sit on his shoulder, and as Jos walked down Riverside Drive Laura would call out, "Left! Right! Left! Right!"

At some time in the early 1930s, the senior manager for Demba at Mackenzie was an American, a Mr. Rucker. Mrs. Leona Rucker established the first Girl Guide and Brownie Troops in Cockatara. At one time, the Whalleys took the small train from Wismar to Rockstone on the east side of the Essequibo River, a journey of about 30 kilometres. The little wood-burning engine was called *Leona*, after Mrs. Rucker. At Rockstone, there were only a few buildings. They had stayed at the Sproston's-built rustic hotel, which could accommodate twelve people, and from which they could view large Gluck Island in the distance. (Early settlers in Wismar had been German: the word "gluck" means "good luck" or "happiness".) Gladys noticed in the hotel log book that one entry was signed by Theodore Roosevelt, who had obviously visited Rockstone long before, more than twenty years earlier, probably by voyaging up the Essequibo River ,and most likely with his friend Dr. William Beebe, who was managing a tropical research laboratory downriver at Kartabo.

In October 1934, Gladys gave birth to a baby girl, Wendy, who was the second white child born in the Mackenzie Hospital. The first white baby was a girl born to the wife of a minister living across the river. Within the next year or two, the first Canadian staff would arrive to work for Demba, Jack Batzold and Jim Wright. Another girl, Margaret, would be born to the Whalleys in 1939. The family would continue to live in Watooka until near the end of the war and would always recall their early youth and first schooling under their Day School teacher, Canadian Jean Tudhope, with great fondness. So much so, that in her retirement, Wendy wrote an excellent book about her family's time in Watooka, *Bauxite, Sugar and Mud*, in which she records her following thoughts as a little girl:

> *All of my memories begin where the river flows past the wharf-like stelling where we used to swim, past the airy house on stilts where we used to live, past the hospital where I was born and the bauxite plant and office where my father used to work, and past the cricket field at Cockatara where my first world ends. Down to the city of Georgetown and out to the wide muddy sea.*
>
> *I lie in bed at night and try to imagine the universe. I tell myself: "I am in a bed in my room. My room is in my house. My house is in Mackenzie. Mackenzie is in B. G. B. G. is in South America. South America is in the world. The world is in the sky. The sky is in the universe. What is the universe in?" For a long time, this is a nightly puzzle, lying flat in the wondrous cave that is my bed draped in a tent of mosquito netting that has an ending like everything else I know has an ending, and for the life of me I cannot imagine anything that cannot be contained by something else. But at least as I lie here I know that I am rooted securely where I am, in the heart of everything that is important, and I never wonder how we got here, and I do not know that one day we will have to leave.*

The Whalley family would leave the country for Jamaica in 1944, under wartime conditions. The airplane had black curtains on its windows, blocking out the light from British Guiana, which had been their sunny paradise. Wendy Whalley later obtained degrees from McGill University, worked in a variety of interesting jobs, and was the curator of the museum in Grand Manan, New Brunswick, where she now lives.

In late 1947, senior engineer Ralph Sinke arrived in Watooka to become the assistant general manager and to live in this house. A widower, he brought with him his very young children, Ralph, Jr., and his younger sister, Gail. Ralph, raised in Three Hills, Alberta, was a mining-engineer graduate of the University of Colorado, where he had also excelled at sports. In the mid-1940s he had been the manager of the Cuyuni Gold Mine in the tropical wilderness up the Cuyuni River, at Aurora Landing, in British

Guiana. The company was headquartered in Vancouver, British Columbia. His wife, Margaret, and children had accompanied him. Margaret had acquired tuberculosis and sadly had passed away, having returned to Canada for unsuccessful medical help. Ralph then returned to British Guiana with his children to work for Demba in Watooka.

In the same month, December 1950, that our family arrived in Watooka, Ralph addressed a large group of black foremen with a motivational speech and a long poem, of which an excerpt follows:

> *Your job is important, don't think it is not,*
> *So try hard to give it the best that you've got!*
> *And don't ever think you're of little account,*
> *Remember you're part of the total amount.*
> *If they didn't need you, you wouldn't be there,*
> *So always, my lad, keep your chin in the air.*
> *A digger of ditches, mechanic or clerk…*
> *Think well of your Company, yourself and your work.*
>
> —Ralph Sinke, Sr., *Mackenzie Miner*

Molly Miller was a pretty, single Canadian lady, born in Summerland, British Columbia, working in Demba's accounting department. She arrived in Watooka prior to Rita Rosinke, another single Canadian woman, who became a Watooka School teacher in 1951. Single women shared accommodation, and were assigned a maid who did their cooking and washing. Ralph Sinke, Sr., married Molly in 1951 and, not long after, Rita married engineer Don Ourom. Ralph and Molly would produce two more children, Roy and Rick, in the next two years, children of Watooka. Stephen would arrive later, in Jamaica.

Molly used to order whole-wheat flour in bulk from Georgetown, share it with her neighbours, and store it in her fridge to prevent the weevils from getting at it. The cook made the bread. She enjoyed eating roasted breadfruit and eating the red mangoes from the tree at the side of their yard. "We used to call the screens on the windows 'meat safes' because they kept the flies outside and away from open meat in the kitchen". On occasions, she would accompany Ralph, Sr., on a rail "chigger" through the bush from the Demerara River over to Rockstone on the Essequibo River to hunt and fish. Ralph, Sr., used to love to hunt, and once shot a spotted jaguar in the bush near the village, which he had skinned and displayed in his home. Gail Sinke's godfather, as for her brother, was Dr. Basil Wong in Georgetown. He and his brother, Dr. Leslie Wong, a dentist, as youngsters in 1929, had represented British Guiana at the third World Boy Scout Jamboree in England.

A sweet and gentle girl, Gail, before she could swim, used a tyre tube around her to float in the Watooka pool. One time she got in the pool without the tube, descending quickly to the bottom of the deep end... where, fortunately, her fast-moving father rescued her. Her brother Ralph, Jr., as a result of swimming almost daily in this pool, subsequently became a swimming champion for his high school in Windsor, Canada.

In 1954, the Evan Wong family arrived in Mackenzie. The Sinke family had just left for Jamaica, so it is most likely at this time that the Wong family moved into this house. Over time, as did many families, the Wongs would live in other homes in Mackenzie. Often change would take place after the family had been away on vacation. Evan brought with him his wife, Chris, and their young children, Robert, and two babies, Linda and Jennifer. Over time, brothers Scott and Douglas would be born in Mackenzie. Evan received his early education at Queen's College at the same time as Linden Forbes Burnham. In fact, they had both been raised in Kitty, and had walked to school together. He would later obtain his engineering degree at the University of Toronto in Canada.

The Wong family would flourish in Watooka, retaining fond memories of it all through their lives. In 1970, Jennifer Wong would become Miss Guyana, attaining the semi-finals at the Miss World Pageant that November in London, England. As I've mentioned previously, very early in 1971, President Burnham held a private meeting with Evan to try to convince him to be the head of Guybau, which would be the new name of Demba when it was nationalised the following July. Evan declined, predicting accurately that Guybau would not have the capability to survive without the Canadians and with government ownership. With sadness, as for so many other Guyanese citizens, the Wongs would leave the country in 1971, having contributed significantly to the country's development and history.

At some time after the Wongs moved to another location in Mackenzie, Theo Hunte and his family moved from near our old home on the river to this larger home further north along Riverside Drive. With his wife, Louie, and daughters Helen and Pat, Hunte had arrived from Trinidad in 1947. Allan would be born in 1949. Theo would rise to become the chief accountant for Demba.

I have had the pleasure to meet the current owners of this house, Wally and Pauline Melville. They have lived there since 1982, when the Bob Wharton family moved out. Pauline was born in Berbice. Wally came from Albouystown on the East Coast with his family around 1942, at nine years of age. The family commenced to live in Christianburg while his father, Joseph, performed bauxite exploration for Demba. As he grew older, Wally became a teacher at Mackenzie High School before he began to work for Demba. Affable and very competent, he ultimately rose to become a senior manager in charge of all administration functions for the company before his retirement. Later, he became Linden's town clerk, responsible for managing all aspects of the growing town's operations.

Wally recalls rescuing a granddaughter who had encountered a yakman snake in the back yard. Green with a yellow underbody, this pretty snake is poisonous and needs to be avoided.

#126 Riverside Drive

This was the home of your author and younger brother, Mike, sons of Jack and Mary Connolly, who lived here from late 1950 until the spring of 1953. It is the home we have always remembered more than any other, for it was a paradise for us. It was all white in colour ,and at the front, on the right-hand side, there had been a two-and-a-half-metre-high concrete vat, also white, that collected water from the eaves troughs for drinking purposes. The water had to be boiled, of course, and then would be stored in bottles in the refrigerator for drinking and brushing teeth. Sometimes Demba's sanitary inspectors would put small guppy/cacabelly fish in the vat to eat mosquito larvae.

Like all the other houses, the house stood on stilts that, in turn, as I described earlier, stood on cement bases with a small moat of Bunker-C oil in them, to help prevent insects from crawling up the posts and into the house. These moats no longer exist. The spacious shady area under the house was used for play purposes, for a huge suspended cage that housed Joseph, our small parrot, for a pile of hardwood firewood used for the kitchen wood stove, and for a table where the maid washed clothes in two galvanised metal tubs.

There were two sets of stairs, including one for the kitchen where Blair, our maid, and Inez, our cook, presided. The house had two huge bedrooms, a very large living and dining room area, and a long wide veranda, where we enjoyed becoming very adept at playing table tennis, using sandpaper bats. Ceiling fans turned on some of the ceilings. I do not recall any glass windows in the house. All apertures were screened, with some windows being jalousied so that, when my brother and I ran around to close them, the torrential rain would be shut out. In these downpours, the nearby river would turn white with millions of bullet-like raindrop splashes, and nothing but a huge roar could be heard in the house with the corrugated metal roof, seen also from within, pounded upon as though at the bottom of a Guyana waterfall. There was a shower and sinks in the house, supplied with water directly from the river. If there was a rare need for hot water, it had to be boiled on the kitchen wood stove.

I have always remembered my first night trying to get to sleep, with the loud unfamiliar sounds of seemingly millions of insects, crickets and singing tree frogs celebrating the arrival of our parents and of two more children of Watooka. Later times, upon wakening early in the morning, we could hear the huge roar of red howler monkeys across the river in the rainforest.

The walls of the house were a single layer of planed greenheart wood painted with a beige or white glossy paint, purposely slippery so that insects would find it hard to climb them. Demba supplied all the rattan, bamboo, and other wood furniture. I recall several men would arrive at times with DDT tanks on their backs to spray the whole house interior. First, they would cover the furniture with sheets, and when they were finished, these same sheets, soaked with DDT, would be used for spraying the next house. After two hours or so we would be allowed back into the house. This practice had been initiated by the world-renowned malarial scientist, Dr. George Giglioli, who had been a Demba employee from 1922 to 1932.

This was the house where we would have an orange tree sprayed with heavy lead-based silver paint for a Christmas tree. We made our own paper ornaments and decorations. My mother freaked out when she opened the bread box one day to find a poisonous coral snake curled up within it. She repeated her alarm when our gallant father used an Amerindian bow and arrow to shoot a bat on their bedroom ceiling one dark evening. The bleeding victim fell on our mother, screaming in the bed, while my brother and I in the next room simulated police car sirens to let her know that help was coming (smile). I also recall struggling with serious malaria for a week in bed under my mosquito net, with two portable fans creating a soothing breeze of warm air on me. Dr. Frank Brent would come from time to time from the hospital to check on me.

Our gardener, Gobin, was a very competent and personable East Indian man who lived in Wismar and came to work every day with his bicycle, using a small boat to cross the river. He was an expert at cutting our lawn with his scythe, sharpening it frequently with a certain stone. He was also responsible for all the garden work for three other houses. Things grow so fast with the heat, rain, and humidity that he was never short of work, trimming bushes, trees, and flowers, and cleaning up fallen petals, branches, and other plant debris. He helped us to make bush huts and teepees out of troolie-palm leaves, and often took us on rainforest hikes, where he was an expert at finding us all sorts of wild fruit and sugar cane. Our expansive back yard was mostly open to the slowly flowing black river, except for a large, mature bamboo tree, which we avoided due to its snake population. Now that tree is gone, replaced with small bamboo and other tropical growth along the river side of the property. Unlike in the past, there is also a fence around the property, as is the case for most of the homes along Riverside Drive today. In our time, crime in the village was unknown.

The dark Demerara River flowed slowly past, and we used to stand on the grass at its bank, mesmerised, wondering what type of evil creatures lurked under its leisurely moving and innocent surface. We could have easily swum across the river and back but hesitated to even wade into the uninviting black water. The river had a tide, and during its ebb we would collect a blue-grey clay with which to make artefacts, hardening them over a fire. Sometimes we painted them, and if not satisfied with the result we would lob them into the river as grenades, pretending to attack an imaginary German submarine.

Our mother and we two boys each had bicycles with baskets on the front handlebars, while our father used a red scooter. We also, as I mentioned before, had one of the seven cars in Mackenzie, a well-used 1930s small green Singer convertible. Any bike in the village that had a bell and a light was considered upscale. Not for us, though. Inez and Blair also had bicycles for their daily work journey from their homes in Cockatara. Riverside Drive was a macadamised road, covered with tar that would display bubbles in the heat of the day. Wearing sandals with no socks, we would often arrive home with black big toes from popping these bubbles. After rainfalls, puddles on the road would often contain dozens of little black tadpoles.

Often, on a weekday night, many families in the village would bicycle down the road to watch the movie at the cinema in the Day School. We would ride home in the dark, and the next morning on the way to school, we would see some carnage on the road from all the bicycles the previous evening: dead frogs, snakes, crickets, beetles, etc.

Our family had returned to the country, and to Watooka, after almost seven years in Quebec, Canada, and in Texas City, Texas. My father, Jack Connolly, became the superintendent of construction and mechanical services. Over the next few years, he would report to Demba managers Vance Echols, Harry Jomini, and Roy Johnson, as they succeeded each other in the post. Jack had originally arrived as an unmarried engineer in early 1940, together with his friend Norm Fraser, previously mentioned, with whom he had grown up with in Sydney, Nova Scotia.

Jack Connolly, upon his arrival in 1940, was accommodated at the Bachelor's Quarters near the far end of Riverside Drive. Mary arrived to marry him in September 1941, after which they lived one of the homes at the south end of Riverside Drive, across the road from the river side—a typical white-painted home on stilts. On the first anniversary of their marriage, they easily accommodated more than 100 guests at this home for a celebration. This should give the reader an idea of the large size of these one floor homes. I was born in the Mackenzie Hospital in January 1943, and our family left the country four months later due to my mother's recurring malaria. Brother Mike was born in Arvida, Quebec, while our father worked at the big aluminium smelter there.

As explained previously, our family moved from British Guiana in May 1953, when my father was promoted to work on the huge project to build an aluminium smelter at Kitimat, British Columbia. Mike and I were too young to know what was going on, but we were certainly saddened to have to leave our little friends and paradise. We were tanned, and had become excellent swimmers and divers, having used the Watooka Clubhouse swimming pool almost every day of our time in Watooka. Brother Mike sported a long-sleeved jacket to hide his ringworm marks so we would have no trouble passing through the border authorities.

We have never forgotten Watooka.

#125 Riverside Drive

During our family's stay in British Guiana, from 1950 to 1953, our neighbours just to the south were the Kreller family. Fred Kreller was a self-taught, practical man who was highly respected for his mining experience and knowledge. He had worked in the mines at Val D'Or in northern Quebec in the 1930s and had subsequently helped to build the Gander Airport and a military highway in Newfoundland. Fred possessed a great sense of humour, including a hilarious repertoire of songs that was always appreciated by adults and children alike. His wife, Lynn, a great North American baseball fan, was the perfect partner for him, always chuckling as Fred would tell "Bobby and Bessie" stories to his children and their friends, while we sat on his knee and around him. Their oldest child, Judy, was my brother's age, and we often played together. Bobby enjoyed riding his tricycle and listening intently to his father's great storytelling. Lynn would accompany my mother to chaperone all of us at the Clubhouse swimming pool in the hot afternoons. A short palm tree grew in their back yard, possibly a troolie palm tree, with reachable broad leaves, which were perfect for our own backyard building projects, intended to simulate primitive native housing structures. Like our family, the Krellers would leave in the late spring of 1953 to live in the new Alcan aluminium smelter town of Kitimat, British Columbia.

Immediately after they left, Bob and May Hendry's family upgraded to this home, after having lived south down the road, not on the river. Bob Hendry was from northern Ontario in Canada, and had a mechanical-engineering degree from Queen's University in Kingston. In British Guiana, the family had first lived at isolated Ituni before moving to Watooka. The children, Jan and Jim, had been taught not to go near the river to avoid snakes and creepy critters. Our adjoining backyards shared the massive bamboo tree at the riverside that was inhabited by snakes. Often our gardener, Gobin, would encounter these snakes as he cut the grass with his scythe anywhere near the tree. On one occasion, Gobin killed a three-foot-long coral snake to show the Hendry children and my brother and me. This one had red, white, and black bands, meaning it was venomous. (There are many types of banded coral snakes, and not all of them can deliver poison.)

Jan and Jim recall that the Costa family lived almost directly across the street from them, the first black family live in Watooka. With daughters Jacqueline and Caroline, they would have moved into the home that the Percival family had vacated in 1954 for Keith to work for Alcan in England.

Somewhat younger, the Hendry children were admired by us. They were active and enthusiastic as playmates, and they had learned to swim in a shorter time than any of the children in Watooka—for a unique reason. My brother and I had learned to swim at the shallow end of the warm pool, swimming underwater at first. Bob Hendry had taught Jan and Jim to swim by tossing them in off the diving board, ready of course to rescue them if necessary. They became excellent swimmers—they could swim like fish. Ultimately, they would move to Jamaica and then back to Canada. Jan and Jim live in Sudbury, Ontario, where Jan was a professor at Laurentian University and Jim continues to head his own successful business.

Norma Howard is the current owner of this large house. While her husband, Doug, who was an accountant for the bauxite operations, passed away some time ago, Norma has lived here for more than fifty years and is well-known and liked within the community. As you'll recall from my earlier account, I first met her raking leaves under a sourie tree at the side of the road. Smiling, she rescued me from the heat by welcoming me to join her underneath her home, to sit and drink coconut water. This I was fortunate to experience on two hot afternoon occasions. As we chatted about past life in Watooka, we watched the dark river flow slowly past, uninviting but beautiful, with the bright sun shining on the still jungle on the far side.

I could recall times, more than sixty-three years ago, when I had played under that same house. I could see the backyard of our old house next door, and admired in wonder the prolific tropical growth present in her yard. The huge bamboo tree I've mentioned, which once shared the boundary at the river of the two homes, was long gone. I asked her to list for me the various flora: hibiscus, sourie, breadfruit, guava, paw paw, plum, lemon, lime, pomegranate, avocado pear, soursop, genip, gooseberry, and young bamboo. Even Suriname cherry, used by Norma to make tea. She could open a food market! On a later occasion, surrounded by its inviting spicy smell, I could almost taste the channa she was cooking upstairs in her kitchen. I was so grateful to meet this special lady and look forward to meeting her again.

#116 Riverside Drive

In October 1962, a young man from Canada arrived to live in Watooka as a new employee of Demba. Although his career would include many interesting and exciting times, perhaps nothing would match that of his next ten years in British Guiana.

At only twenty-six years of age, Tom Wilson was given the above house, along with a cook, maid, and gardener. Literally speaking, he would have the best overall view of the company's, and of the country's, industrial and political events. Tom, whom I've already written about briefly, was to be the first, and only, airplane pilot-mechanic employee for Demba, and a very popular one. Decades later, Guyanese-women friends of mine would recall, with a twinkle in their eyes, when this tall, lanky, and rugged man came into the mail room to pick up his mail. The local Guyanese folks would refer to Tom as "Willow" because of his height and demeanour.

De Havilland management had recommended Tom for the job because the requirement was not just for a pilot, but for someone engineer-qualified to maintain Demba's first new airplane, an eleven-seater De Havilland Otter DCH-3 amphibian. The airplane would be used extensively to serve Demba management, families, and VIPs and for other purposes, such as river gauging. A small metal hangar had been built at the lonely Mackenzie airstrip to house the airplane.

In April 1963, the longest general strike of workers in any country up to that that time commenced in British Guiana. Supplies were drying up in Watooka, and with violence happening nearby, Demba managers Norm Fraser and Bob Rosane called upon Tom Wilson to evacuate most of the non-essential staff workers, and the wives and children of Watooka families by flying them to Paramaribo, the capital city of Suriname. Tom once read to me his flight book, which recorded, over a period of eight weeks, forty-three return trips to Paramaribo, allowing for 347 Watooka residents to have been evacuated. During the strike, Tom also evacuated Lady Baden Powell to Trinidad—she had been visiting the Girl Guide community in the country. The following year, when the *Son Chapman* boat was tragically bombed a few kilometres north of Wismar, Tom used the Otter to help in the recovery process.

In September 1967, another interesting single person would arrive to work for Demba and live in Watooka, in her home adjacent to the north end of the Watooka School. She was Maureen Dunn, who had a strong ability for office administration. In 1962, she been transferred from Alcan's Northern Aluminum Works in Birmingham, England, to Alcanigeria at Port Harcourt in Nigeria. In 1967, Nigeria erupted into civil war, also known as the Biafran War, and the dangerous situation forced Alcan to evacuate its thirteen expatriate families there, as well as Maureen. She was one of the last to go, helping plant manager Bill Coles close the office. It would not be the last time that she would be called upon to evacuate a major Alcan office.

In 1968, the mining area of Mackenzie, including Watooka, was opened for fast access to/from Georgetown by the construction of a paved road from Soesdyke, about thirty-two kilometres south of Georgetown, near the Atkinson Field airport by the river, south for about seventy-three kilometres. The previous year, a bridge had been built across the river at Mackenzie. Soon, the number of vehicles in Mackenzie and across the river would greatly increase. Later that year, Tom Wilson would be laid off from work, because Demba no longer had a need for the Otter on a permanent basis. No longer would Watooka's residents be able to watch Tom glide his Otter down on the river just north of the farm and step-taxi it, producing parallel rooster tails, to the dock at the Watooka Clubhouse.

Tom and Maureen would marry and, as mentioned earlier in this narrative, Tom would form a partnership in Georgetown to commence the charter airplane company Inair. Maureen would then work for Managing Director Jim G. Campbell, and with him would close down the office when the company was nationalised in 1971. In fact, she did all the stenography and typing work required for Demba during the nationalisation negotiations with the government. She and Tom moved to Vancouver, Canada, where Tom would complete fifty years of flying, surviving seven plane crashes.

Before 1970, a young Guyanese engineer and his wife moved into this residence. Never would it have occurred to them or to their fellow citizens that in fewer than twenty-five years they would become the country's prime minister and first lady: Sam and Yvonne Hinds.

As mentioned earlier in my writing, Sam Hinds obtained a Demba Scholarship to study chemical engineering at the University of New Brunswick in Fredericton, New Brunswick, Canada. He arrived in Montreal from British Guiana in late August 1963. An Alcan representative enthusiastically welcomed the young man, and took him to Sears Canada to buy clothing. He later said he had "never had spent so much money in his life at one time" (courtesy of Alcan). He subsequently took a train to Fredericton, where he was met by Dick Grant, dean of student housing. Dick and his family would become long-time friends of Sam. Given his extremely personable manner, Sam quickly became popular with his student colleagues and with university staff. In the summers, he worked in Canada for Alcan and also for Irving Oil—except for the summer of 1965, when he returned to his country to work for Demba. While there, he attended a social event at the residence of Canada's High Commissioner to British Guiana, who would keep this post through the country's independence in 1966. Supposedly, Sam's invitation was somehow connected to the fact that the High Commissioner and his wife were from New Brunswick. At this event he was captivated by a beautiful young woman, born in Bartica, who was actively preparing in Georgetown for her own future: Yvonne. They would correspond until Sam's graduation in engineering and return to Guyana.

High Commissioner Milton Fowler Gregg

Canada's High Commissioner to British Guiana/Guyana during this period was Milton Fowler Gregg, a remarkable person, as was his wife, Erica Deichman Gregg. Milton had been a World War I hero, winning the Victoria Cross. Subsequently, he was a soldier, Member of Parliament, cabinet minister, academic, and diplomat. From 1944 to 1947, he was President of the University of New Brunswick. Erica and her first husband, had become renowned for their outstanding pottery, made in New Brunswick, for which she earned the Order of Canada. When her then-husband died, she married Milton Gregg. Youthful Sam and Yvonne Hinds certainly started out in good company!

At university, Sam obtained academic results that placed him at or near the top of his class. He was fondly referred to as "Skin Man" due to the perfect complexion of his skin. He returned to his country in the summer of 1967, married Yvonne that December, and commenced living in Watooka and working for Demba as a chemical engineer, under the tutorship of Harry Whicher in the chemical laboratory. Bob Rosane, Clarence London, Norm Fraser, and Art Love would also become influential mentors.

Just prior to leaving Canada in 1967, Sam may have visited Expo '67 in Montreal, where Guyana shared a pavilion with Barbados. Millie the Guyanese parrot had been featured there, but only for a short period of time. The parrot, really a macaw, had been present for several weeks before the opening, and from the construction workers had learned foul language in both of Canada's official languages. Officials had been greatly embarrassed and disturbed upon the opening of the pavilion when the parrot let forth major bilingual cussing. The parrot was immediately deported. (That Christmas, the government produced four postage stamps, featuring, not the Virgin Mary or Santa Claus, but Millie! This caused the Catholic Church to raise a fuss about celebrating a cussing parrot.)

(There is a just *possibly* apocryphal corollary to this story. It has been said that Father Bernard Darke in Georgetown had two male parrots who were used to saying the rosary twice a day. When Millie was returned to Guyana, to correct her ways she was put into the cage with Father Darke's two parrots. One of the male parrots squawked, "Wow, our prayers have been answered!" Millie stopped swearing, the two parrots stopped saying the rosary, and they all lived happily ever after.)

Currently, #116 Riverside Drive is occupied by Zallina Jabar. On two occasions, she rescued me from the heat of the day, welcoming me into her house, placing two powerful fans facing me, and providing me with cold coconut water and interesting discussion. She has eight sisters and one brother. Zallina taught at the Watooka School. I was pleased to hear from her that she could walk down Riverside Drive at midnight with no fear of crime. Her father, as I've mentioned previously, was Abdool Jabar, who worked in Demba's Milling Department. As he aged, he took on lighter work, performing maintenance duties at the Watooka Clubhouse.

In my time, our gardener had also been an East Indian man, Gobin, who, according to Zallina, reported to a man named Rahoman. Gardeners then were each responsible for maintaining the expansive yards of four houses. Lawns were cut using scythes, so professionally utilised that modern motorised equipment could do no better. Anita, Zallina's 24-year-old daughter, toured me around the large yard. One could not see the nearby small creek, due to it being buried in overgrown greenery, but it came naturally to keep one's distance, since it appeared risky and has been known to be a home to caiman and snakes. Oranges, sourie, coconuts, correa, sugar cane, jamoo and guava were all pointed out to me. Off the thick grass and mucky river bank, one could catch a variety of fish: lau lau, haimura, yaru, lukanani, butter fish, snapper, trout, and piranha, to mention a few.

#87 Riverside Drive

Welesley "Wes" and Valerie Arthur moved into this house some time in 1970. Of Scottish lineage, he worked at accounting for Demba: many years earlier, commencing in 1927, his father had worked there as a self-taught stenographer. Wes had been "spared the benefits of a modern education", yet was able to advance at work via hard work and self-learning. Born in Georgetown, he grew up mostly in Mackenzie. Valerie was born to the Portuguese Pires family, also in Georgetown. Wes and his family lived at 777 Powell Crescent in Cockatara, where he grew up. Decades later, in 1984, he wrote the following poem/song about his memories of his family home there:

A Long Time Ago

I lived in a house once, a long time ago.
'Twas numbered with sevens, yes three in a row.
The walls they were wooden, had windows all 'round
and it stood on strong pillars eight feet above ground.
And out back behind it was the large levelled field
Where we boys played at cricket and in turn we would yield
So that girls could play rounders, we ran races and all,
And sometimes we had a great tug-o-war haul.
That was a long time ago… a very long time ago.

Out front was a river, Demerara by name,
where the freighters would go by, all their cargoes the same,
bauxite ore they were hauling up Canada way
and they are still doing it to this very day.
And all 'round this house grew a hibiscus hedge.
There were flowery pots on a low, wooden ledge.
The hot sun was shaded by a large mango tree,
and a blossoming citrus was a real joy to see.
That was a long time ago…a very long time ago.

From boyhood to manhood I lived at that place.
From school days to work days that was my base.
I learned to swim in the river out front
and my first car was parked there when the full day was done.
Then one Easter day very close to sundown
a sweet girl walked by, she was not from our town,
and Cupid, he hit me not a moment too soon.
And we have been married for many a moon.
That was a long time ago… a very long time ago.

Oh, I lived in a house once where I had so much fun
in a place far away 'neath the tropical sun.
Yes, I lived in a house once, I remember it so
In a place far away, a long time ago.
Yes, I lived in a house once, I remember it so,
in a place far away… a very long time ago.

Not far down and on the same side of the road lived Mike and Kathy Rogers. Mike had graduated from Howard University, majoring in chemistry, and then joined Demba in 1966. He rose to become the chief chemist in the bauxite lab and was on Demba's last labour-negotiating team before nationalisation. He and Kathy moved to Alberta, Canada, where he is the president of Alberta Technology and Science Inc. The company has provided water-system consulting to all the many oil companies there. Mike's sister, Joy, is married to former Guyanese cricket star Lance Gibbs.

After fewer than two years living in this house, Wes and Valerie decided in 1971 to leave Guyana to work at Alcan's headquarters in Montreal. Demba was being nationalised, and Wes did not want to work for a company that he felt would not survive under government leadership. Five years later, they moved to Bracebridge, Ontario, where Wes worked at Alcan's Wire and Cable Plant until his retirement.

Andrew and Colleen Forsythe are the current owners and occupants of this house. On two occasions I was rescued from the heat of my walk down Riverside Drive to enjoy shandy, coconut water, and interesting discussion with these fine people. I first met Colleen, an attractive homemaker who seemed to be always smiling, while she was in the shade under the house with her beautiful grandchildren. Andrew is a handsome, part Amerindian, man who is also very personable. He told me that he was a long-distance runner in his youth, winning the 5,000-metre competition in Guyana six years in a row. He had been the head of the PPP for this region, Region 10, for some time. I could not recall who had lived in this house, situated not on the river side, during our family's time.

#84 Riverside Drive

This large house is situated directly across the road from the Manager's House. I could not obtain its civic number. The road here is currently in poor shape, and there are gates on the road that prevent vehicle passage at this point, unlike in the distant past. It is the only house in old Watooka that has a guard house, just inside the gate. Lady guards are situated there around the clock—it must be difficult to assume this post without a fan in the heat! The home is currently a hostel for women nurses, who walk in their white uniforms every day to and from the hospital. The old tennis court sits in poor repair just to the north of the home, and youth shoot baskets at a dilapidated basketball hoop with no net. Clothes are hung to dry in the heat every day around the outside of the house.

This is also a storied house, one of the first ones built in old Watooka. I will restrict its tale to one occupant, whose story from the past will give the reader a sample of life at that time. In 1962, a thirty-two-year-old Canadian schoolteacher from Arvida, Quebec, arrived in Georgetown. Lilly Syvaoja was amazed at the heat and at the sights along the road from the airport into Georgetown, as she was transported in a rainstorm via a leaky old

Volkswagen bus (minus window wipers). Demba's pilot, Tom Wilson, later flew her in the Otter to Mackenzie, where she had commenced to teach at the Watooka Day School under the principalship of Charlotte MacLean. A single woman, she lived in the house opposite the Manager's House, which was then occupied by Norm Fraser and his family. Her housemate was another Canadian teacher from New Brunswick, Cathy Arsenault. Other teachers had resided in the home, as would be the case in the future.

Some of Lilly's interesting memories, both written to me and found in her book *Lilly's Travels,* are as follows:

> *Edna, a lovely woman, was our cook and maid. Our houses were on stilts, and she lived in a room under the house. She had to move out temporarily because termites were eating her ceiling (that was my bedroom floor). There was a fan on our sitting room ceiling and Cathy and I had one in our bedrooms. They are a real blessing as it was so hot! Our house was comfortably furnished, and we had an electric fridge and stove in the kitchen. And cockroaches! Our phone number was 395. There was not a pane of glass in the windows... everything was screened. Each bedroom in each house had one large cupboard with a light burning in it all the time. It is the only way to keep clothes dry. Each kitchen had a little cupboard with a light burning in it... to keep coffee, sugar, and salt dry. This was a very humid climate.*
>
> *Mackenzie was infested with lizards up to one foot in length. We had sunshine every day, with a daily downpour that started suddenly and ended just as quickly. There was no twilight, as it gets dark quickly. No one paid cash money for anything here. Everything was charged until the end of the month, when all the bills were deducted from your paycheque. At the Watooka School, there were two ceiling fans in each classroom. The classrooms were screened on the sides and when it rained canvas blinds could be pulled down. Each classroom had a drinking fountain but it was so hot! And everything was rusty... thumb tacks, scissors, paper clips, and paper cutters.*

Sometimes, we went into the bush to attend BBQs. Jeeps and Land Rovers had to be used as cars had difficulty getting through. You should have seen the condition of the cars in Mackenzie. They were real rusty wrecks!

The trains from the bauxite mines practically passed under my bedroom window. What a racket they made! Several times I would awaken during a night and think that I was in the middle of a war. These trains pulled thirty to fifty cars, and when a train stopped the cars bumped into each other and the noise was unbelievable. At school, it was not possible to teach when a train went by.

When I had first come to Mackenzie, I had regularly walked past a certain house on the way to school to hear someone say "Hi!" to me. I could never see who was saying this, but I had always returned the salutation. It had taken me months to realise that the greeter had been a friendly parrot.

While living in the house, Lilly experienced a plant strike and, in 1964, the Wismar Massacre. She was always been comforted because of the nearby guards across the road at the Manager's House.

During her two years in Watooka, Lilly dated British engineer Bill Reilly. It wasn't until 1982 that she would locate him again. They married and spent some years at his banana plantation in the Cayman Islands before residing at other locations, finally retiring in England. During her lifetime, Lilly has lived in and/or visited more than fifty countries.

#61 Riverside Drive

This large and long house is set at an angle to the river. It, too, has had an interesting history. In 1954, Walter Hutt, his second wife, Doreen, and their two children, Melanie and Dexter, a Guyanese family with a multiracial heritage, arrived from Georgetown to settle at this location. Over the next eight years, six more Watooka "mudheads" would be added to the family. Walter became the Superintendent of Stores for Demba. He and his brother, Percy, had been merchant seamen. Walter had been scheduled to work on the last voyage of the Saguenay Terminals Ltd. ship *Proteus* but, in order to spend time with his mother, exchanged the posting with Percy, who then perished when the ship sank in the fall of 1941.

Young Dexter used to enjoy riding his Hopper bicycle on Riverside Drive, particularly when he could hold onto his father's shoulder while he rode his BSA motorbike. He also recalled caddying for a lady golfer who would give him a tip every time she swore. "My hopes always rose as she lined up for her next shot!"

According to Dexter:

I will never forget the hooter... the company's ship-like blast that sounded at regular intervals and could be heard throughout Mackenzie. It regulated the lives of all of us... workers, parents and children. Its blast sounded at quarter to six in the morning to wake the workers, at ten to seven to let them know that they should have left for work, at seven to signal the start of the working day, at eleven a.m. to mark the start of the lunch break, at twelve-fifteen to start the journey back, at twelve-thirty to start afternoon work, and at four-thirty to indicate the end of the working day. It also sounded at quarter to six in the evening. Parents would tell their children to "be sure to be home by the hooter".

At midnight on New Year's Eve, we would listen out for the several blasts of the hooter... the company's way of ringing in the New Year. I often wondered what would happen if the hooter broke down. But, it never did.

I chased the many butterflies in our garden around with my butterfly net, with limited success, until I learned the trick of putting overripe bananas out on a shelf that I balanced between the branches of a small tree in the garden. The butterflies that alighted on the fruit would fly off in a slow, almost drunken state, and then I would pounce with my net. I learned to remove each butterfly carefully from my net, apply one or two drops of methylated spirits until it was still, and then use a pin to mount it on a white cardboard sheet, with its colourful wings spread out.

I remember wandering about everywhere without shoes, never mind socks!

After schooling at Watooka School, Dexter greatly enjoyed his time at the Mackenzie High School in Cockatara, with its high-quality and competitive British education system. Discipline was enforced by the use of a cane that "did the trick". All of this influenced him to become a teacher in England, where he excelled in this profession. In 1988, he became the head of the inner-city poor-performing Ninestiles School in Birmingham and turned it around to become an example-setting high performer. He continued to do so with other schools, using his "Behaviour for Learning" and moral-suasion disciplinary approaches, and in 2004 was knighted by Prime Minister Tony Blair to join what has been called the "UK Guyanese Mafia", which includes renowned Guyanese people who have excelled in Britain, such as Valerie Amos, who was Leader of the House of Lords, and many others. Sir Dexter Hutt later formed his own consulting company, was made a commissioner on the Commission for Racial Equality, and is on the board of the Birmingham City Symphony Orchestra. He has come a long way from being barefoot in Watooka!

Harry Whicher, his wife, Joyce, and four children, Carl, Ken, Sandi, and Cecilia, arrived from Arvida, Quebec, to live in this house in 1961. Harry served as the head chemical engineer, and the family formed an integral part of the community until their departure in 1969. Joyce became prominent in Girl Guide leadership in the country, and Harry would encourage a young academic achiever in Georgetown to accept a Demba Scholarship. That young man later became an engineer who worked for Harry: Sam Hinds. At the swimming pool, Harry's daughter, Sandi, used to jump from the high diving board onto the lower one, and then into the water. "I only missed the lower board once!"

In late May 1964, the Whichers used their house to protect an East Indian family from the violent Wismar Massacre that had occurred across the river. Joyce Whicher related:

> *Ram, an East Indian living with his family in Wismar, who had been a guide for us on a Land Rover expedition, had swam across the river, and surfaced at our dock in Watooka wild-eyed and dripping, to beg for our ballahoo. He, his wife, and their two children had escaped from their burning house and fled into the jungle across the river from us. Our two boys, alone at home, had quickly given him two paddles and some food. That evening, our Afro-Guyanese cook, Wilhelmina, with no discrimination, cooked a meal for us and for our refugees, including Harry's East Indian secretary, whom he had rescued from his office. They all stayed with us that night. That evening,*

we went into our boy's room to find them sound asleep, their faces innocent and vulnerable. Between their beds was a small table and on it, carefully laid out within easy reach, was one BB gun (with a crooked barrel) and two machetes, handles toward each table for quick defence in case of need. When I kissed those precious children, they did not even stir.

Joyce and members of her family returned to Guyana on several occasions over the decades to re-live their fond memories of the past. As I write, she is still alive. in her mid-nineties, in Wiarton, Ontario. Harry passed away many years ago, but not before writing *Rhymes and Notes of an Industrial Chemist*, a book about chemistry and chemists, supplemented with his poetry.

The house is currently owned by Nicholas Chuck-A-Sang, a relatively young professional and entrepreneur. One morning in Georgetown, I ventured over to his Dutch Bottle Cafe on North Street to meet with him. I was impressed by his personal demeanour and the simplicity of his office. We talked about this house in Watooka, and I learned that he rents it out for short periods. It is large, furnished, and has an expansive view of the river scene.

Nicholas is a petroleum engineer and petroleum geologist by training. He told me that he was working as a consultant to oil interests in the Essequibo region, where oil has been recently found in huge quantities off the Guyana coast. Subsequently, in the fall of 2017, he was appointed to be the deputy director of the government's new Petroleum Department, which reports to the Ministry of Natural Resources. With respect to the promising and exciting new oil find, the department will be responsible for formulating, developing, implementing, and evaluating policies that will promote and sustain a vibrant petroleum sector in Guyana.

Nicholas's sister, Renata Chuck-A-Sang, is also an achiever. At one time she was President of the Tourism and Hospitality Association of Guyana. Now she is the Commissioner for the Women and Gender Equality Commission for the country.

#59 Riverside Drive

From 1951 to 1953, this house was occupied by Joe and Doreen Janco, who had no children at that time. Joe was from Saskatchewan, Canada, the oldest boy in a family of twelve children. He was an expert in mineral and ore drilling. Doreen was part-Portuguese, born in British Guiana. For some reason, their home was not built on stilts. It was the last one at that time on the river side of the road. They were the first occupants.

Joe was working for Boyles Brothers Drilling Company (Britain), doing contract drilling for Demba. He was always seen driving a Jeep, and then a Land Rover, as his duties required him to be mostly in the field doing drilling and obtaining information for mapping purposes. He spent much of his time living in bush camps. He was particularly proud of the results that he achieved in training Guyanese foremen and workers in drilling work. He was well-respected for his professional skill, and popular for his relationships with people. Janco is a German name.

Doreen was the daughter of Neville and Olga Schuler. Her father, a German, was an optometrist in Georgetown until the family moved to New Amsterdam, where he managed Schuler's Optometry. Doreen was the secretary to Royal Bank Manager Vivian Sharpe in Georgetown when she met Joe. Her mother, Olga, was the sister of John Fernandes, who, starting in the 1940s with a small shipping company, built what today is one of Guyana's largest group of businesses, employing more than 1,000 people. John Fernandes Limited is a wholly-owned family business that controls Bounty Farm Limited, JPS Trading Inc., Fairfield Investments Limited, Fernandes Holdings Limited, and JP Santos and Company Limited.

In 1962, the company lost its buildings at the wharf at the end of Water Street in Georgetown due to riot-caused fire. After the country's independence in 1966, the company was fortunate to escape nationalisation, unlike Bookers and Sproston's. John's three sons, John, Bonnie, and Chris, took turns managing the company after their father. Chris is the current chairman. He is married to Desiree Yip, who was born in Mackenzie a few months after my birth there. The business has always been interested in the development of Guyana and is known for its charitable generosity.

The Jancos were close friends with my parents, and later with my brother Mike and myself. Doreen recently told me that she may have as many as fifty-six cousins. One of them is Tommy Fernandes, who was the pilot of one of the airplanes that ambushed on the Port Kaituma airstrip during the Jonestown massacre event. He survived. Another cousin, Terry Ferreira, bicycled from Kaieteur Falls in Guyana all the way to Niagara Falls, Canada, in 1996. This journey of more than 12,000 kilometres required almost seven months. When he slept in his tent, he always tied a string from his toe to his bicycle.

Give me my people's company and I am most happy
Give me my country's spirit, give me my people's outlook,
and I am boss in anything I choose.

— Terry Ferreira

The Jancos left British Guiana in 1953 for Vancouver, British Columbia, Canada, where Joe would continue to work for Boyles Brothers Drilling Company and would become well known for his professional work in removing a massive obstacle to shipping at Seymour Narrows, between Vancouver Island and the British Columbia mainland near Campbell River.

This obstacle was an underground mountain with two fang-like peaks just below the surface of the water. More than 120 ships had sunk there over the years. Much expert drilling, some never experimented with before, was required from Joe in order for explosives to be planted. The resulting explosion was one of the largest non-nuclear ones in world history, making a success of the project. During the time leading up to this event, children Meg and Mark were born to the Jancos.

In 1970, Doreen convinced Joe to establish his own drilling-consulting business, which proved to be successful, allowing them to live and work in South Africa, North Rhodesia, and North America. They retired in Phoenix, Arizona, where Joe and my brother, Mike, a metallurgical engineer, used to travel together to visit old mines and to share their geological expertise.

Just north of the Jancos, also on the river, lived Mike Ideman and his wife. He was an American engineer working for Demba who loved to hunt and explore in the rainforest. Part of the underside of their house was enclosed to make a large room where Mike kept native artefacts and others relating to his rainforest travels. I can recall a boa-constrictor snake skin on his wall that was more than six metres in length. His house was always a great museum place for us youngsters to visit. He also had a spider monkey for a pet.

At some time in the early 1950s, Mike had, according to him, pioneered the first vehicle trail through the forest, from Atkinson Field south to Mackenzie, in his Willys Jeep. Later, in 1955, while with Caesar Gorinsky, Frank Lawson, and others at a rum shop in Georgetown, he bet US$1,000, a considerable sum then, that he could drive his jeep from Georgetown, over the Rupununi cattle trail, to Boa Vista in Brazil. Caesar Gorinsky and his wife, Eleanor, a daughter of the original pioneering Melville family, were managing the Good Hope Ranch in the Rupununi...where Ideman, Lawson, and their guide, Gonzales, would rest for a week upon their successful arrival.

The Rupununi cattle trail began building the Rupununi Development Company in 1921, and it was completed in 1930. It covers almost 200 kilometres from the Yakaburi Savannah on the Berbice River south to Annai in the Rupununi. The trail allowed thousands of cattle to be moved to the markets in Georgetown every year from the large ranches in the Rupununi, such as Good Hope, Dadawana, Pirara, and a few others. At the time, there were about 35,000 cattle being raised in the southern savannahs. The trail crossed both the Demerara and Essequibo rivers. The trail closed in 1953, as beef could then be flown from the Rupununi to Georgetown. Ideman would drive his little expedition through the rainforest from Georgetown down to Mackenzie, to meet the old cattle trail near there at the mouth of Arakara Creek. He estimated that the trip of about 280 kilometres would take about seven days.

The expedition proceeded, and things went as expected until they had travelled past Ituni, where the tropical growth slowed them down. When they got to Cannister Falls up the Demerara River, the jeep slipped into seven feet of water. Once the jeep had been rescued, Ideman's mechanical skill got it functioning again. They had to build bridges across creeks, and finally after more than two weeks, they had to abandon the jeep and call for an airdrop of supplies. Meanwhile, they had set off two explosives in water to kill fish to eat. According to Frank Lawson, it was faster to walk than to drive the jeep anyway. They finally walked into the Surama Amerindian village, where they borrowed two ponies to get them to the open Rupununi Savannah and the village of Annai. Eventually they got to the Good Hope Ranch. Pioneer rancher Ben Hart at the Pirara Ranch retrieved and bought the jeep. They never made it to Boa Vista, and it is not clear if the bet was ever paid.

Courtesy: Dmitri Allicock
Watooka Creek Bridge

This structure was built around 1920 in the very early days of Mackenzie. The Watooka Creek then was one of dark water, a natural border to separate the staff village of Watooka from the bauxite plant and the workers' village of Cockatara. In the photo above, the view is looking south, and one can see the Watooka Clubhouse on the far right. For approximately three and a half decades, there was a small hut on the right (north) end of the bridge that housed a constabulary guard around the clock.

At the beginning, there may have been only one car in Mackenzie, driven by the plant manager. Even by 1950, there were only seven vehicles in the area. The traffic on this bridge, aside from pedestrians, would have been mostly bicycles and small motorbikes or scooters. People not living in Watooka were not permitted to cross the bridge south unless their pass indicated they were a servant, gardener, or property maintenance worker. I'm not sure if the residents of Watooka had to present a pass; they were relatively few, so the guards most likely would recognise them—and, of course, they were white. The bridge really did not serve as much of a barrier to anyone who wanted to enter Watooka. Like all members of Demba's constabulary, the guard did not carry a gun. His only weapon might have been a baton. Although I know of no such instances, an intruder could easily have entered the village from anywhere along the river or along the east/south side of the area. They could have crossed the creek easily by other means. Bush traders used to park their small boats next to backyards of houses to peddle their wares: bows and arrows, native craftwork, parrots, monkeys, turtles, etc. Today, it is interesting to note, that there is much more physical security apparent than ever before. Unlike during my childhood, almost every single property is now fenced with a gate.

During our family's time, one could stand on the bridge and clearly see down to the mouth of the creek, where it entered the Demerara River, less than 300 metres away. Demba's boats *Dorabece* and *Polaris* were docked just below the bridge. In his old age, Keith Percival, Demba's personnel manager in the early 1950s, told me that the guardhouse and pass requirement at the bridge were discontinued around 1954. Once the road to Georgetown was completed in the late 1960s, allowing for increased vehicle traffic, another, larger road structure over-the-creek was built just 100 metres east of the old bridge, to handle this traffic along with bauxite ore and logging trucks. It is not clear when the Watooka Bridge was destroyed.

Today, sadly, the creek water cannot be seen, due to bamboo and other dense tropical growth. Perhaps it is just as well, as for many the bridge would serve as a negative symbol of the racial discrimination that existed in the country and in Mackenzie in the past.

HOUSES OF HISTORY—
CHRISTIANBURG, COCKATARA, WISMAR, AND GEORGETOWN

Abandoned and forgotten houses often hide the greatest stories.
— Mehmet Murat Ildan

As I mentioned earlier, Cockatara was part of Mackenzie: the village for the, mostly black, workers of the Demerara Bauxite Company, Demba. When the village was first built, some of the homes had to share outdoor toilet facilities. The houses were constructed of durable greenheart wood, and raised on stilts. They were considerably smaller than the houses built for the staff in Watooka. They had the same corrugated metal roofs, and their walls were similarly made of a single layer of horizontal wood boards, painted on the outside and on the inside. Yet they were still of a higher quality than what most people in other areas of the country had the time, except for some areas of Georgetown.

The houses across the river in Christianburg and in Wismar did not form part of Mackenzie and were not maintained by Demba. Hence, the houses in these villages were, in most cases, similar to those in most of the rest of the country: lower quality, often shacks, often unpainted, on stilts and not on stilts, and placed in an unplanned manner. There were no water, electricity, or septic-system facilities.

Little is known about the early German settlers who probably gave Wismar its name. Germans were amongst the very early explorers of northwestern South America. In the early sixteenth century, the Welser family, German bankers, acquired colonial rights in the province of Venezuela. Their primary goal was to find the lost city of El Dorado. Adventurer Ambrosius Ehringer commenced a search, and was the European founder of Maracaibo in 1539. Other German explorers also failed to find El Dorado. The Welser family called their colony "Little Venice", and 4,000 slaves were brought there to work on plantations. Many of them, together with their German masters, died of disease and from attacks by natives. Germans also settled in other areas of the Caribbean, as well as in Suriname, starting around 1650. By the end of the eighteenth century, a significant percentage of the white European population in Suriname were German. Many Suriname plantations and people's surnames today have German names. Around 1839, a small religious group of Rhinelanders and Wurtenbergers, some from the old city of Wismar in northern Germany, settled on the west bank 105 kilometres up the Demerara River. The historic city of Wismar in Germany obtained its name from a nearby creek, there named Wyssemara. The plantation Christianburg was named after its initial European owner, Dutchman Christian Finet.

My purpose for this chapter is the same as for the previous chapter, but focused on the houses and people of different nearby villages and, in one case, of Georgetown. In 1970, these villages and others would together form the town of Linden. The houses depicted and storied here are not abandoned, and not forgotten. For the most part, multiple families and/or others have lived in these homes, and somewhere in our world those folks who lived in them recall them with special memories and with great fondness. In my childhood, I had had no idea what life was like in the areas outside of Watooka. Now that I am fortunate enough to know many people who grew up around me, it is important and exciting for me to tell some of their deserving stories. They are interesting and form true history.

Lot 1, Section C, Christianburg

At some time in the late 1940s, this house was owned by Sam and Winifred Hinds (not related to former President/Prime Minister Sam Hinds). They had two children, Vashti, and her younger brother, David. I am fortunate to know Vashti, who now lives in Brooklyn, New York. She has strong memories back to three years of age. Their house was separated from the river by a dirt road and was close to, just north of, Katabulli Creek and its bridge. It was served by a wooden outhouse "with a full-moon" opening on the front door. Drinking water, "the coolest and purest", was drawn from the creek in a clay goblet, and a metal pail was used to haul water for other purposes. Winifred would wash clothes by kneeling at the riverside, using Sunlight soap and beating the clothes with a short paddle. A wood stove was used to cook in the upstairs kitchen, while a metal-lined stove was used under the house for baking. There were three bedrooms, with one of them rented out to a young couple. There were many trees in the yard representing the abundant tropical growth: rubber, papaya, mango, avocado, malacca apple, lime, and guava.

While Vashti was born in Buxton on the East Coast, David was born in the Christianburg house. Generally, babies born on that side of the river were born at home with midwife help, since the small hospital across the river was for Demba employees. The hospital would not turn away seriously ill people from anywhere, however, and the few doctors at that time were known to travel outside of Mackenzie to provide medical help. Like many other families, the Hinds practiced their religion seriously, and for them that meant the nearby Adventist Church.

Carmen Barclay Subryan's grandfather, George Garvan Allicock, a.k.a. "Uncle Garvey", lived in the house on stilts next door. His wood mill served the whole area. Many of the wood boards used to build the houses in Mackenzie came from Garvey's Mill. At times, he could be seen building coffins under the peach tree in his yard.

Vashti had an industrious Aunt Orpah, who was a widow taking care of her grandchildren. In those days, Demba's workers went to work at the mines and in the plant very early in the morning. Their wives, in the meantime, would prepare their lunches, and Aunt Orpah would collect them, to transport them to central areas and to the mine-train track scooters for the men to eat at their 11 a.m. lunch period. Demba paid her to do this, but since she was only paid once per month, she had to supplement her income with other work. She sold bananas, ground cocoa beans and rolled them into chocolate sticks (for hot cocoa), and sold cassava bread made with yucca flour farina. She would sweeten it with stewed coconut in the middle.

One day in 1950, Vashti travelled with a family adult friend to New Amsterdam, on the far side of the Berbice River, for a short visit. Her father had given her twelve cents. She bought five mangoes for eight cents and kept the rest. Her visit was interrupted and she was taken home immediately, where she found out why.

One recent morning in July, prior to going to work, her father Sam had attended church, and had sung a song that included two of the following refrains:

Thy way not mine, O Lord,
However dark it be.
Lead me by thine own hand,
Choose thou the path for me.

Hold thou my cup of life,
With joy or sorrow fill.
As best to thee may seem,
Choose thou my good and ill.

The Lord would choose Sam's path very quickly. He was a carpenter and had been working every day across the river to help build the new cinema in Cockatara. The same morning Vashti went to New Amsterdam, he set out to row his ballahoo across the river, in the usual morning river fog. At the same time and at low tide, the bauxite ship *London Mariner* had grounded on a sand bar. Revving its engines, the ship caused wave action that tipped Sam into the water, to tragically be drowned. It was no consolation that ships would no longer be permitted to leave the wharf in conditions of fog.

Vashti returned home to find her mother still crying, and offered her the four cents she had saved to try and console her. The accident would have been seen from the house if not for two large "whitey" trees that blocked the view.

After the loss of her husband, Winifred purchased two cows. With no fence, they would wander everywhere munching grass. When pregnant, they would return home, and Vashti would milk them every morning before going to school. One Sunday morning, having given birth to a calf in a field, a cow plodded over to the church to call the attention of the family and others to the fact she had completed her feat and needed attention.

By 1964, Winifred had remarried, and Vashti found herself, at twenty years of age, in Trinidad, studying to be a nurse. Her brother, David, was also attending school there. Winifred had been in Georgetown and was travelling home on the *Son Chapman* passenger launch. Just after leaving the village of Hooridia, about 23 kilometres downriver from Christianburg, the launch exploded, sabotaged by a bomb. Forty-three Afro-Guianese men, women, and children died, more than half of the people on board. Sadly, Winifred was not among the survivors.

Pilot Tom Wilson landed his Otter airplane, with Demba Manager Norm Fraser and senior military officials on board, near where the launch had sunk. Floating bodies were being temporarily tied to trees while rescue and recovery continued. Tom watched one large lady's body suddenly appear on the water's surface from below. A dredge that had been working nearby moved over to the area of the tragedy to be helpful.

Vashti was a close friend to the Caryll family of seven children. Sadly, their mother also died in the event. The youngest member of the family, 18-month-old Stephen, is now the head surgeon of the Brooklyn General Hospital in New York. He often travels back to Guyana, to other Caribbean countries, and to South Africa to provide voluntary medical service. Vashti has worked in the nursing field for more than fifty years: both are achievers despite great adversity. She, Stephen, and other family members attended the fiftieth-anniversary commemoration of this tragic event, held in old Cockatara in 2014. Vashti's memories of her youth up the Demerara River are wonderfully related in her book *School Daze and Beyond*.

> *In life, a person will come and go from many homes. We may leave a house, a town, a room, but that does not mean those places leave us. Once entered, we never entirely depart the homes we make for ourselves in the world. They follow us, like shadows, we come upon them again, waiting for us in the mist.*
>
> — Ari Berk

Just behind Vashti's house, further from the river, lived the Mosely family, with no road to their home. They used a path to get past the Hinds' home to access the road along the river. Lillian "Dot" Mosely recalls living there as a five-year-old child during the latter part of World War II. Her very small eyes looked like dots to her father, and she has been called Dot ever since.

She remembers the day when an Amerindian woman killed a fourteen-foot water camoodie. The woman turned the snake over on its back, and called for many nearby children to come and see it and touch a foot upon the snake's stomach. By doing this, according to the woman, the child would in the future always be able to see a snake before the snake would see the child.

My mother, at times, fondly mentioned to me the wonderful, and very large, nurse known as "Horsey", who cared for her and myself at the Mackenzie Hospital upon my birth in January 1943. Dot, born three years earlier than me, later grew up to know "Horsey", a.k.a. Nurse Melbourne. "She was a big woman", Dot recalled, "and if any of the men visitors to the hospital gave their women a hard time, she would grab the man by the neck and throw him out!"

After two years or so, Dot and her family moved back over to Cockatara, to a home on Potaro Road near the home in which she had been born. Later in her life, she was in Georgetown and had scheduled herself to travel to Mackenzie on that same fateful day that the *Son Chapman* was bombed. Fortunately, when she had arrived at the stelling she found that her transport had just departed. Disappointed and only three minutes late, she could see the rolling wake behind the southbound boat.

Lot 2, Section C, Christianburg

This house goes back a long way into the history of the area. At one time it was owned by Margaret Blackman, a single mother with two children. She was later joined by George Garvan "Garvey" Allicock, renowned in the region. He was a great-grandson of Robert Frederick Allicock, a Scotsman who was one of the first white settlers in the area, arriving in 1769. R.F. Allicock established a flourishing sugar-production operation at plantation Retrieve on the east side of the river. Subsequently, he also developed a thriving timber business. Retrieve had previously been known as Noitgedacht, and had been owned by Dutch settlers. Allicock would sire nine offspring, one by Hannah Simon, an Amerindian woman, and eight by Ann Mansfield, a free coloured woman.

Garvey inherited his timber mill in Retrieve from his grandfather and father and, like other Allicock families, lived in a modest wooden house nearby. Over the years, he obtained his timber from along the river and from tributary creek areas, with two workers and with his two young sons. Rafts were used to transport the timber, much of which was greenheart, which had to be secured to the sides of the rafts because this timber is so dense that it will sink in water. Not only did he supply boards for much of the building of the Cockatara and Watooka houses, he also supplied wood to fire up the turbines operated by the Demerara Bauxite Company. Prior to moving across the river to Christianburg, he was married for some time to Arabella Stoll, who delivered seven children before dying after her final childbirth.

Allicock family members are still well-known in the Linden area, in Guyana, and as expatriates. Hon. Sydney Allicock is Guyana's Minister of Indigenous People's Affairs. Ricardo Allicock is Jamaica's ambassador to Japan. Aubrey Allicock is an opera star in the United States. Dmitri Allicock is well known for his poetry and writings about the area of Linden.

Carmen Barclay Subryan, also related, whom I mentioned previously (and promised to write more about) is a special friend of mine for whom I have an admiring respect. Garvey Allicock having been her grandfather, she lived in the old Retrieve area for the first decade of her life, and then attended Mackenzie High School, where she was a star netball player and an academic achiever. Ultimately she obtained a Ph.D. at Howard University, where she spent her career as a professor in English and writing. She has authored several books, including *Blackwater People,* which provides an excellent history of her birth area and of her Allicock family. Living now in Maryland, US, she returns regularly to Guyana to provide help and mentoring to Linden school children. One of her latest projects is to obtain funds to support fifteen-year-old Linden athlete Deshanna Skeete, who in October 2017 won a Gold Medal at the South American Games in Chile in the 400-metre race.

Carmen has referred to herself as "the backwater woman who will never cease to get enough taste of the black water".

#52 Constabulary Compound, Cockatara

The Demerara Bauxite Company ensured the security of its operations and of its workers with its own police force, known as the Constabulary. It functioned primarily in Cockatara and Watooka. Prior to and during our family's time there, constables used bicycles, some scooters, and horses for mobility. They were unarmed. As a child, I watched the annual mounted police equestrian show with fascination. In addition to having exceptional riding ability, the police riders could also use lances and pistols with great skill. Playing musical chairs using horses was always popular, and at times hilarious. For the most part, constables were black. Their leader was white and reported to Demba's personnel manager. In 1957, the head of the Constabulary became, for the first time ever, a black person, an exceptional man: Inspector John Leyland Blair. Assumption of this post permitted him to become a member of Demba's privileged "staff".

Inspector John Blair moved into the house located at #52 Constabulary Compound in Cockatara with his wife, Olive, and seven children, Ned, Brenda, Leyland, Newton, Barnett, Elaine, and Cheryl. Eldest daughter Daphne would stay as a nurse in New Amsterdam, and a ninth child, Olive, would be born the following year in Mackenzie. Given the father's police responsibilities with the British Guiana Police Force, the family moved several times, from Georgetown to Fort Wellington to New Amsterdam

John Blair was raised in Hopetown in West Coast Berbice, and formally trained to be a police inspector at Scotland Yard in England. His wife, Olive Hamilton, also born and raised in Hopetown, was trained as a seamstress. John and Olive married in 1936—the largest wedding ever held in the village.

For the next sixteen years after their arrival in Mackenzie, this home would reverberate with the liveliness of this close and remarkable family. The three-bedroom home contained the boys in bunk beds in one room and the girls similarly ensconced in another one. Not for one instant did they consider themselves poor. The children flourished, fully involved in school, church, athletics, and other community activities. Mother Olive, who lived for her children, excelled in the home, cooking, baking, and making dresses for the girls and shirts for the boys. Her children fondly remember accompanying her to the market on Saturdays, her main social event outside of the house, to gather food for the following week. About seventy-five other constables and their families also lived in the police compound. Some of the Blair family neighbours were the Adams, Drake, Farley, and Freso families.

Prior to going to Mackenzie, John Blair was the most sought-after first-aid instructor in the country. In 1950, he trained at Halifax, Nova Scotia, to become a Class One St. John Ambulance Brigade Instructor. Back in his country, his signature courses in first aid were highly pursued by nurses, police, and civilians in the Demerara and Berbice regions. Many of his students became instructors themselves. At the Annual First Aid Competition held in Georgetown, Inspector Blair's team from the Mackenzie Constabulary won the coveted first-place award for three consecutive years, 1957, 1958, and 1959. Once, John saved a drowning child in the Demerara

River near Ituni. He was a Group Scout Master, and formed the first 4H Club in Mackenzie.

The family proved that they had room for yet another child in their home temporarily during the period of unrest following the bombing of the *Son Chapman* in 1964. A young East Indian girl who lived in Wismar and attended school in Mackenzie was sheltered and protected by the Blair family until the racial disturbance had quieted down.

Thanks to Mom and Dad, all the Blair children were healthy, as well as handsome or beautiful. Elaine became a model in Mackenzie and in Georgetown. Leyland, aka "Flash", with Ned's coaching became Guyana's sprint champion, never losing a race. One year, at the Texaco Athletic Games in Trinidad, he placed third in the 200-yard race behind American Olympians Charlie Mays and Mel Pender. Ned taught at Mackenzie Primary School, and later became a supervisor with Demba. Four of his siblings also worked for Demba.

Sadly, John died prematurely in 1966 and, over time, all family members moved to Canada and to the United States. Engrained with the principled values taught them by their special parents, all of the Blair family siblings and their offspring have achieved remarkable success with their lives. Educated at British and North American universities such as Oxford, Harvard, Rutgers, McGill, Howard, the University of Virginia and others, they have assumed posts such as member of the bar of the Supreme Court of the United States and director of project management within the architecture department at Georgetown University. They have been awarded numerous awards for a huge variety of community services. One has performed as a fashion model in Europe, the US, and the Caribbean, and been a TV commercial star. One grandchild attended the University of St. Petersburg in Moscow and is fluent in the Russian language. Another was a triple-jump champion for all of the Catholic high schools in the state of Virginia.

Blair family members give back to Guyana in various ways. Brenda Blair, for example, returns annually to Linden to host a soccer tournament for children, while donating uniforms and equipment. All siblings are contributing members to Guyanese organisations in the areas in which they live. Olive is an anesthesiologist in Gaffney, South Carolina, Barnet is a gifted musician, Cheryl is a lawyer for the Federal government in Washington

D.C., and Daphne is retired after thirty-three years as a head nurse at the Veterans Hospital in East Orange, New Jersey. Leyland obtained an MBA in Engineering Management at Farleigh Dickenson University in New Jersey, and later worked on unmanned air vehicles for Lockheed Martin. Newton, an architect director, has designed buildings and facilities for Georgetown University in Washington D.C. for more than four decades. Remarkably, the marriages of all the original nine siblings remain intact. Ned Blair, who will be given tribute later in my writing, has been instrumental in my writing of this book.

Mother Olive Blair, beloved matriarch of the family, twice named a Distinguished Mother by GUYAID in Washington, DC, passed away at ninety-six years in 2015.

Courtesy: Dmitri Allicock
#61 First Street, Silvertown

As the operations of the bauxite company expanded, particularly with the opening of the alumina plant in 1961, Demba had to build several thousand more houses to accommodate the increase in workers. One of the housing areas, adjacent to Wismar, was Silvertown. Here, Demba built prefabricated homes, made entirely of aluminium except for the floors and stairs. These homes became luminous in the sunlight, and hence the area became known as Silvertown. Most of these simple homes were subsequently replaced. The nearby area called Silver City obtained its name for similar reasons.

The house shown above was built by Stanley Allicock (1920 -2000). Initially he, his wife, Enez, and their children lived on Henderson Road in Cockatara in a Demba-supplied home. Three of the boys were given Russian first names because their birth times coincided with the cold war, Guyana's socialist path was dominating the news, and Stanley thought that it would be a good break in tradition.

In 1959, Stanley began to build a house across the river in Silvertown. He first had to tear down the old all-aluminium house there, and every spare moment afterwards he crossed the river to work on a new home, the one that can be seen above. He first fenced the property, using wallaba wood from nearby Hamilton's Mill and cement purchased in bags from Demba. Greenheart and wallaba wood were hauled to the house lot by donkey carts. It was the first house in Silvertown to have its own septic system.

The family moved into their new home in 1963, just prior to two terrible years of rioting in the area, including the Wismar Massacre in 1964, when the family had to temporarily vacate their home. While several hundred homes were destroyed by fire, their home, by luck and good neighbours, survived. The houses in front of their home had all been burned down, so the Allicocks could see the river. Stanley worked forty-seven years for Demba as a diesel mechanic. Enez continues to live in the house

Stanley and Enez produced seven children, all of whom cherish their beloved parents and their special home. I am fortunate to be a friend of one of them, Dmitri, who lives with his wife, Evadney, and their two children in Florida. He is well-known for his fondness for the area of his birth, and has written innumerable stories, history, and poems related to it. He has had his DNA analysed, and found he has Dutch, British, African, and Amerindian ancestry.

I have read over 100 of his poems, and I choose this one for the reader:

*Gentleness means recognizing that the world around us is
fragile, especially other people. It is recognizing our own capacity to do
harm and choosing instead to be tender, soft-spoken, soft-hearted
and careful. When we are gentle we touch the world in ways
that protect and preserve it.*

*Being gentle doesn't mean being weak; gentleness can be
firm, even powerful. To behave in a gentle manner requires that we stay
centred in our own values and strength—that we are active rather
than reactive. Coming from this centre, a gentle word or touch can channel
our energy into healing or making peace.*

**Courtesy: Tom Wilson
#201 Main Road, Silvertown**

This was the home of Peter and Dolories Haynes. They had seven sons and three daughters. Peter was a Demba employee for many years, with unique responsibilities. Wearing an all-white Captain's uniform, he was the pilot of Demba's *Dorabece* and *Polaris* high-speed motor boats. These boats, instead of the much bigger and slower-moving passenger boat *R.H. Carr*, were used to make fast trips to Georgetown, and for local river destinations.

Often, these boats were used to tour guests around the area and for the pleasure travel of Watooka residents. Peter was also responsible for the maintenance of these boats, which sometimes had been lifted up nose-first at the Watooka Creek bridge for scrubbing and painting work.

When Tom Wilson and Demba's Otter airplane arrived in 1962, use of these boats became much less, so Peter became Tom's right hand man, helping to maintain the Otter and its hangar at the airstrip.

Courtesy: *Kaieteur News*

#48 Blue Mountain Road, Richmond Hill

As Mackenzie expanded with the growth of bauxite production and with the introduction of the alumina plant in 1961, various areas of housing were developed around Cockatara and Watooka. The area east and above Watooka became known as Richmond Hill, where large houses on expansive properties were built. Generally, senior bauxite plant managers lived here. The photo above shows the remains of a beautiful house and surrounding property that were the object of arson in Richmond Hill in 2014. At the time, it was owned by Dunstan Barrow and his family, who were mostly living in Georgetown. Barrow had taken over from Haslyn Parris as the local manager of bauxite operations. As I had walked around the sad quiet remains with Tyrone Peters, I couldn't help but think about the good times that families with children had enjoyed here. A donkey was slowly munching grass near the very large guardhouse inside the tall rusted gates.

One of the first families to live in this house, if not the first, was that of Clarence and Cicely London. Clarence was one of Demba's first Guianese engineers. He had risen from poverty, had excelled at school, and had won a Demba Scholarship to obtain a mechanical-engineering degree at Howard University in Washington, DC. He commenced work for Demba in the late 1950s and married Cicely five years later. They initially lived in Watooka, where Cicely delivered daughters Ayesha and Yollanda. The family subsequently moved into the above property.

During his retirement in Costa Rica, I became a distant friend of Clarence, and we communicated extensively prior to his passing in 2015. He provided me with more 100 pages of his memories, and related to me his interesting genealogical ties to early slavery in British Guiana.

Around 1800, a youngster was born somewhere in West Africa. Enduring horrible conditions, he was brutally and forcibly transported to the colony soon-to-be British Guiana in South America and held as a slave during the prime of his youth. By dint of hard work and/or outstanding leadership qualities, he achieved the position of headman among his fellow slaves, becoming what was known as a slave driver. Initially, he could neither read nor write English, the language of the country. It appears that he may have become a member of the London Missionary Society (LMS), an ardent abolitionist group along the coast, east of Georgetown and west of the Berbice River.

At one time, the young slave driver either took the name Jupiter London on his own, or was baptised into Christianity with that name. He may have been one of the five deacons appointed by LMS Reverend John Smith in 1817 for his congregation at the plantation Le Resouvenir. One of those deacons was a London, a slave from plantation Beterhope.

The LMS sent its first missionary, John Wray, to British Guiana in 1808. Governor Murray and slave owners were apprehensive about and wary of this action, because they did not want the slaves to become educated or given any special status whatsoever. At the time, there were about 80,000 people in the country, 75,000 being slaves, 2,500 being free slaves, and 2,500 being the ruling class, mostly slave owners. Regardless of the apprehension felt about their purpose by others, the LMS missionaries made progress, converting many slaves to Christianity and teaching them that every man should be equal under God.

In 1823, as mentioned before, more than 10,000 slaves erupted into the biggest slave uprising of those times. The revolt started on plantation Success, and spread to more than fifty other plantations. More than 225 slaves were killed by the military and others, and Reverend John Smith, accused of inciting the resurrection, was jailed and sentenced to death.

Unfortunately, he died in jail just prior to the arrival of the decision by the British government that lifted his death penalty.

Just over a decade later, in 1834, slavery was abolished in British Guiana, and Jupiter London was freed. Slaves were given token monetary reparations and symbolic plots of land as part of the 1838 emancipation agreement. Jupiter and seven other freed slaves acquired the abandoned plantation Inverness on the west coast of Berbice, and Jupiter also acquired the nearby plantation Jose for himself. Jupiter married Phoebe, probably born into slavery, and they produced four sons. Christian Jupiter, one of them, later sired Christian Ebenezer, who, in turn, sired Christian Nathaniel— Clarence London's father. In their time, all of the "Christian" men were experts in the making of sugar. Sugar cane from plantation Jose was converted to syrup by crushing it in an animal- or man-driven mill and then boiling the juice in large, open copper pots. The molasses produced was taken to the Bath Sugar Estate and refined into sugar using pan-boiling techniques. The Londons were all well-known for their pan-boiling skill. From this lineage, Clarence on his own jumped out of the old world to become an educated and talented engineer in modern times with Demba.

Clarence would rise to become the head of the large alumina plant, which had more 3,000 employees. In 1976, he was reprimanded by the government for his "attitude" and told he must attend the government's socialism indoctrination program to overcome this impediment. He was also admonished for not having read books authored by the prime minister. Sadly, despite having risen out of poverty, demonstrated high scholarship as a youngster in Cockatara, become a professional engineer abroad, and returned to rise to the highest ranks of his company, Clarence handed in his resignation. He also resigned as chairman of the board of governors for the Mackenzie High School. Together with his family, he left for a successful future in Jamaica, Canada, and Costa Rica. A veritable "family of the soil" forced to find a different earth, they were allowed to take only G$155 out of the country.

Courtesy: Dmitri Allicock
Arvida Road, Cockatara

The house shown above was one of very many built by Demba for worker families. While small, these houses were still better than those of most families in British Guiana. They were owned by the company, and the tenants were chosen and managed by company officials. Initially, they were painted white. This house was occupied by the family of Mr. Joseph "Joe" Solomon, who worked for Demba in the Power House. There were hundreds of houses like these, and they all shared communal outhouses.

The partially shown house on the left was the home of Manly Binning (1899-1986) and his family. A descendant of early settlers in the area, with a Dutch mother and a mixed-race father, he was born at Wiri Bisiri above Malali Falls on the Demerara River. His father owned a timber grant there. After attending Queens College in Georgetown, he married Gloria Millicent Smith, with whom he had ten children. As there is at least fifteen years between the oldest and youngest children, they did not all live in the home at the same time, but in those days, it was quite normal for large families to fill these houses. Manly was a highly respected man who spent much time researching his family's ancestry. Initially he worked for Sproston's, and then joined Demba to work on steam engines. Later he worked in the Power House, and subsequently in the Machine Shop, where he became a foreman. He was known for his ability to fix anything, and could be seen at home repairing appliances. At work, he converted an old steam engine into a pile driver that he had called the "Lord Manly". His daughter Deanna remembered him to me as being "very focused and collected". My father knew and respected this man. Beloved by his family, and everyone, he was buried in Christiansburg, where he had been born.

Courtesy: Debbie Roza-Mercier
#150 Watooka Road

This large house, situated close to the hospital, was home to several doctors and their families. Most likely Dr. George Giglioli and his family were the first tenants, when the hospital opened under his direction in 1925. By the late 1940s, Canadian Dr. Frank Brent lived in this home, employed by Demba as the chief medical officer. At some time during the early 1950s, Dr. Brent, his wife, and their daughter, Barbara, returned to Canada, while Dr. Charlie Roza assumed the post of Chief Medical Officer.

Dr. Roza was born in Berbice, of Portuguese descent, and studied medicine at the University of Edinburgh in the UK. He returned to the country of his birth to work at Georgetown's Mercy Hospital. After his first wife died in an accident, he married Beverley Bunbury, a nurse, and a descendent of the well-known Bunbury business families in Georgetown. Around 1950 they arrived in Mackenzie for him to work for Demba, bringing babies Patrick and Carole with them. Margot and Robert would be born in Mackenzie shortly after.

Dr. Roza became renowned in the area in the interior of the country for his dedication to his profession, for his selflessness, and for his ability to handle almost every medical situation possible. My parents greatly enjoyed their friendship with Charlie and Beverley, as did the whole community, regardless of race. The Charlie Roza Nursing School would later be established in Mackenzie in his honour.

A shocking event occurred in the Mackenzie area in the mid-summer of 1961. Two young children playing near the forest in Wismar heard the cries of a baby. They summoned adults, who discovered a baby left to die on an anthill in the forest. Quickly, the bitten baby, an East Indian girl, was transported across the river for emergency attention by Dr. Roza, who saved her life. The baby was about eight days of age. After an unsuccessful search for any parent, the Roza family adopted the beautiful baby.

The Roza family moved to England in 1972. This was a sad event for them, but the violent times and the socialist government, together with the nationalisation of Dr. Roza's employer, all contributed to this decision. Debbie was ten years of age. His daughter Margot informed me that Dr. Roza was so disheartened at leaving the area he had always referred to as "Paradise" that he did not practice medicine again. He received the Order of the British Empire medal for his medical service to Guyana.

Debbie grew into an attractive young woman who became a BBC drama TV star. She became the first actress to play the receptionist, Susie Mercier, in the long-running *Casualty* comedy series, set in a hospital emergency ward. Now living in Wolfville, Nova Scotia, with her husband, Cal Mercier, Debbie fondly recalls some of her past in Mackenzie, as follows:

> As a child growing up in Watooka, I remember the freedom that we all had...like Mowgli... running barefoot, adventurous and

usually climbing a tree. Mom would scold me for not wearing shoes, so I would always have them on when I left the house, but they were always abandoned at the foot of the front steps.

My best friend at one time was Shani Howard. Adventurous, one time we accepted an offer of a friendly man to come with him in his boat to his family's home across the river. The house was a small shack; his wife and children greeted us warmly and offered us a homemade sweet, but we declined. It was obvious that life on this side of the river was not opulent… Shani and I were both aware that they had only the bare necessities. There was a fire outside that they used to warm water in an old tub. I will always remember this visit and the feeling of being grateful for the advantages we had in our lives on the other side of the river.

I remember that the morgue was across the way from our house and whenever someone died there were women wailing outside. With mesh windows, it was hard to block out the sounds. When the storms would come, my Mom and I would run around the house to pull the furniture away from the windows… and then we would wait until the floors would dry so we could push things back again. Those mesh windows could keep the breezes flowing but they were catch-alls for large moths.

Christmas was always a fun time. Christmas parties and plays seemed to fill the season. Mom and Dad would take us caroling at the hospital next door and we went to Christmas Mass in Mackenzie. Mom used to use Chanel No. 5 and it was a treat to get a dab behind the ear. Santa would come to the Watooka Clubhouse and give out a present to each Watooka child.

Debbie and Cal's daughter, Giverny, is currently a singing star in Halifax, Canada, heading up the popular band Roxy and the Underground Soul Sound.

Courtesy: Bishop Charles Davidson
#573 Ariwa Oval, Cockatara

This is the old home of the Davidson family. Archie Davidson was a mechanic and sheet metal worker for Demba, while Marjorie Davidson was kept busy raising two daughters and two sons. Initially, the family lived on Silverballi Street. A son, Charles Alexander, is of particular interest, given that he is currently occupying a central position of leadership in the country. In his youth at Mackenzie High School, he was a popular student, round-faced and always with a smile on his face. He loved to sing at an early age, and sang with the girls in a choir. His classmates, including John Cush and Cheryl Blair, recall the above with great fondness. According to Cheryl, "He had the voice of an angel".

Charles lived as a neighbour to his boyhood friend Hugh Chapman, and the two of them would walk to and from school together, including at lunch time. Right from his early youth, Charles wanted to become a priest. His family attended the Anglican Christ the King Church in Cockatara, where he would have been in the choir and acted as an altar boy. Easter Sunday would have been very special for him at this beautiful little church by the river. Perhaps it would also have been an early dream for his friend Hugh to become a priest, since he and his family also attended this church. At thirteen years of age, Charles was sent to Georgetown to attend school, and he subsequently went to Codrington College in Barbados to obtain his priesthood via theological/divinity studies.

Codrington College opened in 1745, named after its benefactor, Christopher Codrington III, who died much earlier, in 1710. Initially, the land for the college was the plantation Codrington, where Christopher had been born. The land had its name chained to Society, its slaves branded with the word "Society" on their chests. Christopher always had an empathy for the slaves, and desired their conversion to Christianity and for them to learn to read and write. Upon his death, he bequeathed his substantial wealth for the establishment of a Christian learning facility to meet his wishes.

Charles Davidson was ordained as a priest in 1978 and subsequently worked for thirteen years in the Bahamas and in the Turks and Caicos Islands. Upon moving to the United States, he practiced his Christian profession first at Jacksonville, Florida, then at New Haven, Connecticut, and finally in Philadelphia, Pennsylvania. In 2015, he was unanimously elected to become the Bishop of Guyana, Suriname, and Cayenne. In March of that year, he was ordained Bishop at St. George's Cathedral in Georgetown, an event overflowing with parishioners, including many VIPs, such as President David Granger and his wife, Sandra. His childhood friend Hugh Chapman, by then also an Anglican priest, gave the sermon.

The Davidsons, Charles and Maureen, now live in the beautiful Anglican Residence, Austin House, in Kingston, Georgetown. He has realised his dream, and has come a long way from old Cockatara.

Courtesy: John Cush
#640 Industrial Area, Cockatara

Wow. I found myself talking on the telephone again with world-class tennis coach Bill Adams, who was speaking enthusiastically from the clay surface of one of his six tennis courts at Miramar, Florida. Now and then he would break off the conversation by shouting instructions to a student tennis player—he drives them hard. Here is the interesting story that relates to the house shown above.

When Bill was born in 1950, his Guianese family was living in Christianburg, on the Wismar Main Road, across the river from Mackenzie's bauxite plant. His father, Vivian Rupert Adolphus Adams, was doing pork-knocker gold prospecting and carpentry work. Wilhemina, his mother, had been the head seamstress at the New Amsterdam Hospital prior to meeting Bill's father in Georgetown. In 1951, Bill's father, mostly referred to as "R.A. Adams", or just "R.A.", was working as a carpenter on the new Crescent Cinema for Cockatara when his contractor boss had a heart attack. In spite of his lack of formal education, R.A., gifted with an ability to analyse complexities and provide solutions, was asked to take over the construction project. He also led the building of the Sports Club that same year. He then formed R.A. Adams Construction, and built homes all over the area, including at the south end of Riverside Drive in Watooka and up on Richmond Hill.

The most important house that he built was the house at #640 Industrial Area in Cockatara, into which his family moved from their original house in Christianburg. Outside of Watooka, according to Bill, their new house was the first to have both hot and cold water. Young Bill, his brother, Keith, and his sisters, Roxanne, Pat, and Paulette, would all spend their formative years here.

R.A. Adams had a "range" or "batchy" (bunkhouse) at the back of his house, where some of his workers used to sleep. One of these workers was well-known Basil Chong, who lived in the range for several years. On one occasion when the range was being moved, a nest of about twenty snakes was found under the mattress. Apparently, Basil had not been concerned.

While attending Mackenzie High School, Bill excelled at track and field, was captain of the school soccer team, and was on the national under-twenty-one soccer team. He also began playing tennis on the two courts across Riverside Drive from the Watooka Clubhouse, and played on the YWCA courts in Georgetown. His father had been a friend of President Burnham, but things had turned so difficult in the country that Bill decided to leave for higher education in the United States. His father had steered his brother Keith to learn dentistry, and wanted Bill to become a medical doctor. Many of Bill's friends had chosen to go to Howard University in Washington, DC, but Bill, with a chuckle, states that he was a maverick and looked on a map to see what university was the furthest from Howard... which is why he commenced studies at the University of Oregon. He shortly determined that medicine was not for him, and he, along with his friend Victor Wright (who later became an engineer) ended up in warm California, where he became enamoured with tennis.

His tennis ability was noticed by Darlene Hard, who was a tennis instructor and also worked for the University of California. Unable to pay for her instruction, he made an agreement whereby he would look after her property in return for tennis coaching. He was fortunate to have found a person of superb capability. Darlene was ranked as one of the top women tennis players in the world between 1957 and 1963. She was runner-up to tennis star Althea Gibson at Wimbledon in 1957, and became the US

Women's tennis champion in 1960 and 1961. Indeed, Bill was in good coaching company. He later joined the US Army, became their tennis champion, and soldiered with them in Germany and at Tucson, Arizona, where he coached tennis at an academy. He left the army, and found himself in Florida, where he met renowned tennis player and coach Harry Hopman, who owned multiple tennis coaching academies, including one in Italy.

Impressed with Bill's coaching ability, Hopman ("my second Dad", Bill calls him), convinced him to go to Italy to coach at his tennis academy there. Bill then coached Italy's Davis Cup team, and all of Italy's tennis stars. Hopman was from Australia, where he had been revered. He and his teams had won fifteen Davis Cups from 1950 to 1967, after which he established his tennis coaching academies. He coached world tennis stars John McEnroe, John Newcombe, Rod Laver, and others. When Hopman died in 1985, Bill Adams took over managing his facility in Italy, and then in 1987 moved to Florida to facilitate his daughter's education.

By coincidence, Bill, his wife, Carol, and their daughter would have Richard and Oracene Williams and their five daughters as neighbours in Del Ray, Florida, recently arrived from ghetto living in California. Two of the daughters, young teenagers Venus and Serena, were exceptional tennis players, and the Williams family invited Bill to coach them. The two girls became the best women tennis players in the history of the sport.

Bill established the Bill Adams International Tennis Academy in Florida, which he continues to own and to operate. At any given time, he has twenty to thirty young tennis stars from many countries in his program. As would be expected, he is intense and demanding in his training style. He credits his father and Harry Hopman as being the two greatest influences in his life.

#4 Pike Street, Kitty, Georgetown

The property shown above does not now contain a house: the stilted house was removed many years ago, replaced by a children's playground that has now been abandoned. It is interesting nevertheless to mention the old invisible house on this property because two renowned, but unrelated, people were born at this location. All the surrounding houses in this area were built on stilts. The house in the background is the home long owned by Roger Luncheon and his family.

In 1923, this now missing house was being rented by James and Rachel Burnham from Bhawani, and Lily Persaud. James was the headmaster of the local Methodist school. Rachel's maiden name was Sampson. In February of that year, a son was born to them in the house: Linden Forbes Sampson Burnham. He would be followed by two sisters, Flora and Jessica.

Many interesting families lived on or near Pike Street, and as time went by their children would congregate for play activities underneath the house. The Agard family lived at #60 Pike Street and the Williams family at #28 Pike Street. The Aaron family lived on nearby Gordon Street. Recently, I have been fortunate to come to know members of all these families. Evan Wong and his family also lived nearby, and Evan recalls walking to school often with young Burnham.

On several occasions, I have talked to Dr. Roger Luncheon, who lives next door to the 4 Pike Street property, on Stanley Place Street. He is a medical doctor, a graduate of Howard University, who specialised in kidney illnesses. Known as an astute academic, he has spent much time in government, and was the former PPP head of the Presidential Secretariat, and Cabinet Secretary. He was a great fan as a child of Linden Forbes Burnham's father, James, who was a devout Methodist. As a hobby outside of his schoolmaster work, James enjoyed working as an artisan, making house furniture. He also delighted the young boys in the area, such as Roger, by making toy wooden rifles for them. The property was loaded with fruit trees and sea grapes, which helped feed neighbourhood children. According to Roger, the house had been removed by the time he returned from Howard University in 1980.

Burnham rose to become the Executive President of the Cooperative Republic of Guyana. Rather than implement the democratic socialism that he had been taught in England by Harold Laski, he chose to attempt cooperative socialism—and failed. During his time, Guyana and Cuba were the only socialist countries in the Caribbean. His story is well known and is well documented in lawyer/socialist/author Ashton Chases's book *Guyana, A Nation In Transit: Burnham's Role*.

Burnham did have many achievements, but they were far outweighed by bringing the country to economic and social ruin. No one can argue this, particularly when so many members of the then existing and future middle class of the country, many of whom had originally voted for him, were forced to emigrate, taking their tremendous current and potential capability with them...resulting in the country's current situation of struggle almost three decades after Burnham's death.

A major difference between the failed Burnham and his successful student colleague of socialism in England, Lee Kuan Yew, was integrity and character. Singapore's remarkable rise to economic and social achievement was largely due to Yew's humble and modest dedication to helping his people and city-state, whereas Burnham, of equal mental brilliance, as succinctly stated by Ashton Chase, "was devoted to causes; but he was his greatest cause". Two interesting examples of Burnham's self-promotion (of innumerable ones) follow.

In 1974, Burnham arranged for diplomatic relations to be made with North Korea and its leader, Kim Il-Sung. Subsequently, North Korea gave materials and supplies to Burnham's failing country, including farm and boat equipment, infrastructure projects, and food. Duplicating Kim Il-Sung's self-idolatry, Burnham introduced Mass Games to Guyana in 1980, which would continue for twelve years. Thousands of children lost much school time practicing their gymnastics, singing, dancing, and drama performances, with the situation upsetting their parents and school authorities. For the first Mass Games, according to Moe Taylor, the North Koreans brought eight tons of decorations, and Guyana's government distributed 200,000 pins displaying Burnham's visage. Arrangements were made at these events to ensure that heaps of praise were showered upon the president, the anti-imperialist imperialist.

Recently, at his Guyanese father's well-attended funeral service in Ottawa, Canada, I met artistic Keith Agard, who lives in Jamaica. We spent some time together at his sister Joy Mighty's home, where he described some of his beautiful oil paintings on her walls to my wife. Carolyn. and me. He also creates amazing sculptures. In 1980, Burnham searched for a prominent Guyanese artist to create artwork for the Mass Games, and invited Keith to do so. Admirably, he politely declined.

Burnham, a smoker, developed a throat illness. In August 1985 he entered the Georgetown Public Hospital for a supposedly routine operation. He refused to allow himself to be treated by Guyanese doctors, and so was being aided by medical practitioners from Cuba. He did not survive the procedure. As he had desired, he was entombed in purple glass, copying that of Vladimir Lenin in Moscow, and was placed at the Site of the Seven Ponds at the Botanical Gardens. Due to many shortcomings in creating an environment to preserve his body, his remains were subsequently transported to Moscow, where embalming treatment was applied at the Laboratory of the Lenin Mausoleum in Moscow. Vladimir Lenin had been a socialist hero for Burnham, and purple had been Burnham's favourite colour. While the embalming process was taking place, a mausoleum was built to house Burnham's remains at the Site of the Seven Ponds. He would be pleased about this. Compare it with the modest gravesite of the hugely successful Lee Kuan Yew at the Kranj State Cemetery in Singapore.

By 1932, the Burnham family had moved to another home in Kitty, and the Persauds were renting the house at #4 Pike Street to their son Bhawani "Bhoney" Persaud and his wife, Betty. That year, Betty gave birth in the house to a daughter, Indrani.

Bhoney was a champion tennis and cricket player. He had starred for British Guiana at the world-class level in cricket, and put a racquet in daughter Indrani's hands when she was a youngster. She often played tennis with her father and, even though much younger, also played with Linden Burnham. Athletic star Ian McDonald related to me, "I knew Bhoney Persaud well...a feisty little competitor on the tennis court and on the cricket field. He was a stubborn cricket batsman and a defensive get-the-ball-back baseline tennis player. He was a great character at both games, which he played with great heart and great credit at Club level. I liked him very much".

Indrani's mother died when she was only two years of age. Her grandmother mostly helped to raise her. She attended the Kitty Methodist School, head-mastered by Burnham's father, and then attended St. Joseph's Convent High School. Subsequently, she went to England to study law. While there, she met Trinidadian Donald Gayadeen, who had already obtained his dentistry education at Northwestern University in the United States, and who was then taking post-graduate studies in England to become a dental surgeon. Indrani and Donald married, and when he completed his studies, they went to Bihar in northeastern India for three years, where he practiced his profession. Subsequently, President Burnham asked them to come to Guyana for Donald to practice. They did so in the late 1950s, starting out with a mobile dental van and then establishing a clinic.

At some time in the early 1960s, when politics got violent, they moved to Toronto, Canada, but a few years later found themselves back in Guyana. Indrani was a judge for the Miss Guyana Pageant for several years, and voted for Shakira Baksh, the winner in 1967. She was friends with sisters Dolly and Molly Singh. Dolly Singh became the Governor of the Bank of Guyana. Her signature, even after her retirement in 2011, can still be found on some of the country's paper money notes.

Northeastern India left an indelible mark on the Gayardeen couple. They were able to accumulate funds to travel back to India, often several times a year, for Indrani to help people with leprosy. She became renowned for her work, and established clinics and hospitals to deal with leprosy. She became known as "Mother Indrani", and her Mother Indrani Hospital in Bihar took on her name. She also became a close friend of Mother Teresa. Wherever she travelled, even in London, England, she always had bodyguards. She recalls fondly the times when she would sit at Benares on the Ganges River to feed the poor.

> *It has always been my concern to touch people with leprosy, trying to show in a simple action that they are not reviled, nor are we repulsed.*
>
> — Princess Diana

Given Donald's passing some time ago, Indrani lives in Toronto, and is still active and generous. At eighty-six years of age, in 2017 she was working with monks to establish some drinking wells for villages just outside of Calcutta, India. She has three daughters and a son, all well-educated and with families, who live nearby and give her great joy. She has just written a historical novel about a Guyanese woman, *Arshana*. The title is a blend of the first name of her three daughters. I have been grateful to meet this gracious lady and to converse with her on many occasions. "Indrani" means "Queen of the sun". She has said to me, "I only have one prayer: 'Thy will be done'". She says with a chuckle that she feels the reason Burnham was good looking was because his mother was part East Indian.

And all of this started at #4 Pike Street in Kitty.

* * *

Every house has a story. Every family and every person has a story. One could write whole books about the houses, families, and people on any street in the world: endless interesting stories.

Guyanese Rudy Insanally rose to become Guyana's Permanent Representative to the United Nations, and later became Guyana's Minister of Foreign Affairs. Amongst many other awards, he has received Japan's prestigious Order of the Rising Sun. Rudy Insanally grew up living next door to Mother Indrani on Pike Street.

GUYANA—THE FUTURE

It's amazing how a little tomorrow can make up for a whole lot of yesterday.

— John Guare

Yesterday is gone. Tomorrow has not yet come. We have only today. Let us begin.

— Mother Teresa

So, why has it taken so long for Guyana to recover from President Burnham's rule since his death in 1985? Over three decades have passed, with many people feeling that little progress has been made.

While not everyone may agree, and although the response to this question can be complex, I believe it stems from two main reasons. The first is the fact that the country, primarily in the 1970s and 1980s, lost most of its middle class to emigration. In fact, to some extent, this is still happening, as the population has continued to decrease. These people, for the most part, were well-educated in Guyana's excellent education system— or, being still very young, had the potential to become educated high contributors to society. The skill of this middle class, lost to Guyana, has been demonstrated by its exceptional expatriate success and achievements in countries across the world.

Even at the time of independence, Guyana's middle class was not yet ready to accomplish such. When Britain permitted more than forty former colonies to achieve western-type governments and France did the same for more than twenty-five former colonies, the results were initially poor, and in many cases that remains the case. As Lee Kuan Yew has postulated, a people must have achieved a high level of education and economic development and must have a sizeable middle class, and life must no longer be a fight for basic survival, before a western-type constitution will work.

After Burnham's passing, his PNC party continued to govern for seven more years before the PPP government took over, presiding for most of the remaining time until 2015. No matter what government has been in place, I am of the opinion that, until much of the lost educated middle class is replaced to a large degree, full recovery, even to the level that existed in 1953 (before internal politics commenced), will not be achieved. However, I believe that this *will* happen: slowly, very slowly, but surely.

The loss of so many middle-class people has weakened all aspects of the country's government, business capability, and overall economy. With insufficient pools of educated, experienced, and motivated people to draw from, there has been no choice but to promote less-qualified people into positions of leadership and at worker levels. This is not to say that there are not some very talented and capable people now in the country—there certainly are—but there are nowhere near enough of them.

Guyana, for example, must fill High Commission and Consulate posts in many countries. When the new coalition government was elected in 2015, it could not immediately replace the leadership in these posts due to a lack of qualified and experienced candidates. It took approximately one year to do so, with mostly diplomatically inexperienced people.

Hoping and pleading for capable expatriates to return home to contribute their skills to Guyana's future is a pipe dream. For the most part, those who emigrated are now aged, and if not retired are close to being so. Their children are used to first-world benefits and generally are not willing to step backwards into a comparatively more difficult lifestyle. Certainly, some expatriates have returned or are finding other ways to contribute to the country, but these laudable efforts are far from making a sustainable recovery on their own.

Middle-class recovery must and will happen within the country by continuing and improving the current education system, and by retaining the young citizen graduates of this education system by attracting/supporting private enterprise to employ them. This will be a slow process but is entirely achievable with competent, enthusiastic, and incorruptible leadership. Guyana's leaders have one important ingredient available to them already: the country's youth. We all know that providing a solid education to any race will produce improved human beings. Look, for example, at what happened with the bauxite industry in Mackenzie/Linden when Guyanese men, of several races, were given educational opportunities, took advantage of them, and rose to become the top management in the industry.

I have been so fortunate to have met many senior Guyana government officials who have been extremely well-educated in countries such as in England, Canada, the United States, and Russia. Most that I have met, or know of, have been drawn from the fields of law, economics, politics, medicine, education, and finance, as is the case in most countries.

A weakness for many well-educated leaders, in my opinion, is that they have not been trained to achieve results. I was trained as an engineer, and only by learning and experience did I achieve a respected capability to achieve results, using tools and techniques, not to mention extremely hard work and persistence. Using Management By Objectives techniques, supplemented with computerised critical-path networking and short-interval scheduling tools, was a normal practice, necessary to produce results in the extremely competitive and very stressful computer-systems design and development environments that I worked in for thirty-five years. Activities for a project that fell behind schedule were identified quickly and had to be immediately restored back to schedule by corrective action, often requiring overtime/weekend work. This is how the Americans first landed a man on the moon. One of my mentors was a Texan who was the head of system testing for Apollo 9 through Apollo 13.

This weakness in achieving results in well-educated folks is prevalent in governments and in businesses to varying degrees everywhere, not just in Guyana. I have a good Guyanese friend who is known for her academic skill and intelligence: Dr. Joy Agard Mighty, Associate Vice President of Teaching and Learning at Carleton University in Ottawa, Canada. She has functioned well in the world of Masters of Business Administration (MBA) education at various universities for a long time. She agrees with the need to complement knowledge skills with achievement skills, and is designing her MBA programs to accomplish this. The Doctrine of Praxis is to enact, engage and apply theory and knowledge to realise achievement.

The second cause for slow progress, in my opinion, has been political racial discrimination, promoted and demonstrated primarily by East Indian and Afro-Guyanese politicians and party members. To a lesser extent, it also continues to occur amongst the general population, although I sense some improvement at this level. People are still voting by race. Some argue that the discrimination situation might be worse than that which had existed during British governorship.

In October 2017, the Canadian Chapter of the PPP, commonly known as the ACG (Association of Concerned Guyanese) and consisting mostly of East Indians, held a strategic planning session over many days in Toronto, Canada. I have several friends who were present. At one associated Gala event, more than 850 people attended: including, unfortunately, fewer than twenty Afro-Guyanese people. Does one think that the PNC party, whose members are mostly Afro-Guyanese people, functions any differently?

Every major Canadian city has Guyanese cultural associations. In most cases, but not all (e.g. Calgary), these are not consolidated—they are separate with members being clustered into Afro-Guyanese, Hindu, and Muslim associations. They have a birth country in common, but not much else. Each group has many outstanding and contributing members. How wonderful it would be for these groups to consolidate and work and socialise together under their common culture and Guyana flag.

The heart never knows the colour of the skin.

— Chief Dan George, Canada

On a positive note, the current government has placed the responsibility for fostering multiculturalism with the Ministry of Social Cohesion, which is also responsible for culture, youth and sports.

> *The task allotted to the Ministry of Social Cohesion is a great one: to ensure that individual and community relationships are nurtured to have a unified Guyana. Unifying Guyana, of course, goes beyond differences of race and ethnicity and includes every aspect of our social lives, religion, age, geographical location...and all other similar factors that divide us. Social cohesion therefore means bridging those gaps, to promote the development of a country where all diversities are embraced, conflicts are resolved, where equity is promoted and all decision making processes lead to equal opportunities for all of Guyana.*
>
> — Guyana Chronicle, *October 22, 2016*

I was in Guyana when I had read the above article. Every resident in the country and every expatriate should work hard to support the important goal of achieving cultural unity, which will also lead to more mature politics and a more stable economy. Additionally, it is positive to note that the portion of the population that is of mixed race is now at twenty percent, and is rising. As Guyanese youth increase interracial marriage and appreciate the wonders of diversity, perhaps they may overcome the current dysfunction to set an example for other countries to follow.

> *The problem is how to create a situation where the minority, either in ethnic, linguistic or religious terms, is not conscious that it is a minority; where the exercise of its rights as an equal citizen is so natural and so accepted a part of our society that it is not conscious of the fact that it is sharing, within this wider whole, equal rights with the dominant ethnic groups who accept its equality as a matter of fact.*
>
> — Lee Kuan Yew

> *Whatever our race or religion, it is what we produce that entitles us to what we get, not our race or religion. Developing the economy increasing productivity, increasing returns, these make sense only when fair play and fair shares make it worth everyone's while to put in his share of effort for group survival and group prosperity.*

— Lee Kuan Yew

Religion cannot be a force for national unity. Indeed, secularism is essential for religious harmony for our multi-religious community.

— Lee Kuan Yew

There are many wonderful opportunities available for Guyana and for its people. In no particular order, I will enthusiastically address several of them below, but one must know that there really is no limit to favourable possibilities.

TOURISM

People across our wonderful world have innumerable choices for leisure travel. Their travel decisions depend on their personal interests and their knowledge of potential destinations. Guyana is relatively unknown as a tourist attraction but is unique and remarkable with its composition of people, culture, history, flora, fauna, and much more. Caribbean islands are indeed pristine and beautiful, but although of course I am biased, I would choose to visit the raw beauty of Guyana rather than only a Caribbean island. It is a much bigger country, and there is simply much more to see and to do for visitors. It can also be very exciting.

Guyana's Cheddi Jagan International Airport experienced a record 572,000 arrivals for 2016. Of these, 235,000 were recorded as tourists. This number has fortunately increased from 66,000 in 1998 and is expected to reach 300,000 by 2020. Seventy-five per cent of the tourists come equally from the United States and the Caribbean. Tourism contributes about seven per cent to Guyana's GDP—much less than many other Caribbean countries. For example, the island of Barbados, with forty per cent of Guyana's population and less than one per cent of Guyana's land area, receives more than 600,000 tourists each year.

Guyana's government recognises the opportunities for increasing tourism, and is taking steps to do so, taking advantage of the country's unique nature and adventure offerings. Note that about 30 million tourists visit the Caribbean every year...about the same number that annually visit Niagara Falls in Canada.

Convincing world-recognised airlines to establish routes to Guyana will be important. This will be greatly aided by the planned significant expansion of the airport. Also, there is a huge opportunity to encourage cruise ships to stop in Guyana. Currently, fewer than ten small cruise ships per year make an appearance. That can be increased with customised touring options provided for passengers. Larger cruise ships could be accommodated more easily with the development of a deep-sea port, which is also needed for the future oil business, for enhanced access by Brazil to North America, and for other purposes. Ship and airline arrivals can be arranged to coincide with the seemingly endless festivals in which the Guyanese people of six races colourfully participate. Imagine ships arriving off the coast at Easter to join in the flying of tens of thousands of kites. Guyana's National Trust organization has identified more than 400 historical sites of interest.

It must be understood that all initiatives to improve the country for increased tourism require funding, which is very scarce in a third-world country. Even in a first-world country, it can be difficult to find the funding for museums, libraries, historical-site maintenance, and cultural facilities. Often these are funded by philanthropists, who are scarce in Guyana. Private industry can be called upon to help. Even today, some international travel agencies include Guyana in their repertoires. Norway has signed a landmark agreement to provide Guyana's government with US$50 million for each of five years, in return for Guyana preserving its tropical rainforest and environment. Guyanese Desmond Sears, who worked in the bauxite industry for twenty years and who is Norway's Honourable Consul to Guyana, is hopeful that this mutually beneficial agreement will set an example for other countries to follow. In return for its financial support, Norway expects that Guyana will keep its deforestation rate one of the lowest in the world, will implement forestry management reforms, and will fully transform its energy sector to clean and renewable energy. The government has identified seventy-two sites that may be considered for development of hydroelectric power. Amerindians will be reimbursed to preserve their forest, and funding will be provided to enable Amerindian land titling.

Guyana's government and most opposition parties want to build a highway all the way south to Brazil. Although this will happen inevitably, I have mixed feelings about it. It is so important for Guyana to continue to protect its rainforest: the country has one of the highest proportional forest coverages in the world and has successfully maintained a very low deforestation rate. Its rainforest contains a high level of diversity, but many vertebrate and plant species are endangered, not to mention other rainforest species. (I have read that a single pond in nearby Brazil can sustain a greater variety of fish than is found in all of Europe's rivers.)

> *The beauty, majesty, and timelessness of a primary rainforest are indescribable. It is impossible to capture on film, or to explain in words, or to explain to those who have never had the awe-inspiring experience of standing in the heart of a primary rainforest.*
>
> — Leslie Taylor, *The Healing Power of Rainforest Herbs*

The above words are in line with my first paragraphs in my opening chapter re my own personal musings while finding myself in wonder in the midst of the Guyana rainforest. It is paramount for Guyana to preserve its rainforest.

The idea for a highway through the rainforest, from Manaus on the Amazon River in Brazil to Georgetown, to my knowledge arose more than one hundred years ago, so it is not a new one. It arose more for the benefit of the rubber business in Brazil (possibly the coffee business as well) than for any particular need for the then British Guiana. A new highway would definitely improve trade between the two countries and would provide Brazil with a much shorter route to Caribbean and North American markets. For this reason, Brazil is interested in helping fund the highway. Lethem in Guyana is situated at the border with Brazil, and the distance from there to the city of Bonfim, Brazil, is only seven kilometres. A modern highway already exists from there for 133 kilometres to the large city of Boa Vista, 260,000 people, and from there to Manaus.

Boa Vista is growing much faster than Georgetown. Imagine population from here expanding north into Guyana with a new highway. This will cause more border issues and controls. Brazilians have not demonstrated capability to conserve their own rainforest. Be careful, Guyana. My thoughtful son, Todd, feels that perhaps a train route from Brazil to Georgetown with no/few stops within the rainforest, instead of a highway, might be an option.

While Brazil has its own social and financial challenges, it can afford to help fund a highway in Guyana for its shared benefit. Brazil has about thirty-five billionaires. Guyana has none. Most people are not aware that wealthy Brazilians, amongst many other interests, own Tim Hortons, Burger King, H.J. Heinz, and Kraft Foods via 3G Capital, a multi-billion-dollar global investment firm, whose principals are Jorge Paul Lemann, Carlos Alberto Sicupira, Marcel Hermann Telles, and Roberto Thompson Motta, all Brazilian billionaires. The first two Burger King restaurants opened in Guyana in latter 2017. Minister Raphael Trotman informed me that funding discussions with Brazil have already commenced, as have discussions with China, to access its multi-billion-dollar China Select Fund.

A modern north-south highway down the middle of Guyana would also certainly open the country to increased tourism. But it would also facilitate an "easier" type of tourism, and thus would take away the more exciting and current raw/wild form of vacation experience. It would also guarantee increased peopling of the rainforest, resulting in deforestation and everything else that comes with people. It would facilitate increased flora and fauna smuggling, drug smuggling, illegal mining, and water pollution. The government already struggles with these matters, not having the resources to address them adequately. Much thought must be given to these concerns in order to mitigate them.

Eco-tourism is already in place and strongly supported by the government. This should continue and can even be enhanced. Ninety percent of Guyana's population lives along its coast. There is much work that can be done to improve infrastructure in Georgetown and towns and villages all along this coast—decades of useful and exciting future work to enhance and beautify this part of the country. Population increase is necessary to develop Guyana, and this area is where new population should reside. It is my strong opinion that this approach, rather than to opening up and populating the rainforest, is the more prudent, unique, and sustainable way to move forward. Some areas, such as Linden, could be exceptions, of course, and these locations can also be developed into centres for eco-tourism.

> *Only when the last tree has been cut down, the last fish caught, the last river poisoned... only then will we realise that we can't eat money.*
>
> — Cree Indian proverb

HEMP

One great opportunity to help save Guyana's rainforest, and to simultaneously kick-start all sorts of businesses while also increasing export revenue, would be to grow industrial hemp, and to do so on a large scale, as is currently being done in Chile and Uruguay in South America, as well as in Canada and many other countries, but not in the United States yet. Half of the trees that are cut annually across the world are used to make paper, and this pressure for deforestation can be hugely alleviated by alternatively using hemp to produce paper. It is important to note that hemp, although of the same species as cannabis, is not psychotropic (i.e., it contains negligible THC, the chemical that gives one a high) and is used for different and vastly diverse applications. To the amateur, hemp and cannabis plants can look very much the same, except hemp can grow much taller, to more than three metres.

Hemp can be used for thousands of uses, including biofuel (and, through gasification, electrical power), car vehicle components (including body composites, interior panels, and dashboards), fibre board, load-bearing beams, building construction, textiles, cosmetics, hemp-seed oil, food, rope, biodegradable plastics and composites, hempcrete, soap, insulation, highway soundproofing, paper, shoes, and much more. The paper money used in Guyana is made from hemp. Drafts for the development of the Constitution and the Declaration of Independence for the United States were written on hemp paper by Thomas Jefferson, and that country's flag was made out of hemp by Betsy Ross. That nation's settlers rolled west in hemp-covered wagons. Gutenburg's printing presses in Europe printed the

Bible for widespread reading on hemp paper. The renowned *USS Constitution* carried hemp sails while using sixty tons of hemp rigging—and the *Mayflower* was also powered by hemp. Slaves used to tie cotton bales with cheap hemp rope.

During October 2016, I found myself with Syeada Manbodh at the beautiful home of Dr. Turhane and Vedika Doerga in Georgetown. It was the night of Diwali, the Festival of Lights, and the outside of their house was nicely lit up with dozens of small, burning diyas for the celebration. Vedika pointed to her neighbour lady's driveway, telling me how a gunman had pointed his pistol at her the previous day to steal the groceries she was bringing into the house.

Turhane is from Suriname and holds a Ph.D. in Industrial Development. He is well known in Guyana and has worked at the executive level in the rice industry for a long time. He explained to me that, while the rice industry has been producing rice at record levels, not enough markets have been developed for its exportation. He was very concerned about the management of the industry. He is also the head of the Guyana Hemp Association, and we had a long and interesting discussion about the possibilities and benefits of growing hemp in the country. He believes that unemployment could be reduced by at least 5,000 workers and entrepreneurs in the short term if the government would change its regulations to permit the growing of industrial hemp.

Hemp is a fast-growing crop, and in Guyana's tropical environment, three crops could be grown per year, compared to one crop for Canada, where he has travelled to obtain knowledge and advice about hemp growing/business. Whereas for rice it has been difficult to find markets, there is a huge demand for hemp in the world. It requires relatively little fertiliser compared to other fibre plants and suppresses weeds while growing. It improves the soil, and after harvesting leaves the soil immediately ready for another crop. Its foot-long roots allow it to thrive in drought-damaged soil, and it can be used for erosion control. It is relatively free from disease and pests. Promoters of industrialised hemp in the United States feel that their country will soon allow full hemp production. States such as Kentucky, Arkansas, and others will plant hemp on old eyesore mine sites to recover past beauty and restore the soil. Dr. Doerga feels this can also be done for

Guyana's old moonscape-like open-pit bauxite-mine properties. His birth country of neighbouring Suriname has commenced a pilot project to grow hemp. He is quick to say that regulators and the public must not confuse hemp with marijuana, known as "ganja" in Guyana, because (as noted) hemp does not have the chemical in it that gives its smoker a "high". He refers to the fact that Dubai, an emirate of the United Arab Emirates, was of less consequence than Guyana before it discovered oil. He says that Guyana is fifty-two times the size of Dubai and has many more resources which, together with the new oil discovery, can make the country one of the wealthiest nations in the world. Guyana's politicians need to move expeditiously to take advantage of the enormous opportunity to grow hemp.

I will always remember this wonderful evening hosted by these special new friends for another reason. Attractive Vedika prepared a spicy and very tasty variety of supper dishes. I bit into a small round ingredient lurking in one of the dishes, and lit up like a giant diya. I had encountered my first wiri wiri pepper! I had had to stand up, greatly perspiring, with tears in my eyes. A large glass of cold water barely helped, but I survived, and I still consider the whole experience to have been quite humorous. Hemp, hemp hooray! *No buss da peppa!*

SPORTS

The village of Plaisance lies nine kilometres east of Georgetown on the coast. Its original settlers were French, who gave the area its name. In 1842, the families of sixty-five emancipated slaves bought this area to settle upon—they used a wheelbarrow to bring their hard-saved money for payment. I have been fortunate to meet Beryl "Bobby" Adams Haynes, who was born and raised in Plaisance prior to her career in teaching in England. Her excellent book *Plaisance: From Emancipation to Independence and Beyond* gives a full history of the village. Gulliver Bunbury was one of the sixty-five freed slaves who purchased the land, and ever since the Bunbury name has been associated with Plaisance.

Alex Bunbury was born in Plaisance in 1967, the youngest of thirteen children. He was often teased by his older brothers for his lack of skill at soccer, but this challenge and his determination allowed for him to become a local star player after his family moved to Montreal, Canada, in 1976. At seventeen years of age, he joined Canada's National Soccer Team to become a scoring star. A stamp was issued to commemorate his renown. Later, he played in England, Portugal, and the United States. He and his family live in Minnesota, US, and his son Teal has played for the US National Team and plays soccer professionally. Youngest son Mateo is also progressing in soccer. Daughter Kylie is a Hollywood actress.

Bunbury, internationally respected and well connected, has formed the Alex Bunbury Sports and Academics Academy (ABSAA), which is now focused on building a US$100-million Sports Academy in Linden, Guyana. Wow. It would be built near Ituni, south of Linden, where my uncle Bruce Hay was the mining engineer/manager in 1945. It is anticipated that some 4,000 to 6,000 jobs would be created for the impoverished Linden area. The almost 100-hectare facility will have a 24,000-seat stadium, a 7,500-square-metre training facility, ten training fields, a co-ed sports academy, an eighteen-hole golf course, a 6,000-seat amphitheatre, retail and business centres, a healthcare facility, and a five-star resort with 120 rooms and 100 onsite residences.

Britain and other European soccer and cricket teams could train at this facility during their off-seasons. So could other northern countries, such as Canada and Japan. Tennis, baseball, basketball, swimming, track and field, bicycling, hockey, and other sports will similarly take advantage of the facility...the opportunities are limitless. As more and more visitors became familiar with the academy, the environment, and the country, it would lead to a natural marketing of Guyana to people across the world. Wealthy athletes would spend locally and invest in property and businesses. Youth from across the country, following in the footsteps of Guyanese athletic heroes and heroines of the past, could easily travel to the Sports Academy for accommodation and training purposes, thus contributing to the local economy. Major sporting events would attract thousands of fans from within and external to the country.

Imagine the potential of expanding this project to enhance the old Watooka Clubhouse, and the Manager's House and other houses in old Watooka. The old stelling at the Clubhouse could be restored and expanded to handle boats and small amphibian airplanes, together with a helicopter pad. A modern hotel could be established close by, together with a promenade gardens. River tours could be customised for tourists to eco-explore upriver native villages, waterfalls, blackwater creeks, and rainforest areas of interest. On several occasions in the early morning, I have walked around the Watooka Clubhouse grounds and stood at the riverside, imagining into what a beautiful historical resort the property, and other Watooka properties, could be transformed. Much government support and hard work remain to bring this dream to reality.

Baseball Guyana has also announced its project to establish a US$33-million sports facility. The first of three phases will consist of a high school, two lighted baseball fields, a soccer field, and a huge multi-sport indoor recreational building, all powered by solar energy. The facility will be located, growing from ten hectares to forty hectares, at Georgetown, and is expected to commence construction in 2018.

OIL

In 2017, Natural Resources Minister Raphael Trotman was able to confidently state that, "Guyana is rising from potential to prosperity. We stand at the cusp of a great transformation". True. Commencing in 2015, a consortium of three companies made a series of tremendous oil discoveries about 160 to 320 kilometres off the west coast of Guyana. ExxonMobil (forty-five percent), Hess (thirty-five percent) and CNOOC Nexen (twenty five percent) have found huge high-quality oil deposits within the offshore 26,800-square-kilometre Stabroek Block areas of Lisa, Payara, Snoek, and Turbot. This consortium is continuing exploration, and the Repsol, Eco Atlantic, and Tullow companies are also exploring for oil off the coasts of both Guyana and Suriname. The oil has been found at a depth of more than 5,000 metres (including a water depth of about 1,800 metres). Production is expected to start in 2018 and is expected to exceed 100,000 barrels per day.

All of this presents a marvellous opportunity—and challenge!—for the country. Although it may change, my understanding of the financial agreement between the consortium and the government is a combination of revenue sharing and profit sharing. Guyana will receive a two-percent royalty on gross revenue and will share net profit, after expenses and depreciation, on a 50/50 basis. Minister Raphael Trotman has confirmed this to me. The annual income for the country will be significant and the government has the enviable, but very responsible, duty to spend it well after consultation with citizens and others. For starters, some of the income will be needed to make up for the diminishing income from the declining sugar industry. Major infrastructure projects are being considered to benefit from the oil revenue source, such as the Linden to Lethem highway, high-span concrete bridges over the Essequibo, Demerara, and Berbice rivers, at least two power plants, and a deep-water seaport. One of the main reasons that the alumina plant in Linden was shut down in 1981 was a shortage of power. With oil in the future for power, and depending on markets and other factors, perhaps the old alumina plant could be rejuvenated.

More than 300 Guyanese workers are currently engaged by the oil consortium. This number will grow until production commences, when it will be reduced. Guyanese people from overseas are already applying to come back to work in the new petroleum industry. Existing businesses and new businesses will benefit from the need to support the industry with a supply and logistics base. The government is backing the US$500-million establishment of a deep-sea port on Crab Island at the mouth of the Berbice River, to be known as the Berbice Port Project, by CGX Energy, a Canadian oil and gas exploration company. The company has signed a fifty-year land lease for an area of 22 hectares, with 600 metres of water frontage. The facility will support the offshore exploration industry in the Guyana-Suriname Basin, and will be the largest port in northeast South America. Huge Panamax oil tankers will be serviced, and perhaps even cruise ships for the tourism industry. This would also be the port for opening up Brazil's land-locked northwest, in combination with a new north-south highway. It is expected that as many as 600 new jobs can be created. It will be in a position as well to create a ship-repair industry, emulating the industry that Singapore so successfully achieved decades ago.

Crab island, so-named because of the numerous crabs found there, has an area of only five square kilometres. It is situated only ten kilometres from the open Atlantic Ocean, and part of its river surroundings have the deepest draft of any of Guyana's rivers.

> *The green island was like a pillow on which both streams could lay their heads after a long and tortuous journey to the coast.*
>
> — Jan Carew, *Potaro Dreams*

The government of Guyana has decided that it will not fund an oil refinery, which has been estimated to cost US$5 billion. The Petrotrin oil refinery in Trinidad and the Staatsolie refinery in Suriname were built to handle heavy crude oil, and not the light sweet oil that will be produced in Guyana. Other factors relating to use of these refineries would also have to be considered. Of significance, a new Guyanese company, Prime Energy, led by Dr. Turhane Doerga, is planning to build a modular refinery, at a capital cost of from US$100 million to US$200 million, to produce gasoline, diesel, and asphalt. The refinery would be located at Linden and would also provide fuel for the power needed to use the local bauxite to make aluminium and related end products. Many new jobs will be created, local power costs will be reduced, and huge savings for foreign currency export will result. ExxonMobil will be shipping its oil to US Gulf Coast refineries. Modular refineries are used in many places in the world, are more affordable, and are a solution for remote areas. Guyana has been importing its oil from Curacao and Venezuela for a long time. Its new light, sweet oil is relatively easy to refine.

Under the leadership of Guyana's Minister of Finance, Winston Jordan, the government is working to establish a Sovereign Wealth Fund to manage oil revenue. The government has looked closely at Uganda's legislative framework, and has been seeking advice from the International Monetary Fund and the Inter-American Development Bank, together with the Commonwealth, United Kingdom, and United States. Minister Raphael Trotman has confirmed that the public will also be consulted. The Fund will have three specific purposes: stabilisation of the fund given unstable oil prices, infrastructure development, and intergenerational saving.

I have met with Minister Trotman and have communicated with him on several occasions. He is young, bright, well-educated, enthusiastic, and responsive. Guyana is fortunate to have him in charge of natural resources.

He is also the co-founder and leader of the Alliance for Change political party and has considerable influence with the youth of the country. Importantly, he supports diversity and social cohesion.

There is a potentially major obstacle that must yet be dealt with: the border dispute with Venezuela, which has not been fully resolved ever since the Venezuelan Ambassador in London, England, formally requested the conclusion to a Treaty to define the boundary between Venezuela and British Guiana in 1944, claiming that Venezuela owns the land west of the Essequibo River, almost sixty percent of what is now Guyana. Even though two tribunals have ruled in Guyana's favour, Venezuela has refused to accept the outcomes. The new oil discoveries lie in the ocean north of the disputed land, and this situation has caused Venezuela to vigorously raise the dispute to the forefront again.

At Guyana's request, the UN appointed a Norwegian diplomat in 2017 to mediate. However, this did not resolve the matter, and now the issue is before the International Court of Justice. Guyana's greatly respected former Commonwealth Secretary-General and former Minister of State and Minister of Foreign Affairs for Guyana, Sir Shridath Ramphal, an expert and author on this topic, feels strongly that Venezuela has been incorrect and offensive with its claim. Brazil also supports Guyana in this matter and has promised Guyana military support if ever required.

In 1896, Venezuela hired Washington, DC, lawyers William L. Scruggs and James J. Storrow as counsel to the Venezuela Boundary Commission. I can confirm that their voluminous report, while siding for Venezuela, and even if fault may be found with it, makes for great reading relative to the early history of the two countries.

In the late nineteenth century, an Arbitration Tribunal, consisting of two Americans, two British, and one Russian, carefully reviewed much history, together with the submissions of Venezuela and Great Britain. Each side was represented by four counsels. One of these for Venezuela was former US President Benjamin Harrison. In 1899, this tribunal ruled in favour of Great Britain/British Guiana, and determined the exact marking of the border that exists today.

Legal issues and petroleum industry regulations need to be addressed and many obstacles must be overcome yet, but there is huge potential for success and country transformation.

BAUXITE

One morning I had walked less than a corner down the street from the Rainforest B. & B. and into a large, two-story, well maintained house-like building at 278 Forshaw Street. My meeting with Russian bauxite company RUSAL's Head Representative in Guyana had been scheduled, and the receptionist welcomed me to take a seat. She may have noticed a smile on my face, because I was chuckling to myself after having immediately noticed the large circular pillar at the bottom of the curved steps descending from upstairs--a special pillar for me. Let me explain.

This building, for decades, belonged to the Demerara Bauxite Company. On one occasion in 1952, our family was accommodated upstairs. I was nine years old, and was upstairs sleeping with my brother, Mike, while a lively party was going on downstairs. I walked down the stairs in my pyjamas, in my sleep, and sauntered up to the pillar...to pee. I will always recall my astonished mother walking me back up the stairs, while there was much hilarity heard from the adult party attendees, led most likely by my father.

Jim G. Campbell, Demba's last Managing Director in Guyana, and past close friend of my father, sadly cleared out the house when the company was nationalised in 1971. Assistant Maureen Dunn had helped him pack. I do not know the further history of the building, except that President Burnham's wife, Viola, lived there for a short period after his death in 1985, according to Maureen Mondonza, who lives across the street. Bharat Jagdeo and his family, when he was Minister of Finance, subsequently lived in this house prior to becoming the country's president. The house is owned by the government and rented to RUSAL.

I soon found myself hosted in a conference room by a congenial Vladimir Permyakov to talk about bauxite. United Company RUSAL is the world's second-largest aluminium company by primary production output, next to China's Hongqiao Group. It operates in more than thirteen countries and has more than 60,000 employees. In 2006, RUSAL acquired the assets of the Aroaima Bauxite Company from the government of Guyana and formed the Bauxite Company of Guyana, giving the government a ten-percent ownership share. They are mining near the old Kwakwani mining area on the Berbice River, where Reynold's Bauxite Co. operated decades ago. They have leased land from the Hururu Amerindians to open the relatively new Kurubuka mine. Processed bauxite is transported downriver on barges to seagoing vessels that deliver the ore to the Nikkolayev Alumina plant in the Ukraine, and to the Aughinish Alumina plant in Ireland. Approximately 500 permanent employees and 200 contracted people work, with about twenty Russians placed in key positions. Metallurgical grade bauxite is primarily produced, compared to the primarily refractory grade bauxite produced by Bosai on the Demerara River.

Annual production has been around 1.6 million tons, with bauxite reserves estimated to be 50 million tons. The company has incurred losses every year, and costs are significant compared to bauxite mining costs in other countries, due to the high cost of removing overburden. RUSAL has mining facilities in Guinea, Africa, where bauxite deposits are close to the ground surface, reducing costs significantly. Guinea has the largest bauxite reserves in the world. Local people at Hururu are concerned about the removal of forest but appreciate the opportunity for employment.

Given continuing losses, it is not clear what the future may hold for this particular bauxite operation. With the oncoming oil availability, cost reductions may result thanks to cheaper power and the possibility of producing aluminium and other end products locally.

I greatly appreciated my time with Vladimir. He is fluent in four languages, including Vietnamese. He had worked in France, and nine years in Vietnam. I told him the story of the pillar, and we had both chuckled as we glanced at it while I was escorted to the door.

A very promising new US$50-million bauxite mining operation will soon be brought into play by Canadian company First Bauxite Corporation in the Bonasika area. Exploration and core sampling/analysis work over several years have resulted in the finding of several large bauxite deposits. These may be compared to those seen in the Linden region, which now produces refractory bauxite, as well as chemical- and cement-grade bauxite.

Bonasika is located about seventy kilometres southwest of Georgetown, between the Essequibo and Demerara rivers. Construction will start in 2018, and production will commence twelve months later. Reserves have been determined sufficient to last for at least twenty-five years of mining operation.

Tropical rainforest areas will have to be cleared for open-pit mining using excavators—no drilling or explosives will be required. Some of the bauxite is found at the surface, while other deposits range from a depth of twenty to sixty metres. Backfilling of pits with overburden will be performed. The ore will be transported by truck to an area called Sandy Hill, on the west side of the Demerara River, where it will be crushed and dried. Subsequently, the processed ore will be barged to Soesdyke, not far north across the river, where it will be loaded to ships. The ore will be shipped to Louisiana, where it will be processed into proppants: engineered ceramic pellets used for hydraulic fracking. Louisiana was chosen for end processing because doing so there would have less environmental impact than in Guyana. This new mining enterprise will employ more 150 Guyanese workers.

Minister Raphael Trotman enthusiastically accepted my recommendation that his people seek advice from Canadian Alberta oil sands companies to find new technology to remove overburden. This would greatly aid the mine companies working the rich, but deep, bauxite deposits along the Berbice and Demerara rivers in reducing costs for improved competitiveness on world markets.

OTHER

The Guyanese economy has exhibited moderate economic growth over recent years and is heavily dependent on six commodities that make up about sixty percent of the country's US$3.5-billion (2016) GDP: bauxite, gold, rice, shrimp, sugar, and timber. While the sugar industry is struggling with reduced output, gold production has been accelerating, moving to more than 700,000 ounces for 2017. Gold's rise has been due to more investment, mining improvements, and the fact that enhanced government regulations and policing are causing gold production to be better and more fully reported. This upward trend is expected to continue.

The Canadian-owned Omai Gold Mine, which closed in Guyana in 2006, was previously the largest one in South America. It is now being resurrected by Mahdia Gold Guyana Inc., also Canadian-owned. Licensed to explore/mine about 2,800 hectares, the operation, after construction, is expected to provide work for 650 employees, and will also provide significant increased revenue for the government.

Guyana's mineral heritage also includes deposits of semi-precious stones, kaolin, diamonds, silica sand, soapstone, kyanite, feldspar, mica, ilmenite, laterite, lithium, columbite, manganese, molybdenum, tungsten, copper, nickel, and others. In 2016, Bosai Minerals Group Co. bought the rights to the significant manganese deposits at Mathew's Ridge in northwest Guyana. After a two-year construction period, production will commence, and the mine will employ from 300 to 400 workers. Reserves are expected to last for 15 to 35 years, depending on extraction rates.

Canadian-based company Guyana Strategic Metals Inc. is working with Greenpower Energy of Australia to search for anticipated lithium in the Cuyuni-Mazaruni area.

The unique white silica sand found in vast quantities in Guyana, and certainly as overburden for the bauxite mines, is angular, ideal for making cement. Cement production is an opportunity for Guyana for sure, and is being considered as an industry in Linden. Guyana is also ideally situated near the equator for implementation of solar-generated power. Georgetown is sunny for fifty-six percent of its daylight hours, with a lower intensity of sun, but still significant, during cloudy periods. In line with the government's commitment to renewable energy, Guyana Power and Light Company is already experimenting with solar power generation, and some businesses are also starting to thus generate power.

"Guiana" means "land of many waters", and the country is blessed with seemingly endless natural water resources. The Caribbean islands import great quantities of bottled water from various continents over long distances: Perrier water from France, for example. Within the Caribbean area, Guyana is in an excellent position to develop a very competitive and successful bottled water industry. Also, this industry can ramp up to provide water on a large scale to countries whose water sources are drying up, such as the southern United States.

On one occasion in Linden, I had the opportunity to meet with Dianna Plowell and her pretty daughter, Whitney, who live at Amelia's Ward. Dianna is an example of excellent entrepreneurship that bodes well for small business in the country. She concocts and sells colourful pepper sauces, both sweet and hot, in professionally labelled, attractive bottles, calling her business Pleasurable Flavours. Her products are sold in specialty shops and in supermarkets. She uses tiger-teeth peppers, which have about the same pungency (spicy heat), measured in Scoville heat units, as do wiri wiri peppers. As they mature, both of these Guyana peppers go from green to orange to red. They are small and very hot, similar to bird peppers, but not quite so hot as are Scotch bonnets. (I cannot eat even one of any of these peppers. They are much, much hotter than original Tabasco sauce.) Peppers such as the Carolina reaper, Trinidad scorpion "Butch T", and the chocolate bhutlah are ten times hotter, on the top of Scoville heat unit scale. Police-strength pepper sprays are even hotter—for sure, one does not want to be a target of these. Wiri wiri peppers, round, marble-sized, and also known as the "Guyana pepper", are a staple of Guyanese cuisine.

Hot peppers are cultivated in all ten regions of Guyana. There is tremendous scope for expansion of hot pepper production for both local and export markets. As peppers grow, they may go from green to yellow, orange and/or red, increasing in spicy heat as they age. Therefore, the specific colour demanded in the market will determine when they are harvested. The burn of a pepper comes from a substance called capsaicin, which is a natural poison designed to protect the plant by making it inedible. Wild chili peppers are spread by birds that do not have receptors in their mouths to sense the heat. All chili peppers, even ornamental varieties, are edible. One fresh green chili pepper has as much vitamin C as six oranges. Oleoresin, the colour extracted from very red peppers, is used in everything from lipstick to processed meat.

Once, after eating an extremely hot spicy sauce, resulting in a burning/suffering mouth, I was coached to put some white sugar on my tongue…and was immediately restored to normal. Cold water is not a solution. Guyana's unique tropical produce allows for people like Dianna Plowell to flourish.

I will write about rum in the following chapter.

As I write, there is a booming world demand for coconuts, and a looming global supply shortage. Health-conscious consumers are driving huge market growth for high-value products like virgin coconut oil and coconut water. In the past decade, the world-wide market for coconuts has grown by more than 500 percent. Some have said that the world needs to plant one billion new trees to meet future demand. It takes six to ten years for a new tree to produce coconuts in fertile soil. Tall coconut trees can produce from thirty to seventy-five fruit per year, and reach peak production in fifteen to twenty years. They can live 100 years.

Guyana is well positioned to grow coconuts, and current production, according to Essequibo-born Trevor Daniels, will grow significantly over the next five years. Daniels, now based in the United States, is in the process of cultivating 3,000 acres of coconut trees, initially at the Greenfield and Barama Profit plantations in the Pomeroon where he was raised. This enterprise will employ from 80 to 100 workers, mostly from the local area. Others will follow.

Drone technology is already being employed in Guyana, and there are many useful opportunities that lie ahead for its deployment. A few entrepreneurs have already started businesses to provide drone services, and policemen have been, and continue to be, trained to use drone devices. While at the Watooka Clubhouse, a young Filipino man showed me work he had completed as a consultant for Bosai to do land mapping. For the whole area of Linden, he showed me maps indicating land heights and depressions, from both aerial and cross-section views.

Guyana has serious problems, needing to regulate and police illegal mining, logging, fauna removal, drug movement, pollution, and land infringement. The Wapishana natives in the Rupununi have trained themselves to use drones to curtail illegal logging. Scientists, if they aren't already, will be using drones to monitor the movement and habits of tagged fish and wildlife. Just as blimps were used in World War II to search for German submarine activity, drones can now be used to search for illegal shipping off Guyana's coast.

China is making huge investments in the Caribbean, an area of great strategic interest, since it sits between North and South America. In 2017,

China committed to investing US$250 billion in the area. Already one can see its progress in Guyana, with growing investments in bauxite, manganese, power generation, infrastructure, building, and retail. Two downtown streets in Georgetown are sometimes referred to as forming a mini-Beijing. China is the single largest destination for Guyana's timber products. The economies of Antigua and Barbuda have already moved significantly forward because of Chinese investment.

It is only a matter of time before the initiatives outlined in this chapter, and many others, come to fruition. Successes will build upon successes, challenges will be overcome, and the synergistic result will help to replace the lost middle-class population, while projecting Guyana into the future and into being a first-world country.

> *There is a glorious rainbow that beckons those with the spirit of adventure. And there are rich findings at the end of that rainbow. To the young and the not too old, I say look at the horizon, find the rainbow, go ride it. Not all will be rich; quite a few will find a vein of gold; but all who pursue that rainbow will have a joyous and exhilarating ride and some profit.*
>
> — Lee Kuan Yew

EPILOGUE

Sometimes a short walk down memory lane is all we need to appreciate who we are today.

— Susan Gale

I returned to Guyana for a third time in April 2017. I wanted to be there for one of the country's biggest annual events: Easter. I had recalled the Easters there as a child, mostly having to do with church events and with playing children's games and competitions at the Watooka Clubhouse. There, we had had crawling races while pushing potatoes with our noses, hopping races in crocus sacks, and swimming races. We hunted for coloured eggs that my mother and her colleagues had dyed, the silver egg being the one most sought after. Our fathers pushed our mothers in wash tubs while swimming, racing them two lengths of the pool, and competed in horseshoe throwing and egg catching. In our tropical environment, all of this had been very colourful and much fun.

At that time, there were only about twelve children at the Watooka elementary school. At Easter time, I was always paired for a swim race against Ralph Sinke, Jr., a talented but overly aggressive boy. Well-tanned and very capable swimmers, we were both very competitive. Half a century later, we cannot agree on the outcomes of these races.

As I took my place at the head of the pool to commence a race, I did not then know that my opponent would later become a high-school swimming champ in Canada, and later a champion swimmer at St. Leo's University in Florida. He would also become an MVP for several years playing water polo for the US Marines. More incredibly, he would become one of the most highly decorated US Marines in the Vietnam War, wounded fourteen times, earning five purple hearts, two presidential citations and much more. (But he still didn't beat me in the pool!)

I was fortunate that the popular Rainforest guest house had room for me again, and my usual and familiar room was available. Syeada greeted me enthusiastically. Jerry was still away in the United States. Everything seemed normal. Syeada's interesting friends and house staff were coming and going as usual, and she was focused on her latest animal-rescue project. Three monkeys, including bad-behaving "Jack", found somewhere in the city, had been taken under her care until she could find a way to return them to the wild. In the meantime, she had arranged to keep them at the nearby Zoological Park. In addition, she was upset because armadillos were being sold at a roadside stand for food.

Early Easter Sunday morning, two days later, found me at Mass at St. George's Anglican Cathedral. The huge edifice was mostly full of well-dressed folks, the ladies in colourful dresses, with many fanning themselves even though large turning fans are secured to the massive pillars. Pigeons were cooing while resting high up on various beams, and I noticed some pigeon feathers and dried whitish droppings on the unvarnished, but otherwise very clean, greenheart wood floor. Easily recognised as a visitor by being the only white person in the church, I was warmly welcomed by those around me. I was so grateful for this, and thanked God for allowing me to have somehow found my way back to this wonderful country of my birth.

Looking around, I was truly mesmerised. Several of the priests I knew were present: Father Raymond Cummings, Archdeacon George Spencer, Canon Thurston Riehl, and the Very Reverend Andrew "Andy" Carto, who is the dean of the church. At the closing of the Mass, a long line of the clergy and assistants formed to perform the closing procession down the centre aisle. I was surprised, amazed, and humbled when Canon Riehl stepped out of the line to reach over and shake my hand to welcome me back. Wow. (I think most of them know that I am a Catholic, smile.)

It was noon that same day when I walked into the Herdmanston Lodge, just to see what might be happening. The dining room was full of well-dressed guests partaking of an Easter lunch. Incredibly, a seated handsome couple waved me over to their table, and asked me to sit with them. I did not know them, and I am still puzzled as to why they befriended me. I was so fortunate to meet these people, Stanley and Cheryl Moore, and we had a lively and interesting discussion for some time.

Stanley had been an admired judge with the Eastern Caribbean Supreme Court. Cheryl showed me a photo of her as a pilot standing beside an airplane, and another photo of a Guyana postage stamp, commemorating her achievement of being Guyana's first female commercial pilot, together with Beverley Drake, who was also Guyana's first female military pilot, and who was also commemorated on a postage stamp. The two women trained together in 1978 at the Embry Riddle Aeronautical University in Florida, then the world's best pilot-training school. Drake had later worked for more than thirty years investigating airplane accidents for the US National Transportation Safety Board.

Stanley, looking very fit in his early eighties, had been the President of the Guyana Amateur Boxing Association, and a sports commentator for cricket and soccer. He and Cheryl were very proud of their son Alex, who is a magistrate. I walked back to the Rainforest thanking my lucky stars for having met these remarkable people.

I spent Easter Sunday afternoon at the seawall with tens of thousands of people flying kites all along the coast. Wow. All sorts of kites...singing kites, giant kites, fighting kites, Chinese kites, box kites, broken kites...of all shapes and sizes. As the wind blew in from the sea, the kites were all flying inland, often getting entangled in trees, landing in water or amongst vehicles, and even getting loose in the air in free flight. Kite strings and tails crossed and tangled in the air and on the ground. Food and drink stalls abounded, and children frolicked along the seawall and in the parks. Vehicles were parked on both sides of roads for kilometres, and packed into every available park space. This celebration would continue also in full force the following day, Easter Monday.

As planned, I met young Christopher Taylor on a seawall bench to catch up on our activities and to watch the kite-flying excitement. I gifted him an excellent book about graphics design to help him in his aspiring profession. Afterwards, I was approached by an older Portuguese man on his bicycle who may have overheard us and who introduced himself as Paul "Pablo" Gonzales. He has a good sense of humour, and it turned out that we have some friends in common—the Beharrysingh family. He was able to relate the names of most of the now-adult children of this family, and chuckled as he recalled the mischievous times that he had had as a friend of Derek, the youngest member of this family, in their youth. I can assure you that Derek also has a good sense of humour. On occasion, they used to imbibe at the South Central bar, a place of questionable renown, using Derek's policeman-father's old Vauxhall car for transportation. They had had so much fun together.

(Over the next few days, I felt the urge to locate the South Central bar in order to have a drink and to imagine the good times that Pablo and Derek had had there, Pablo interested in knowing more about Derek's sisters and Derek interested in other girls and hoping that no one would notice his father's car parked outside the pub. While taking taxis to go here and there in Georgetown, I asked about the South Central pub and its location. In all cases, I received a similar response, "Don't go there! You will come out horizontal… and naked! If you have any gold in your teeth, you will lose it! They'll chop your fingers off for your rings… and they won't give your fingers back!" I later learned that the pub had closed down after someone had been murdered there. Oh, well.)

Just before noon on Easter Monday, I took a taxi to the Guyana Veteran's Legion on Carifesta Avenue, not far from the Police Headquarters. It was quiet there…some folks were preparing for an afternoon barbecue…but I was enthusiastically welcomed to a table of three Guyanese men sharing a bottle of vodka. One of them was "Skeffers", the elderly, but very lively, manager of the Legion and of its bar. We all had a jovial time, with Skeffers admiring my new running shoes and trying to convince me to trade them for his beat up plastic clogs. I controlled myself to minimise my drinking, as the day was yet early, although this was difficult, given the great camaraderie. (Unlike the Tower Hotel and Duke Lodge, the Legion doesn't use a computer to measure liquor leakage the following morning.) That afternoon I found myself sitting under a tree in the hot, hot afternoon at the National Park, not far across the road from the Legion, with Skeffers and some of his buddies. His much younger girlfriend was very busy selling channa food and drinks from her portable cart. The huge park was packed with families picnicking and flying kites everywhere in the air. An entourage of black limousines appeared, moving slowly amongst throngs of people cheering and waving small Guyana Arrowhead flags. Skeffers jumped up excitedly, "It's President Granger!" I enthusiastically followed the crowd and watched with great interest as the well-guarded president emerged from his car to walk through the park, shaking hands endlessly and posing for photographs with his country's citizens. It was all very colourful and moving for me.

A day or two later, after a very early weekday-morning Mass at St. George's Cathedral, I sauntered over to greet three priests who had been sitting together in the pews to one side of the church: Archdeacon George Spencer, Canon Thurston Riehl, and the Very Reverend Andrew Carto. They each have a great sense of humour, are very well educated, and exude intelligence. I was grateful to have some time with them. Canon Riehl's wife, Clarissa, is an acquaintance of mine—she is currently Guyana's High Commissioner to Canada and, amongst many other achievements, has been Speaker of the House in Guyana's parliament. Canon Riehl, this year, was celebrating his fiftieth anniversary as an Anglican priest. He graduated from Penn State University in the US, majoring in physics.

The huge cathedral was undergoing an initial phase of costly renovation, with carpenters removing the old greenheart siding off one of the side walls. I suggested to Father Carto the church consider having the old wood made into artefacts to sell to help pay for church expense: i.e. miniature crosses, framed crosses, miniature carvings of the church, etc., just as remnants of the Berlin Wall were crafted for sale. Of interest, special approval and arrangements have been made to use kiln-dried greenheart wood from the Iwokrama rainforest for the new siding.

I kidded the Very Reverend Carto, chuckling that he is the only priest I know who is a member of the board of directors of a booze company, Banks DIH. In fact, he is also an employee, functioning as the director of human resources.

I would like to now relate some interesting information about liquor production in Guyana, particularly that for which it is renowned: rum.

The Caribbean area is the largest producer of rum in the world. Rum is a heritage industry in Guyana that continues to produce acclaimed rum spirits, popular across the world. All of this is accomplished by two large companies, Diamond Distillers Limited, DDL, and Banks DIH Company. Together, indirectly and including bars, hotels, and "rum shops" they provide employment for more than 20,000 workers. Their El Dorado and XM brands are internationally recognised and awarded. Production is continuously growing, particularly in the aged-rum category. North America is a major export destination, and much opportunity lies ahead to penetrate additional markets, such as India, which is the country that consumes the most rum in the world.

Rum production commenced in what is now Guyana in the 1640s, and increased dramatically in the following decade, when British planters introduced the process of distilling. Rum is made by fermenting sugar cane juice and then distilling it to produce a clear liquid. Dark rum results from aging in charred oak barrels. The longer the aging, the darker the rum. Sometimes, molasses, burnt sugar and/or caramel are added. White rum is aged in stainless-steel casks, and has a slightly lower alcohol content than dark rum.

Over time, almost every sugar plantation established a still house using the molasses product of their sugar-making industry, so that by the 1700s more than 300 distilleries were present. Again, as time continued to pass, market and other situations arose that called for a consolidation of all the distilleries, resulting in the formation of DDL in 1992. It was also in that year that the company became the first rum producer in the world to market a premium-quality aged rum: El Dorado 15-Year-Old Special Reserve. This extraordinary product has been voted the world's best rum on at least eight occasions, and has become the internationally recognised benchmark for aged rums. The company is located on the old Diamond estate on the east bank of the Demerara River, close to shipping and customs facilities.

In 1655, just after the British defeated the Spanish momentously in Jamaica, the British Royal Navy introduced rum as a portion of the rations issued to sailors, for both celebratory and medicinal reasons. It helped to replace drinking water on ships, which turned rancid. Rum got its name from "rumbullion", meaning fight or disturbance. In the old days it was also called "kill devil" and "grog".

Rum for the British Royal Navy was obtained from various locations in the Caribbean. One of these rum sources was the Diamond Distillery at the Diamond plantation/estate on the east bank of the Demerara River, which commenced operations in 1670. Another destination for this rum was Abraham Hart's rum-producing company in Cornwall, England. In 1804, his grandson, Lehman "Lemon" Hart, established Lemon Hart & Son Rums Co., which produced the world renowned Lemon Hart rums. It had been in that same year that this rum became the first official rum of the British Royal Navy. Over time, the brand has changed hands a few times, and is now owned by the Canadian company Mosaiq, while still being barrel-aged and blended by DDL in Guyana.

In the 1840s, Portuguese Jose Gomes D'Aguiar formed a rum company that commenced to prosper in British Guiana. In 1896, his four sons formed a partnership to buy the Demerara Ice House (DIH) a business/building that housed a hotel, soft-drink plant, and liquor bars. It got its name by also housing ice imported to the country by schooner from Canada. In 1934, youngest son Peter D'Aguiar took over as head of DIH, and further prospered the company by focusing on rum and soft-drink production. In 1942, the company became the first to obtain a Coca Cola franchise in South America. In 1969, the company merged with popular Banks Breweries to become Banks DIH. Its XM rum name is derived from "eXtra Mature", and its premium quality is making a name for itself. Sales commenced in the United states in 2015. The company headquarters is located at Thirst Park on the east bank of the Demerara River. Banks beer is hugely popular in Guyana and in the Caribbean.

Fifteen men on a dead man's chest...
...Yo-ho-ho and a bottle of rum!
Drink and the devil had done for the rest...
...Yo-ho-ho and a bottle of rum!

— Robert L. Stevenson, *Treasure Island*

One afternoon on the police headquarter grounds, I noticed many recruits outside over at the Felix Austin Police College and decided to walk over there to explore the premises and to visit the Police Museum. Two young men were shooting baskets while more than fifty recruits looked on, sitting in the shade drinking cold bottled water. I cannot dance, sing, or do many things, but even in my 75th year, I can still shoot a basketball well. I challenged the two recruits to a shooting contest in spite of the very hot sun, and so we proceeded. After half an hour, I had lost...barely. My opposition were not particularly good shooters, but the hoop had been crooked and there had been no net. Excuses, for sure. The recruit onlookers had been cheering for me (probably because of my age!). Afterwards, I enjoyed regaling them with humorous stories.

A fast tour of the museum was like visiting a large garage storage area. I was disappointed, finding only poorly presented artefacts and no documentation of any kind. I wondered how the recruits could study in buildings that were not air-conditioned, and also wondered why the college had been named after the first police commissioner who had served after independence, rather than after Kunj Beharrysingh, who had founded the college. Perhaps it had been a racial matter.

Just before noon on a weekday, my taxi dropped me off at the historic Cara Lodge on Quamina Street.

> *To become a guest at Cara Lodge is to become part of its illustrious history. To savour the ambience of its cultural wealth and diversity is to be in touch with the very soul of Guyana.*
>
> — Cara Lodge

I was there for a very simple but special event for which I was fortunate and very grateful: lunch with Major General Joe Singh. Prior to his availability, I had opportunity to wander around the neat and tropical-like premises, as well as to talk to folks in the Bottle Restaurant, with its outstanding collection of Dutch bottles.

Known originally as the Woodbine House, the structure was built in the 1840s as a home for the Meservey family and for their servants. It was sold in the last decade of the nineteenth century to George Forshaw, a solicitor who became the first mayor of Georgetown. The house served as a centre for high-society events, and later became a favourite place for distinguished artists and writers of Guyana and the rest of the Caribbean.

In 1996, two Irish Guyanese, Paul Stephenson and Shaun McGrath, who had acquired the property, opened its doors under its current name. Over time, England's Princes Charles, Andrew, and Edward, Mick Jagger, and US President Jimmy Carter have been amongst many renowned people who have stayed here. I admired the ficus tree planted by Jimmy Carter upon his stay to monitor the well-handled election of 1992.

Major General Joe Singh greeted me graciously and with enthusiasm. How fortunate I was to meet with him! We have some commonality, in that we are both storytellers and both of our wives are named Carolyn. Other than that, we greatly differ, given that he is renowned and I am not. A very solid and handsome man, he was wearing his tropical brown military uniform, and welcomed me to sit with him at a table in the Mango Tree Patio. The patio is open to the sky in the middle of the premises, allowing guests to be comfortably placed in hardwood furniture amongst tropical foliage, centred by a large eighty-year-old mango tree.

Joseph Singh was born to East Indian parents, both teachers, on the Plantation Ogle sugar estate just to the east of Georgetown. After attending Queen's College, he was among the first group of Guyanese chosen by the British army in 1965 to attend officer-cadet training in the UK in preparation for the establishment of the Guyana Defence Force (GDF) for an independent Guyana. His service as a commissioned officer spanned thirty-four years, during which he performed admirably and with great leadership, discipline, and respect. In 1986, then-President Desmond Hoyte promoted him to head the GDF, a position he held under four more presidents, until his retirement. He was Chairman of the Guyana Elections Commission in 2001 and has held other leadership responsibilities since, including being CEO of the Guyana Telephone and Telegraph Company. At our meeting he provided me with his business card, which informed me that he was currently Adviser to the President.

We settled into a non-stop, interesting discussion covering many topics. I confirmed much of what I had known about him. I doubt if there is anyone in Guyana who knows every inch of ground in the country as well as he does. As a conservationist, it is good for the country to have such influence at the top echelon of government. He is calm, thoughtful, and confident in his manner, while exuding common sense and an empathy for people, particularly for the youth of Guyana. *The country is fortunate to have this man*, I thought, and I wish that he could be multiplied a thousand times over.

We exchanged books, and I looked forward to reading his book *Growing Up in British Guiana 1945-1964*. After our delightful repast, Major General Singh graciously offered for me to be chauffeured by him and his bodyguard to my next destination.

One evening, Dr. Ian Gorin and I walked from the Rainforest several long corners to the home of Terry and Greta Fletcher. Terry is a retired engineer. We were also fortunate to meet their other guests, Dr. Maurice and Valerie Odle, well-educated and well-known senior officials in the Guyana government. Maurice is the Chairman of the Board for NICIL, and Valerie is a senior official for the CARICOM Secretariat. We had had a lively evening sharing cold Banks beer and interesting discussion.

Maurice served with distinction at the UN, and later as economic adviser to CARICOM's Secretary General. He had been Chairman of Guyana's Tax Reform Committee. An economist, he was educated at London's School of Economics. He related a humorous story of how, as a student at Queen's College, he and two of his student colleagues were hauled off to the principal's office for fighting. The longest-serving principal ever at the College, Captain Nobbs, selected one of his three types of canes and had caned the boys. Restoring his cane to its place of rest, he then asked, "So, what did you boys do?"

The time had come for another visit to Linden and old Watooka. Horace James picked me up at the Rainforest, and off we went. I noticed the trash again along the lonely highway. Horace would rarely travel at night on this road, to minimise the risk of negative occurrences. We talked bauxite and about bauxite people, some of whom are called "OBEs" (Old Bauxite Engineers). Horace has given much to the Linden community. In addition to his bauxite career, he has been CEO of the Linden Electricity Company, Director of the Linden Technical Institute, and the first Regional Chairman. At one time, a car travelling in front of us displayed some words on its bumper: "DO NOT DESPISE MY ACHIEVEMENTS, WE ALL HAVE 24 HOURS." I could not help but think of Singapore's Lee Kuan Yew.

EPILOGUE

Once again, I enjoyed a stay at the Watooka Clubhouse, which I used as a base for getting to better know the sixty-three houses of old Watooka and some of their inhabitants over several days. I could not get enough of this. At supper one evening, I was fortunate to dine with two visiting evangelical pastors, Ellsworth Chester and Fitzroy Tyrell. They invited me to join them that evening at the Calvary Temple for a religious celebration; Mayor Carwyn Holland, with two of his four young boys, would chauffeur us.

This event turned out to be a floor-stomping, arm-raising evening of "Hallelujah!" While I greatly enjoy this type of event, I am not competent at it, and I felt uncomfortable placed in the front row (smile). Pastor Tyrell blew the roof off with his powerful sermon, and at one time roared something to the effect of, "We people of God need to get out of our churches and get into our communities to spread the word and transform the community...just like Brother Connolly has infiltrated the school system with his book!" Really? Wow. Hilarious.

I was asked to speak at the pulpit after this, and calmed things down. My family, together with the Blair family, had donated 3,500 books to the high-school children of Linden for the past Christmas. Ten-year-old Carwyn Holland, Jr., had also spoken at the podium, giving an amazing lecture of religious content, for which he obtained a big ovation. I asked him afterwards if he aspired to be a minister, and he seriously responded, "No, I want to be the president". Wow. The country needs future presidents like him.

> *Your life is not the sum total of your circumstances...it is the sum total of your choices.*
>
> —Pastor Fitzroy Tyrell

On Sunday morning, I was offered a ride to the Anglican Christ The King Church on the river in old Cockatara. I was welcomed in the yard by an attractive and smiling Afro-Guyanese lady with long dreadlocks—Gloria Britton. And I was ushered into the church to sit beside gentle Pamela Butcher. I admired the interior of the small church, designed and built by Demba under the leadership of our family friend Gordon Johnson, and opened in June 1951. I admired the simple church interior: no glass windows, but rather wooden louvered walls, with eaves that extend outside for a good length, thus offering both water protection and excellent air flow in the constant heat. A new pastor, Reverend Montell Alves, gave an excellent sermon, and I was later invited up to the pulpit to introduce myself and to speak about the history of the church: all very special for me, and for which I remain grateful.

After I had subsequently been introduced to several parishioners, Gloria drove Pamela and me to nearby Christ The King Catholic Church, also situated on the river. This building, a twin of the Anglican church building, also opened in June 1951, with its construction having been led by my father. Mass had just ended, but I was able to meet Deacon Berchmans and several other neatly dressed folks. Gloria then drove us to the market area by the river. The village was colourfully decorated for Linden Town Week, which is hugely celebrated every year at this time. Pennants hung over the streets, and the Guyana Golden Arrowhead flag was prevalent. Gloria had recently won Guyana's Medal of Service award for her contribution to education. She had been headmistress of Mackenzie High School, and the District Education Officer. She continued touring us around, and walked me briefly around the Mackenzie High School grounds. Her deceased husband, Harold, had been a Demba electrical engineer. On another occasion, NICIL's Tyrone Peters would tour me around to visit certain residents of old Cockatara, and later we would stop briefly at Gloria's very nice walled property in Fair's Rust. She is a fine lady.

The previous evening at the Watooka Clubhouse had been a highlight of this visit to Guyana. It was Saturday evening. After a hot afternoon walking down Riverside Drive to visit folks, I had showered, put on a fresh shirt jac, and descended to the bar area for a Banks beer and to talk to some interesting people seated on the stools around the curved bar. I mentioned that many people in Guyana did not pay their property or income taxes, searching for comment, which came quickly from a friendly patron named Raoul. "How can you get water out of stone?" I quickly switched the subject, relating some of the history of the large unused, tarped, and somewhat derelict billiard table standing in the corner.

EPILOGUE

> **Winston "Famous" Blair**
>
> As I write in December 2017, a very special person has just passed away in Brooklyn, New York. A generous, jovial, soft-spoken, and intelligent old bauxite engineer—OBE—Winston "Famous" Blair loved to play billiards, and often did so at the Watooka Clubhouse.
>
> Winston obtained his "Famous" nickname by being modestly brilliant, especially in mathematics, at Mackenzie High School. He obtained his chemical engineering degree at McMaster University in Canada, then returned to work at the bauxite operations in Linden, Guyana. As he had risen in the ranks, he had travelled much of the world to market Guyana's bauxite with Sam Hinds, who has just praised Famous, eulogising, "We fought a good fight to make and keep bauxite profitable".

I was also allowed to review a very precious document, the Watooka Clubhouse Guest Book. The entries went as far back as 1962, and I was amazed to see the signature of Evelyn Waugh for January 8 of that year. He was the well-known British author who, amongst many other books, wrote *Ninety-Two Days*, about his three months of travel in British Guiana in the early 1930s.

> *It was as keen a physical sensation as I have ever known, excluding nothing, to sit on a lucuba across a fast flowing mountain creek, dabble one's legs knee-deep and pour calabash after calabash of cellar-cool water over one's head and shoulders, to lie full length on the polished rocks and let the stream flow over one, eddying and cascading...*
>
> — Evelyn Waugh, *Ninety-Two Days*

As the darkness arrived and the dissonant nighttime noise ascended from outside of the screened windows, my special guests began to arrive. I was to host the seven of them for a private supper, to make a presentation of a large plaque for a wall in the Clubhouse. Each guest had been born in and/or had worked in the area of Mackenzie/Linden. The three ladies were well-educated and accomplished in their deeds and reputations, and five of us were engineers, educated separately in four different countries. We were all friends, with much in common.

During World War II, 1942 was the worst year for German submarine activity in the Caribbean. Bauxite ore ships and oil tankers were being torpedoed at a rapid rate. The Watooka swimming pool had opened late to schedule in April of that year, with a special celebration that included my parents. One can still see the small square ceramic tiles that line the pool at its water level, except for a few that are missing. Two bauxite ships in succession, returning from Canada and carrying tiles for the pool, were torpedoed, burying the tiles in Davy Jones's locker. I had designed and donated a large plaque to commemorate this event. As we—Emmet, Horace, Lauren, Nancy, Paula, Sam, Victor, and myself—had our cocktails, dined, and shared lively discussion, I thanked God for this wonderful and truly mesmerising and mellifluous experience.

Late that evening, Sam, the longest-serving prime minister ever in the Caribbean, and his guards drove me back to the Rainforest. Syeada's four beloved dogs behind the gate, all former strays, went berserk, setting off the howls of a dozen other dogs down the street, confirming that I would be a failure in the burglar profession. Gratefully, so gratefully, I waved farewell to personable and honourable Sam.

I had returned to Guyana three times in the past year, after sixty-three years of absence and after seventy-three years since my birth here, for highlights of my life. I had learned so much more about the country's history and had met innumerable and wonderful people. I was so fortunate. How could I ever explain all of this to anyone?

That is why I wrote this book.

The journey is the treasure.

— Lloyd Alexander

My Guyana, Eldorado

My Guyana, Eldorado
Best of all the world to me
In my heart where'er I wander
Memory enshrineth thee;

All my hopes and aspirations,
All my longings only tie
Everlasting bonds around us
As the fleeting years roll by.

My Guyana, times unfolding
More and more thy destiny,
To redeem in lasting splendor
All the years had lost to thee;

And the dawning of thy glory
O'er the long long night is cast
O arise triumphant, glorious,
From the ashes of the past.
O arise triumphant, glorious,
From the ashes of the past

— Walter MacArthur Lawrence

ACKNOWLEDGEMENTS

Knowledge is in the end based on acknowledgement.

— Ludwig Wittgenstein

This book originated primarily from the publishing of my first book, *Children of Watooka,* and from my resulting three visits to Guyana within one year, totalling thirty-five exhilarating days in the country. Counting people quoted, historic explorers and past people of renown, current Guyanese people at all levels of society, domestic and expatriate, friends and acquaintances, more than 800 people have been touched upon in my writing. Many have contributed directly and others indirectly to the content. Most of us form a society that is bonded and has a common interest and fondness for the country of our birth...Guyana. Obviously, it is not possible for me to individually acknowledge each contributor: you know who you are, and in various manners you are given tribute/mention in the book. I am extremely grateful to each of you. Thank you.

Nevertheless, I will make a few exceptions.

This year, 2018, marks the fiftieth anniversary of marriage for Carolyn and me. In total, we have lived more than 150 years. While we equally share in the leadership of our family, it is patently clear that she, as she long ago declared, is the uncontested CEO of our large farmhouse. When one writes a book, it is near-impossible—in fact, it *is* impossible—to do so with a clear desk and a clear floor. Hundreds and hundreds of notes, letters, email print-outs, photos, and much more cannot simply be stacked/boxed, stored in the barn, and easily retrieved endless times per day. Look at the bibliography...dozens of books must be at hand, off the shelves of our large library, for easy/quick reference. And many books must be referred to that are not even in the bibliography.

My little Carolyn does not agree.

According to her, just like in the future of Guyana, everything is possible. So, we have had to compromise. It is to her that I am most grateful for allowing me to write.

I must thank my great parents, Jack and Mary Connolly, for having come together and for having provided me and my brother, Mike, with a wonderfully unique and fortunate beginning to our lives. Our father's leadership, our mother's ability to be an outstanding mother, and their loyalty and devotion to each other over a period of fifty-five years, gave us exceptional stability and mentorship. Both always cherished their start and time together in British Guiana. They never had to lecture their sons to appreciate, to foster, and to enjoy diversity in the world. They demonstrated it. In particular, I am grateful to my mother for the exceptional notes that she left behind. She lived two years longer than our father. Attending to her at her death bed in 1998, I asked her endless questions about our early past, knowing that it would be my last chance. Even so, in writing both of my books, I have learned that I never came close to asking her enough questions.

> *As I was growing up, when I began to read of the angels of heaven, it never occurred to me to doubt that they could be anything other than beings made in the mold of my mother, invested with immortality and sent to do the biddings of the Maker of the Universe.*
>
> — A.J. Seymour, *Growing Up In Guyana*

By nature, I am gregarious. Wherever I go, I try to make my day as interesting as possible. If I walk into a pub, restaurant, train, or airplane, I will always seek out a seat close to a person and/or people with whom I may strike up a conversation. Naturally, my manner has allowed me to meet many of those featured in my writing. However, there is one Afro-Guyanese individual to whom I am indebted for indirectly enriching the content of this book via his own gregarious and charming manner, which has permitted him to have endless close friends and contacts in the Guyanese and other Caribbean communities of the Caribbean, Canada and the northeastern United States: Ned Blair.

I first met tall and handsome Ned when he organised the Fiftieth Anniversary Reunion of the Mackenzie High School in Toronto in 1996. He asked me to be a speaker, and more than 500 people attended. We did not meet again until my book *Children of Watooka* was published twenty years later, and Ned contacted me to order four dozen books.

Ned Blair was born as the eldest Blair-family son on Anira Street in Georgetown in 1939. Later, in New Amsterdam, he attended St. Aloysius Primary School, and subsequently studied at Berbice High School. After his family moved to Mackenzie, he attended Echols High School (later Mackenzie High School), before becoming a teacher at Mackenzie Primary School around 1960. He was assigned to preside over the Scholarship Class, which included some very bright youngsters, including future Bishop Charles Davidson.

Around 1965, Ned was hired to become a supervisor at Demba's alumina plant, where he remained until he moved to Toronto in 1972. Over many decades, he was responsible for managing quality-assessment functions at American Can Company, and later for Steelcase Canada.

Ned has been given countless awards for his volunteerism and community building, including the prestigious Harry Jerome Award for Community Service. He founded and remains president of the Organization of Black Tradesmen and Tradeswomen of Ontario. He founded and presided over the Alliance of Guyanese Canadian Organizations. He remains a vice-president of the National Ethnic Press and Media Council of Canada, which has more than 800 members. He was awarded the Queen Elizabeth II's Diamond Jubilee Medal for his outstanding service to his community.

Ned and I communicate many times a week. He will ask me if I want to communicate with anyone within the Caribbean community, and, given a name, will immediately arrange for a three-way conference call. If I don't suggest a name, he will…and away we go. Many of the multi-race folks mentioned in this book were introduced to me by my friend…people at all levels of society: professors, doctors, old bauxite engineers (OBEs), clergy, business men and women, government ministers, and even his friend Freundel Stuart, prime minister of Barbados. And guess what…his special wife, Myrna Williams Blair, was raised at #28 Pike Street in Kitty!

Thank you, Brother Ned.

I would like to greatly thank the six endorsers/Preface writers of my writing as highlighted at the front of this book. You were carefully chosen for your achievements and for the mutual love that you have for the country of our birth. Thank you so much for your friendship.

A big thanks to our son, Todd, for his natural intelligence and technical skills, which helped me on many occasions to overcome dilemmas with my computer. Thank you, Todd. Even though one needs to be careful with validation, the Internet has become an indispensable tool for writers, for both research and communication purposes. Today, the difficulty and effort that ancient authors were confronted with to produce a written document is unimaginable.

Our doctor daughter, Julie, has brought more than 1,500 babies into this world. However, five of them are her own…our own…and just thinking about them all has given me great motivation to leave them with some documented family history. Thank you, Julie.

By coincidence, today is Christmas Day 2017. In ten days, I will reach 75 years of age. Most of all then, I thank God for my life.

BIBLIOGRAPHY

Knowledge like air is vital to life. Like air, no one should be denied it.

— Alan Moore

Agard, William Oscar. *Called To Be More: Windows On The Work and Witness of the Anglican Church in the Diocese of Guyana.* Toronto, ON: 1994.

Amrine, Douglas. *The Wit & Wisdom of Lee Kuan Yew (1923-2015).* Singapore: Editions Didier Millet Ltd., 2015.

Bacchus, Gordon Scott. *A Historical Analysis of the Socio-Economic Forces Which Shaped a Small Industrial Town in Arkansas.* Arkadelphia, AR: Ouachita Baptist University, 1968.

Bahadur, Gaiutra. *Coolie Woman: The Odyssey of Indenture.* Chicago, IL: The University of Chicago Press, 2014.

Beckert, Sven. *Empire of Cotton: A Global History.* New York, NY: Vintage Books, 2015.

Black, Jeremy. *Slavery: A New Global History.* London, UK: Robinson, 2011.

Burnham, Jessie. *Beware My Brother Forbes.* Georgetown, Guyana: Jessie Burnham, 1964.

Caine, Michael. *The Elephant to Hollywood*. New York, NY: St. Martin's Press, 2011.

Campbell, Duncan C. *Global Mission: The Story of Alcan, Vol I*. Toronto, ON: Ontario Publishing Co. Ltd., 1985.

Campbell, Duncan C. *Global Mission: The Story of Alcan, Vol. II*. Toronto, ON: Ontario Publishing Co., 1990.

Campbell, Khalilah, and Liverpool, Compton. *Foundation of the Guyana Defence Force: A Soldier of Valour Story*. Bloomington, IN: AuthorHome, 2016.

Carew, Jan. *Potaro Dreams: My Youth in Guyana*. London, UK: Hansib Publishing Ltd., 2014.

Carew, Joy Gleason. *Episodes in My Life: The Autobiography of Jan Carew*. Leeds, UK: Peepal Tree Press Ltd., 2015.

Chagnon, Napoleon A. *Noble Savages*. New York, NY: Simon & Schuster Paperbacks, 2013.

Chase, Ashton. *Guyana: A Nation in Transit—Burnham's Role*. Georgetown, Guyana: Ashton Chase, 1994.

Chin, Godfrey. *Nostalgias*. Gotha, FL: Chico Khan Publishing, 2007.

Connolly, Steve. *Children of Watooka*. Hertford, UK: Hansib Publications Ltd., 2016.

Craig, Christine, and Watson, Dennis. *Guyana at the Crossroads*. New Brunswick, NJ: Transaction Publishers, 1992.

Cuadros, Alex. *Brazillionaires*. New York, NY: Spiegel and Grau, 2016.

Da Costa, Emilia Viotti. *Crowns of Glory, Tears of Blood: The Demerara Slave Rebellion of 1823*. New York, NY: Oxford University Press Inc., 1994.

Davis, Irvin, and Walcott-Quintin, Paula. *Bauxite Century Magazine: Observing the 2016 Centennial of Guyana's Bauxite Industry*. Trinidad: 2016.

Dindayal, Vidur. *Guyanese Achievers, USA and Canada*. Bloomington, IN: Trafford Publishing, 2011.

Fine, Doug. *Hemp Bound*. White River Junction, VT: Chelsea Green Publishing, 2014.

Foundation, Rainbow. *Rainbow Over Westminster*. Hertford, UK: Hansib Publications, Ltd., 2014.

Gayadeen, Indrani. *Arshana*. Streetsville, ON: In Our Words, Inc., 2017.

Haynes, Beryl "Bobby" Adams. *Plaisance: From Emancipation to Independence and Beyond*. Guyana: F&B Printing Establishment, 2010.

Hewitt, Guy. *Fathering a Nation: Barbados and the Legacy of Errol Barrow*. Hertford, UK: Hansib Publications Ltd., 2016.

Hoyles, Asher and Martin. *Caribbean Publishing in Britain: A Tribute to Arif Ali*. Hertford, UK: Hansib Publications, Ltd., 2011.

Ishmael, Odeen. *The Guyana Story: From Earliest Times to Independence*. Bloomington, IN: Xlibris Corporation, 2013.

Jagan, Cheddi. *The West on Trial*. Berlin, DE: Seven Seas Publishers, 1966.

Jagan-Brancier, Nadira. *Cheddi Jagan*. Milton, ON: Harpy, 1998.

Kirke, Henry. *Twenty-Five Years in British Guiana*. London, UK: Sampson, Low, Marston & Company, Ltd., 1994.

Krampner, Jon. *Creamy & Crunchy*. New York, NY: Columbia University Press, 2013.

Kurlansky, Mark. *Salt: A World History*. New York, NY: Walker Publishing Company Inc., 2002.

Lall, GHK. *Guyana Elections 2015: Hard Truths, Harder Challenges*. Georgetown, Guyana: GHK Lall, 2016.

Layton, Deborah. *Seductive Poison: A Jonestown Survivor's Story of Life and Death in the People's Temple*. New York, NY: Anchor Books, 1998.

McDonald, Ian. *A Cloud of Witnesses*. Guyana: The Caribbean Press, 2012.

McDonald, Ian. *Essequibo*. Calstock, UK: Peterloo Poets, 1992, and Brownsville, OR: Story Line Press, 1992.

McDonald, Ian. *Mercy Ward*. Calstock, UK: Peterloo Poets, 1988.

Morisset, Lucie K. *Housing for the "Magic Metal" City: The Genesis of a Vernacular Home*. Montreal, QC: School of Management, University of Quebec, 2014.

Ramphal, Shridath. *Guyana in the World: The First of the First Fifty Years and The Predatory Challenge*. Hartford, UK: Hansib Publications Ltd., 2016.

Reilly, Lilly. *Lilly's Travels*. UK: Self-published, 1996.

Robinson, Rowan. *The Great Book of Hemp*. Rochester, VT: Park Street Press, 1996.

Rodney, Walter. *A History of the Guyanese People, 1881-1905*. Baltimore, MD: The Johns Hopkins University Press, 1981.

Rodway, James. *In the Guiana Forest*. London, UK: T. Fisher Unwin, 1895.

Roth, Vincent. *A Life in Guyana: Volumes I & II*. Leeds, UK: Peepal Tree Press, 2003.

Scruggs, William L. and Storrow, James J. *Brief for Venezuela*. Venezuela: Counsel for the Venezuela Boundary Commission, 1896.

Sears, Elizabeth L. *Behaviour Characteristics of the Africanized Bees,* Apis mellifera scutelata. Abstract. Earthlife.net. https://www.earthlife.net/insects/afr-bees.html.

Seymour, A.J. *Collected Poems 1937-1989*. Brooklyn, NY: Blue Parrot Press, 2000.

Seymour, A.J. *Growing Up in Georgetown*. Georgetown, Guyana: Labour Advocate Printers, 1976.

Seymour, A.J. *I Live in Georgetown*. Georgetown, Guyana: Labour Advocate Printers, 1974.

Seymour, Elma. *A Goodly Heritage*. Georgetown, Guyana: Labour Advocate Printers, 1987.

Singh, Joseph G. *Growing Up in British Guiana 1945-1964*. Georgetown, Guyana: Sheik Hassan Printery Inc., 2011.

Swan, Michael. *British Guiana: The Land of Six Peoples*. London, UK: Her Majesty's Stationery Office, 1957.

Subryan, Carmen. *Black Water People*. Beltsville, MD: Demerara Press, 2003.

Talbert, Tony. *Rum, Rivalry and Resistance*. Hartford, UK: Hansib Publishing Ltd., 2010.

Taylor, Conrad. *Path to Freedom*. US: TCF Business Group, 2011.

Tourism and Hospitality Association of Guyana. *Explore Guyana 2015*. St. Lucia: Lokesh Singh, 2015.

Tourism and Hospitality Association of Guyana. *Explore Guyana 2017*. St. Lucia: Lokesh Singh, 2017.

Watson, Cynthia. *Ecology and Conservation of Arapaima I Guyana: Recovery of a Giant Fish in Distress*. Syracuse, NY: State University of New York, 2011.

Waugh, Evelyn. *Ninety-Two Days*. London, UK: Duckworth and Penguin Group, 1934.

Williams, Denis. *Giglioli in Guyana 1922-1972*. Leeds, UK: Peepal Tree Press, 1973.

Williams, Dr. Eric. *Capitalism & Slavery*. Kingston, Jamaica: Ian Randla Publishers, 2005.

Williams, Dr. Eric. *Documents of West Indian History*. Buffalo, NY: EWORLD Inc., 1963.

Yew, Lee Kuan. *From Third World to First: The Singapore Story 1965-2000*. New York, NY: HarperCollins Publishers, 2000.

Young, Mathew French. *Guyana the Lost El Dorado*. Leeds, UK: Peepal Tree Press Ltd., 1998.

AUTHOR

Author Steve Connolly was born in 1943 in Mackenzie, British Guiana, to Canadian parents.

His family left British Guiana when he was only four months of age when they subsequently had lived in Arvida, Quebec, Canada, and then in Texas City, Texas, U.S.A.

The family returned to British Guiana in 1950 for three years, and it is this period of time that the author fondly remembers and that gave him the impetus to write *Children of Watooka* and *Journey Back to Watooka*.

The author enjoyed his teenage years at Kitimat, British Columbia, starting in 1954. He obtained his degree in advanced electrical engineering from the University of British Columbia in 1965 and since then obtained management training at several other universities.

Upon graduation, he worked almost five years for Computing Devices of Canada in Ottawa helping to design/develop anti-submarine warfare technology for Canadian destroyer ships. By 1982, he had risen to the V.P. level at the Bank of Montreal in Toronto in the function of computer systems and operations. Later, he managed large informatics organizations in two ministries of the Federal government in Ottawa before his last work posting as Assistant Commissioner for Informatics with the Royal Canadian Mounted Police.

After forty years in the field of computer systems, he retired with his wife, Carolyn, at their farm in the Gatineau Hills of Quebec. They have two children, Todd and Julie, and five grandchildren.

CPSIA information can be obtained
at www.ICGtesting.com
Printed in the USA
LVHW01s1317110418
573008LV00003B/3/P